PRECEDENT IN NIGERIAN COURTS

TO

MY MOTHER MADAM
BRIGID OBOT IN
APPRECIATION OF
HER LOVE AND SACRIFICES
FOR ME

Precedent In Nigerian Courts

By

P. U. Umoh

Fourth Dimension Publishing Co., Ltd.

First Published 1984 by
FOURTH DIMENSION PUBLISHING CO., LTD
16 Fifth Avenue, City Layout. PMB. 01164, Enugu, Nigeria.
Tel+234-42-459969. Fax+234-42-456904.
email: fdpbooks@aol.com, fdpbooks@yahoo.com
Web site: http://www.fdpbooks.com.

Reprinted 2002

ISBN 978-156-017-7

Design and Typesetting by
Fourth Dimension Publishers, Enugu

CONTENTS

PREFACE

This book is based on a thesis which I submitted to the University of London in 1977 for the award of a Ph.D. degree (Laws). It is the first full-scale study of the doctrine of precedent as applied in the Nigerian courts and is divided into three parts. Part One deals with the nature of judicial precedent and its importation from its English home into, and development in, Nigeria. Part Two examines the various factors which determine the worth of a judicial precedent and in Part Three an attempt is made to forecast the future of the doctrine in Nigeria in the light of various forces.

The author of a textbook must of necessity ask himself what objective he is trying to achieve by writing it. A cursory glance at the text will show what the purposes are. I have tried to show that there is nothing obscure about the meaning of judicial precedent by drawing analogies with events in everyday life, have distinguished precedent from *res judicata* to avoid confusion for law students and have discussed the various modes whereby the doctrine was introduced into the country, thereby debunking the traditional view that it came simply with the common law.

I have also indicated how the doctrine has influenced the growth and development of the common law, equity and customary law and how it has been twisted to retard the growth of the latter. A plea for a distinctively Nigerian common law and equity has also been entered for the purpose of solving those legal problems that are peculiarly Nigerian.

The 'reception' clauses of some of our High Court Laws and the Interpretation Act, 1964, have been analysed and I have tried to show what vintage of the English rules of common law and doctrines of equity was received in Nigeria. In this regard, two suggestions have been made to remove ambiguity. A redrafting of the 'reception' clauses has been suggested and an illustration has been provided. Alternatively, I have suggested to the Supreme Court, if the debate continues, to make a declaration on the lines of that made by the House of Lords in 1966 over the vexed question of *stare decisis,* indicating what vintage of the rules and doctrines has been accepted.

The subject of the *ratio decidendi* has been treated in full and cases have been chosen to illustrate the various factors that determine the worth of a *ratio*. A distinction has been drawn between *obiter dictum* and *dictum* and I have tried to show why the two terms should not be used interchangeably and why *dictum* should be binding.

On law reporting I have advocated the scrapping of regionally based reports and urged the setting up of a National Council of Law Reporting in order to reduce the incidence of oversight of authorities and encourage a national approach to precedent. An annual compilation of the rubrics of important cases to assist in the tracing of important authorities has also been suggested.

A comprehensive treatment of the doctrine of *stare decisis* has been undertaken in Chapter 8 and a solution to the problems presented to lower courts by decisions *per incuriam* has been suggested. In Chapter 9 the problems created by overruling decisions have been given prominence and circumstances justifying overruling have been adumbrated and solutions to the problems have been offered. Lastly, I have to mention that the doctrine of precedent in the non-law-making courts, that is, customary courts and magistrates' courts, has also been dealt with in full.

The above remarks bring into focus some, but by no means all, of the points dealt with in the text. It remains to add that this treatise is a plea for a more creative use of precedents by our courts in order to ensure justice. Whether my efforts have succeeded is left to the verdict of history.

But I hope the book will be found useful by law students who study Nigerian legal system and jurisprudence in our universities. Young lawyers will find the book a valuable friend and counsellor when they come to deal with the problems which arise in daily practice through the use of precedents. I am sure it will teach them the art of using precedents and how to handle cases of first impression. Scholars who are interested in comparative jurisprudence will, I am sure, find the book equally useful.

In conclusion, I have to pay tribute to all those who have helped to make this work possible. My mother, Madam Brigid Obot, to whom this book is dedicated deserves first place in my list of benefactors. I am most grateful to her for the enduring sacrifices she made to train me singlehandedly and give me the necessary basic education upon which I built my legal studies. Her fortitude, understanding and endurance during the lean years when I had to stint myself and the family in order to win academic laurels by self-education are commendable. Special gratitude is due to the chiefs and people of Midim who helped me financially to study at the Bar for two years in England. Without their help my training and call to the Bar would have been impossible.

To Professor A. N. Allott of the School of Oriental and African Studies, University of London, I owe a special debt of gratitude. The University of London appointed him as an adviser on my thesis and I have benefited immeasurably from the advice and suggestions of this prolific mind. Mr. E. S. Ekpe, Librarian of the Ministry of Justice, Calabar, Cross River State, helped with some of the books and periodicals that I used for background reading. To him and those lawyer-friends who were kind enough to lend me their books I am very grateful.

Lastly, I have to thank my one-time secretary, Mrs. Grace J. Esiet, who showed personal interest in the work on the thesis and typed my awkwardly written manuscript accurately and with complacency and devotion. Grateful thanks also go to Mr. U. J. Edimoh, my secretary in the Ministry of Justice, who typed the revised version of the work before it went to press.

Lastly, I have to mention that I am deeply impressed by the speed and efficiency with which the publishers have handled this work. It is refreshing to see a publishing house being so smart and business-conscious. They have answered to every word of the description which Professor Umozurike, Dean of the Faculty of Law, University of Calabar, who recommended them to me put upon them.

I shall be grateful for useful comments and constructive criticisms of this work from the Bar, Bench and the Law Faculties in our Universities.

P. U. UMOH

Attorney-General's Chambers,
Ministry of Justice,
Calabar,
Cross River State.
November, 1980

TABLE OF CASES

Anamali v. Ijirigho (1960)
Anani v. The King (1951)
Andrei v. Agbebi (1931)
Andrews v. Styrap (1872)
Angu v. Attah (1974)
Anya v. The State (1965)
Arayi v. Ojubu (1956)
Are v. The Attorney-General of Nigeria (1958)
Arinze v. Arinze (1966)
Aromire v. Oresanya (1938)
Asani v. Adeosun (1966)
Ashogbon v. Oduntan (1935)
Asiyanbi v. Adeniji (1966)
Attorney-General v. Butterworth (1963)
Attorney-General v. John Holt (1910)
Attorney-General for Ontario v. Canada Temperance Federation (1946)
Attorney-General v. Palm Line Ltd. (1958)
Atu. v. C.O.P. (1970-71)
Auzinawa v. Kano N.A. (1956)
Awe v. Alabi (1970)
Aworeni v. Akinyele (1967)
Ayinule v. Abimbola (1957)

B

Bakere v. Coker (1935)
Bakhshuwen v. Bakhshuwen (1952)
Balogun v. Balogun (1943)
Balogun v. Obisaanya (1956)
Bamgbose v. Daniel (1954)
Bank of the North Ltd. v. Intra Bank S.A. (1969)
Barclay's Bank, D.C.O. v. Hassan (1961)
Barretto v. Oniga (1961)
Bassey v. Cobham (1924)
Benson v. Ashiru (1967)
Beverges v. Sandeman (1902)
Board of Customs and Excise v. Bolarinwa (1968)
Board of Trade v. Cayzer, Irvine & Co. Ltd. (1927)
Bolton v. Bolton (1949)
Bosah v. British American Insurance Co. Ltd. (1972)
Boys v. Chaplin (1968)
Bradshaw v. Waterlow & Sons Ltd. (1915)
Briggs v. Briggs (1957-58)
British Reinforced Concrete Engineering Co. Ltd. Re (1929)
Brown v. Brass and Ambrose (1949)
Brown v. Chapman (1848)
Bryars v. Canadian Pacific Steamships, Ltd. (1956)
Butterfield v. Forrester (1809)

C

Carpenter v. Ebblewhite (1938)
Chairman, L.E.D.B. v. Adewale (1966)
Chairman, L.E.D.B. v. Olopinkwu (1959)
Chairman, L.E.D.B. v. Oyewo (1969)
Chawere v. Aihenu (1935)
Chellaram & Sons v. G.B. Ollivant Ltd., (1944)
Chetwynd's Estate, Dunn Trust Ltd. v. Brown (1937)
Chime v. Elikwu (1965)
Chiokwa v. The State (1979)
Codling v. Mewlem (1913)
Coker v. Coker (1954)
Coker v. Jinadu (1958)
Cole v. Cole (1898)
Cole v. Folami (1956)
Coleman v. Shang (1961)
Coleshill and District Investment Co. Ltd. v. Minister of Local Government (1968)
Commonwealth Trust v. Akotey (1926)
C.O.P. v. Potts-Johnson (1947)
C.O.P. v. Igwe (1961)
Cox v. English, Scottish and Australian Bank Ltd., (1905)
Cross v. British Oak Insurance Co. Ltd. (1938)
Crowcour v. Salter
Curtis Moffat Ltd. v. Wheeler (1929)

D

Dabipi v. Anyabogwu (1962)
Dabiri v. Gbajumo (1961)
Danby v. Beardelog (1880)
Danmole v. Dawodu (1958)
Deane, Re (1888)
Dede v. African Association Ltd. (1910)
Dede v. United Arab Airlines (1969)
Doherty v. Abubakar (1961)
Doherty v. Balewa (1961)
Donoghue v. Stevenson (1932)
Duclaud v. Ginoux (1969)

E

Echefu v. Obi (1966)
Ede v. Inspector-General of Police (1960)
Edet v. Attorney-General (1957-58)
Edet v. Esien (1932)
Edmeades v. Thames Board Mills Ltd. (1969)
Edwards v. Jones (1947)
Egbe v. Eagle Group (1970-71)

Egokor v. Agbeyegbe (1933)
Egri v. Uperi (1973)
Ejiamike v. Ejiamike (1972)
Ekechukwu v. C.O.P. (1966)
Ekpendu v. Erika (1959)
Eleko v. Officer Administering the Government of Nigeria (1931)
Emodi v. Commissioner for Lands (1972)
Ephraim v. Asuquo (1923)
Epi v. Aigbedion (1972)
Erikitola v. Alli (1941)
Esan v. Faro (1947)
Esien v. Okori (1973)
Estate of James Sholu (1932)
Evans v. Bakare (1974)
Eve v. Dunn (1890)
Eyamba v. Holmes (1924)
Eze v. Ilonse (1962)
Ėzeani v. Njidike (1965)
Eziukwu v. President, Ibinta Improvement Union (1972)

F

Fairman v. Perpetual Investment Building Society (1923)
Fatoyinbo v. Williams (1956)
Federal Administrator-General v. Adeshola (1960)
Ferguson v. Duncan (1953)
Fetuga v. Western Nigeria Housing Corporation (1968)
Fisher v. Ruislip-Northwood U.D.C. (1945)
Flione v. Oladipo (1934)
Folarin v. Williams (1942)
Folawiyo v. Folawiyo
Fonseca v. Passman (1958)
Foster v. Baker (1910)
Fulani v. Bornu N.A. (1966)

G

Gachi v. The State (1965)
Galli v. Lee (1969)
Garvin v. City of London Police (1944)
Gath v. Shoesmith (1939)
George v. Walken & Co. Ltd. (1926)
Giwa v. Erinmilokun (1961)
Gokpa v. Insp.-Gen. of Police (1961)
Gottschalok & Co. Ltd. v. Spruce Manufacturing Co. Ltd. (1956)
Gottschalck & Co. v. Elder Dempster & Co. (1917)
Grant v. Australian Knitting Mills Ltd. (1935)
Green v. Owo (1936)
Guri v. Hadejia N.A. (1959)

Kano N.A. v. Obiora (1959)
Kareem v. Ogunde (1969)
Katsina N.A. v. Kogo (1930)
Kirk v. Todd (1882)
Kofi v. Twum (1938)
Koloko Imports and Exports Co. Ltd. v. African Continental Bank (1977)
Kudiabor v. Kudanu (1932)
Kufeji v. Kogbe (1961)

L

Lang. v. London Transport Executive (1959)
Laoye v. Ojetunde (1944)
Larinde v. Afiko (1940)
Laragun v. Funlayo (1955-56)
Lateju v. Lanihun (1958)
Laurie v. Raglan Building Co. (1942)
Law, Re (1894)
Lawal v. Younan & Sons (1961)
Layanju v. Araoye (1961)
Layiwola v. Bello (1965)
Lewis v. Bankole (1908)
Liddel's Settlement, Re (1936)
Lloyd v. Guibert (1865)
London, Midland and Scottish Railway Co. v. Anglo-Scottish Railways Assessment Authority (1933)
London Street Tramways v. London County Council (1898)
Lopez v. Lopez (1924)
Lyndon's Trade Mark, Re (1886)

M

Machi v. Machi (1960)
MacIver & Co. Ltd. v. C.F.A.O. (1917)
Maizabo v. Sokoto N.A. (1957)
Maja v. Chief Secretary to the Government (1948)
Makanjuola v. Khalil (1958)
Manama v. Bornu N.A. (1961)
Manko v. Bonso (1936)
Mary Kingston (1948)
Matthew v. The State (1972)
Maurice Goualin Ltd. v. Aminu (1957)
Mehemet Ali v. R. (1958)
Mckenzie v. Findlay (1966)
Mercantile Bank of India Ltd. v. Central Bank of India Ltd. (1938)
Millar v. Porter (1939)
Miller Brothers Ltd. v. Ayeni (1924)
Minister of Lands and Housing v. Obe (1964)
Minister of Pensions v. Higham

Mokelu v. Federal Commissioner for Works and Housing (1974)
Moore v. Tayee (1933)
Morelle Ltd. v. Wakeling (1955)
Motayo v. Commissioner of Police (1950)
Mpi v. Secretary to the Teachers Disciplinary Council (1960)
M-T. v. M-T. (1949)
Muhammed v. C.O.P. (1967)
Munday v. Munday (1954)
Murmansk State Steamship Line v. Kano Oil Millers Ltd. (1974)
Musa v. Insp.-Gen. of Police (1962)

N

Negro v. Pietro Bread Co. Ltd. (1933)
Newbiggin-By-The-Sea Gas Co. v. Armstrong (1879-80)
Ngwo v. Monye (1970)
Nicholas v. Penny (1950)
Nifa. The (1872)
Nkambule v. R. (1950)
Noble v. Southern Railway Co. (1940)
Norske Atlas Insurance Co. Ltd. v. London General Insurance Co. Ltd.
Northmoor Steamship Co. v. Holland (1903)
Nwafia v. Ububa (1966)
Nwafor v. Nduka (1972)
Nwankwo v. Chukwueke (1972)
Nwankwo v. Okoyeocha (1962)
Nwaribe v. President, Orlu District Court (1964)
Nwokeleke v. Onicha (1955-56)
Nwugwu v. Ogbonna (1965)

O

Obadara v. C.O.P. (1965)
Obaji v. The State (1963)
Obi v. Maduabuchuku (1957)
Ochonma v. Unosi (1965)
Odebode v. Ashaka (1944)
Odeneye v. Savage (1964)
Odiase v. Agho (1972)
Odiase v. Odiase (1965)
Odigbo v. C.O.P. (1972)
Odume v. Nnadi (1964)
Odunjo v. Odunjo (1964)
Odunsi v. Ojora (1961)
Oduntun v. Adefunmilayo (1958)
Offiong v. C.O.P. (1966)
Ofunne v. Okoye (1966)
Ogbuanyinya v. Okudo (1979)
Ogo v. Ogo (1964)

Peacock v. Amusement Equipment Co. Ltd. (1954)
Pearce v. Aderoku (1936)
Pierce v. Hopper (1810)
Pepper v. Platt (1922)
Pepple v. Federal Administrator-General (1958)
Perkins v. Stevenson (1939)
Perry v. Equitable Life Assurance Society (1929)
Phillips v. Eyre (1890)
Phillips v. Homfrey (1883)
Phillip v. Phillip (1946)
P.Z. & Co. Ltd. v. Pepple (1933)

Q

Queen, The v. Akpakpan (1956)
Queen, The v. Adelani (1959)
Queen, The v. Fadina (1958)
Queen, The v. Governor, Eastern Nigeria, Ex-parte Warri (1960)
Queen, The v. Governor, Western Nigeria (1959)
Queen, The v. Itule (1961)
Queen, The v. Mboho (1964)
Queen, The v. Ogodo (1961)
Queen, The v. Ogor (1961)
Queen, The v. Olagunju (1961)
Quinn v. Leathem (1901)

R

R. v. Abbot (1955)
R. v. Adegboyega (1937)
R. v. Adekanmi (1944)
R. v. Ajani (1936)
R. v. Car-Briant (1944)
R. v. Denny (1963)
R. v. Elechi (1958)
R. v. Fitzgerald (1924)
R. v. Golder (1961)
R. v. Herliky (1956)
R. v. Johnson (1962)
R. v. Landow (1913)
R. v. Podola (1960)
R. v. Quinn (1944)
R. v. Sabri (1956)
R. v. Selkirk (1925)
R. v. Sharp & Johnson
R. v. Stockesley (Yorkshire) Justices, Ex-parte Bartram (1956)
R. v. Taylor (1950)
R. v. Treanor (1939)
R. v. Wise (1924)

R. v. Young (1957)
Read v. Joannon (1890)
Rex v. Aliechem (1956)
Rex v. Aniogo (1943)
Rex v. Eka (1945)
Rex v. Northumberland Compensation Appeal Tribunal (1951)
Rex v. Sala (1938)
Robins v. National Trust Co. Ltd. (1927)
Rookes v. Bernards (1964)
Royal Court Derby Porcelain Co. Ltd. v. Russell (1949)
Rumbold v. L.C.C. (1909)
Runka v. Katsina N.A. (1950)

S

Sabbach v. Bank of West Africa (1962)
Salako v. Ordia (1958)
Salako v. Salako (1965)
Salami v. Salami (1957)
Sam Offiong v. C.O.P. (1973)
Sanmabo v. The State (1967)
Sarkis v. Sarkis (1923)
Scott v. Avery (1865)
Scruttons v. Midland Silicones (1962)
Seluade and Beckley, Re (1943)
Seriki v. Solaru (1965)
Shokunbi v. Mosaku (1969)
Shokoye v. Insp.-Gen. of Police (1962)
Sholu, Re (1932)
Simidele v. C.O.P. (1966)
Slack v. Leeds Industrial Co-operative Society (1923)
Smith v. Selwyn (1914)
Solanke v. Somefun (1974)
Stapley v. Gypsum Mines Ltd. (1953)
State, The v. Akpan (1972)
State, The v. Akpan (1976)
State, The v. Dushi (1967)
State, The v. Egbe (1972)
State, The v. Ete (1976)
State, The v. Nelson (1972)
State, The v. Odunsi (1966)
State, The v. Odunsi (1969)
State, The v. Ogon (1972)
Steven, v. Midland Counties Railway (1854)
Suberu v. Sunmomu (1936)
Sule v. The Queen (1959)
Sun Insurance Office Ltd. v. Ojemuyiwa (1965)
Suwa v. The State (1965)

T

Taiwo v. Lawani (1961)
Taiwo v. Sarumi (1913)
Tapa v. Kuka (1945)
Taylor v. Cummings (1941)
Taylor v. Williams (1935)
Terry v. Sweeting (1899)
Tewari v. Singh (1908)
Thompson v. Charnock (1799)
Thynne v. Thynne (1955)
Tiamiyu v. Ashiru (1955)
Tijani v. Secretary, Southern Nigeria (1921)
Toriola v. Arewa (1949)
Trimble v. Hill (1879-80)
Tsamiya v. Bauchi N.A. (1957)
Turquand, Ex parte (1884-85)

U

Ubom v. The State (1972)
Uka v. Insp.-Gen. of Police (1962)
Ukaegbu v. C.O.P. (1972)
Ukwa v. Awka Local Council (1966)
U.A.C. Ltd. v. Umeugo (1959)
United Kingdom Tobacco Co. Ltd. The v. Carreras Ltd. (1931)
Usifo II v. Oke (1957)

V

Velasquez Ltd. v. I.R.C. (1914)
Victorian Railway Commissioners v. Coultas (1888)

W

Waghoreghor v. Aghenghen (1974)
West Ham Union v. Edmonton Union (1903)
Williams v. Att.-General of Nigeria (1932)
Williams v. Akinwumi (1966)
Williams, Re (1941)
Wokoko v. Molyko (1938)
Worthington & Co. Re (1880)

Y

Young v. Abina (1940)
Young v. Bristol Aeroplane Company Ltd. (1944)
Younghusband v. Luftig (1949)

Z

Zaidan v. Mohssen (1973)
Zaria v. Small (1973)
Zeidman v. Owen (1950)

TABLE OF STATUTES

The Statutes are arranged alphabetically for ease of reference. The statutes listed are those referred to by the courts in the course of judgment or by the writer in the course of exposition.

Abolitionof the Osu System Law, 1956
Administration of Estates Law (Mid-Western State)
Appellate Jurisdiction Act, 1876 (English)
Appointment and Deposition of Chiefs Ordinance, 1948,
  s. 3(a)
  s. 3(b)
Constitution of the Federal Republic of Nigeria, 1963
  ss. 4, 5
  s. 26(1)
  s. 117
  s. 120
  s. 127
  s. 158
Constitution (Amendment) No. 2 Decree, 1976
  s. 1
  s. 3(1), (2)
Constitution of the Federal Republic of Nigeria, 1979
  s. 6
  s. 7
  s. 9
  s. 212
  s. 213
  s. 215
  s. 217
  s. 219
  s. 242, 247
  s. 258
  Fourth Schedule
Criminal Code Act, 1958
  s. 283, 318
  ss. 283, 284
Criminal Procedure Act, 1958
  s. 363
  s. 287
  s. 288

s. 12
High Court Law (Eastern Nigeria) 1963
s. 14
s. 15(2)
s. 16
s. 17
High Court (Civil Procedure Rules) (Eastern Nigeria)
Order 35, r. 1
Order 56, r. 15
High Court (Civil Procedure) Rules (Western Region)
Order 35, r. 10
Illiterates Protection Ordinance, 1958
Indian Code of Criminal Procedure s. 498(1)
Interpretation Act, 1964 s. 45
Jury Ordinance, 1958
Land Registration Act, 1958
Land Transfer Acts, 1875-1897 (English)
Law of England (Application) Law, 1959
s. 3
Law Reform (Married Women and Tortfeasors) Act, 1934, (English)
Limitation of Dowry Law, 1956
Magistrate's Court (Lagos) Ordinance, 1958
s. 14(2)
Magistrate's Court Edict, 1966 (East Centeral State)
s. 18(1)
Marriage Ordinance, 1948 s. 35
Matrimonial Causes Act, 1950 (English)
Matrimonial Causes Decree, 1970
Money-Lenders Act, 1927 (English)
Money-Lenders Ordinance, 1948 s. 12(1)
Native Courts Law (Northern Region) No. 6 of 1956
s. 20(1)(b)
Native Courts Ordinance No. 44 of 1933
Nigeria (Constitution) Order-in-council, 1954
s. 138
s. 142
Nigeria (Constitution) Order in Council, 1960
s. 2
s. 114
Protectorate Courts Ordinance, 1933
s. 32
Statute of Distribution, 1670
Recognition of Chiefs Law, 1957 (Western Region)
Recognition of Chiefs Law, 1960 (Eastern Region)
States Creation (Transitional Provisions) Decree, 1967
s. 1(5)

States Creation (Transitional Provisions) Decree, 1976
Supreme Court Ordinance, 1948
s. 14
s. 16
s. 17
Supreme Court Act, 1960
s. 9
Supreme Court Ordinance No. 12 of 1960
s. 9
Supreme Court Rules Order 27, r. 11 (English)
Town and Country Planning Act, 1947 (English)
s. 12(1)
Western Nigeria Constitution Amendment Law, 1963
Western State Court of Appeal Law, 1967

BIBLIOGRAPHY

Books and papers consulted in the course of preparation

Allen, Law in the Making, 7th edition

Allott, Essays in African Law, 1960

Ayandele and others, The Growth of African Civilization, Vol. 2, 1971

Brott, Stare Decisis in Nigeria - Some Random Thoughts, (1965) 6 Nigerian Bar Journal, 74

Chambers Twentieth Century Dictionary

Clerk and Linsell, Torts, 13th edition

Cowen, The Binding Effect of English Decisions Upon Australian Courts, (1944) 60 L.Q.R. 378

Craise, Statute Law, 7th edition

Daniels, The Common Law in West Africa, 1964

Dias, Jurisprudence, 3rd edition

Dias and Hughes, Jurisprudence, 1957

Dickinson, The Law Behind Law, (1929) 29 Columbia Law Review 113

Elias, Groundwork of Nigeria Law, 1954

Elias, Colonial Courts and the Doctrine of Judicial Precedent, (1955) 18 M.L.R. 356

Elias, The Nature of African Customary Law, 1956

Elias, (ed.) African Indigenous Law, 1975

Ellis Lewis, The History of Judicial Precedent, (1930) 46 L.Q.R. 207

——— The History of Judicial Precedent, (1931) 47 L.Q.R. 411

——— The History of Judicial Precedent, (1932) 48 L.Q.R. 230

——— The "I Think" Doctrine of Precedent (1950) 66 L.Q.R. 374

Ezejiofor, Stare Decisis in the Nigerian Courts (1972) 6 Nigerian Law Journal, 47

Freeman, The Protection Afforded Against the Retroactive Operation of an Overruling Decision (1918) 18 Columbia Law Review, 230

Glanville Williams, Learning the Law, 5th edition and 7th edition

Gooderson, The Rule in Young v. Bristol Aeroplane Co. Ltd. (1948-50) C.L.J. 432.

Goodhart, Precedent in English and Continental Law, (1934) 50 L.Q.R. 40

——— Precedent in Divisional Courts (1946) 9 M.L.R. 257
——— Precedents in the Court of Appeal, (1945-47) 9 C.L.J. 349
——— Essays in Jurisprudence and the Common Law (1931)
Halsbury, Laws of England, 2nd edition, Vols. 14 and 36
Hood Phillips, A First Book of English Law, 6th edition
Ijalaye, Chime v. Elikwu; Judicial Precedent; Conflicting Decisions of a Higher Tribunal (1971) 9 N.B.J. 63 (case comment)
Keay and Richardson, Native and Customary Court of Nigeria
Keeton, The Law of Trusts, 8th edition
Kiralfy, The English Legal System, 1954
Llewelyn, The Bramble Bush
Lloyd, Introduction to Jurisprudence, 2nd edition
Lord Wright, Precedents (1944) 8 Cambridge Law Journal 118
Nnaemeka-Agu, in African Indigenous Laws, 1975.
Oxford Advanced Learner's Dictionary of Current English
Park, Sources of Nigerian Law, 1963
Paton, A Textbook of Jurisprudence, 3rd edition
Paton and Sawer, Ratio Decidendi and Obiter Dictum in Appellate Courts (1947) 63 L.Q.R. 461
Radcliffe and Cross, The English Legal System, 3rd edition
Salmond, Jurisprudence, 11th edition
Simpson, The Ratio Decidendi of a Case (1959) 22 M.L.R. 453
Snell, Principles of Equity, 26th edition
Spencer Bower and Turner, The Doctrine of Res Judicata, 2nd edition
Stone, Stare Deçisis in the Divisional Court (1951) 14 M.L.R. 219
The Nigerian Bar Journal (1966) Vol. 8, p. 74.
The Times, Friday, September 24, 1976
Winder, Divisional Court Precedents (1946) 9 M.L.R. 257

ABBREVIATIONS USED IN THE TEXT

A.C.	Appeal Cases
A.E.R.	All England Law Report
A.-G or Att.-Gen. . . .	Attorney-General
ALL E.R.	All England Law Report
ALL N.L.R.	All Nigeria Law Report
APP. CAS	Appeal Cases
Cap.	Chapter (in reference to statutes)
C.A.R.	Criminal Appeal Report
C.F.A.O.	Compagnie Francaise Afrique de Occidentale
Ch.	Law Report of the Chancery Division
Ch. D.	Law Report of the Chancery Division
C.O.P.	Commissioner of Police
C.L.J.	Cambridge Law Journal
D.C.O.	Dominion, Colonial and Overseas
E.C.S.L.R.	East Central State Law Report
E.N.L.R.	Eastern Nigeria Law Report
E.R.N.L.R.	Eastern Region of Nigeria Law Report
F.C.A.	Federal Court of Appeal
F.S.C.	Selected Judgments of the Federal Supreme Court
G.L.R.	Ghana Law Report
Insp.-Gen.	Inspector-General of Police
Ir. Rep.	Irish Law Report
I.R.C.	Inland Revenue Commissioners
K.B.	Law Report of the King's Bench Division
L.C.C.	London County Council
L.E.D.B.	Lagos Executive Development Board
L.J.	Law Journal
L.L.R.	Lagos Law Report (Law Report of the High Court of Lagos)
L.Q.R.	Law Quarterly Review
M.L.R.	Modern Law Review
N.A.	Native Authority
N.B.J.	Nigerian Bar Journal
N.L.R.	Nigeria Law Report
N.M.L.	Nigeria Military Law
N.N.L.R.	Northern Nigeria Law Report
N.R.N.L.R.	Northern Region of Nigeria Law Report
P.C.	Privy Council Judgment
Q.B.D.	Report of the Queen's Bench Division

S.C.	Cyclostyled Judgments of the Supreme Court
T.L.R.	Times Law Report
U.A.C.	United Africa Company
W.A.C.A.	West African Court of Appeal Reports
W.L.R.	Weekly Law Report
W.N.L.R.	Western Nigeria Law Report
W.R.N.L.R.	Western Region of Nigeria Law Report
W.S.C.A.	Western State Court of Appeal

SUMMARY

I

THE NATURE OF JUDICIAL PRECEDENT AND ITS DEVELOPMENT IN NIGERIA

1

THE NATURE OF JUDICIAL PRECEDENT

The words "judicial precedent" import a technical concept. To make it intelligible to lawyer and layman alike we must preface its discussion and exposition with what is meant by precedent in common parlance.

1. Precedent in Common Parlance

There is good counsel in the injunction that we must work from the known to the unknown. In every field of human endeavour where an enquiry has to be conducted into a realm hitherto unknown the enquirer must find his premises and initial data before he starts. This confers a fourfold advantage. First, he will have a clear conception of his goal. Secondly, he will be able to understand and appreciate the significance and value of his discoveries. Thirdly, his initial knowledge and outlook will enable him to make a critical appraisal of his discoveries in the light of the purposes they are intended to achieve and to decide how they can be manipulated to achieve these purposes. Fourthly, since some subjects of scholastic exercise are not meant solely for the expert but also for the general reader, the latter will find it less difficult to assimilate the less familiar details of the result of the investigation.

This treatise on the doctrine of judicial precedent as applied in the Nigerian Courts will therefore be preceded by a definition and explanation of what precedent is in common parlance and what purposes it serves in everyday life. This basic knowledge will equip a newcomer to the study of judicial precedent with a vision of what to look for and what to expect from his study.

Chambers's *Twentieth Century Dictionary* defines a precedent as "that which precedes; a past instance that may serve as an example." From this definition two ideas clearly stand out. One is that a precedent must be the first happening of its kind in point of time. Another is that this happening may serve as an example for future happenings of a similar character. These two conceptions are the dominant elements in the idea of precedent. Dias and Hughes define a precedent as "any set pattern upon which future conduct may be based." They go on to say:

> This is a device which we constantly use in our daily lives, and it is but natural that we should find it employed by the law.[1]

Llewelyn would have us believe that:

> A precedent consists in an official doing over again under similar circumstances substantially what has been done by him or his predecessor before. The foundation, then, of precedent is the official analogue of what, in society at large, we know as folk-ways, or as institutions, and of what, in the individual, we know as habit.[2]

This definition would equate precedent with repetitive practice which it is not. It is not a subsequent instance or instances of an "official doing over again" what has been done before that constitute a precedent. The first happening is what is required. Again, it would be unnecessarily restrictive and short-sighted to limit precedent to what is "official," since, as Llewelyn himself admits, instances also occur in private lives. Whether in the private life of the individual or in the public life of the nation, the question is whether there is an occurrence that can be seized upon as an example for emulation for good or evil.

Advantages of Precedent

Lord Wright has said:

> Precedents are what they are because men faced with a problem ask "Have we not had this before or something like it"?[3]

Now let us ask: Why should people contemplating an action look for a precedent?

[1] *Jurisprudence*, 1957, p. 52.
[2] *The Bramble Bush*, p. 65.
[3] "Precedents" (1944) 8 Cambridge Law Journal, 118, 144.

The search for precedent has several purposes in view. First, there is the need for guidance. This is necessary to eliminate or reduce the tendency to error. This advantage becomes manifest to a later generation in one or two ways. The precedent act might have been flawless, in which case subsequent pursuers of similar conduct would have found a sure and infallible guide. Alternatively, their predecessors might have had some problems to grapple with before the precedent action succeeded, in which case the later generation would have learnt from their efforts. Professor Dennis Lloyd[4] regards precedents "as guides to future conduct."

The second reason for a search for precedent is to save time. Every decision involves some mental and painstaking efforts which can be obviated when there is a precedent in point to draw upon.

> To take the same course as has been taken previously, or as has usually been adopted in the past, not only confers the advantage of the accumulated experience of the past but also saves the effort of having to think out a problem anew each time it arises.[5]

The opinion of Kiralfy is equally cogent and worthy of note:

> It is waste of time and energy to decide every point that arises in daily life by tracing it back to first principles, like the propositions of geometry.[6]

To the above opinions we will add that not only persons planning a course of action similar to the precedent one will find it useful as a model but also all those who plan an improvement or edifice upon the precedent action. Such people will find that they do not have to crack their brains or waste their time about the fundamentals of their proposals, but that they can go straight ahead and build on a foundation that has already been laid for them. In this way their time and efforts are reserved for the challenges posed by the unknown and untried venture.

The third justification for precedent is orthodoxy. One's conduct may be criticised by one's fellows. They may daub it eccentric or utopian. They may seek to forestall it, or even mobilise public

[4] *Introduction to Jurisprudence*, 2nd edition, p. 366.
[5] *Ibid.*
[6] *The English Legal System*, 1954, p. 104.

opinion against it, but if its protagonist has a precedent to point to he will silence his critics. The precedent will persuade them and others whom they would otherwise influence that the conduct is orthodox, being precedented.

Lastly, those who look for precedent look for perfection. If the conduct to be emulated has won approbation or at least subserved its ends those seeking to emulate it will do so free of constraints. Moreover, they will be able to feel that what they are doing is best and practicable and that having succeeded once it will succeed again. Above all, there is an invaluable lesson to learn from the success story of the pioneers in the field.

Examples of Precedent in Everyday Life

Examples of precedent abound in everyday life. A referendum has never formed part of the British political machinery, but circumstances compelled Harold Wilson's administration to employ it in 1975 to determine the question of whether Britain should stay in, or withdraw from, the European Common Market. This machinery for ascertaining the views of the electorate was found to be a signal success. Later, following agitation by Scottish and Welsh politicians it was used again to determine the question of Scottish and Welsh independence.

The native administration system was introduced into Nigeria by Lord Lugard in 1914 and applied uniformly throughout the whole country while Nigeria remained a unitary colonial state. With the introduction of federalism and the consequent break-up of the country into three States in 1954, each State Government established its own system of local administration. Difficulties and problems which were not present during the unitary rule started to emerge. Then the country under the military administration went back to the uniform system of local administration with a strong devolution of powers and discretion to the States. The 1979 Constitution has carried forward the idea.[7]

In the above examples the agitation for the use of a referendum to decide the question of independence for Scotland and Wales stemmed from the fact that it was used once and was found to be

[7] See Section 7 and the Fourth Schedule.

successful. The return by Nigeria to the uniform system of local administration is encouraged by the experience gained during the period of indirect rule associated with the colonial administration. The native administration system established common directives for the whole country, but each governmental unit was free to stress its own peculiarities within the broad framework. Similarly, the present local government system is concerned with uniformity of objectives and not of administration.[8]

Precedent and its Dangers

We have seen that precedents are useful. They also have their dangers. Unless the precedent to be followed is a paragon, adherence to it may be a perpetuation of vice. The foolishness and the ignorance of the past may be repeated in the present. Again, an uncritical adherence to precedent may inhibit progress and dampen the spirit of experiment. To quote Professor Lloyd:

> There is, however, an inevitable danger that this tendency to follow past precedents may lead to stereotyped procedures and so stultify progress, and much of the working success of any organisation may depend on its ability to apply precedents creatively.[9]

Thirdly, a thing may be right and proper when done because the conditions of its age and environment are propitious. But conditions and circumstances do not remain static, and if the same action is done in future under different conditions and circumstances it may cease to command the respect and approval which it received when it was first done.

At present in the United Kingdom opinion seems to be current that a referendum ought not to be made a regular feature of British political life as it interferes with the sovereignty of Parliament. Further, it is argued that:

> holding a referendum on Scottish independence, not long after the EEC referendum would make it almost impossible to refuse to grant similar votes on other important issues.[10]

[8] Broadcast by Brigadier Yar' Adua, Chief of Staff, Supreme Headquarters, Lagos, Monday, October 4, 1976.

[9] *Introduction to Jurisprudence*, 2nd edition, p. 366.

[10] *The Times*, Friday, September 24, 1976.

These strictures merely emphasize the evils that can be expected from an over-indulgence of precedents.

2. Precedent in Legal Parlance

Now that we have seen what a precedent is and what it stands for in everyday life we will go on to define and discuss the central subject of our enquiry—precedent in Nigerian Courts. There are broad similarities between both concepts. A judicial precedent is a judicial decision which serves as a paradigm for future decisions.

> English courts make a habit of following their previous decisions within more or less well-defined limits. This is called the doctrine of precedent.[11]

Dr. Goodhart has written that:

> all legal systems follow precedents, for it is a natural practice of the human mind, whether legal or non-legal, to accept the same pattern in similar or analogous cases.[12]

To be useful as a precedent the material facts of the precedent case must be similar to the material facts of the case in which the precedent case is being invoked so that the same principle of decision will apply. In the unreported case of *Adewoyin v. Adeyefa*[13] the facts were exactly like those of the subsequent case of *Asiyanbi v. Adeniji.*[14] In both cases a head chief granted hunting rights over a piece of land to one family and later granted farming rights over the same piece of land to another family. The Supreme Court in each case decided that such a grant was improper. In *Asiyanbi v. Adeniji* the case of *Adewoyin v. Adeyefa* was cited as a precedent in point, the facts being similar.[15]

The two cases referred to above are exceptional in point of exact similarity of facts. Such cases are rare, and if such close similarity as existed in the above cases were required before the first could be a

[11] Glanville Williams, *Learning the Law*, 5th edition, p. 64.

[12] "Precedent in English and Continental Law" (1934) 50 L.Q.R. 40, 41.

[13] F.S.C. 167/62 decided on January 28, 1963.

[14] (1966) N.M.L.R. 106.

[15] See Dias and Hughes, *Jurisprudence*, 1957, p. 74, where the learned authors stated: "If in a later case the material facts coincide with or are contained within the material facts of the earlier case, then the earlier case is a precedent in point."

precedent for the second there would be a dearth of judicial precedents. In actual fact exactitude of constituent facts is not required. What is required is the coincidence of material facts.[16]

Thus, in *Duclaud v. Ginoux*[17] a wife, with the general authority of the husband, drove the latter's car for her own purposes and in a road accident the plaintiff who was a passenger in the car was injured. It was held on appeal that vicarious liability did not attach to the husband as the wife was not driving the car as an agent of the husband nor for his purposes. In so holding the Supreme Court relied upon the precedent decision in *Hewitt v. Bonvin*[18] in which a father was held not liable for the tort of his son in similar circumstances.

In the first case a wife was alleged to have committed a tort with her husband's car, while in the second it was a son who did so with his father's car. Again, in the first case a woman passenger was injured, while in the second case the injured passenger was a man. In applying the second case as a precedent in point in the first case the Supreme Court did not consider these differences to be material since they did not in any event influence the principle of law governing the cases. What was important was the "legally material facts"[19] which determined the law applicable to the cases. The law so laid down is known as the *ratio decidendi.*[20]

When lawyers say that one case is a precedent for another, what they mean is that the *ratio decidendi* of the one case can be followed in the other case. In other words, they mean that the first case has established a rule of law which the later case can look upon as an example and follow. The rule so laid down should be a right rule, but this is not always so, and instances are many in the law reports in which bad decisions are followed.[21]

[16] See Chapter 10.

[17] (1969) 1 All N.L.R. 26.

[18] (1940) 1 K.B. 188.

[19] Glanville Williams, *Learning the Law*, 5th edition, 1954, p. 64.

[20] See Glanville Williams, *Learning the Law*, 5th edition, pp. 65–69. The subject of *ratio decidendi* has a whole chapter to itself in this work—Chapter 10.

[21] Such instances are discussed in Chapters 8, 9 and 10.

2

PRECEDENT AND *RES JUDICATA*

Before we proceed further with our enquiry it is necessary to distinguish the doctrine of judicial precedent from another doctrine of Anglo-Nigerian law—that of *res judicata*. The possibility of confusion between both concepts is very real to the uninitiated student of precedent. A few significant differences exist between the two doctrines, but before a discourse on this is embarked upon we must cast our glance at definitions. A precedent as we have seen, is a judicial decision which later courts can regard as guides to decisions on cases pending before them. *Res judicata*, on the other hand, is a rule of estoppel which prevents a matter which has been finally determined between the parties in the same interests from being reopened.

At this juncture it is pertinent to quote Spencer Bower and Turner:

> In English jurisprudence a res judicata, that is to say a final judicial decision pronounced by a judicial tribunal having competent jurisdiction over the cause or matter in litigation, and over the parties thereto, disposes once and for all of the matters decided, so that they cannot afterwards be raised for re-litigation between the same parties or their privies.[1]

The main differences between precedent and *res judicata* are as follows. *Res judicata* is founded on the judgment of any competent court, however low in the judicial hierarchy, provided it has authority by law to make binding decisions. Thus, a judgment of a native court was held to constitute *res judicata*.[2] But only the higher courts create precedents.[3]

[1] *The Doctrine of Res Judicata*, 2nd edition, p. 1.

[2] *Seriki v. Solaru* (1965) N.M.L.R. 1.

[3] Dias, *Jurisprudence*, 3rd edition, p. 61; Dias and Hughes, *Jurisprudence* 1957, pp. 60–61.

In *res judicata* it is the last of the conflicting judgments of courts with equal jurisdiction over a subject matter that creates an estoppel.[4] But, generally speaking, this is not the rule when precedents of equal jurisdiction conflict. Where the conflicting precedents emanate from the High Court, lower courts have the liberty to decide which of them to follow, but are not bound to follow the last.[5] Where there is an unnoticed conflict between two decisions of a court higher than the High Court the same rule prevails and the High Court can follow either. But where the conflict has been noticed by the higher court and a definite pronouncement made, it is only the decision that is owned up and approved that represents the law.[6]

Thirdly, for *res judicata* to apply it must be shown that the parties, issues and subject matter are the same in the previous action as those in the action in which the plea is raised.[7] But the doctrine of precedent is law for the whole world and binds every litigant coming before the court with facts similar to those in the precedent decision.[8]

Fourthly, a court has no power to reassess and evaluate the evidence in the previous case when a judgment is tendered in proof of *res judicata* in order to decide whether the plea of *res judicata* is well founded.[9]

When, on the other hand, a case is cited as a precedent a court has the right and the power to study the facts as disclosed in the evidence in order to decide whether the *ratio decidendi* is born out by the facts, and if not, it can reconstruct the *ratio*.[10]

Fifthly, as *res judicata* is a question of facts, not law, it must be pleaded and evidence led on it.[11] But the applicability of a precedent

[4] *Makanjuola v. Khalil* (1958) W.R.N.L.R. 82.

[5] Salmond, *Jurisprudence*, 11th edition, pp. 169–170.

[6] *Fisher v. Ruislip-Northwood U.D.C.* (1945) 2 A.E.R. 458; *Johnson v. Lawanson* (1971) 1 N.M.L.R. 380; Dias and Hughes, *Jurisprudence*, 1957, pp. 66–67.

[7] *Alase v. Ilu* (1965) N.M.L.R. 66.

[8] Glanville Williams, *Learning the Law*, 5th edition, p. 64; Dias and Hughes, *Jurisprudence*, 1957, p. 74.

[9] *Waghoreghor v. Aghenghen* (1974) 1 S.C. 1.

[10] See Allen, *Law in the Making*, 7th edition, pp. 259–260; Dias, *Jurisprudence*, 3rd edition, pp. 63–64.

[11] *Agyako v. Zok* (1944) 10 W.A.C.A. 277; *Chellaram & Sons v. G.B. Ollivant Ltd.* (1944) 10 W.A.C.A. 77.

to the facts of a case is a question of law and is not required to be pleaded.

Sixthly, *res judicata* takes effect after the right to appeal against the decision is lost.[12] But a case is a precedent as soon as judgment is pronounced.

Seventhly, *res judicata* need not proceed from a statutory court; any body of persons to whom the parties voluntarily take their dispute and agree to abide by their decision can make a binding decision capable of operating as an estoppel.[13] Again, the regular courts are not the only bodies capable of making decisions that can work an estoppel, for it has been held that a registrar of titles can make such a decision.[14] But a judicial precedent must of necessity proceed from a court of law of superior jurisdiction.[15]

In the eighth place, a decision operating as *res judicata* from the lowest court binds even the highest court to the extent of precluding it from entertaining the same matter as that affected by the *res judicata*.[16] But a precedent of subordinate authority does not bind a higher court.[17]

The ninth difference is this. It appears that *res judicata* does not come into being as a result of an interlocutory decision, but only when the decision is final.[18] Precedent, on the other hand, can be created when the decision is not only final, but also interlocutory.[19]

Lastly, we agree with Spencer Bower and Turner that while the doctrine of *res judicata* is part of the doctrine which states that it is in the public interests that there should be an end to litigation, that of

[12] Not as Dias and Hughes say "after the time for appealing against the decision is past," for there is always a provision for an appeal out of time (*Jurisprudence*, 1957, p. 53). A right to appeal may be lost through factors other than effluxion of time.

[13] *Onwurike v. Onwurike* (1962) VI E.N.L.R. 10; *Inyang v. Esien* (1957) 2 F.S.C. 39.

[14] See *The Nigerian Bar Journal* (1966) Vol. VII, p. 74.

[15] Dias, *Jurisprudence*, 3rd edition, p. 61.

[16] See *Ngwo v. Monye* (1970) 1 All N.L.R. 91; *Onisango v. Akinkunmi* (1955–56) W.R.N.L.R. 39.

[17] *Itsekiri Communal Land Trustees v. Warri Divisional Planning Authority* (1973) 11 S.C. 235.

[18] *Olawoyin v. C.O.P.* (1961) All N.L.R. 130.

[19] *Kufeji v. Kogbe* (1961) All N.L.R. 113; *Egbe v. Eagle Group* (1970–71) 1 E.C.S.L.R. 64. In these cases precedents in interlocutory injunctions were followed.

precedent is only concerned with "the desirability of certainty and uniformity in the law."[20]

In conclusion, we have to admit that while there are differences between the two doctrines there are also broad similarities. One of these is that both doctrines proceed from bodies exercising judicial functions. The other is that each doctrine is designed for a definite, though different purpose.

[20] *The Doctrine of Res Judicata*, 2nd edition, p. 15.

3

THE DEVELOPMENT OF JUDICIAL PRECEDENT IN ENGLAND

The development of judicial precedent in England was fortuitous, not planned. By this we mean that no English lawyer or judge made up his mind to rely on previous decisions from the beginning of the judicial system. All cases that came before the royal courts were cases of first impression and the judges had to decide them in the light of custom, common sense, natural justice and public utility. Neither judge nor counsel at this stage troubled himself about precedents, for either there was none to invoke or no importance was attached to them for the purpose of subsequent litigation.[1]

But in the process of time, as litigation increased different departments of social, economic, commercial and political life came under judicial regulation. As events repeated themselves and came before the courts it became necessary to have recourse to earlier decisions for purposes of guidance, and between the twelfth and the thirteenth centuries we find evidence of citation of authorities by counsel and writers on common law.[2]

However, apart from Bracton who listed some two thousand cases in his Note Book and employed five hundred of these in his exposition of the law, some of the "institutional writers" employed none and some others one each. Bracton was, therefore, the most prolific and influential of the early writers. He had a purpose to serve in employing these cases. His view was that the basic principles of the common law as previously established were being distorted by the profession and he cited old and new cases to illustrate the principles that were being distorted.[3]

[1] Ellis Lewis, "The History of Judicial Precedent" (1930) 46 L.Q.R. 207, 215.

[2] See Allen, *Law in the Making*, 7th edition, p. 188; Dias and Hughes, *Jurisprudence*, 1937, p. 54.

[3] Allen, pp. 187–189, Dias and Hughes, pp. 54–55.

Perhaps Bracton's use of cases had a profound influence on the development of the doctrine of precedent. He succeeded in persuading his contemporaries that the legal importance of the cases was not limited to the parties but extended to the world at large because they provided guidance as to the lines which future cases based on similar facts should take, as well as material for professional and academic study. Right from the last quarter of the thirteenth century we find the Year Books coming into being. They are thought to be notes compiled by students of law on points of practice to remind them and their successors of what the law was on these points. The Year Books bore no true resemblance to our modern law reports; they did not contain the facts of the cases, arguments, or decisions thereon and reasons for the decisions, though according to Radcliffe and Cross:

> in the course of time they improved very much in quality. Those of the fifteenth century are generally distinctively superior to those of the fourteenth.[4]

But it would be a mistake to think that the Year Books were authoritative, for they were private collections of cases of which the authors were aware and must have been based on memory. At this time the theory of binding precedent did not evolve. Cases were, no doubt, cited from the Year Books, but they were intended merely as guidelines and not that the judges should be bound by them. Nevertheless, as we saw in the case of Bracton, the Year Books contributed in no small measure to the development of English jurisprudence since they record evidence of the development of the binding doctrine of precedent.[5]

With the exit of the Year Books in the sixteenth century came an era of private law reports. During this period the reports of Dyer, Plowden, Coke and Burrow figure prominently, among others. But those of Burrow are thought to be the best of them all and to show resemblance with our modern law reports and, in fact, paved the way for them.

[4] *The English Legal System*, 3rd edition, p. 95.

[5] For the influence of the Year Books see Radcliffe and Cross, pp. 363–364, Allen, pp. 190–203, Dias and Hughes pp. 55–56 and Ellis Lewis (1930) 46 L.Q.R. 207.

> They distinguish clearly between argument, facts, and decision and give proper reports of the judgments.[6]

Despite the attempts of the various law reporters of the period before the nineteenth century to make knowledge of decided cases common property there was no clearly evolved system of binding precedents. This was because the hierarchy of the courts was unsettled, and in the absence of such a settlement it was impossible to say which court bound which court. Apart from the decisions of the Court of Exchequer Chamber which commanded great respect because of the number of judges who sat to give them, no other court was able to claim such respect for its decisions. Particularly looked down upon were decisions of judges of *nisi prius*, both because they were decisions of single judges only and because they were given on the spur of the moment and not reserved.[7]

Even the House of Lords at the time—the highest court of appeal in England—could not win any respect for its decisions. About precedents in the House of Lords during this time Salmond has this to say:

> Whatever may be thought of the rule as applied to modern decisions, it can hardly be said that all the old decisions of the House are of high intrinsic authority.[8]

This was so for at least two reasons. First, the speeches contained only facts, arguments and judgments, but without the grounds on which the judgments were predicated. Secondly, no distinction was drawn between the House as a legislative body and as a court, for all the Lords, both laymen and professionally qualified lawyers, took part in its judicial work. About this time the quorum in the House was three and the other two members were men not trained in the law who always endorsed the view of the only qualified professional lawyer on the panel.[9]

To make decisions binding and authoritative two sets of reforms were carried out. One was to increase the legal element in the House

[6] Dias and Hughes, p. 57.
[7] Radcliffs and Cross, pp. 176–177.
[8] Salmond, *Jurisprudence*, 11th edition, p. 176.
[9] Salmond, p. 177.

of Lords from one to two.[10] Another was the passing of the Judicature Acts, 1873–1875. To quote Radcliffe and Cross:

> Under the Judicature Acts the Court of Chancery, the Courts of Queen's Bench Common Pleas and Exchequer, the Court of Probate, the Court of Divorce and Matrimonial Causes, the Court of Admiralty and the London Court of Bankruptcy were consolidated and united together in one Supreme Court of Judicature, which was divided into two parts, the High Court of Justice and the Court of Appeal.[11]

At the apex of this pyramid was the House of Lords as a final court of appeal created by the Appellate Jurisdiction Act, 1876.

Under these legislative arrangements it became evident which court bound which. The principle of the binding force of precedent took definite shape at this time, and in the practice that was evolved all lower courts were bound by higher courts[12] and the House of Lords considered itself bound by its own decisions.[13]

1. Reasons for the Doctrine

Twelve reasons (collected from the opinions of jurists and judges) have been assigned for the existence of the binding force of precedent.[14] These are: (1) that they are the principal and most authoritative evidence of the custom that forms part of the law; (2) that it is the culmination of a deep-laid conspiracy to oppress the people; (3) respect for one's ancestors; (4) practical expediency; (5) flexibility; (6) convenience; (7) *elegantia juris*—scientific development of the law; (8) prevention of errors of individual judgment; (9) prevention of partiality or prejudice; (10) prevention of inequality; (11) the mischief that will result from an overruling of a case that has been persistently followed and on which citizens have based their

[10] *Ibid.*

[11] *The English Legal System*, 3rd edition, p. 288.

[12] Radcliffe and Cross, p. 364.

[13] See *London Street Tramways v. London County Council* (1898) A.C. 375. But by a Practice Statement of 1966—see (1966) 3 A.E.R. p. 77—the House of Lords declared that it reserved the right to reconsider any of its decisions if there was the need to do so.

[14] See Goodhart, "Precedent in English and Continental Law," (1934) 50 L.Q.R. 40.

transactions, and (12) certainty in the law. Although all these reasons have been effectively debunked by Dr. Goodhart and other writers we shall single out some of them for additional short comments. The claim in (3)—respect for the opinion of one's ancestors—is misconceived. Several better methods of paying homage to one's ancestor are available. One is to write his biography; another is to compose an epitaph extolling his virtues in other respects. But to follow a bad judicial precedent established by one's ancestor as a mark of respect for him is the most damaging method of displaying his ignorance and lowering his esteem in the opinion of generations of lawyers.

The view in (8)—prevention of the errors of individual judgment—is tenable so long as the original precedent represents the law, but if it is wrong, to follow it would be to perpetuate the error. In (10) we are told that the reason is to prevent inequality. True, it is an elementary principle of justice that like cases should be treated alike. But why should an error made in the first case be repeated in the second? And why should generations of litigants suffer injustice because the first judge made an error from which later judges feel they cannot deviate?[15]

2. How the Doctrine is Applied in England

From a study of the history of judicial precedent in England it is clear that the doctrine applied to decisions only of the High Court and the higher courts which thereby bind all lower courts.

> County Courts and Magistrate's Courts do not create binding precedents.[16]

But a decision of one High Court judge is of persuasive authority only when invoked before another High Court judge, though in practice he will not depart from it unless he is clearly convinced that the decision is wrong.[17] When two High Court Divisions decide the same point of law differently the latter is not thereby overruling the

[15] Further comments are reserved for Chapter 8 where merits and demerits of *stare decisis* are treated.

[16] Dias and Hughes, *Jurisprudence*, 1957, p. 60.

[17] *Huddersfield Police Authority v. Watson* (1947) 2 All E.R. 202.

former, but the two decisions stand side by side until the "legal antinomy" is resolved by a higher authority.[18] Until such resolution lower courts are free to follow whichever they prefer.

A Divisional Court binds itself. This was the position taken in *Huddersfield Police Authority v. Watson*[19] when counsel invited the Court to overrule its previous decision in *Garvin v. City of London Police*.[20] Lord Goddard, C.J., said:

> In any event, whether it was rightly decided or not, I am clearly of opinion that we ought to follow it. This court is made a final court of appeal in these matters . . .; and I can imagine nothing more disastrous than, where the Court has given a decision on the construction or application of this Act, that another Court should give a contrary decision so that there would then be two conflicting cases and no finality in the matter at all.[21]

It appears, however, that this inflexible stand will not be maintained where the precedent case has not been argued on one side[22] or on both sides.[23] That these exceptions have been recognised is a salutary development; the spirit of the common law would be killed by an uncritical adherence to precedent by a court which is a final court of appeal in cases originating in the Magistrates' Court. As Dr. Goodhart has observed:

> There is an obvious antithesis between rigidity and growth, and if all the emphasis is placed on absolutely binding cases then the law loses the capacity to adapt itself to the changing spirit of the times which has been described as the life of the law.[24]

The Divisional Court is not bound by the decision of a single High Court judge,[25] but will treat it with respect. A Divisional Court hearing civil cases is bound by the Court of Appeal (Civil

[18] Salmond, *Jurisprudence*, 11th edition, p. 1671; Dias and Hughes, *Jurisprudence*, 1957, p. 61.
[19] (1947) 2 A.E.R. 193.
[20] (1944) 1 A.E.R. 378.
[21] P. 195.
[22] *Edwards v. Jones* (1947) 1 A.E.R. 830.
[23] *Nicholas v. Penny* (1950) 2 A.E.R. 89.
[24] "Precedent in Divisional Courts" (1948) 64 L.Q.R. 40, 41–42.
[25] Dias and Hughes, *Jurisprudence*, 1957, p. 62.

Division)[26] and by the Court of Appeal (Criminal Division) in respect of criminal cases.[27]

The Court of Appeal (Criminal Division) binds all inferior Criminal Courts. Its decisions are binding upon itself, except in cases where the liberty of the subject is involved.[28] It does not bind the Court of Appeal (Civil Division) because it is of co-ordinate jurisdiction; nor is it bound by the latter for the same reason. When one of its precedents is challenged, the court sits as a full court to consider the matter. This is what happened in Taylor's case.[29] Three judges normally constitute a court, but a full court would be five or more.[30]

It is difficult to see what greater powers a full court has over a division of that court. The law in granting it power to hear and determine appeals from the High Court does not distinguish between a full court and a division of the court. The practice of assembling a full court to consider a precedent that is under attack has no statutory basis and is based on convention. Power to depart from precedent is again not conferred by statute. In the circumstances we shall conclude that a decision by the so-called full court does not destroy the precedent, but only scathes it since the full court has no greater powers than a single division of the court and cannot, therefore, overrule the previous decision.[31] Both are laws though the later decision gains more in weight than the first because of the greater number of judges taking part in it and because of the change of front it represents. It needs the axe of the House of Lords to kill it and wipe it off the legal plate. Otherwise there is nothing to prevent a later court of co-ordinate jurisdiction from adopting and following it.

We now turn our attention to the Court of Appeal (Civil Division). It binds all lower civil courts and also binds itself. But in *Young v. Bristol Aeroplane Company*[32] the court, while declaring that it was bound by its previous decisions, stated three exceptions

[26] *Read v. Joannon* (1890) 25 Q.B.D. 300, 302–303.
[27] *Hawke v. Mackenzie* (1902) 2 K.B. 225, 231.
[28] *R. v. Taylor* (1950) 2 A.E.R. 170.
[29] Supra.
[30] Salmond, *Jurisprudence*, 11th edition, p. 193.
[31] See Winder, "Divisional Court Precedents" (1946) 9 M.L.R. 257, 264.
[32] (1944) K.B. 718 (C.A.); (1946) A.C. 163.

under which it might depart from them. Under the rule the court will not be bound by its previous decision if it is in conflict with another decision of the court, or if, in the opinion of the court, it is in conflict with a subsequent decision of the House of Lords, or if the earlier decision was given *per incuriam*, that is, in ignorance of statute or rule having statutory force.

Under the first of these exceptions the court will choose between its previous inconsistent decisions. Under the second the court will prefer the decision of the House of Lords, and under the third a decision which is in consonance with the statute or rule having statutory force will be worked out.

But these exceptions do not appear to exhaust the circumstances in which the court should be impelled to consider its previous decisions. Previous decisions are not considered for fun. They are to be considered when the interests of justice demand it, and it cannot be said that the totality of interests served by justice fall within the three exceptions stated in *Young's case*. Their Lordships have not even said whether they consider the interests of justice paramount or those of legal certainty. As Dr. Goodhart rightly observes, the Court of Appeal did not consider "the wisdom of the rule or the grounds on which it was based" but talked of the undesirability of the court to depart from its previous decision given on a question of principle.[33]

Lastly, we shall consider the application of the doctrine in the House of Lords. For some years before 1898 considerable controversy had raged in the House about the question of whether the House should stick to its previous decisions, whatever the circumstances, or not.[34] But in *London Street Tramways v. London County Council*[35] whatever doubt remained of the position was cleared when the Lords declared avowedly that they were bound by their previous decisions.

Since then the Lords have pursued two undesirable lines. One is to adhere to precedent however wrong it is and leave it to Parliament to alter the law if thought fit to do so.[36] Another is to indulge in

[33] Goodhart, "Precedents in the Court of Appeal" (1945–47) 9 C.L.J. 349, 350–351.

[34] See quotations from decided cases in Salmond, *Jurisprudence* 11th edition, p. 175.

[35] (1898) A.C. 375.

[36] See Salmond, p. 183.

spurious distinguishing to escape from an inconvenient precedent. But all these are roundabout and costly ways of solving the problem created by the doctrine of *stare decisis*. It is roundabout in that the House of Lords is trying to share its judicial functions with Parliament and abdicate its responsibility to that body. It is costly in that such abdication of responsibility and self-effacement could, in a totalitarian state, mean executive encroachment and usurpation of judicial power. Again, the trend, if continued, will cost the House its fame as the world's repository of legal wisdom.

Happily enough the statement of practice by the Lords in 1966[37] engendered a sigh of relief in the profession as a whole. It declared:

> Their Lordships regard the use of precedent as an indispensable foundation upon which to decide what is the law and its application to individual cases. It provides at least some degree of certainty upon which individuals can rely in the conduct of their affairs, as well as a basis for orderly development of legal rules.
>
> Their Lordships nevertheless recognise that too rigid adherence to precedent may lead to injustice in a particular case and also unduly restrict the proper development of the law. They propose therefore to modify their present practice and, while treating former decisions of this House as normally binding, to depart from a previous decision when it appears right to do so.
>
> In this connexion they will bear in mind the danger of disturbing retrospectively the basis on which contracts, settlements of property and fiscal arrangements have been entered into and also the especial need for certainty as to the criminal law.
>
> This announcement is not intended to affect the use of precedent elsewhere than in this House.

This practice statement is a welcome one. For the first time it has held out the hope that the House, as the final court of appeal, will not hold blindly on to the doctrine of *stare decisis*, but will review its previous decisions where it considers it right to do so. Human vision is strictly limited. A decision which is right today in the present circumstances may turn out to be wrong and unjust tomorrow because of change of circumstances. A judicial system

[37] (1966) 3 A.E.R. 77.

which is appointed to dispense justice must adapt itself to some change. A system that is averse to change is a monument of injustice.

Welcome as the practice statement is, it is of limited value. It is limited only to the House of Lords; it does not apply to other courts below it. Although the Divisional Court, the Court of Appeal (Civil Division) and the Court of Appeal (Criminal Division) have declared their stands at various times it is submitted that two constraints still remain. One is that the circumstances in which these courts say they will be free to depart from their previous decisions are inadequate, being too much circumscribed. They should be as liberal as the House of Lords, declaring that a departure will be registered when it appears right to do so without specifying the particular circumstances in which this will be done. Alternatively, if it is feared that there may not be agreement between the Bench and the Bar as to "when it appears right" to depart from a previous decision it is suggested that the totality of the circumstances which may justify a departure from precedent should be spelt out.[38] The light of experience makes it possible to locate such circumstances.

The other constraint is the rule that lower courts are bound by higher courts. True, it is undesirable for lower courts not to be bound by a higher authority to which appeals lie from the lower courts. Appellate jurisdiction would be nugatory in such circumstances. But suppose the higher court has made a mistake as is sometimes the case. How can its decision be followed without perpetuating an error? It is suggested that there should be established a machinery whereby it would be possible for a lower court to bring to the notice of a higher court, preferably the House of Lords, the point of law involved, indicating the reasons why it considers it wrong and asking for second thoughts on the decision. The technique will remove not only anomalies in the law and ensure justice, but will also promote the much-canvassed legal certainty.

A word must also be said about the peculiar position of the Privy Council. It is not part of the hierarchy of English courts in the ordinary sense but is a final appellate court for British colonies and dependencies. Formerly it also heard appeals from the dominions,

[38] Contrast this with the practice recommended for Nigeria where no such declaration has been made (see Chapter 8).

but most of this jurisdiction is now gone as the dominions prefer to have final appellate courts on their own soil.[39] The relationship between the Privy Council and the English legal system is summed up by a learned writer as follows:

> it is not an appellate tribunal from the ordinary courts of England and Wales, other than ecclesiastical and Admiralty, nor, of course, from Scotland. English courts, therefore, of whatever degree, theoretically reserve to themselves independence in respect of Privy Council decisions.[40]

The reason why English courts are not bound by the decisions of the Privy Council are not far to seek. It is appointed to settle points of law other than English law, and where the points it has settled have some resemblance to English law its decisions have only a persuasive effect.[41]

[39] Nigeria, for example, stopped appeals to the Privy Council in 1963; see section 120 of the 1963 Constitution.

[40] Allen, *Law in the Making*, 7th edition, pp. 249–250.

[41] The decisions of the Privy Council aspect of the Nigerian legal system up to 1st October, 1963, will be treated in Chapter 13.

4

THE MODES OF INTRODUCTION OF THE DOCTRINE INTO NIGERIA

In Chapter One we discussed the meaning of judicial precedent and, in Chapter Three, its origin and development in England. In this chapter we are going to discuss the different modes in which the doctrine came to be imported into Nigeria from its English home.

1. Introduction of the Common Law

Following the establishment of British rule in Nigeria between 1861 and 1914[1] English law was introduced into different parts of the country at different times by a series of proclamations and ordinances.[2] English law started with the Lagos Settlement which later became a colony on cession to the British Crown in 1861. Later, when British rule extended farther into the mainland that area was constituted into the Protectorate of Southern Nigeria. A separate administrative unit was being established to the north of the Southern Protectorate and this was called the Protectorate of Northern Nigeria. In 1914 Lord Lugard "brought the northern and southern portions of the country under one administration."[3]

In the same year the Supreme Court Ordinance was enacted which superseded all former ordinances and proclamations and "became applicable to the whole of Nigeria on the amalgamation of

[1] See Ayandele and others, *The Growth of African Civilisation*, Volume 2, 1971, Chapters 4 and 5.

[2] See Elias, *Groundwork of Nigerian Law*, 1954, pp. 17-18; Daniel, *The Common Law in West Africa*, 1964, pp. 54-62.

[3] See p. 155 in the textbook mentioned in note 1 above.

Northern and Southern Nigeria with effect from January, 1914."[4] The last of such ordinances which survivea up to the time that Nigeria became a federation in 1954 was the Supreme Court Ordinance,[5] section 14 of which provides:

> Subject to the terms of this or any other Ordinance, the Common Law, the doctrines of equity, and the statutes of general application which were in force in England on the 1st January, 1900, shall be in force within the jurisdiction of the Court.

When the country became a federation the above provision was repealed and re-enacted in the High Court Laws of the respective regions which were carved out of the country.[6] In Lagos which was then a Federal territory and not a region the High Court of Lagos Ordinance (now Act) governed the question of reception.

In this way English common law and equity came to have a foothold in Nigeria. The question now for us to consider is the date of reception. Authorities are agreed that the statutes of general application were received on 1st January, 1900, as part of Nigeria's *corpus juries.*[7] But there is no agreement among textwriters as to whether this limiting date also applies to common law and equity. Dr. T. O. Elias[8] and Professor A. N. Allott[9] are of the opinion that the same date applies to both. Mr. A. E. W. Park proffers the contrary view.[10]

According to Mr. Park the current common law and equity in force in England is meant to be in force in Nigeria. He claims

[4] Elias, *Groundwork of Nigerian Law*, 1954, p. 18. "In this way," continues Elias, "were introduced into the Colony and Protectorate of Nigeria the rules of English Common Law, the principles of English Equity and 'Statutes of general application which were in force in England' on 4 March 1863 (as regards Lagos Settlement) and 1 January 1900 (as regards the whole country)."

[5] Cap. 211, Vol. 6 of the Laws of Nigeria, 1948.

[6] See Eastern Region High Court Law No. 27 of 1955, S. 15; Western Region High Court Law, 1955, S. 14; Northern Region High Court Law No. 8 of 1955, S. 28; High Court of Lagos Ordinance No. 25 of 1955.

[7] *Lawal v. Younan and Sons* (1961) All N.L.R. 245; Textwriters—Allott, *Essays in African Law*, 1960, p. 29; Elias, *Colonial Courts and the Doctrine of Judicial Precedent*, 1955 18 M.L.R. 356; Park, *Sources of Nigerian Law*, 1963, pp. 19–23.

[8] "Colonial Courts and the Doctrine of Judicial Precedent" (1955) 18 M.L.R. 356.

[9] *Essays in African Law*, 1960, Chapter 2.

[10] *Sources of Nigerian Law*, 1963, pp. 19-24.

support from the wordings of the various statutes which make the law applicable. With reference to section 45 of the Interpretation Act which reads in part:

> the common law of England and the doctrines of equity, together with the statutes of general application . . .

Mr. Park says:

> Here the substitution of "together with" for "and" effectively separates the relative clause from the first two types of law.[11]

In support of this contention Mr. Park makes further references to the wording of two separate statutes. With reference to section 28 of the Northern Region (now Northern States) High Court Law Mr. Park says that the fact that the different bodies of received law—common law, equity and statutes of general application—are listed in separate paragraphs and marked off from one another by semicolons is evidence that the reception date applies to the statutes only.

> Moreover, [says Park] section 3 of the law of England (Application) Law of Western Nigeria, which receives only the Common Law and Equity contains no limiting date.[12]

This argument has great force. In the Northern States, High Court Law the fact that the words "which were in force" follow "statutes of general application" in the same paragraph in which these words occur strongly indicates that the limiting date applies to "the statutes of general application" only and not to common law and equity. The same impression seems to be created by the above Western Nigeria Law[13] to which he has referred and which adopts only the common law and equity without any limitation as to date. The view that the limiting date applies to statutes only and that only the Common law and equity presently current in England is received has the support of another learned writer.[14]

Park rejects the view that only the pre-1900 English cases are received in Nigeria on the ground that it will "compel the courts to

[11] *Ibid.*, p. 21.
[12] *Ibid.*, p. 22.
[13] Laws of England (Application) Law, 1959 (Cap. 60); Laws of Western Region, 1959.
[14] See Daniels, *The Common Law in West Africa*, 1964, pp. 123–124.

observe outdated rules." His view has some merits. If the current English common law and doctrines of equity are what the various statutes enjoin in Nigeria then the Nigerian legal system stands to benefit (as it is in fact benefitting from the richer experience of the better developed British system.) Nigerian Courts would be saved the tedium and drudgery of having to think out problems anew as they have the richer English *corpus juris* to draw upon. Again, our courts would not need to grope for authorities because these are abundant and are reported in one English Law Report or the other.[15]

On the other hand, if only the pre-1900 case-law is received, some difficulties might arise. The Nigerian courts might find themselves without guidance on questions that have not been decided in England since English case law at that date was not as rich as it is today. Again, where the English courts have overruled the pre-1900 cases in post-1900 decisions the Nigerian courts might be building on foundations that had been abandoned in England.

It is not true, however, that Nigerian courts are being called upon to "observe outdated rules." The statutes which enjoin the application and observance of these rules were not enacted for the first time when Mr. Park wrote in 1963. They were enacted and came into effect soon after the date of reception[16] and the doctrines of common law and equity in force in England a short time before were to be received and not those "which existed over sixty years ago"[17] as Mr. Park claims in 1963. The intention was to give the Nigerian courts a base to build on and to develop the Nigerian common law and equity independently of Britian, but *pari passu* with her. In other words, the reception was of the common law and equity as operating in England at the time, and from the date of reception the Nigerian legal system was to develop along its own lines.

Park's "current law reception" theory (to be so called hereafter) is not without support from judicial circles. Thus in *Osumanu v.*

[15] Our courts in fact have these benefits at their disposal, for nearly all English Law Reports are available in this country.

[16] See Elias, *Groundwork of Nigerian Law*, 1954, pp. 17–18, from whose account it is possible to conclude that English law was introduced into the different parts of the country not more than two years from the time each part was acquired by the British.

[17] Park, p. 20.

Seidu[18] the West African Court of Appeal followed the principle laid down by the English Court of Appeal in 1944 in *Young v. Bristol Aeroplane Co. Ltd.*[19] and declared:

> the position , so far as this court is concerned, is that it is bound to follow previous decisions of its own, as well as those of Courts of co-ordinate jurisdiction.

Blackall, P., who delivered the judgment of the court stated the exceptions to the rule just as the Court of Appeal stated them, and in the second exception he declared that the court will not be bound by "a decision of its own which, though not expressly overruled, cannot, in its opinion, stand with a decision of the Judicial Committee of the Privy Council or the House of Lords." In *Motayo v. C.O.P.*[20] the same court declared:

> This court will adopt in criminal matters the principle enunciated by the Court of Criminal Appeal . . .

All of the authorities cited in *R. v. Ajani*[21] were post-1900 English decisions, but the West African Court of Appeal felt compelled to follow them and observed:

> it is for the legislature and not for this court to effect an alteration of the law, and we feel bound to give effect to the law as we find it.

Again, the English case of *R. v. Abbott*,[22] a post-1900 decision of the Court of Criminal Appeal, was followed in *Adisa v. C.O.P.*[23] and *R. v. Ajani* (supra) was not referred to. In *Dede v. United Arab Airlines*[24] Holden, J., refused to apply the *dicta* of Bairamian, J.A., in *Ojemuyiwa v. Sun Insurance Office Ltd.*[25] on the ground that "it came before the very clear judgment of the Court of Appeal in the

[18] (1949) 12 W.A.C.A. 437.
[19] (1944) K.B. 718; (1944) 2 A.E.R. 293.
[20] (1950) 3 W.A.C.A. 114. The English Court of Criminal Appeal case was *R. v. Taylor* (1950) 2 A.E.R. 170; (1950) 2 K.B. 368.
[21] (1936) 3 W.A.C.A. 3, 7.
[22] (1955) 39 C.A.R. 141.
[23] (1961) W.N.L.R. 81.
[24] (1969) 1 N.M.L.R. 75.
[25] (1965) N.M.L.R. 451.

Post Office case."[26] The case of *Smith v. Selwyn*[27] was applied in *Tiamiyu v. Ashiru*[28] and the principle of law stated there approved.[29]

All of the above cases that have been followed are post-1900 English cases, and with them in view it is easy to agree with Park that only the current common law and equity are in force in Nigeria. This is all the more so when the Nigerian courts treat such cases as if they are binding upon them. Thus in *Shokoye v. Insp. Gen. of Police*[30] Onyeama, Ag. C.J., Lagos (as he then was), in allowing an appeal against a conviction for affray when self-defence was set up before a magistrate, said:

> The attention of the learned magistrate was not drawn to two cases, namely, *R. v. Sharp* and *R. v. Johnson* both of which are reported in (1957) 1 Q.B. 552.

From the quoted remarks it would appear that the learned Ag. C.J. was implying that the two post-1900 cases were binding on the magistrate. If this is what he meant and if all superior courts in this country took the same attitude to English precedents in the magistrate's court then the doctrine of precedent in Nigeria would face a grim future for three reasons. One is that magistrates' courts have too much on their hands; another is that the standard of advocacy in these courts is lower than in the High Court, and a third is poor library, especially in the areas outside the State headquarters, where recent English cases cannot be expected.

Further support for Park's view is found in the Eastern Nigeria High Court Law[31] which is presently in force in all four States which formerly formed Eastern Nigeria. Section 15(1) of this Law provides:

> Subject to the provisions of this Section and except in so far as other provision is made by any law in force in the Region, the common law of England, the doctrines of equity and the statutes of general application that were in force in England on the first

[26] That is, *Post Office v. Norwich Union Fire Insurance Co. Ltd.* (1967) 2 W.L.R. 709.

[27] (1914) 3 K.B. 90.

[28] (1955) 21 N.L.R. 42.

[29] The principle of the case was also approved in *Eze v. Illonse* (1962) 6 E.N.L.R. 79, but it was held not to apply to the case.

[30] (1962) 2 All N.L.R. 119, 121.

[31] Cap. 61, Vol. IV of the Laws of Eastern Nigeria 1963.

> day of January, 1900, shall, in so far as they relate to any matter for which the Legislature of the Region is for the time being competent to make laws, be in force within the jurisdiction of the court.

This section as worded is a fundamental departure from its predecessor in the Supreme Court Ordinance. The crucial words are "in so far as they relate to any matter for which the Legislature of the Region is for the time being competent to make laws." To which of the three bodies of law do these words refer? Certainly not to "common law" or "the doctrines of equity," for it is difficult to envisage any matter dealt with by the common law or equity for which the legislature of the Region was not competent to make law.

The expression can, therefore, be taken to refer to statutes of general application exclusively, since, under the federal constitution of Nigeria, there is an allocation of power between the Federal legislature and the state legislatures and a state legislature can make laws for some matters and not for others. The expression specifies what "statutes of general application that were in force in England on the first day of January, 1900," can come within regional competence. It excludes statutes dealing with subjects essentially within federal competence. From this analysis it can be presumed that the legislature intends that the current common law and doctrine of equity should be received and that Park is correct.

The view of Park and the practice of the courts are not, however, free from difficulties and dangers. First, it is clear from section 14 of the Supreme Court Ordinance[32] that the English common law and equity as at 1st January, 1900, were intended to be in force. If, in subsequent legislations, the legislatures of Nigeria have changed their minds, express words should have been used. It is difficult to accept the view that a legislature would adopt foreign laws that are not yet in existence and of whose scope and limitations it has no idea.

Secondly, since the original statutes and current statutes use the words "shall be in force" the legislative intention there is that this "received" law is mandatory and has obligatory force, the provision being absolute.[33] This being so, the current decisions of the English

[32] Cap. 211, Vol. VI of the Laws of Nigeria, 1948.

[33] See Craise, *Statute Law*, 7th edition, pp. 260–261.

High Court are binding even on the Nigerian Supreme Court as Nigerian statutes. English courts would be making laws for Nigeria which Nigerian courts must swallow hook, bait and sinker. A Nigerian court, even the Supreme Court, would not have power to overrule an English High Court decision or even refuse to follow it. Every case overruled by a Court of Appeal in England would cease to represent the law in Nigeria even when it has been followed in a Nigerian decision.

Thirdly, the Nigerian courts would have to exercise *exacta diligentia* in coming to decisions, exploring every avenue to make sure that there is no contrary English decision in point, or they would be caught by the doctrine of *per incuriam.* Every decision given in ignorance of an English case and inconsistent with it would be given *per incuriam.* Where a Nigerian court happens to differ from an English court the Nigerian court would be committing a breach of statute and its decision would be *ultra vires* and, therefore, null and void. In the circumstances, rights acquired and duties imposed under such a judgment would lack the concomitant attribute of legal enforceability. Executions levied in consequence of such judgments would be void as having no basis on which to operate and sheriffs would be exposed to the danger of civil actions for trespass and conversion.

A situation like this is horrible to contemplate. It is inconceivable that the legislature would have liked to produce it, or that, in enacting that section of the statute and investing it with the meaning attributed to it by Park and Daniel, it did not have in contemplation these possible consequences. The "current law reception" theory, if tenable at all, is only tenable in the Western States because of the special provision of the Law of England (Application) Law, Section 3, with the possible consequences we have adumbrated above.[34]

But the "current law reception" theory appears untenable. As Elias states[35] the first reception date was 1st January, 1863, by an Ordinance of that year. Subsequently the date shifted from 1863 to 24th July, 1874, and lastly to 1st January, 1900, where it remains till today. Subsequent legislations have not changed the date again.

[34] It is, however, unlikely that any court will ever give the section the interpretation we have put upon it. But the question is arguable.

[35] See his *Groundwork*, pp. 17–18.

It is a perfectly possible construction to hold that if the date of reception applies only to statutes of general application and not to common law and equity the shift in date would have affected only the former and not the latter. Why should the provision for all three bodies of law be contained in the same section and shift together with every shift in date? It is submitted that the same reason which prompted the reception of the statutes of general application also prompted the reception of the common law and equity. The reason was to provide colonial and primitive Nigeria with a legal system with which to start.

To hold that the legislature meant current common law and equity is illogical, for many common law rules which existed in England on 1st January, 1900, have been overtaken by post-1900 statutes[36] and modified versions of these rules are not applicable in our courts.[37] Further, in view of statutory invasion of the province of the common law there is an appreciable contraction of its sphere of influence in English legal system and an adherence to the "current law" theory would mean the stultification of common law growth in Nigeria. The fact that Nigerian courts follow English common law decisions which are not affected by post-1900 statutes supports this thesis.[38]

That current English decisions apply in Nigeria there is no doubt, but these are limited to special cases where Nigerian statutes adopt current English statutes and English practice and procedure. In that event, it is desirable that there should be uniformity of decisions and that English precedents should be followed.[39] The confusion is worse confounded by the attitude of our courts. As far as the present writer is aware there is no reported case in which the pre-1900 theory is openly avowed or the "current law" theory openly rejected. Most of the cases in our reports cite and follow English decisions without distinction of dates with the same relish as they follow Nigerian cases. Whether only pre-1900 cases are binding and post-1900 cases

[36] E.g. Law Reform (Miscellaneous Provisions) Act, 1934; Law Reform (Married Women and Tortfeasors) Act, 1934.

[37] See *Pepple v. Federal Administrator-General* (1958) L.L.R. 42; *Lawal v. Younan & Sons* (1961) All N.L.R. 245, 250.

[38] See note 2 above. l

[39] See sections 2 and 3 of this Chapter.

are not binding or are only persuasive is not plainly stated by our courts. In short, no judicial thought has been addressed to the distinction.

Dicta can, however, be found in our reports which suggest that English decisions are not binding or are of persuasive authority only without stating the grounds on which such decisions are so treated. First, we have the case of *Chime v. Elikwu*[40] in which Idigbe, the then Ag. C.J., of the Midwestern State of Nigeria, when applying post 1900 English decisions[41] to the facts of the case before him, said:

> The above decisions are weighty and of considerable authority . . . although I am not bound by them . . .

The Supreme Court commenting on the House of Lords decision in *Rookes v. Bernards*[42] which deals with the question of exemplary damages observed:

> it is of strong persuasive authority.[43]

None of the above decisions has solved our dilemma. Idigbe, Ag. C.J. did not say which of the decisions in the English cases he had consulted were not binding on him. The Supreme Court did not say why the House of Lords' decision was merely "persuasive." Or, was it for Beckley, J., in *Alli v. Okulaja*[44] to explain why English cases are persuasive and not binding? In that case when a decision of Lord Justice Denning was cited to the learned judge he observed:

> I do not think that this court can be held bound by that authority of the Court of Appeal of England, this country now being an independent sovereign state but judgment of an eminent judge like Lord Justice Denning, Master of Rolls, would certainly be of the most persuasive authority and would be followed except

[40] (1965) N.M.L.R. 71, 80.
[41] The decisions were *Munday v. Munday* (1954) 2 A.E.R. 667; *Bolton v. Bolton* (1949) 2 A.E.R. 908; *Re British Reinforced Concrete Engineering Co. Ltd.* 45 T.L.R. 186.
[42] (1964) 2 W.L.R. 269.
[43] See *Ezeani v. Njidike* (1965) N.M.L.R. 95, 98.
[44] (1970) 2 All N.L.R. 35, 44.

the court feels otherwise strongly about the ratio decidendi of such decision.[45]

The reason given by Beckley, J., for not being bound by the English decision is hardly convincing and does not solve our problem. Is the reason for Nigerian courts not being bound by English decisions the fact that Nigeria is now "an independent sovereign state?" Were Nigerian courts ever bound by post-1900 English decisions[46] when Nigeria was a colonial appendage of Britain? The decisions of the West African Court of Appeal in *Osumanu v. Seidu*[47] would tend to suggest that this was so. In that case the court declared that it would not be bound by a previous decision of its own which, though not expressly overruled, could not stand with a decision of the "Privy Council or the House of Lords." The same impression seems to be created by decisions which rest exclusively on English authorities.[48]

It is difficult, however, to see how this somewhat difficult problem could be so disposed of with a wave of the hand. The Nigerian courts were not part of the same judicial hierarchy as the English courts, the special position of the Privy Council excepted. Even if they were so treated, this would only afford partial answer as to why English decisions were binding on the courts in Nigeria prior to October 1, 1960. It will not tell us anything about the significance of the date of reception (January 1, 1900) which is our central problem in this chapter. Again, no satisfactory basis, statutory or conventional, has been shown for such identification of pre-1960 Nigerian courts with the English judiciary which would make post-1900 but pre-1960 English decisions binding on Nigerian courts. Nevertheless such a basis exists.[49] But Beckley, J., has not addressed his mind to it and so could not explain it. No court has grappled with this problem nor with the problem of the status of pre-1900 English decisions in our courts.

[45] The English decision was *Edmeades v. Thames Board Mills Ltd.* (1969) 1 Lloyd's Report 221.

[46] Apart from those of the Privy Council and the House of Lords on points of English Law.

[47] (1949) 12 W.A.C.A. 437, 428, cited above.

[48] See, for example, *R. v. Ajani*, 3 W.A.C.A. 3, 7.

[49] See Chapter 13.

This is a serious abdication of responsibility on the part of our judiciary. Even the Supreme Court and the earlier intermediate courts of appeal have fought shy of the matter. Only textwriters have tried to construct a legal order out of chaos.[50] But in the absence of a consensus among them it is impossible for the courts to be guided and persuaded to accept one view rather than the other. Textwriters cannot be persuaded to sink their differences. Rather, our submission is that the ball is in the court either of the legislatures or of the courts.

The various provisions of the sections of our statutes dealing with reception should be redrafted to show clearly what body of law is being received and at what date. The confusion and obscurity that has resulted from existing provisions stem from the fact that the reception of common law and equity and statutes of general application is done by the same section or subsection with one limiting date, without showing clearly whether the same date applies to all, or whether common law and equity is to be governed by one date and statutes of general application by a different date.

We will therefore suggest the following drafts. If the legislature's intention is to receive the three bodies of law at the same date—1st January, 1900—the provision in the case of a State law, should be worded as follows:

> Subject to the terms of this or any other law, the common law and the doctrines of equity which were in force in England on the 1st day of January, 1900, and the statutes of general application also in force at the said date, shall be in force within the jurisdiction of the court.
>
> Provided that in the case of statutes of general application only such statutes as relate to matters for which the legislature of the state is for the time being competent to make laws shall be so in force.

If, on the other hand, the intention is to limit the reception of the statutes of general application to 1st January, 1900, and to adopt the current common law and doctrines of equity in England, as Park claims, the wording should read:

[50] Elias, Allott and Park in their respective works already noted.

(I) The rules of the Common Law and the doctrines of equity currently in force in England and such rules and doctrines as may be substituted for them from time to time shall be in force within the jurisdiction of the courts.

(II) The statutes of general application which were in force in England on the 1st day of January, 1900, shall be in force within the jurisdiction of the court.

Then a proviso similar to the above should be added.

In the case of the Interpretation Act, 1964, which is an enactment of the federal legislature, the provision of section 45 which deals with this question of reception should be amended to read like either of the above suggestions according to intention, but subject to the following amendments. For the words, "within the jurisdiction of the court" there should be substituted "within the federation." In the proviso the words "Federal legislature" should be substituted for "the legislature of the state."

The above suggestions are being offered as a modest contribution to the solution of the problem of uncertainty which at present bedevils our legislative enactments on the question of reception. But, if the legislatures are too tardy or unwilling to act, an alternative solution should be found by the courts. And the court best able to do this is the Supreme Court. By a practice statement on the lines of that made by the House of Lords over the vexed question of *stare decisis*[51] the Supreme Court can put academic debate to rest and make it possible for judges and lawyers to know with what effect they are relying on and citing post-1900 English decisions. It is suggested that the statement should declare as follows:

> Since Nigerian courts form a separate and distinct system from the English judiciary and independent of it, the post-1900 decisions of the latter (except those of the Privy Council and the House of Lords up to 1963) are not and have never been binding on the Nigerian courts, but are treated as persuasive only.[52] When such decisions are followed by Nigerian courts they, of course, form part of Nigerian law. But, except as stated, Nigerian courts are not legally obliged to follow post-1900 English decisions. The only English decisions which Nigerian courts are obli-

[51] See (1966) 3 A.E.R. 77.

ged to follow are the pre-1900 decisions and it is these that form part of the law of Nigeria, by virtue of the various "reception" provisions of Nigerian statutes.[52]

A practice statement in this vein will show what the judicial attitude to the question has been all along and in what light the courts have understood the various provisions of the respective statutes. For those who may argue that such a course as here suggested may raise a question as to the constitutionality of the statement if not tied to a concrete case the practice statement of the House of Lords can be cited as a precedent.[53] On the other hand, the Supreme Court should watch for suitable opportunity (which of course frequently occurs) to make the declaration in a concrete case before it. It will infuse sanity into, and rationalise, judicial attitude to the question.

2. Statutory Provisions Importing English Practice and Procedure

Although the doctrine of precedent is a necessary concomitant of the common law the importation of the common law into Nigeria is not the sole instrument by which the doctrine becomes operative in this country. There are certain statutory provisions in our law which pray into service English rules of practice and procedure where our law does not make provisions on the point.[54] Such rules are in force in this country both in criminal and in civil causes and matters. The tendency is for the courts of Nigeria to follow English decisions based on the rules the legislatures have imported. This they do for two reasons. First, where the rules of practice and procedure are statutory, the decisions afford the safest guides to the actual meaning

[52] But see Chapter 13 where English decisions have been shown to have been binding on Nigerian Courts before 1963. Such a declaration would, therefore, not be free from difficulties.

[53] See Hood Phillips, *A First Book of English Law*, 6th edition, p. 182.

[54] Examples are Criminal Procedure Act, section 363; High Court Law of Eastern Nigeria, S. 16; High Court of Lagos Act, S. 12; High Court Law of Northern Nigeria, S. 26. Each of these laws is in force in the new states carved out of its former area of operation by virtue of the States Creation (Transitional Provisions) Decree, 1967, S. 1(5) as subsequently amended by the States Creation (Transitional Provisions) Decree, 1976.

and application of the rules. Secondly, where the rules are conventional and rest on the common law the decisions constitute the actual rules themselves.

It is sufficient to illustrate this last point by a few Nigerian cases. Our law makes no provision for the discharge of any accused person who has no case to answer at a jury trial. But the Criminal Procedure Act by section 363 provides for the application in our High Courts of the rules of "procedure and practice for the time being in force in the High Court of Justice in England in criminal trials." Now the English rule and practice is based on the common law and not on statute. In *The Queen v. Olagunju*[55] the trial judge had discharged one of the accused persons tried with a jury at the end of the case for the prosecution, saying that he had no case to answer. The Federal Supreme Court held the procedure to be wrong since there was no provision in our law regulating the matter and urged that English practice should have been resorted to. The court observed:

> The Jury Ordinance does not lay down what is to be done in such a case, and what the learned judge did was to withdraw the case from the jury and himself discharge the accused. We consider that under Section 363 of the Criminal Procedure ordinance he should have followed the practice of the High Court in England. There, a person once given in charge to a jury can only be acquitted or convicted by the jury: *R. v. Heyes* (1951) 1 K.B. 29; and the correct course would have been to direct the jury, as a matter of law, that they must bring in a verdict of Not Guilty.

Another English rule of practice which has no statutory basis but depends on the common law was applied in *Sanmabo v. The State*[56] by the Western State Court of Appeal. In that case a trial was held to be a nullity when one judge took the plea and another continued the hearing. The court observed *obiter* that the only exception was where a judge had died after delivering judgment but before passing sentence, in which case another judge might pass sentence after hearing the accused or his counsel as regards sentence. For this view the court relied upon the English case of *Pepper v. Platt*[57] and observed:

[55] (1961) All N.L.R. 21.
[56] (1967) N.M.L.R. 314.
[57] (1922) 16 C.A.R. 12.

> This English practice would appear to be in force in this State by virtue of the provision of Section 363 of the Criminal Procedure Ordinance . . .[58]

In *The Queen v. Ogor*[59] a rule of English practice on the question of an accused person suspected to be insane was followed in which it was held that the investigation of the issue must be taken up as soon as the question arises. The case relied upon was *R. v. Podola.*[60] The question as to what factors the court must consider before granting bail to a convicted person pending appeal was resolved in *Sam Offiong v. C.O.P.*[61] on the basis of English decisions. The combined effect of these decisions is that there must be a reasonable chance of success for the appeal of the appellant.[62]

So far we have been considering the rules applicable in criminal cases. Now we are going to consider examples of rules of English practice and procedure which have to be followed in civil cases. In *Fetuga v. Western Nigeria Housing Corporation*[63] the Supreme Court of Nigeria followed the practice of the Court of Appeal in England of asking counsel for the defence if he would have called evidence if the trial judge had asked him if he wished to do so at the close of the case for the plaintiff. The English case relied upon was *Laurie v. Raglan Building Co.*[64]

The practice whereby the Court of Appeal in England amends proceedings to accord with the facts proved in evidence in the court below was followed by the Western State High Court in *Shokunbi v. Mosaku*[65] in an appeal from a Magistrate's Court. The rules of practice of the Court of Appeal were contained in *Clark v. Wood*[66] and *Thynne v. Thynne*[67] and these were followed in the *Shokunbi case* in which the High Court allowed the name of a party to be amended.

[58] *Sanmabo v. The State* (1967) N.M.L.R. 314, 317.
[59] (1961) All N.L.R. 70.
[60] (1960) 1 Q.B. 325.
[61] HT/5CA/73. An unreported case decided by Ete, J., at the Ikot Ekpene High Court on 25-3-74.
[62] See *R. v. Wise* (1924) 17 C.A.R. 17; *R. v. Fitzgerald* (1924) 12 C.A.R. 147; *R. v. Selkirk* (1925) 18 C.A.R. 172.
[63] (1968) N.M.L.R. 233.
[64] (1942) 1 K.B. 153.
[65] (1969) 1 N.M.L.R. 54.
[66] (1882) 9 Q.B.D. 272.
[67] (1955) P. 272.

The case of *Smith v. Selwyn*[68] has been invoked in Nigerian courts several times for the purpose of staying civil proceedings in cases where felonies have been disclosed until the felonies have been prosecuted.[69] In *Okwodu v. Alli*[70] following English practice in *Cross v. British Oak Insurance Co. Ltd.*[71] and *Herbert v. Railway Passengers Assurance Co.*[72] the Western Nigeria High Court in 1958 held that a plaintiff who had obtained judgment against a defendant in a running-down action could only proceed against the defendant's insurer by action and not by motion.

In all the above instances the English rules of practice and procedure are created by the cases cited and where our law enjoins that these rules should be followed what it means is that the cases should be followed. In this way English decisions on common law practice and procedure of English courts automatically become binding on Nigerian courts. We cannot approbate and reprobate. We cannot make English decisions in this area of practice mandatory on us and then turn round and refuse to follow such decisions, however inconvenient they might be. This is another avenue through which the doctrine of judicial precedent came to this country.

From here we will proceed to consider the other wing of this question—rules of practice and procedure statutorily laid down by Act of Parliament or under an Act of Parliament and required by Nigerian statutes to be applied in Nigerian courts. In *Ogunleye v. Arewa*[73] there was no Western Nigeria High Court Civil Procedure rule corresponding to the then Order 27, Rule 11 of the Supreme Court Rules in England which permitted a plaintiff in default of defence to apply to the court by motion of summons for judgment in terms of the statement of claim. But Order 35, rule 10, of the former Western Nigeria High Court (Civil Procedure) Rules permits a recourse to English rules in such circumstances. It was held that the plaintiff was entitled to judgment on his motion for final judgment without leading evidence.

[68] (1914) 3 K.B. 98.
[69] See *Eze v. Illonse* (1962) VI E.N.L.R. 79 in which other Nigerian authorities are cited.
[70] (1958) W.R.N.L.R. 28.
[71] (1938) 1 A.E.R. 383.
[72] (1938) 1 A.E.R. 650.
[73] (1960) W.N.L.R. 9.

Atu v. C.O.P.[74] was a case in which a convicted prisoner applied by summons under section 123 of the Criminal Procedure Law of former Eastern Nigeria for bail to the High Court pending appeal from the Magistrate's Court. Following the unreported case of *The State v. Odunsi,*[75] Agbakoba, J., held that a provision of the English Rules applied and that the applicable procedure was contained in

> Form 35 rule 29A Article 963 at page 357 of 36th Edition of Archbold by virtue of Section 363 of the Criminal Procedure Law and Section 16 of the High Court Law.

Giving a catalogue of the various English rules that become applicable in Nigeria by virtue of the "reception" provisions of our law would be beside the point having regard to the field of our enquiry. Our primary purpose is to consider the significance of these rules from the point of view of judicial precedent. How do the Nigerian courts treat the English decisions on these rules? Do they regard the decisions as persuasive and assume the freedom to consider their meaning and application afresh? Or, do they regard the decisions as authoritative and therefore binding?

In support of the first view it is possible to argue that the Nigerian courts adopt the rules and not the English courts' constructions on them. In other words, it is the rules that form part of Nigerian law and not the cases. In the circumstances, the Nigerian courts are free to ignore the cases and consider and place whatever interpretation they deem right upon the rules. But this can only be so in those cases where the rules are statutory and not based on case-law. In this way there may well be two different lines of decisions on the same rules, and although no appeal lies from one set of courts to the other the resulting lack of uniformity would be undesirable.[76]

As against the first view there are obvious practical reasons why support should be mustered for the second view. First, if English statutory rules are good enough for Nigeria, then English decisions on them should be good enough and should be received along with the rules.[77] The rules are exclusively English rules, but become

[74] (1970–71) 1 E.C.S.L.R. 7, 9.

[75] Decided in Ijebu-Ode on 25/11/69 by Abina, J.

[76] See Craise, *Statute Law*, 7th edition, pp. 19–20.

[77] This view is consistent with that expressed by Professor Allot in his *Essays in African Law*, 1960, p. 41.

Nigerian by adoption. Being English rules only English courts have the final say on their meaning and application and whatever the English courts decide should be binding on Nigerian courts. The Nigerian legislatures must be deemed to have received the rules with such interpretations as shall be placed upon them from time to time by the English courts, there being no limiting date for the reception. The only exception is the legislature of former Eastern Nigeria which received "the law and practice . . . observed in England in the High Court of Justice on the thirtieth day of September, 1960."[78] In this case not only the rules which were in vogue in England on this date form part of the law of Eastern Nigeria,[79] but also all the decisions on the rules up to that date.

3. Construction of English Statutes in Force in Nigeria

The treatment of this topic follows the same lines as the treatment of the statutory rules of procedure and practice. What matters to us is the decisions on the statutes, not the statutes themselves. Two classes of statutes can be distinguished: those statutes of general application which were in force in England on the 1st day of January, 1900, and those currently in force in England and received as part of Nigerian law by different Nigerian statutes.

The statutes of general application in force in Nigeria were referred to in the consolidated case of *Lawal v. Younan and Sons*[80] by Brett, F.J., and the decisions which established them as such were cited.[81] These pre-1900 statutes currently in force in England and received by Nigerian legislature have been applied in Nigerian courts from time to time. The real question in issue is whether English decisions on their meaning and application are binding on Nigerian courts. According to Professor Allott[82] decisions on pre-1900

[78] Eastern Nigerian High Court Law, S. 16, Vol. IV of the Laws of Eastern Nigeria, 1963.

[79] Now, Imo, Anambra, Rivers and Cross River States. See States Creation (Transitional Provisions) Decree, 1967, S. (5) and subsequent legislation.

[80] (1961) All N.L.R. 245, 254–255.

[81] Statutes of general application have ceased to apply in Western Nigeria and therefore Bendel State (formerly Midwestern State) and Ogun, Oyo, and Ondo States. See Law of England (Application) Law, 1959, S. 3.

[82] *Essays in African Law*, 1960, pp. 40–41.

statutes of general application before the reception date are binding since the legislature must be deemed to have taken the statutes with the decisions thereon, but that those decisions taken after the date of reception are not binding but persuasive. With regard to post-1900 statutes, on the other hand, Professor Allott says that the decisions thereon should be binding in the interests of uniformity.[83]

To agree with the learned Professor, decisions on the pre-1900 statutes should be binding because the legislature is deemed to have been aware of them before the statutes which they construed were received as part of our law. But constructions after 1900—the date of reception—should not bind our courts since the legislature is not deemed to know before hand what they would be.

When we come to post-1900 statutes the position is different. The legislature is deemed to have taken "the benefit with the burden." English and Nigerian courts cannot be heard to sing discordant notes on the same subject; there must be uniformity of interpretation and English decisions should be binding on Nigerian courts according to status.[84] It is doubtful, however, whether English courts would accept Nigerian interpretations as binding on them.

But if not, why not? A simple explanation might be that English statutes are made in England for English people and that only English courts with English background can properly interpret them. No other court without a similar background experience of English social, economic and political conditions is equipped to interpret them in a manner acceptable to the English people.

If the English courts adopt this kind of approach it should be understandable to the Nigerian courts, for Nigerian statutes even empower our courts to construe English statutes applicable in Nigeria "with such verbal alterations, not affecting the substance, as may be necessary to make the same applicable to the proceedings before the court.'[85] Moreover, Nigerian statutes provide that such

[83] *Ibid.*, p. 41.

[84] See Elias, *Groundwork of Nigerian Law*, 1954, p. 33.

[85] See High Court Law, S. 15(2)(b) in Vol. IV of the Laws of Eastern Nigeria. Similar provisions occur in the High Court Laws of the other States. They were taken from the Supreme Court Ordinance, S. 16 (Cap. 211, Vol. 6) of the Laws of Nigeria, 1948.

statutes "shall be in force so far only as the limits of the local jurisdiction and local circumstances permit."[86]

In the light of the above analysis it is difficult to expect that the much-looked-for uniformity of interpretations can always be achieved. Starting with pre-1900 statutes we find that "children" and "wife" under the Fatal Accidents Acts 1846 are given different interpretations by English and Nigerian courts. In England, "wife" means the wife of a monogamous marriage and "children" means children born in lawful wedlock. In Nigeria the position is different. A wife under native law and custom and children born thereunder or born without customary marriage of parents but acknowledged as legitimate by their putative father are entitled to benefit from the death of the deceased husband or father under the Acts.[87] In *Bamgbose v. Daniel*[88] the word "children" under the Statute of Distribution, 1670, which is a statute of general application in force in Nigeria was construed in such a way as not to limit its local application in Nigeria to children who are the issue of monogamous unions.

Coming to post-1900 English statutes we find that the jurisdiction in probate and matrimonial causes to be exercised by the court must be in "conformity with the law and practice in force in England on the 30th day of September, 1960."[89] The Matrimonial Causes Act, 1950, applied in Nigeria up to 17th March, 1970, when it was replaced by the Matrimonial Causes Decree 1970. The English probate laws also apply. In cases such as these, strict conformity with English law and practice is required and verbal alterations should not be permitted especially in matrimonial causes. The reason is that such laws relate to matters essentially peculiar to English social life and a country adopting them must be prepared to follow English law and practice with regard to them as well as decisions thereon.[90]

86 Section 15(2)(a), *ibid.*

87 *Lawal v. Younan and Sons* (1961) All N.L.R. 245, 250–251. For the position at customary law see *Phillip v. Phillip* (1946) 18 N.L.R. 102.

88 (1954) 14 W.A.C.A. 116.

89 High Court Law of Eastern Nigeria, S. 17.

90 But see Daniel, *The Common Law in West Africa*, 1964, p. 143, where the practice is criticised. "The two societies are socially and culturally different. When members of the United Kingdom Parliament are debating on such Bills they think primarily of the social conditions in England."

In this instance again we find that the English judiciary is a dictator *vis-a-vis* Nigerian courts. Two other instances have already been observed; they are pre-1900 common law and equity and English practice and procedure where our law makes no provision. In *Trimble v. Hill*[91] the Privy Council said:

> it is of the utmost importance that in all parts of the empire where English law prevails the interpretation of that law by the courts should be as nearly as possible the same.

Although there is no known instance in which English High Court decisions have been dissented from in Nigerian courts in probate and matrimonial causes and matters, it is submitted that special weight should be given to the decisions of the House of Lords and the Court of Appeal in these cases. In *Hunt v. Fripp*[92] it was observed by the Privy Council:

> that, although not in the strict sense of the word binding, the decisions of the Court of Appeal in England are regarded with the highest respect in the courts in the colonies, and that substantially you are entitled to look at the English decisions turning upon the construction of similar statutes as giving the law which, should the precise point arise, the courts in the Australian colonies would act upon.

The above *dicta* were uttered in cases which examined colonial statutes similar to the English statutes on the same subjects. They apply with greater force to English statutes which are in force in Nigeria for the reasons we have seen. Reference to "empire" and "colonies" in the *dicta* makes no difference since the Privy Council did not mean that English decisions should be followed because Britain was the imperial power. The idea is to promote consistency and uniformity in the interpretation of such laws.[93]

Now let us take a point. When Britain is the imperial master the need for consistency and uniformity is apparent since colonial decisions going on appeal to the Privy Council are going to be looked at in the light of English interpretations,[94] and non-conformity will

[91] (1879–80) App. Cas. 342, 345.

[92] (1898) 1 Ch. 675, 679.

[93] Allott, *Essays in African Law*, 1960, p. 41.

[94] See Cowen, *The Binding Effect of English Decisions Upon Australian Courts* (1944) 60 L.Q.R. 378, 381–382.

be penalised by overruling. But where a country is independent and no appeal lies to the Privy Council, what is the sanction that non-conformity will attract? True, there is no supranational authority to oversee the practices of the courts and enforce conformity. But in these days of increasing interest in the study of comparative jurisprudence .lack of uniformity will attract comments which may be adversely weighted against the country noted for oblique decisions. Furthermore, the "donor" country will not feel able to follow the interpretations of the "donee" country which run radically counter to their basic ideas of what the law is.

The reasons given above are cogent enough to make uniformity a desideratum. But the circumstances of individual countries may require individual approaches and if occasion arises the courts of this country should be prepared to sacrifice uniformity to justice.

4. The Professional Ethos of Judges and Lawyers

It is tempting to conclude that the three methods we have seen above, namely, the reception of the common law in Nigeria, the statutory importation of English practice and procedure and of post-1900 English statutes, are the only avenues through which the doctrine of precedent found entrance into the Nigerian legal system. But this is not so. A fourth route is available: the professional training and attitude of the judges and lawyers who administered and still administer the law in Nigeria.

Up to about the early 'fifties the judges appointed to administer law and justice in Nigeria were British citizens, born and bred in England, the home of the common law and trained in her Inns of Court. Added to them were the lawyers, some British and many others Nigerians, all of whom had and still have their training in the common law. It is therefore natural that they should imbibe common law discipline and be influenced by it and allow this discipline to influence their work and their attitude to work. This discipline is that habit of legal thought which delights in precedent and the search for it.

The tools of their trade—textbooks and law reports—contain common law methods of legal thought and are the chief instruments for laying down legal rules. No lawyer with a common law training—

be he an advocate in court or a textwriter—will feel satisfied until he can find an authority for his legal proposition. In these circumstances it is easy to see why the doctrine of precedent would still have come into this country even without any of the above three methods. That this is so is shown by the fact that the doctrine of precedent also applies to decisions on customary law which is home grown and not imported and which has never developed its own systematic doctrine of precedent.[95]

In fact, we can submit without fear of contradiction that it is the thinking habit of lawyers and judges, more than anything else, that brought the doctrine into Nigeria.[96]

[95] See Elias, *The Nature of African Customary Law*, 1956, pp. 256–258. The learned author rightly says: "African judges do not, as modern English judges do, regard themselves as being under a legal obligation to follow previous cases, except that they would be loath to disregard well-established ones for fear of seeming perverse or recalcitrant."

[96] See Dias, *Jurisprudence*, 3rd edition, p. 55.

5

THE DEVELOPMENT OF THE COMMON LAW IN NIGERIA THROUGH THE DOCTRINE

We saw in Chapter Four the four methods by which the doctrine of judicial precedent was imported into this country. We saw in that chapter that one of the means of importation was through the introduction of the common law. In this chapter we are going to study its development in the Nigerian legal scene after importation. But before doing so we must explain what we mean by common law in the context of this chapter. According to Salmond[1] common law may bear a "more extended sense, meaning the principles of English law as they have been adopted in the other 'common law' countries, like the United States of America, Canada, Australia, New Zealand and the Irish Republic." The list could be extended to include Nigeria, for Nigeria has adopted English common law in this sense and it is the development of common law in this sense that we are going to treat in this chapter.

Thus we will deal with (a) common law in "a form of case law having its source in the judicial decisions of the old courts of King's Bench, Common Pleas and Exchequer and of the modern courts by which the system so established is now administered and developed"[2]; (b) principles of equity established by the Court of Chancery; (c) English Practice and Procedure; and (d) English statutes in force in Nigeria.

1. Growth and Development of the Common Law

When these principles of English law were received by the Nigerian legislature they grew and developed through judicial

[1] *Jurisprudence*, 11th edition, p. 99.
[2] Salmond, *Jurisprudence*, 11th edition, p. 96.

decisions. We can see with our eyes closed these various rules of English law overlaying the Nigerian legal system, and we can see them in their pure, unadultrated English form. Immediately thereafter Nigerian courts start to decide Nigerian cases between Nigerian parties on Nigerian facts, but following the imported English decisions and interpreting the imported English statutes. The decisions retain the essential characters of English doctrines, but they also partake of Nigerian character through association with Nigerian circumstances.

Thus England donates its law to Nigeria. The Nigerian legislature receives it, and Nigerian courts develop the law through judicial decisions. In other words, English law provides the humus out of which the seeds of Nigerian decisions grow. There are decisions on common law, equity, English statutes and English court practice and procedure.

Decisions on Common Law

Under this heading we deal with decisions on common law in the narrow sense. Common law in the narrow sense is limited to decisions based on sources other than equity and statutes, e.g. custom, reason, public utility, practical expediency, etc. Such decisions constitute the common law mentioned in the receiving statutes in the last chapter and on which Nigerian courts have erected further edifices of judicial doctrine and in that way cause it to grow and develop. We will give a few illustrations of such development in areas of the common law relating to trade marks, contract, false imprisonment, malicious prosecution, negligence, conflict of laws, etc., using Nigerian cases based on pre-1900 English precedents.

In *MacIver & Co. Ltd. v. C.F.A.O.*[3] the Nigerian Full Court of the Supreme Court, relying upon English decisions held that the trademark of the defendant so resembled that of the plaintiff that the Nigerian public was likely to be deceived by the defendant's trademark and so ordered refusal of registration. In coming to this conclusion the court based its decision on pre-1900 English cases,[4] and Speed, C.J., observed:

[3] (1917) 3 N.L.R. 18, 22.

[4] *Eve v. Dunn* (1890) 15 A.C. 25; In *re Lyndon's Trade Mark* (1886) 32 Ch.D. 109; In *re Worthington & Co.* (1880) 14 Ch.D. 8.

> These decisions are of course binding on us but they must be construed having regard to the local conditions which are widely different from those that obtain in England.

At page 19 of the Report, Webber, J., remarked:

> Judges of the Supreme Court of this Colony have consistently administered these laws with due regard to local conditions and I think we should embrace this opportunity of expressing our unqualified approval of their decisions.

A modern decision that has adopted the principles of earlier decisions is *Gottschalck & Co. Ltd. v. Spruce Manufacturing Co. Ltd.*[5] In that case Foster Sutton, F.C.J., approved the *dictum* of Butler Lloyd, J., in *The United Kingdom Tobacco Co. Ltd. v. Carreras Ltd.*[6] where the latter said:

> It is a well established principle, not only in this country, that the likelihood of deception varies with the intelligence and education of the consumers . . .

and then agreed with the cases which Butler Lloyd, J., cited in support of the above principle.

Another instance of the development of judicial precedent in Nigeria after importation can be given from contract. In *Gottschalck & Co. v. Elder Dempster & Co.*[7] there was a bill of lading which contained the terms of a contract for the carriage of goods. Plaintiffs sought to extend the defendant's liability by giving evidence of the custom of the port. The lower court refused to admit such evidence. On appeal to the Full Court reliance was placed on two pre-1900 English cases and one post-1900 case,[8] and Speed, C.J., delivering the judgment of the Court, said,

> . . . it is a well established rule of law that no evidence of custom can override the terms of a written contract.

Speed, C.J.'s, "well established rule of law" cannot refer to any other rule than the one that can be extracted from the cases cited and

[5] (1956) 1 F.S.C. 42.
[6] (1931) 16 N.L.R. 1, 2.
[7] (1917) 3 N.L.R. 16.
[8] *Helman v. Wade, The Times*, 11th May, 1887; *The Nifa*, 62 L.J., p. 12; L.R. (1892) p. 411, *Northmoor Steamship Co. v. Holland* (1903) 2 Ir. Rep. 657.

others establishing a similar principle. This "well established" rule was imported into Nigeria by an act of the Nigerian legislature and was helped to size by recognition and enforcement in *Gottschalck and Co. case*.

The received law on false imprisonment has also been helped to grow by Nigerian decisions. A case in point is *Oduntun v. Adefunmilayo.*[9] In that case it was held on appeal, reversing the lower court, that merely giving information to the police about a crime and saying that the defendant suspects the plaintiff is not enough to render the defendant liable in an action for false imprisonment. Such an expression of opinion is no more than putting the police on a trail upon which they can work instead of leaving them in the dark, and subsequent investigations may and may not lead to an arrest. All the authorities relied upon by Ademola, C.J., were pre-1900 cases.[10] He said that the appellant had not put the law in motion against the respondent simply by giving such information and referring to *Danby v. Beardelog*, he stated:

> This appears to be a case on all fours with the claim before the learned Magistrate.[11]

In developing our law of malicious prosecution we find both pre-1900 and post 1900 English cases being relied upon. Typical examples are *Usifo II v. Uke*[12] and *Ilo v. Nwokolo.*[13] In the first case the defendants, though found to have acted out of spite in prosecuting the plaintiff, were nevertheless held to have had an honest belief in the guilt of the plaintiff.[14] In the second case the defendant was found liable. Betuel, J., delivering judgment said:

[9] (1958) W.R.N.L.R. 31. l

[10] *Chivers v. Savage* (1855) L.J. Q.B. 85; *Brown v. Chapman* (1848) 6 C. and B. 365; *Danby v. Beardelog* (1880) 43 I.T. 603.

[11] P. 32.

[12] (1957) W.R.N.L.R. 46.

[13] (1959) 3 E.N.L.R. 62.

[14] The following cases were followed: *Steven v. Midland Counties Railway* (1854) 10 Ex. 352, 356, where Baron Alderson said that the proper motive for a prosecution was a desire to secure the ends of justice; *Bradshaw v. Waterlow and Sons Ltd.* (1915) 3 K.B. 527, 535, where Pickford, L.J., said there could be no absence of reasonable and probable cause where the facts were fairly put before the Attorney-General for the purpose of obtaining his fiat; *Cox v. English, Scottish and Australian Bank, Ltd.* (1905) A.C. 168, 175, where the Privy Council said

> I think that if a defendant asserts falsely to a policeman that his bicycle and money have been stolen by the plaintiff and others and, as a result of the assertion, the plaintiff is prosecuted for stealing, he has instigated a prosecution falsely and maliciously, and he only aggravates his guilt by stating that he was only defending himself against a charge of breaking down a wall (Per Hawkins, J. in *Hicks v. Faulkner* (1878) 8 Q.B.D.; *Brown v. Hawkes.* (1891) 2 Q.B. 233; and *Payin v. Abinah* (1953) 14 W.A.C.A. 267).

Pepple v. Federal Administrator-General[15] was an action in negligence against an administrator of a deceased's estate for personal injuries caused to the plaintiff in a motor-car accident by a car owned by the deceased. The action was brought after the death of the owner of the vehicle and was not pending at his death as required by the common law. In reliance upon three pre-1900 English cases which denied relief to the plaintiff in such circumstances,[16] Onyeama, J., held:

> it follows, in my opinion, that the present action by the plaintiff against the estate of A. O. Thomas is governed by the common law rule and cannot be maintained and it must therefore be dismissed.[17]

Further evidence that the received common law rules have developed and are developing in Nigeria is afforded by the following two cases. In *Benson v. Ashiru*[18] the plaintiff/respondent sued the defendants/appellants under the Fatal Accidents Act, 1846, claiming damages for injury suffered as a result of the deceased's death by the deceased's husband. The Fatal Accidents Act as a statute of general application had ceased to apply in Western Nigeria and had been replaced by a locally enacted Fatal Accidents Law with effect from 1st July, 1959. The action was brought in a Lagos High Court where the latter statute was not in force. On appeal it was contended that,

that the onus of proving absence of reasonable and probable cause was on the plaintiff; and *Hicks v. Faulkner* 8 Q.B.D. at p. 171 where Hawkins, J., defined reasonable and probable cause.

[15] (1958) L.L.R. 42.

[16] *Kirk v. Todd* (1882) 21 Ch.D. 484; *Terry v. Sweeting* (1899) 1 Ch. 387, and *Phillips v. Homfrey* 24 Ch.D. 454.

[17] P. 44.

[18] (1967) N.M.L.R. 363, 365.

the Fatal Accidents Act not being in force in Western Nigeria where the injury occurred, the plaintiff could not sue. In reply Brett, J.S.C., delivering the judgment of the Supreme Court observed:

> The rules of the common law of England on question of private international law apply in the High Court of Lagos. Under these rules an action of tort will lie in Lagos for a wrong alleged to have been committed in another part of Nigeria if two conditions are fulfilled; first the wrong must be of such a character that it would have been actionable if it had been committed in Lagos; and secondly it must not have been justifiable by the law of the part of Nigeria where it was done *(Philips v. Eyre* (1890) L.R. 6 Q.B. 1). The conditions are fulfilled in the present case.

The other case is the unreported case of *The State v. Uwem Dan Akpan.*[19] The argument for the defence in that case was that since the information charged the accused with having killed the deceased on the day on which the injury was administered and the evidence disclosed that the deceased died on a different day, the date of death was not proved and the accused should be discharged. Ita, J., giving judgment, stated:

> the old English common law rule which is also the law in Nigeria is that where A injures B and in consequence of that injury B dies within a year and a day of having received the injury A can be convicted of the murder of B.

The above instances are enough to show that the Nigerian courts are busy developing the received common law through an application of the doctrine of precedent. We have chosen to confine our discussion strictly to decisions based on pre-1900 English cases in order to show how the latter have developed as part of the law of Nigeria through the structures built on them by the Nigerian courts. Further examples will appear later.

Decisions on English Court Practice and Procedure

We now turn our attention to common law in the extended sense and under this heading we want to deal with one of two aspects of it-

[19] Uyo High Court Charge No. HU/17C/72 in which judgment was given on 10/11/72.

decisions on English court practice and procedure. We have seen in Chapter Four, section two, how English decisions were imported into this country through certain provisions in our statutes which authorise recourse to English practice and procedure. This happens where our laws do not make any provision about what practice and procedure to follow when certain matters arise. And we made reference to English decisions which Nigerian courts had to follow in these matters. It will serve no useful purpose to repeat those discussions here, and insofar as they illustrate the development of judicial precedent in Nigeria we adopt them here and go on to consider other examples.

Decisions on practice and procedure borrowed from English courts are proliferating in this country and thereby help to develop the law in this area of the legal system. In addition to examples seen in Chapter Four we have the following additional ones. Section 15 of the High Court Law, 1963, of former Eastern Nigeria and Order 25, Rule 10 of the High Court (Civil Procedure) Rules of former Western Region of Nigeria make provision permitting a recourse to English practice and procedure where our law is silent. In *Ogunleye v. Arewa*[20] the plaintiff had filed his statement of claim and had it served on the defendant who failed to file his defence despite the fact that he had ample opportunity to do so. The Western Region High Court Rules made no provision as to what would happen in such circumstances. But Order 35, Rule 10 provided that "the procedure and practice in force for the time being in the High Court of Justice in England shall so far as can be conveniently applied, be in force in the Court."

An application for judgment in terms of the statement of claim was made by the plaintiff under Order 27, Rule 11 of the Supreme Court Rules in England and the trial judge granted the prayer. On appeal to the Federal Supreme Court it was held that the judgment was in order. Quashie-Idun, Ag. F. J., delivering the judgment of the court, said:

> As the defendant failed to deny these allegations of the plaintiff, we think that the provisions of the Western Region High Court Rules would be rendered ineffective if Order 27 rule 11 of the

[20] (1960) W.R.N.L.R. 9.

> Rules of the Supreme Court, England were not applied, for it would mean that even though no defence has been filed in answer to material averments by the plaintiff, the court would still be bound to hear evidence as if no statement of claim has been filed. This would also reduce the Rules and Practice of pleadings to absurdity.[21]

This decision was followed in the Eastern Nigerian case of *Ibiono Rural District Council v. Udo*[22] in which judgment was accordingly given for the plaintiff.

It appears that circumspection is necessary to ensure that English practice and procedure should be resorted to only where our laws do not make a provision. Thus in *Are v. The Attorney-General of Nigeria*[23] recourse to English procedure in seeking redress by petition of right was held to be incompetent as the law in Western Nigeria had made a provision in that regard. In the case of Eastern Nigeria the Supreme Court held in *Odume v. Nnadi*[24] that section 15 of the High Court Law of Eastern Nigeria should be understood as meaning that English rules should be consulted only where the rules of court in Eastern Nigeria are silent.[25]

Following English rules of practice and procedure when we ought not to do so is to follow the wrong precedents. This will introduce chaos and uncertainty into the law and will rob us of the very advantage we want to achieve—guidance as to the right thing to do in particular cases. The practice will also render the existing provisions of our law nugatory. English rules of practice and procedure are meant to be our servants and not our masters.

On the other hand, it is submitted with respect, that some of our judges do not seem to advert to the provisions of our laws which receive English rules of practice and procedure when occasion demands it. Thus on the question as to what procedure should be

[21] P. 11.
[22] (1961) 5 E.N.L.R. 69.
[23] (1958) W.R.N.L.R. 126.
[24] (1964) 1 All N.L.R. 329.
[25] The Supreme Court has made a similar ruling in the Northern Nigeria case of *Bank of the North Ltd. v. Intra Bank S.A.* (1969) 1 All N.L.R. 91. At page 96 of the Report the Supreme Court said "It is therefore clear that in a proper case where the rules of law are silent, it should be competent to the court to turn to English practice."

adopted in an application for bail pending appeal by a person convicted by a Magistrate different judges have held different views. In *Musa v. Inspector General of Police*,[26] Reynolds, J., held that such an application was properly brought by motion under Order 35, Rule 1 of the High Court Rules of former Eastern Nigeria which deals with interlocutory applications. He observed:

> with regard to the procedure whereby such application should be brought in the High Court I think the application clearly is an interlocutory application in the appeal and by rule 1 of Order 35 of the High Court Rules 1955 interlocutory applications may be made by motion at any stage of a cause or matter.

Against this stand, Agbakoba, J., in *Onyeama v. Commissioner of Police*,[27] when the above case was cited to him, held that the proper procedure was to invoke section 363 of the Criminal Procedure Law which invited a recourse to the procedure and practice followed in England in the High Court of Justice where the law of former Eastern Nigeria (which is still in force) makes no provision. Accordingly, he held as follows:

> I have very profound respect for Reynolds, J., but I am unable to follow the *ratio decidendi* in the judgment which considers an application for bail pending the hearing of an appeal yet in its inchoate stage as "an application in the appeal." It was because the learned judge held that such an application was "an application in the appeal" that he also held it was interlocutory.

Agbakoba, J., was, however, dealing with a case of bail after committal for trial when the decision of Reynolds, J., in *Musa's case* was cited to him by counsel. Not finding the law laid down in that case agreeable he refused to apply it and took occasion to discredit it in the way he did. It is submitted that Agbakoba, J., is right in holding that an application for bail pending appeal in the circumstances of *Musa's case* could not by any stretch of the imagination be deemed to be interlocutory, especially as the appeal in the case did not yet reach the High Court. Furthermore, the proceedings in the Magistrate's Court had come to an end and there was nothing left

[26] (1962) 6 E.N.L.R. 149.
[27] (1970) 1 E.C.S.L.R. 10.

over to be done except the appeal which had not yet reached the High Court.

This conflict of decisions could be avoided if we had self-contained laws and rules which do not appeal to external sources. There is no doubt that having to invoke English rules of practice and procedure places at our disposal the richer experience of the English judiciary. But let us ask ourselves: Has the time not come for us to take an inventory of our borrowings from the English courts and to codify them and limit ourselves to them for all time?

It may be objected that codification may not be far-sighted enough to take care of all the different situations that may face our courts. The short answer to this is that the code only provides for what is easily foreseeable. Unforeseen circumstances can be taken care of as they arise. The English courts, as we have seen, are not dependent solely upon their written rules; the so-called inherent jurisdiction is invoked to deal with situations that have arisen *ex improviso*.

Again, another question arises. If the code provides no guide and we have ceased to follow English practice, what is there to prevent one judge from following one practice and another judge from devising another practice in the exercise of inherent jurisdiction? We can see that in this situation the doctrine of precedent would be put to flight and certainty and consistency would suffer. And having regard to our experience in matters of bail to convicted persons the conflict is a real possibility. A possible way of avoiding a conflict is for the judge to adjourn and report the matter to the Chief Judge of the state and ask for practice directions.

But this arrangement might produce certainty in the decisions of the courts of one state only while other states might follow different practices. It is therefore suggested that there should be established an institutional machinery whereby novel points not covered by existing rules of practice and procedure should be referred by all courts in the country to the Federal Court of Appeal,[28] for practice directions. It was Lord Justice Brett who said "that in matters of practice not provided for by the Rules, that practice which upon consideration appears to be the best ought to prevail."[29] It is submitted that the

[28] Set up October, 1976. See Decree No. 43 of 1976 and Section 217 of the 1979 Constitution.

judges of the Court of Appeal can work out convenient rules of general application to meet unforeseen situations and, acting with enough despatch and expedition, they can prevent individual cases being held up for too long. In this way uniformity of decisions would be enforced.

Decisions on English Statutes in Force in Nigeria

This is the second aspect of common law in the extended sense as received in the country. Two classes of English statutes are in force in Nigeria; one class comprises the so-called statutes of general application; the other consists of statutes currently in force in England. Decisions on these statutes are our centre of interest here.

With reference to decisions on statutes of general application we have to distinguish two aspects. The first is decisions on what really constitutes statutes of general application. A consideration of both aspects will help to illustrate how far the doctrine of precedent has developed in Nigeria.

To start with, no statute has defined the words "statutes of general application." The task of definition is left to the courts to perform. In *Attorney-General v. John Holt*,[30] Osborne, C.J., delivering the judgment of the Full Court, referred to a previous decision in which the words were defined. We quote from the judgment:

> No definition has been attempted of what is a statute of general application within the meaning of Section 14, and each case has to be decided on the merits of the particular statute to be enforced. Two preliminary questions can, however, be put by way of a rough, but not infallible test, viz.: (1) by what courts is the statute applied in England? and (2) to what classes of the community in England does it apply? If, on the 1st January, 1900, an Act of Parliament were applied by all civil or criminal courts, as the case may be, to all classes of the community, there is a strong likelihood that it is in force within the jurisdiction. If on the other hand, it were applied only by certain courts (e.g., a statute regulating procedure), or only to certain classes of the community (e.g. an Act regulating a particular trade), the probability is that it will not be held to be locally applicable.

[29] *Newbiggin-by-the-Sea Gas Company v. Armstrong* (1879–80) 13 Ch.D. 311, 312.

[30] (1910) 2 N.L.R. 1, 21.

The above observation was made about statutes of general application generally. *Dicta* are available which show how different judges have viewed individual statutes. In the *Estate of James Sholu*,[31] Webber, Ag. C.J., in the Divisional Court sitting in Lagos, reaffirmed his view in *Dede v. African Association Ltd.*[32] and held that the Land Transfer Act, 1897, was not a statute of general application and added: ". . . this Act does not apply to Nigeria."

The case of *Dede v. African Association Ltd.* went on appeal to the Full Court. At page 133 of the Report the Full Court held *obiter* that the Land Transfer Acts 1875 and 1897 are "even more restricted than other Acts mentioned in the Report because they "are applicable in England only and not in Scotland or Ireland." The West African Court of Appeal in *Young v. Abina*[33] unhesitatingly overruled *in re Sholu*. Said the Court:

> With all respect to the learned and experienced judge who decided this point in the Divisional Court we are unable to agree with his decision.
>
> The Land Transfer Act of 1897 applied quite generally to all estates in England of persons dying after 1st January, 1898. It is difficult to see how a statute could be of more "general application" in England than that, and it was in force in England on 1st January, 1900.

The court went on to explain the meaning of "general application" further, adding:

> It seems to us that the word "of general application" are used with reference to the matter of the statutes and not only geographically. Also it seems to us that under Section 14 England is the test of geographical generality.

With this last decision it appears that the controversy has been clinched. What is a statute of general application is no longer open to doubt, for *Young v. Abina* has laid down the tests by which such a statute can be identified. But the case itself has left an important doubt in the wake of overruling *in re Sholu*.

[31] (1932) 11 N.L.R. 37, 38.
[32] (1910) 1 N.L.R. 130—on appeal against Webber, Ag. C.J.'s decision.
[33] (1940) 6 W.A.C.A. 180, 183–184.

The doubt relates to the status of *Dede's* case, not in the Full Court because the observation there was *obiter* and was not a decision, but in the court of first instance where there was a decision that the Land Transfer Act was not a statute of general application. It was the first decision on the point and *in re Sholu* was based on it. But in *Young v. Abina* it was *in re Sholu* that was overruled and not *Dede's case*. Is the latter still an authority for what it decided at first instance?

The answer is probably in the negative. This is a case of implied overruling which is just as effective as an overruling openly carried out.[34] But the West African Court of Appeal should have tackled the problem from the root and not left room for doubt.

Decisions on other statutes—this time the Statutes of Limitations—are also available. *Pearce v. Aderoku*[35] and *Green v. Owo*[36] have decided that the Statutes of Limitations are statutes of general application and in force in Nigeria. Both are decisions of courts of first instance by different judges. In fact *Pearce's case* was based on *Bakere v. Coker*[37] decided by Sir Donald Kingdon, C.J., who himself followed his previous decision on *Egokor v. Agbeyegbe*.[38]

To sum up, the fact that there is a consensus among three judges that statutes of limitations are of general application and that they are applicable in Nigeria establishes beyond doubt that the view is sound and that it represents the law in Nigeria. Again, the fact that one of the judges has found it possible to maintain his ground and follow his previous decision before he got to know, if at all, of the decisions of the other two judges further strengthens this view of the law.[39] Furthermore, the fact that a higher court[40] has laid down conditions which a statute must satisfy in order to fall within the pale of statutes of general application clears the way for other courts faced with similar problems in the future.

[34] See Chapter 11, section 2.

[35] (1936) 13 N.L.R. 9.

[36] (1936) 13 N.L.R. 43.

[37] (1935) 12 N.L.R. 31.

[38] Suit 194/1933 of the Divisional Court, Lagos (unreported).

[39] There is nothing to prevent a judge from reversing his stand and refusing to follow a previous decision of his own when found to be wrong. See *Barclay's Bank v. Hassan* (1961) W.N.L.R. 293 at p. 296.

[40] That is, W.A.C.A. in *Young v. Abina*, supra.

We now turn our attention to precedents on construction. In *Nwafor v. Nduka*[41] the Supreme Court had to consider what constituted allowable deductions under section 7 of the Fatal Accidents Law of Eastern Nigeria. It found a precedent in the English case of *Heatley v. Steel Co. of States Ltd.*[42] which construed an "equivalent provision of the English Fatal Accidents Acts" and declared:

> that no deduction was to be made where the widow lived with her children in the house inherited from her husband.

It is pointless to consider at length decisions on English statutes received in Nigeria for several reasons. One is that the courts in Nigeria would naturally follow such decisions for the reasons we have seen in Chapter Four.[43] Another is that most of our decisions on the received statutes do not cite the English cases they follow in reaching their conclusions.[44]

2. Is There a Distinctively Nigerian Common Law?

We now pass on to consider a most important matter. Now that we have witnessed the importance of English precedents in the development of common law in Nigeria we have to go further and consider whether the common law in Nigeria is a carbon copy of the English common law, or whether the Nigerian courts have developed a distinctively Nigerian common law. In what ways have the Nigerian courts moulded these principles into decisions with characteristics peculiar to Nigeria? We will pursue our enquiry from three perspectives:

[41] (1972) 1 All N.L.R. 307, 313.

[42] (1953) 1 W.L.R. 405.

[43] See also Allott, *Essays in African Law*, 1960, p. 40.

[44] See for example cases like *Ali v. Ali*, 5 W.A.C.A. 94; *Folawiyo v. Folawiyo*, 10 W.A.C.A. 259; *Folarin v. Williams*, 8 W.A.C.A. 142; *Millar v. Porter*, 5 W.A.C.A. 151; *Taylor v. Cummings*, 7 W.A.C.A. 21, all on the construction of Wills under the Wills Act, 1837; on the Fatal Accidents Act 1846 and 1864 see *Lawal v. Younan and Sons* (1961) All N.L.R. 245; *Alawode v. Semoh* (1959) 4 F.S.C. 27; on Land Transfer Act 1897 see *Pratt v. Haffner*, (1959) 4 F.S.C. 82 and many other examples.

Adaptation of English Precedents

In the trade mark field English decisions have been adapted to suit Nigerian circumstances. In *MacIver v. C.F.A.O.*[45] the Full Court allowed the appellant's appeal against the decision of the Divisional Court which allowed the registration by the respondents of a trade mark very similar to that of the appellants and therefore likely to deceive the majority of the Nigerian public who are illiterate. Webber, J., observed:

> To the trained eye of a civilised community there is undoubtedly a considerable difference in the two designs set side by side and the one would hardly be likely to be mistaken for the other, but while the broad principles laid down in English cases should be applied, the Trade Marks laws of this country should be administered with due regard to local conditions and, as stated by Osborne, Chief Justice, in the *Houtman case,* "with a view to protecting not only a vast illiterate population little acquainted with pictorial representations, but also the pioneers of trade who have earned a reputation among these illiterate folk by the quality of goods associated with some recognised mark such as a particular bird, animal, tree or other objects." Judges of the Supreme Court of this colony have consistently administered these laws with due regard to local conditions and I think we should embrace this opportunity of expressing our unqualified approval of their decisions.

At page 21 of the Report, Ross, J., remarked:

> In a highly intelligent and civilised community I should have no hesitation in saying that the likelihood of confusing the two marks is so very negligible that no one could reasonably say that the respondents' mark is calculated to deceive: however, I cannot but feel in coming to a decision in this case that attention must be paid to surrounding circumstances and local conditions.

And Speed, C.J., added:

> It seems clear that the learned Judge in the court below was inclined to refuse registration of this mark and would have done so had he not felt constrained to a contrary conclusion by the

[45] (1917) 3 N.L.R. 18.

> decisions of the English Courts. These decisions are of course binding on us but they must be construed having regard to the local conditions which are widely different from those that obtain in England.[46]

The above case and others deciding a similar point were followed in *The United Kingdom Tobacco Co. Ltd. v. Carreras Ltd.*[47] where it was held that the likelihood of deception varies with the intelligence and education of the customers. Butler Lloyd, J., was of the opinion that "these decisions may seem a little startling to an English mind." A more modern case is *Gottschalck & Co. Ltd. v. Spruce Manufacturing Co. Ltd.*,[48] a decision of the Federal Supreme Court in which Foster Sutton, F.C.J., delivering the judgment of the Court, had this to say:

> If the dispute regarding these marks was taking place in England I should have no hesitation in agreeing with the judgment in this case, but it is not, and I am of the opinion that the standards by which such matters must be judged in Nigeria are entirely different.

The conclusion to be drawn from these decisions is that they all paid regard to local conditions. Although as Speed, C.J., said, the English cases were binding on the Nigerian courts, yet they had to be adapted to suit the peculiar social circumstances and conditions in Nigeria. In this way they have acquired a distinctively Nigerian character which distinguishes them from their English prototypes. The difference lies in the fact that, while these decisions are plausible in Nigeria, no English court would follow them back because they are tailored to Nigerian conditions. This is one way in which a Nigerian common law has developed.

Alteration of Pre-1900 Common Law by Post-1900 English Statutes

If a post-1900 British Act of Parliament alters a rule of the common law which was in force in England on the 1st January, 1900, the alteration only changes the common law rule for Britain. It is not

[46] *Ibid.*, p. 22.
[47] (1931) 16 N.L.R. 1.
[48] (1956) 1 F.S.C. 42.

effective to change that rule for Nigeria because the rule has already been merged into our *corpus juris* before the alteration. Thus, in *Pepple v. Federal Administrator-General*,[49] Onyeama, J., refused to apply any rule other than the pre-1900 common law rule to a claim by the plaintiff for damages for the negligent driving of a motor car by a servant of the deceased owner who died before the action was brought. The learned judge applied the common law rule that a personal action dies with the person and not the post-1900 Law Reform (Miscellaneous Provisions) Act, 1934, which altered the common law rule and made the action maintainable.

In *Lawal v. Younan and Sons*[50] which was a claim for damages under the Fatal Accidents Acts, 1946 and 1864, Ademola, C.J.F., observed:

> In England prior to 1934 when the Law Reform Act was passed, an illegitimate child could not claim under the Acts: *Dickinson v. The North Eastern Railway Co.* L.T.R. Vol. 9 New Series, 1863. This latter Act certainly does not apply to Nigeria as it is a statute, though of general application, passed after 1900. When considering the present action, therefore, it is not possible to go beyond English Law in 1900.

From the above examples we can see that common law development may take two different lines in Nigeria and Britain owing to the intervention of statute. The development in Nigeria follows the pre-1900 pattern, while that in England is dictated by the intervening statute. This is one of the ways in which Nigerian common law can be decidedly different from its English counterpart, but it cannot be said that it has in that way acquired Nigerian characteristics and flavour. It is only the Nigerian-developed version of a rule which the exporting country, England, has rejected.

Where English Statutes of General Application are Interpreted in the Nigerian Sense

This is the third way in which the common law in Nigeria can acquire a distinctively Nigerian flavour and pursue its own line of

[49] (1958) L.L.R. 42.
[50] (1961) All N.L.R. 245, 250.

development. Under section 16 (1) of the Supreme Court Ordinance.[51] "All Imperial Laws declared to extend or apply to the jurisdiction of the court shall be in force so far only as the limits of the local jurisdiction and local circumstances permit . . ."

What this provision means is that the courts in Nigeria have power to interpret these statutes in such a way as to give such a meaning to the words in the statutes as is warranted by local circumstances. In other words, the meaning of the words is not what a court in England thinks it is, but what a Nigerian court, in the light of the values and social circumstances of the country, thinks it to be.

Thus, in *Bamgbose v. Daniel*[52] the English concept of legitimate children was extended to include children of polygamous unions domiciled in Nigeria and such children were held to be entitled to share in the estate of an intestate under the Statute of Distribution. In that case the Privy Council said:

> In the present case the Statute of Distribution is a statute applying to a limited class of persons domiciled in Nigeria. As a matter of construction and on the authorities referred to it cannot in their Lordships' opinion be limited in its local application to children who are the issue of monogamous unions.

In the Ghana case of *Coleman v. Shang*[53] the words "wife" and "widow" were given interpretations different from those in England and Lord Tucker remarked:

> Apart from the Interpretation Ordinance, their Lordships would hold that, in the application of those statutes to Ghana, the courts of that country would be entitled to apply the words "wife" and "widow" to all persons regarded as lawful wives or widows according to the law of Ghana.

[51] Cap. 211, Vol. 6 of the 1948 edition of the Laws of Nigeria. Similar provisions were re-enacted in the High Court Laws of the respective States. The provisions of the Law of each of the States are in force in each of the new States carved out of it by virtue of the State (Creation and Transitional Provisions) Decree, 1967, S. 1(5). This does not, however, apply to the four States carved out of former Western Nigeria in view of the Laws of England (Application) Law, 1959, which made English Statutes inapplicable in the West.

[52] 14 W.A.C.A. 116, 121.

[53] (1961) 2 A.E.R. 406, 411.

In the Nigerian case of *Lawal v. Younan & Sons*,[54] a suit under the Fatal Accidents Acts, 1846 and 1864, the Federal Supreme Court in principle recognised the right of wives of a polygamous union to claim under the Acts, but held that their marriage to the deceased was not proved.

From the above cases we find that the law in Nigeria and, in fact, in other countries that have inherited the common law in the way Nigeria did may be quite different from English law on certain topics depending upon the way statutes common to both countries are interpreted by the courts. If this "benevolent" interpretation were commonly applied, little quarrel would be had with the common law as real justice would be done to a people with a different social background from the English. And common law and statutes so adapted would become true local Nigerian law.[55]

3. Growth and Development of Equity

We have seen that one of the three classes of legal rules received by Nigeria into her *corpus juris* on the 1st January, 1900, was the doctrines of equity. The doctrines of equity are nothing more than decisions of English courts based on equitable principles.

It may be asked why equity was specifically mentioned in the reception clause. Express mention of equity was wise, otherwise it might be taken as though only the common law in the narrow sense was to be received, and this interpretation would have placed Nigerian courts in the same predicament as the English courts before the evolution of the rules of equity with no power to grant reliefs such as equity came to provide, e.g. specific performance of contracts, rescission, injunction, etc.[56]

Furthermore, the dichotomy of courts and jurisdiction, which featured in the English judicial system before the merger of 1873–75 was avoided for Nigeria. In lieu of it, the Nigerian courts were permitted to administer common law and equity as a single body of

[54] (1961) All N.L.R. 245.

[55] See Ekow Daniels, *The Common Law in West Africa*, 1964, p. 335.

[56] See Snell, *Principles of Equity*, 26th edition, pp. 635–736; Dias and Hughes, *Jurisprudence*, p. 160. For Nigeria see Supreme Court Ordinance, section 18.

law in the same courts, which came to be the system in England only after 1875.[57]

Like the common law, equity depends for its development upon precedent. This is so in England[58] as well as in Nigeria. A brief glance at Nigerian decisions shows that the principles of equity are as much part of our law as they are of English law. We can pick examples at random.

Delay Defeats Equity

There is a general rule of equity that delay defeats equity. This means, in the words of Lord Camden, L.C., that a Court of equity "has always refused its aid to stale demands, where a party has slept upon his right and acquiesced for a great length of time."[59] A claim for specific performance of a lease was rejected on the grounds of delay in the Nigerian case of *Ibeziako v. Abatu.*[60] Quoting a passage in Halsbury's *Laws of England,*[61] Reynolds, J., observed:

> In my opinion, having regard to all the circumstances of the case, the second defendant, if ever he had a right to specific performance, by reason of his delay lost that right and consequently the whole basis of the appeal goes.

In *Erikitola v. Alli*[62] the sort of delay which precludes a Court of equity from coming to the aid of a party claiming equitable relief was defined as follows:

> Laches consists of standing by while an infringement of one's right is in progress.

And Snell[63] defines "Laches" as:

> Delay which is sufficient to prevent a party from obtaining an equitable remedy.

[57] Dias and Hughes, pp. 168–169; Radcliffe and Cross, *The English Legal System*, 3rd edition, Chapter XVII.

[58] See Allen, *Law in the Making*, 7th edition, pp. 380–382.

[59] See Snell, p. 37.

[60] (1959) 3 E.N.L.R. 24, 27.

[61] Vol. 13, 2nd edition at page 218. The passage was "In certain classes of claim a strict rule prevails and the claim to relief in equity must be made with special promptitude."

[62] (1941) 16 N.L.R. 56, 58.

[63] Page 37.

Unless there is an invasion of plaintiff's rights, he is under no obligation to incur the expense of bringing an action. Thus in *Taylor v. Williams*,[64] Graham Paul, J., said:

> It is certainly not laches and acquiescence on the part of the plaintiff if he chooses to ignore a bad devise until the devisee to her prejudice does something under the devise.

But the plaintiff in *Ephraim v. Asuquo*[65] was held not entitled to a revocation of the letters of administration granted about two years earlier in respect of an estate that was properly administered. Webber, J., considered the grounds advanced for the revocation of the grant and asked:

> Are they sufficient to justify a court not in revoking a grant under which the Defendant, the present Administrator, has been operating for nearly two years?

He answered his question, "I am of opinion that I can at the outset refuse to revoke the grant."

Equitable Estoppel

The doctrine of estoppel has also been developed in this country. The rule as stated by Snell is as follows:[66]

> Where by his words or conduct one party to a transaction makes to the other a promise or assurance which is intended to affect the legal relations between them, and the other party acts upon it, altering his position to his detriment the party making the promise or assurance will not be permitted to act inconsistently with it.

A party may be estopped by acquiescence in a certain state of affairs. Thus, in *Lateju v. Lanihun*[67] family property was lost through a sale by the head of the family in which the other members of the family were deemed to have acquiesced. In that case Ademola, C.J., said:

[64] (1935) 12 N.L.R. 67, 69.
[65] (1923) 4 N.L.R. 98.
[66] *Principles of Equity*, 26th edition, p. 627.
[67] (1958) W.R.N.L.R. 106, 108.

> If the family became aware of the sale of the family land and did nothing to set aside this sale but left the purchaser in possession for upwards of seventeen years, they cannot, in my view, now be heard to say that they did not acquiesce in the sale.

In so holding the learned Chief Justice relied upon two decisions of the West African Court of Appeal.[68] The gist of the doctrine is whether the defendant has altered his position to his detriment in reliance upon plaintiff's conduct: *Ukwa v. Awka Local Council*.[69] There is no acquiescence if this has not happened.

Equitable Doctrine of Pledge

The doctrine dealing with the redemption of a pledge has also witnessed development. A pledge is the transfer of possession of property by the pledger to the pledgee in consideration of a loan of money, on repayment of which the right to possession of the pledgee in the pledge will cease.[70] It follows therefore that possession in the pledgee continues as long as the loan remains unpaid and that on repayment the pledgee is under a legal obligation to surrender possession to the pledger. In *Ikeanyi v. Adignogu*[71] it was held that "in native customary jurisprudence as in English law if a piece of land is pledged the pledger will have his right of redemption no matter how long the land has been pledged, for once a pledge always a pledge." Irwin, J., in *Laragun v. Funlayo*[72] ruled:

> Lapse of time, in this case over thirty years, is not a bar to recovery of land which has been pledged; in *Agbo Kofi v. Kofi Addo* (1933) 1 W.A.C.A. page 284, it was so held.

Equality is Equity

There is a doctrine that equality is equity. This doctrine has been applied by our courts especially in cases involving the distribution of

[68] 3 W.A.C.A. 93 and *Oshodi v. Balogun* 4 W.A.C.A. 1. The last was a Privy Council decision on appeal.

[69] (1966) N.M.L.R. 41.

[70] See Snell, p. 479–481.

[71] (1957–58) E.R.L.R. 38.

[72] (1955–56) W.R.N.L.R. 167.

intestate estates.[73] But in *Taiwo v. Lawani*[74] an attempt by counsel to get the principle of equal division accepted was rejected by the court which accepted the rival principle (Igikankan or Idi-igi) by which the estate was divided, not according to the number of children (ori-ojori), but according to the number of mothers. The court felt that the latter mode of distribution was strongly entrenched in native customary law of succession.

The Equitable Doctrine of Ademption

The doctrine of ademption was invoked without success in *Ojule v. Okoya,*[75] but the principle was recognised and explained. Coker, J.S.C. delivering the judgment of the Supreme Court, stated:

> Surely, the doctrine of ademption was conceived in equity so that of many children or those to whom a testator stood in loco parentis, one should not at the expense of the other or others take a double portion (see *in re Tussand's Estate, Tussand v. Tussand* (1878) 9 Ch. D. 363.

In the above case the plaintiffs contested the right of the defendant to take his devised share in the residuary estate of the testator after he had received a benefit *inter-vivos* and argued that the legatee's interest under the will was adeemed by the gift *inter-vivos.* The Supreme Court held that the argument was unsound because there was no proof that the legatee was a person whom the testator was under an obligation to provide for in which case the doctrine would apply.

The Doctrine of Bona Fide Purchaser

The doctrine of *bona fide* purchaser is one of the applicable doctrines. Snell says "that a purchaser for valuable consideration who obtains a legal estate at the time of his purchase without notice of a prior equitable right is entitled to priority in equity as well as at law."[76] Equity developed this doctrine with a view to the protection

[73] *Andrei v. Agbebi* (1931) 10 N.L.R. 79; *Phillip v. Phillip* (1946) 18 N.L.R. 102. See *Danmole v. Dawodu* (1958) 3 F.S.C. 46.

[74] (1961) All N.L.R. 703.

[75] (1972) 1 All N.L.R. 385, 388.

[76] P. 32.

of such a purchaser. But where an agent of the purchaser of a legal estate had notice of a judicial sale of a prior equitable interest in mortgaged property it was held that the purchaser must take subject to the equitable interest.[77] Where no notice of a prior equitable estate has been received by the subsequent owner of a legal estate the right of the latter prevails over that of the former.[78] In *Omosanya v. Anifowoshe*[79] the owner of an equitable estate sought to fix the subsequent purchaser of the legal estate with notice of it by showing that their common vendor knew that he was the owner thereof. Mbanefo, F.J., in delivering the judgment of the Federal Supreme Court, stated:

> The whole basis of the equitable principle of a *bona fide* purchaser for value without notice is to protect a purchaser from the fraud of his vendor. If the Eyisha family had notice of the appellant's interest there is no evidence that the respondent had any such notice. Notice to the vendor is not notice to the purchaser.

Equitable Remedies

There are remedies which are only provided by equity. One of the most common is the injunction. It is an order by the court to a party to do or refrain from doing an act. When it commands the doing of an act it is called mandatory; and when it merely prohibits the doing of an act it is called prohibitory.[80]

In *Ayinule v. Abimbola*[81] there was an application for an injunction against the defendant to prevent him from doing an act outside the jurisdiction of the court after having been properly served with the writ outside jurisdiction. Onyeama, J., considered a number of English authorities, among which was *In re Liddel's Settlement*[82] and concluded:

[77] *Ollivant Ltd. v. Alakija* (1950) 13 W.A.C.A. 63.

[78] *Cole v. Felami* (1956) 1 F.S.C. 66; *Omosanya v. Anifowoshe* (1959) 4 F.S.C. 94.

[79] (1959) 4 F.S.C. 94, 97.

[80] See Snell, p. 695.

[81] (1957) L.L.R. 41, 42.

[82] (1936) 1 Ch. 365.

> In view of this statement of the law, I am of the opinion that notwithstanding that the respondent Abimbola was resident in Ghana, he was precisely in the same position as a person within the jurisdiction of this court when he was properly served the writ issued from this court. In such a case it would be competent for this court to decree an injunction against him restraining him doing an act in Ghana.

The remedy by injunction is a discretionary remedy.[83] In *Sabbach v. The Bank of West Africa*[84] it was held that no injunction would be granted to prevent a mortgagee from exercising his legal powers of sale and the English case of *Beverges v. Sandeman*[85] was followed in so holding.

Trust

One of the most important creations of equity is the institution of the trust. A trust comes into existence when one person holds property for the benefit of another.[86] In Nigeria it has been decided that a personal representative, on completion of administration, becomes a trustee of the property under his control.[87] This is also the law in England.[88] As trustee he has power to grant a lease.[89] In England a beneficiary who has instigated a breach of trust and benefits from his action cannot later be heard to complain about the breach.[90] This principle has been followed in Nigeria and the doctrine, among others in equity, is well founded.[91]

A full discussion of the development of the doctrine of precedent in common law and equity in Nigeria will require a separate volume and we have to stop our enquiry here. The little we have seen so far is enough to illustrate our theme—that after reception the doctrine has been unfolded by our courts and the received law developed.

[83] Snell, p. 702.
[84] (1962) L.L.R. 174.
[85] (1902) 1 Ch. 579.
[86] For the definition of Trust see Keeton, *The Law of Trusts*, 8th edition, p. 3.
[87] Pratt v. Haffner (1959) 4 F.S.C. 82.
[88] See Snell, p. 109.
[89] Pratt v. Haffner, supra.
[90] *Re Deane* (1888) 42 Ch.D. 9.
[91] *Pratt v. Haffner*, supra.

4. Is There a Distinctively Nigerian Equity?

But developed as it is, how far have the Nigerian courts evolved equitable principles of their own? In other words, what new doctrines of equity have we devised for the purpose of solving such legal problems as are peculiarly Nigerian? Sir George Jessel stated "that the rules of Courts of Equity are not, like the rules of the Common Law, supposed to have been established from time immemorial . . . they were invented for the purpose of securing the better administration of justice."[92] Dias and Hughes define equity as "the means whereby the law and its administration are made to approximate as closely as possible to the ideal of justice."[93]

From these remarks about equity two basic ideas emerge. One is that equitable principles are a modern invention. The other is that they are designed to fulfill the demands of ideal justice. It was only in 1952 that the English Court of Appeal recognised a new equitable interest in land valid against the whole world.[94] There are black spots in our law relating to intestate succession by children who are not the issue of monogamous unions. There are also others in the law of paternity, seduction, slander and so forth, which ought to be erased, just as the English Chancellors were erasing black spots in English common law by improvising and applying principles which came to be known as the doctrines of equity. Have our courts evolved equitable principles of their own?

Inheritance by Natural Children

The rule that natural children are not entitled to share in the estate of their intestate father who had contracted a monogamous form of marriage and had children by that marriage and that it is only the latter that are entitled was laid down in *Cole v. Cole.*[95] This doctrine was followed in a whole line of cases.[96] But its ghost was finally laid to rest by the judgment of the Privy Council in *Bamgbose*

[92] *Re Hallett* (1879) 13 Ch.D. 696, 710.
[93] *Jurisprudence*, 1957, p. 150.
[94] *Errington v. Errington* (1952) 1 A.E.R. 149.
[95] 1 N.L.R., p. 15.
[96] See, for example, *Adegbola v. Folaranmi*, 3 N.L.R. 89: *Coker v. Coker* (1954) 21 N.L.R. 14; *Haastrup v. Coker* (1927) 8 N.L.R. 68.

v. Daniel[97] in which the injustice of the rule was considered and the rule abrogated. This was followed in *Alake v. Pratt*[98] in which a Yoruba custom was proved whereby natural children acknowledged by their father during his lifetime were considered to be legitimate and it was held that such children were entitled to share with children born in wedlock.

All the above cases were decided on the basis of the Statute of Distribution, 1670, which governed the right of succession. In English law, as it stood at the time, children meant legitimate children and legitimate children meant those born in wedlock (monogamous marriage). Section 36 of the Marriage Ordinance[99] provides for the distribution of the estate of the married couple in accordance with the Statute of Distribution in the event of intestacy. This would mean that only children of a monogamous marriage would inherit, and so if the intestate father had a second wife by customary marriage the children of the latter marriage would not share in the estate.

But fortunately for the Nigerian children of customary unions the English common law rule of private international law recognises legitimacy as dependent upon domicile. It is this principle that was invoked in *Bamgbose v. Alake cases.* But suppose the English common law did not recognise such a principle, would our Courts not have devised their own equitable rule to meet the justice of the case?

Law of Paternity

Another black spot is on the law of paternity. It is a well recognised and deeply entrenched customary law of Nigerians that the children of a married woman whenever and by whomever born belong to the husband unless the latter's price on her has been refunded before their conception and birth.[100] The decision in *Edet v. Esien*[101] to the contrary is a rebellion against the values and

[97] 14 W.A.C.A. 116.

[98] 15 W.A.C.A. 20.

[99] Now Act.

[100] See *Nnaemeka Agu in African Indigenous Laws*, 1975, ed. by Elias and others, p. 263. This is the opinion of all the Customary Courts in Eastern Nigeria where *Edet v. Esien* originated.

[101] 11 N.L.R. 47.

custom of the people and to our knowledge no customary court in any part of Nigeria has followed the doctrine.

A decision antithetic to the rule in *Edet v. Esien* was reached by Egbuna, J., in the case of *Nwaribe v. President Orlu District Court*,[102] who tried to distinguish the latter case from the former. Let us quote the learned judge:

> I have carefully considered the authority cited by Mr. Igwebe and I am satisfied that the circumstances of this case are different from that case of *Ekpenyong Edet v. Nyong Esien* reported in XI N.L.R. page 47.
>
> In that case the applicant was married to his wife under Native Law and Custom. His wife left him and went to live with the respondent. Two children were born of the union between the respondent and the wife. The respondent did not pay to the appellant the money which the appellant had paid in dowry on the wife. The appellant therefore claimed that the children were his.
>
> It was held that it was contrary to natural justice, equity and good conscience to allow the appellant to claim the children of another man merely because the other man had deprived the appellant of his wife without paying dowry for her.
>
> This is not so in the present case. In this case under consideration, the woman stayed with the husband until his death. After his death the woman decided to stay in the late husband's compound and did not leave to go and find another husband. It was whilst she was so staying that she was conceived but before she gave birth she had left to stay with her people. There is no question of any man coming in the show until she took action for divorce in the Native Court.

It is difficult to see what material difference the learned judge was able to discern in the two cases. The mere fact that the woman in *Edet v. Esien* had left the husband and lived with another man is of no moment since the husband's price had not been refunded and the marital bond not severed. With respect, the learned judge was simply repeating the history of judges indulging in unscientific and spurious distinctions in order to escape an obnoxious precedent.[103]

[102] (1964) 8 E.N.L.R. 24, 25.

[103] See Brett, "Stare Decisis in Nigeria—Some Random Thoughts" (1965) 6 Nigerian Bar Journal, 74, 76; Salmond, *Jurisprudence*, 11th edition, p. 180.

He was trying to keep his decision in line with popular opinion and values, and there was nothing to prevent him from taking the bull by the horns and saying in the process that he considered *Edet v. Esien* to be wrong and harsh law.

Law of Seduction

The third black spot is on the law relating to seduction. The average Nigerian parents are proud of their infant daughters and will do anything to protect their chastity. Any violation of their chastity is considered a fatal wound to their parental pride and brings the family into public ridicule. And when the common law insists upon proof of loss of service before an action for seduction can succeed they cannot but feel disrespect for English law.[104] Public opinion holds in derision not only the errant girl but also the family from which she comes. If damages cannot be recovered for any other reason at least it should be recovered for loss of face, wound to family pride and social opprobrium which the seduction involves.

Law of Slander

The fourth black spot shows itself on the law of slander. In customary jurisprudence slander is actionable without proof of special damage. But in English law special damage must be proved except in certain well-defined instances, namely, imputing criminal offence, imputing disease, imputing unchastity to a woman and slander of a man in his calling.[105]

A decision that is in line with customary legal opinion is *Ogo v. Ogo*,[106] in which Mbanefo, C.J. (as he then was), said:

> In arguing the appeal, appellant's counsel has referred me to a number of English authorities and textbooks on what a plaintiff must prove before he could succeed in a case of slander. The essence of an action for defamation is publication and in the case of spoken words the exact words or something as close to them as possible must be proved by evidence. Is such strict proof

[104] Most of these cases go to the Customary Courts and the Magistrates' Courts. In the latter courts English rules of evidence are applied and the claims rarely succeed.

[105] See *Clerk and Lindsell on Torts*, 13th edition, pp. 940–942.

[106] (1964) 8 E.N.L.R. 17.

> necessary in a case of slander in the Customary Court? It has not been suggested that slander as a cause of action is not known in Customary Court. Any words spoken of a person which expose him to hatred, ridicule and contempt would appear in Customary Law to be actionable.[107]

The above decision correctly states the customary law on the matter. But why should our present common law of slander not give way to customary law with which the generality of Nigerians are familiar and which they were born to see and which approximates more to "the ideal of justice?" Why should the fate of the injured plaintiff be contingent upon the nature of the court before which he chooses to bring his action? Before courts applying English law[108] he must prove special damage in order to succeed unless he can bring his case within an exception. But before a customary court all he needs to prove is that the words are defamatory. It is submitted that the time is ripe for a reconsideration of the common law rule and that the customary rule should, in equity, replace the common law.

5. CONCLUSION

Any equitable principles evolved to meet each of the above cases should take account of social policy and values. We should not depend upon English law to recognise legitimacy in our law, but should be guided by considerations of fairness in the distribution of intestate estate to wives no matter how married and to children acknowledged as such by their father no matter by whom they are born. Our courts should also recognise as unjust and destructive of communal accord and public peace a rule which makes a man the legal father of a child born by another man's wife. Such a rule is unknown to customary jurisprudence.

Furthermore, proof of service in an action of seduction should be seen for what it is—a foreign imposition unrelated to our custom and therefore inadmissible. In equity, damages should be recovered for injured feelings and loss of parental and family pride and of the

[107] *Ibid.*, p. 18.

[108] That is, English Common Law and Equity and these range from Magistrates' Courts to the Supreme Court.

prospect of winning a suitable suitor and breach of customary law generally. The common law notion of service should not be entertained. In slander the easily injured feelings of the average Nigerian and the propensity on the part of the Nigerian public to ridicule slandered persons without caring whether the words are true or false should be the governing considerations. Decisions along these lines would "approximate as closely as possible to the ideal of justice."

6

THE DEVELOPMENT OF CUSTOMARY LAW IN NIGERIA THROUGH THE DOCTRINE

Customary law is one of the six classes of laws which Nigerian superior courts are empowered to administer and enforce.[1] Decisions by these courts on customary law constitute law for the country.[2] Being law they are cited and the tendency is for the courts to follow their previous decisions, for "The instinct of inertia is as potent in judges as in other people."[3] In so doing they extend to customary law the doctrine of judicial precedent which is said to be a preculiarity of the common law.[4]

The application of the doctrine of judicial precedent to decisions on customary law has played a dominating part in its standardisation. In this way, customary land tenure, succession, administration of estates, matrimonial causes and matters, matters arising from or connected with customary union, custody of children and matters relating to chieftaincy have become subject to fixed and ascertainable rules.

1. The Doctrine of Frequency of Proof

But unlike the practice in common law, a single decision on customary rules is not sufficient to create a precedent without

[1] The other classes are common law, the doctrines of equity and the statutes of general application in force in England on the 1st January, 1900, and other imperial statues specially designated. See Supreme Court Ordinance Cap. 211, SS. 16 and 17 and succeeding High Court Laws of the respective States. The sixth class consists of locally enacted statutes.

[2] See Dias, *Jurisprudence*, 3rd edition, p. 61, where it is said that only High Court decisions constitute law.

[3] Lord Wright, *Precedents* (1944) 8 C.L.J. 118, 144.

[4] See Elias, *Groundwork of Nigerian Law*, 1954, p. 31; Salmond, *Jurisprudence*, 11th edition, p. 162; Ekow Daniels, *The Common Law in West Africa*, 1964, p. 173.

frequent proof. This principle was laid down in the case of *Larinde v. Afiko.*[5] Following the Privy Council[6] the West African Court of Appeal observed:

> The decision of one case in 1892 cannot be said to be "frequent proof in the courts" enabling the courts to take judicial notice of this particular alleged Awori custom. It therefore had to be proved, and it was not. This is a second reason why the judgment of the court below cannot stand.

The *dictum* of the Privy Council upon which the West African Court of Appeal relied was that of Sir Arthur Channel which was as follows:

> The land law in the Gold Coast Colony is based on native customs. As is the case with all customary law, it has to be proved in the first instance by calling witnesses acquainted with the native customs until the particular customs have, by frequent proof in the courts, become so notorious that the courts take judicial notice of them.

In *Giwa v. Erinmilokun*[7] the Federal Supreme Court followed the principle enunciated above, and in an obvious reference to the above authorities observed:

> It is a well established principle of law that native law and custom is a matter of evidence to be decided on the facts presented before the court in each particular case, unless it is of such notoriety and has been so frequently followed by the courts that judicial notice would be taken of it without evidence required in proof.

It is remarkable that up till now the fallacy in the reasoning of the West African Court of Appeal has not been discovered, for in 1969 the Supreme Court decided *Adegboyega v. Igbinosun*[8] on the same principle.

[5] (1940) 6 W.A.C.A. 108, 110.

[6] See the Gold Coast (now Ghana) case of *Angu v. Attah* in Gold Coast Reports P.C. (1874–1928) referred to at page 110 of 6 W.A.C.A.

[7] (1961) All N.L.R. 294, 296.

[8] (1969) 1 All N.L.R. 1.

An uncritical adherence to this principle has led to grotesque results, for in *Odunsi v. Ojora*[9] the Federal Supreme Court refused to follow two previous decisions on the effect of capping a chief as a White Cap Chief even though these decisions settled the very issue that was before the court in the appeal and even though they were decisions of which the court did not disapprove.[10] In that case the court ruled:

> Native Law and custom being a question of fact in an action in the High Court, it is true that the findings in these cases are not binding as precedents, and it is also true, as has been pointed out by Mr. Oseni on behalf of the respondents, that however learned and experienced the judges whose judgments are relied on may have been, they could only act on the evidence which the parties in the cases concerned chose to call before them.

By this ruling the court has thrown to the winds the celebrated doctrine of precedent. It means that on all other issues precedents are to be followed, but not where native law and custom is concerned. In such cases the custom must be proved again and again even though the custom now in issue is the same custom operating in the same area and affecting the same circumstances as the custom covered by the precedent decision. But we look in vain for a decision that constructs a tariff of the frequency with which a custom must be proved to become law.

It is submitted with respect that the above stream of authorities from *Larinde v. Afiko* down is based on error. Our reason for this submission is this. Section 14(3) of our Evidence Act which deals with the proof of customs contains no reference to "frequent proof." The section reads:

> Where a custom cannot be established as one judicially noticed it may be established and adopted as part of the law governing particular circumstances by calling evidence to show that persons or the class of persons concerned in the particular area regard the alleged custom as binding upon them.

[9] (1961) All N.L.R. 283, 287.

[10] The decisions were *Akodu v. Omidiji* (1927) 8 N.L.R. 55 and *Aiyedun v. Oresanya* (1938) 14 N.L.R. 116.

A reasonable interpretation to be placed upon these words is that once evidence is adduced to show that persons or class of persons concerned in the particular area regard the custom as binding upon them the decision of the court based on such evidence forms part of the law. This interpretation is supported by the wording of subsection one of the section which reads:

> A custom may be adopted as part of the law governing a particular set of circumstances if it can be noticed judicially or can be proved to exist by evidence.

If this interpretation is accepted as correct (which we think is correct) then it is clear that a single proof is enough to turn the custom into binding law, and as law judicial notice can then be taken of it under subsection two. This subsection provides for the judicial notice of a custom:

> if it has been acted upon by a court of superior or co-ordinate jurisdiction in the same area to an extent which justifies the court asked to apply it in assuming that the persons or the class of persons concerned in that area look upon the same as binding in relation to circumstances similar to those under consideration.

The question now arises: To what extent must a court act upon the custom before another court is justified in assuming that the "persons or the class of persons concerned in the area" regard the custom as binding? Would a single instance of proof not be sufficient especially where there is no appeal against the findings? Again, would the fact that the rival version of the custom set up by the other party is palpably absurd not be sufficient to discredit the rival custom and hold out the successful version as the only legitimate custom?

The doctrine of frequency of proof, if insisted upon, may produce a stalemate. Under subsection two a court would be justified in assuming that the custom is binding "if it has been acted upon by a court of superior or co-ordinate jurisdiction in the same area to an extent which justifies" the assumption. If these words mean that a court of superior or co-ordinate jurisdiction must have had the custom frequently proved before it before later courts would be justified in assuming it to be the law of the people then a situation in which such assumption would be justified may never arise, for there is no guarantee that two or more judges may agree on the same custom, and even where there is an agreement a higher court may flout the unanimous opinion of the judges of the lower courts and uphold the contrary custom which the lower courts have discredited, as happened with the decision of the Federal Supreme Court in *Danmole v. Dawodu.*[11]

The attitude of the court in that case is a flagrant contradiction of the doctrine of frequency of proof established in *Larinde v. Afiko* since the superior court's decision is not based on the unanimous decisions of lower court judges but on a custom which none of the lower court judges had thought fit to uphold as law. It was after this Federal Supreme Court decision that lower courts started to uphold the custom.[12]

Another obnoxious but logical consequence of insistence upon the doctrine is that subordinate courts would be free to declare that they are not bound by the findings of the superior court on the ground that the extent to which the later court has acted on the custom is not such as justifies them to regard the custom as binding on the people concerned in the area. And we do not think it would be impolitic if one day a lower court challenged the Supreme Court on its rule in *Danmole's case.* If this attitude were taken up it would deal a devastating blow on the doctrine of *stare decisis.*

Notwithstanding its decision in *Danmole v. Dawodu* the Supreme Court appears to stick to the doctrine of frequency of proof. This is evidenced by its decisions in *Giwa v. Erimilokun* and *Adegboyega v. Igbinosun, supra.* It is difficult to see how frequently a custom must be proved before a decision on it can be regarded as a precedent. In *Larinde v. Afiko* one proof was held not sufficient. In *Odunsi v. Ojora* two independent decisions following two independent and separate proofs were held not sufficient. And we have not been able to lay our

[11] (1958) 3 F.S.C. 46 in which the F.S.C. brushed aside all the concurrent decisions of other courts relied upon by Jibowu, Ag. S.P.J., in deciding in favour of Ori-Ojori custom as against Idi-Igi custom and preferred the latter after hearing further evidence on it. It should be understood that before now no other court has held this custom to be valid.

[12] See, for example, *Salako v. Salako* (1965) L.L.R. 136, where Adefarasin, J. (as he then was), discredited the custom but nevertheless felt bound to uphold it because of the F.S.C. decision and *Taiwo v. Lawani* (1962) All N.L.R. 703, where Udoma, J., followed F.S.C. and upheld the custom.

hands on any reported decision in which the number of proofs regarded as adequate has been stated.[13] Rather, we have the disquieting decision of the Federal Supreme Court in *Danmole's case* which set at nought all lower courts and reached a decision that is in direct conflict with the doctrine.

If this decision had been the last word on the matter we would be justified in concluding that at last the Supreme Court had seen the error and redirected its steps to the path of sanity and rectitude. But the cases of *Giwa* and *Adegboyega* make it impossible for us to reach this conclusion. We, therefore, suggest that the Supreme Court in its characteristic forthright and revisionist spirit[14] should watch for an opportunity to correct the error.

Be that as it may, we will proceed now to consider how the doctrine of judicial precedent has influenced the development of customary law and how true and faithful the Nigerian courts have been to the doctrine in *Larinde v. Afiko* in the respective fields in which customary law has been allowed to function.[15]

Decisions on Customary Land Tenure

The whole basis of customary land tenure in Nigeria was clenched in *Tijani v. Secretary, Southern Nigeria*[16] in which the Privy Council stated:

[13] Even in *Kareem v. Ogunde* (1969) 1 All N.L.R. 73, 80, where the Supreme Court said: "The law reports are replete with cases which establish firmly the entitlement of a Yoruba person's children to succeed in Lagos to his property intestate . . ." and mentioned five relevant cases, it did not say positively that these were enough to dispense with further proof, for it proceeded as follows: "The evidence given by the plaintiff in this case was more than sufficient to support their claim to entitlement and the learned trial judge was wrong to have ruled against them on this point." Why evidence again if there are cases which "firmly" establish the custom?

[14] A Privy Council decision was overruled in *Johnson v. Lawanson* (1971) 1 N.M.L.R. 380 by the Supreme Court for a wrong interpretation of Section 129 of our Evidence Act.

[15] The limitation of customary law to the fields enumerated below came with the successive Native Court Ordinances, the last of which was Cap. 142 in Vol. 4 of the Laws of Nigeria, 1948. Section 8 and the schedule to this Ordinance limited the jurisdiction of Native Courts, as hereunder, except chieftaincy matters of which there is no mention. The respective customary courts laws of the different States have reaffirmed this jurisdiction in material particulars as well as the Magistrates' and High Court Laws.

[16] (1921) 2 A.C. 399, 404.

> In the instance of Lagos the character of the tenure of the land among the native communities is described by Rayner, C.J., in the Report on Land Tenure in West Africa, which that learned judge made in 1898, in language which their Lordships think is substantially borne out by the preponderance of authority: "The next fact which it is important to bear in mind in order to understand the native land law is that the notion of individual ownership is quite foreign to native ideas. Land belongs to the community, the village or the family, never to the individual. All the members of the community, village or family have an equal right to the land, but in every case the Chief or Headman of the community or village, or head of the family, has charge of the land, and in loose mode of speech is sometimes called the owner. He is to some extent in the position of a trustee, and as such holds the land for the use of the community or family. He has control of it, and any member who wants a piece of it to cultivate or build a house upon goes to him for it. But the land so given still remains the property of the community or family. He cannot make any important disposition of the land without consulting the elders of the community or family, and their consent must in all cases be given before a grant can be made to a stranger.

According to the Privy Council there were abundant materials including "decisions" which supported the conclusions in the Report quoted. This shows the influence of precedents in the development of the doctrine of communal ownership of land in West Africa. Although the Privy Council has mentioned "decisions" as part of the materials it had to consider before being led "to the conclusion that the view expressed . . . in the language just cited is substantially the true one," it is not clear how many of such "decisions" had to be made in each individual area of West Africa before the custom of communal ownership could be established as binding on the native community and therefore capable of affording the precedents they did afford.

A corollary of the doctrine of communal ownership as reflected in the passage cited is that the head of a family cannot sell family land without the consent of the principal members of the family. This was decided in Nigeria in *Adedubu v. Makanjoula*,[17] an Ibadan

[17] (1944) 10 W.A.C.A. 33.

case, on an appeal from an Ibadan High Court, and it was a pronouncement on an Ibadan custom. Viewed from the spectacle of *Larinde v. Afiko* there are two things about this case that strike us. One is that there is no reference in the record to any decision on the same custom in Ibadan previously. In fact the West African Court of Appeal did not talk of a previous decision on this Ibadan custom, but of "native law and custom throughout West Africa in regard to the alienation of family land."

Another is that in the later case of *Esan v. Faro*,[18] a case which concerned family property in Ebute Metta, a distinct jurisdiction from Ibadan, the decisions in *Adedubu v. Makanjuola* and the Ghana case of *Manko v. Bonso*[19] were followed. Now the law is that in land matters the customary law of the area where the land is situated shall be applied.[20] How did the court in *Esan v. Faro* prove that the law of land tenure in Ebute Metta, Lagos, was the same as the law of land tenure in Ibadan and Gomoa Assria in the then Central Province of the Gold Coast (now Ghana) such that the decisions in *Adedubu* and *Manko's cases* were authorities in point? Again, if the doctrine of frequency of proof is the creed of our courts, why did the West African Court of Appeal follow *Adedubu's case*?

The decision of the Federal Supreme Court in *Ekpendu v. Erika*,[21] though commendable in some respects, further complicates matters in so far as the frequency doctrine is concerned. The court in that case stating the general law of customary tenure, said:

> It is material to mention that *Esan v. Faro* (2) was decided in Lagos with reference to land in Lagos, and *Agbloe v. Sappor* (3) in Accra, and that the latter case arose on a point of Fanti customary law. Nevertheless, the judgment in the latter case is not based on any native law and custom peculiar to the Fanti tribe, and it is clear that the pronouncements of the Court are generally applicable to family land, whether it is situate in Fanti territory or in Nigeria.

[18] (1947) 12 W.A.C.A. 135.

[19] (1936) 3 W.A.C.A. 62.

[20] See Customary Courts Law of Western Region, No. 26 of 1957, S. 20(1); Cross River State Customary Courts Edict No. 9 of 1969, S. 13(3) and S. 15; Northern Nigeria Native Courts Law, No. 6 of 1956, S. 20(1)(b); Eastern Nigeria Customary Courts Law, 1963, S. 23(1)(a).

[21] (1959) 4 F.S.C. 79, 80.

By what means has the court, if it adheres to the decisions in *Larinde v. Afiko* and *Odunsi v. Ojora*, ascertained that the laws of customary land tenure in the over two hundred ethnic locations in Nigeria have been "so frequently proved" as to justify this judicial notice?

It is submitted with the greatest respect that the highest court of this land is contradicting itself in this question of proof of local customary law of land tenure. When proof of the custom of particular areas is forthcoming as in *Larinde v. Afiko* and *Odunsi v. Ojora* it refuses to accord such custom judicial notice on the ground that one or two instances of proof are not enough, but it is prepared to admit that "the pronouncements of the court are generally applicable to family land, whether it is situate in Fanti territory or Nigeria."

We agree with this "generally applicable" approach and submit that it is the sane thing in the circumstances. The "frequency of proof" approach makes nonsense of the doctrine of judicial precedent in its traditional concept. If it is insisted upon in a particular local area, not only will it encourage a multiplicity of litigations, but it will also make it impossible even for the same judge to preach a consistent doctrine, for he will decide each case in the light of the evidence before him and might find himself giving conflicting decisions on the same custom. In that event the situation will be worse confounded and the law would be robbed of its character as a science.

An adherence to the doctrine of frequency would have a further adverse effect on the doctrine of precedent since it would prevent the development of case-law on our customs and thereby accentuate the very problems with which the doctrine already bristles. Let one decision constitute a precedent.[22]

It would appear, however, that in this respect customary law in this country is not treated differently from customary law in England. There are judicial decisions to the effect that frequent proof is necessary for English customs to attract judicial notice.[23] But while frequent proof is necessary to be sure what a custom exactly is, we

[22] See Allott, *Essays in African Law*, 1960, p. 89, where the learned author says: "If customary law is truly law, a single decision of a court would be a precedent of binding or persuasive authority for the future; but the method of case-law has been little used, except, in the native courts."

[23] *Ex parte Turquand* (1884–85) 14 Q.B.D. 636; *Crowcour v. Salter* 18 Ch.D. 30.

must not lose sight of the possibility that evidence may differ from case to case and so fail to produce a consistent determination.

Divested of the doctrine of frequency of proof, case law on Nigerian customary land tenure can grow and gather strength from decision to decision. Thus in *Lewis v. Bankole*[24] the idea of individual ownership of land foreshadowed in *Tijani v. Secretary, Southern Nigeria* was held to be "of course inevitable" in "a progressive community." The learned judge[25] continued:

> The institution of communal ownership has been dead for many years and the institution of family ownership is a dying institution and it is idle to expect this Court at this time to make use of a power which was given to it in order to avoid or mitigate the the individual hardship and injustice which would necessarily be incidental to the abolition of a primitive native system and the immediate substitution of modern methods, in order to perpetuate or bolster up what is at the best only an interesting relic of the past.

The trend towards the break-up of communal or family ownership is being accentuated by various factors. One is that on a joint sale by the principal members of the family the purchaser purchases an estate equivalent to a fee simple: *Alade v. Aborishade*;[26] another is where there is a *partition.*[27]

Unfortunately, however, this trend towards an improvement and rationalisation of customary land tenure has been set in reverse by the decision in *Miller Brothers Ltd. v. Ayeni*[28] in which Van Der Meulen, J., held that property acquired by a native in accordance with a conveyance in English form may nevertheless become subject to customary tenure on the death intestate of the acquirer and descend upon his children. The learned judge said at page 44 of the Report:

> . . . it is true that the father of the claimants and the defendant held this property under an English title, and if he had so wished he could have disposed of it either by sale or by will without

[24] (1908) 1 N.L.R. 81.
[25] Speed, Ag. C.J., at p. 83.
[26] (1962) W.N.L.R. 74.
[27] *Balogun v. Balogun* (1943) 9 W.A.C.A. 78.
[28] (1924) 5 N.L.R. 42.

> consulting any other person; he did not, however, do this, and, as stated above, it has been admitted that on his death his children succeeded to the property according to native law. I am therefore unable to understand why having succeeded according to native law, these persons should thereafter hold the property according to English law instead of native law.

The institution of communal or family ownership is, without doubt, inconvenient and unprogressive and necessarily imposes a restraint on freedom of alienation. But the above case as a precedent on reversion from individual ownership back to family ownership has established a vicious circle. It cannot, however, be said that the situation is of the judge's making. He could not help giving the sort of judgment that he gave, for it was a decision imposed by the intestate's personal law. Until local customs change the law will remain as it is.

Decisions on Succession to Property on Death

This is the second topic of interest on which the doctrine of judicial precedent has developed. The rule that Idi-Igi method of distribution of intestate estate was an integral part of Yoruba customary law of succession was established in *Danmole v. Dawodu*[29] by the Federal Supreme Court. Two rival methods competed for recognition in the lower court, the other being Ori-Ojori. The latter is a method whereby the property of an intestate father is divided among his children according to their number. The former is a method by which the property is divided according to the number of the wives of the intestate with children.

Defying a consensus of lower court decisions in favour of Ori-Ojori the Supreme Court opted for Idi-Igi, and in reply to the trial judge's preference for Ori-Ojori on the ground that "Equality is Equity" the Supreme Court observed, "Idi-Igi is not repugnant to natural justice, equity and good conscience."[30]

In the later case of *Taiwo v. Lawani*[31] where the facts were similar the defendants preferred Ori-Ojori and their counsel urged

[29] (1958) 3 F.S.C. 46.
[30] P. 49.
[31] (1961) All N.L.R. 703, 708.

the court to reject Idi-Igi contended for by the plaintiffs on the ground that "this custom is repugnant to natural justice, equity and good conscience as the same contravenes the well known maxim of equity that 'Equality is Equity'."

In rejecting counsel's contention the learned trial judge, Udoma, J., said:

> I have found nothing in this custom which is repugnant to natural justice, equity and good conscience, and I hold that it is not so repugnant. Indeed, there is nothing in the evidence to justify my taking the contrary view.
>
> I am fortified in holding that "IGIKANKAN" is not repugnant to natural justice, equity and good conscience by the judgment of the Federal Supreme Court in *Sawebatu Damorola and others v. Yisa Dawodu and others,* 3 F.S.C. 46, in which the custom of succession known as "IDI-IGI" was upheld. The rule of distribution of the estate of a deceased Yoruba person dying intestate and leaving him surviving many wives and children which was found and sustained in that case is similar in all respects to, and may be said to be "on all fours" with the rule of "IGINKANKAN." Both "IDI-IGI" and "IGIKANKAN" would appear to be one and the same customary rule of succession.

Adefarasin, J., as he then was, doubted the decision in *Danmole's case*, but nevertheless followed it because he felt bound to do so.[32]

With respect it is submitted that the doubt is justified, especially when we consider the injustice worked by the Idi-Igi method and the harmonious relationship which Ori-Ojori is calculated to promote among the children. The doubt as to the justice of the rule in *Danmole v. Dawodu* is accentuated by the very *dictum* of the court itself. It says:

> The witnesses for the defendants respondents substantially agreed that Idi-Igi was always observed in former times, but stated that it has now been to some extent superseded by Ori-Ojori, the change having come about to preserve cordial relationships between the children. Those who, under Idi-Igi, received a smaller share than their half-brothers and half-sisters felt aggrieved and this often resulted in the estate of the intestate being depleted by the expense of litigation. To avoid this, therefore, Ori-Ojori was

[32] *Salako v. Salako* (1965) L.L.R. 136.

> adopted in some instances. The upshot of this evidence is, in my opinion, that Ori-Ojori is a fairly recent innovation introduced to avoid litigation.

But is it a bad thing to avoid litigation? Law does not exist for its own sake. It is part of an instrument of government and its objective is to ensure peace and order in society.[33] If Ori-Ojori method of distribution will remove jealousy and ensure harmonious co-existence among the children, then the law would have served its purpose.

The view that Oro-Ojori is to be preferred to Idi-Igi is vindicated in several partition cases which decided that family property should be divided equally among those entitled on the death intestate of the ancestor. There is, first, the case of *Sule v. Ajisegiri*[34] in which Butler Lloyd, J., remarked:

> . . . I am not prepared to depart from the principle which has been followed in scores of partition actions before myself and other judges of this Court in accordance with which in cases of this kind partition or distribution of the proceeds of sale has been ordered equally between those intitled irrespective of sex.

The above case was followed in *Salami v. Salami*[35] which was itself followed by Fatayi Williams, J. (as he then was), in *Barretto v. Oniga*[36] in which case the learned judge said:

> Bearing in mind the decision in the above cases, I find as a fact that all the surviving children of Chief Ipsu . . . were entitled equally to Chief Ipsu's estate at the time of his death.

In the case of *Lopez v. Lopez*[37] a contrary opinion was expressed and in *Sule v. Ajisegiri*, supra, the contrary opinion was doubted, the learned judge stating:

> . . . while the case of *Lopez v. Lopez* N.L.R. Vol. 5 page 47 lends some colour to his suggestion, I prefer the reasoning of Mr. Justice Webber in *Andre v. Agbebi and Others* N.L.R. Vol. 10 page 79. . . .

[33] Lord Wright, "Precedents" (1944) 8 C.L.J. 118, 140.
[34] (1937) 13 N.L.R. 146, 147.
[35] (1957) W.R.N.L.R. 10.
[36] (1961) W.N.L.R. 112.
[37] (1924) 5 N.L.R. 50.

The effect of doubting a case and preferring another to it is to isolate the first and clothe the second with weight and authority. Dias and Hughes have stated:

> If one decision of the High Court has not been followed in a whole line of subsequent High Court cases, which have taken a different view of the law, the authority of the case which has been persistently ignored is, of course, gravely weakened.[38]

This is certainly the fate of *Lopez v. Lopez* because at least three cases have avoided it since it came into being.[39]

There is another line of useful cases from the point of view of the doctrine of precedent. In *Taylor v. Williams*[40] the question was whether native law and custom recognised the right of a party to dispose of her undivided share in family property by will or otherwise. Graham Paul, J., holding that she could not, observed:

> It has been for long settled law in this court that a member of a family in these parts cannot alienate his or her undivided share in the family property. . . .

In *Johnson v. Macaulay*,[41] Lambo, J., following the above case and other cases, declared the property involved in the suit to be family property and held that the testatrix "had no disposable interest in the said property which she could alienate by will." The earlier case of *Ogunmefun v. Ogunmefun*[42] established the same point.

The fact that these cases deal with family property in Lagos may lend support to the doctrine of frequency of proof about which we had something to say earlier. But none of the cases has raised this question and each succeeding case followed the first in the ordinary way. From this and other instances we have so far seen, it appears that this doctrine is raised only when it is convenient for the courts to do so.

[38] *Jurisprudence*, 1957, p. 86.

[39] The cases are *Sule v. Ajisegiri*; *Salami v. Salami* and *Barretto v. Oniga*, referred to above.

[40] (1935) 12 N.L.R. 67, 69.

[41] (1961) All N.L.R 743, 746.

[42] 10 N.L.R. 82.

Decisions on Administration of Estates Subject to Customary Law

Under this heading the first thing we want to consider is the right of an administrator under customary law to sue in the High Court. In *Lawal v. Younan*[43] the Federal Supreme Court held that an administrator appointed under customary law could not sue under the Fatal Accidents Acts 1846 and 1864 to enforce a right conferred by English law, his powers being limited to claims under customary law. But in *Adeyemo v. Ladipo*[44] Doherty, Ag. J., held that such an administrator could sue.

There does not appear to be any conflict in the two decisions. The first was an action started in the High Court as a court of first instance; the second was an action started in the Native Court which granted the authority and went to the High Court only on appeal. A case that seems to be in conflict with *Lawal v. Younan* is *Obi v. Maduabuchuku.*[45] In that case the plaintiff brought an action under the Eastern Nigeria Fatal Accidents Law which is substantially the same as the Fatal Accidents Act 1846 and 1864 of England. The plaintiff had no grant of administration or probate either under English law or customary law. At the close of the evidence for the parties counsel for the defence raised the question. The learned trial judge adjourned to enable the plaintiff to satisfy him by motion and affidavit that he could so sue under native law and custom. On being so satisfied the judge gave judgment for the plaintiff.

Here there is a clear case of conflict. The facts are precisely similar to those in *Lawal v. Younan* and yet the decisions are different. *Lawal's case* seems to have overruled *Obi's case* by implication since the latter was not referred to in the former case and both are irreconcilably in conflict. For this reason it does not appear to be an authority for what it decided, and as a decision of a court of interior jurisdiction it must submit to the overriding authority of *Lawal v. Younan*.

The next thing to consider is the right to administer estates in customary law. In *Aileru v. Abini*[46] it was held that customary law does not permit a widow to administer the estate of her husband. In

[43] (1961) All N.L.R. 245.
[44] (1958) W.R.N.L.R. 138.
[45] (1957) 2 E.R.L.R. 46.
[46] (1952) 20 N.L.R. 46.

a recent case from the former East Central State, *Ejiamike v. Ejiamike*,[47] Oputa, J., as he then was, accepted the evidence of a witness as to the native custom of Onitsha that only an "Okpala" (eldest son) can administer the property of his deceased father and not the widow "except where the Okpala is a small boy."

From the two cases cited above it is clear that the custom about the right of a widow to administer the estate of her intestate husband is the same on both sides of the Niger. A somewhat difficult question was raised in *Fonseca v. Passman*.[48] In that case the deceased was a Portuguese resident in Nigeria. The plaintiff claimed to be his widow by native law and custom and sought representation in respect of his estate. The court—Hedges, J.—held that the deceased was domiciled in Portugal and could not marry by native law and custom, that even if he could there was no proof of the marriage and that therefore the plaintiff was not entitled to representation.

The learned judge did not find it necessary to decide whether a wife by customary law has the capacity to administer the estate of her deceased husband. He appears to have been preoccupied with the question of whether a domiciled European could contract a valid customary marriage in Nigeria. It is impossible to say whether, if he thought that such a marriage was possible, he would have decided in favour of a grant to the plaintiff.

Decisions on Customary Matrimonial Causes and Matters

The customary courts law of the respective States of Nigeria provide for exclusive jurisdiction by customary courts in these matters[49] and the High Court Laws except jurisdiction in matrimonial causes and matters subject to customary law.[50] Decided cases are to the effect that High Courts have no jurisdiction in such matters except when the issues are raised collaterally, as when a caveat is entered by a party to a customary marriage to prevent a further marriage under the Marriage Act by the other party.[51] In claims

[47] (1972) 2 E.C.S.L.R. 11, 16.

[48] (1958) W.R.N.L.R. 41.

[49] See for example the Customary Courts Law, First Schedule in Vol. 2 of the 1963 Laws of Eastern Nigeria.

[50] E.g. Eastern Nigeria High Court Law (in Vol. 4 of 1963 Edition) S. 14.

[51] In *re Seluade and Beckley* (1943) 17 N.L.R. 59 and the authorities cited thereunder.

under the Fatal Accidents Acts it is permissible to raise and prove the issue of customary marriage in order to determine the classes of people entitled.[52] It is also permissible to prove that children who are claiming a benefit under the estate of their intestate father are the issue of a customary union.[53]

It would appear that the half-hearted doctrine of frequency of proof does not apply here perhaps because the existence of a system of marriage under customary law is admitted by the legislature and the courts.[54]

Decisions on Matrimonial Causes and Matters Arising from or Connected with Customary Union

The present heading raises a different question from the last one. It does not deal with marital relations as such, but with questions of paternity and legitimacy. In *Nwafia v. Ububa*[55] it was held that if the issue to be determined was whether a man was the eldest son of another (Okpala) it was an issue relating to family status and that therefore the jurisdiction of the High Court was ousted under section 14 of the High Court Law of former Eastern Nigeria.

Section 18 of the Magistrate's Court Law of Eastern Nigeria contained a provision which prevented a Magistrate from exercising original jurisdiction:

> in any matter which is subject to the jurisdiction of a native court relating to marriage, family status, guardianship of children, inheritance or disposition of property on death.

It was held in *Briggs v. Briggs*[56] that a claim by A in slander against B that B accused him of being illegitimate and an attempt by B to prove that A was in fact illegitimate raised a question of family status and so could not be entertained under Section 18 of the Magistrate's Court Law.

The above authorities are based on the interpretations of statutes. But there are two related cases on strict customary law to which we

[52] *Lawal v. Younan* (1962) All N.L.R. 245.
[53] *Bamgbose v. Daniel* (1952) 14 W.A.C.A. 111.
[54] Marriage Act, S. 35.
[55] (1966) N.M.L.R. 219.
[56] (1957–58) 2 E.R.L.R. 6.

will pay attention now. The first is *Edet v. Esien.*[57] This is a case in which a woman left her lawful husband by customary marriage to live with another man by whom she had two children and who had not refunded the husband's price paid on the woman. On a claim by the husband for the children it was held by Carey, J., that a native law and custom which permitted such a state of affairs must be "overruled . . . as being repugnant to natural justice, equity and good conscience." Carey, J., came to this conclusion in spite of the fact that a Native court in the same case had ruled to the contrary.

A decision proceeding in the opposite direction was given in *Nwaribe v. President, Orlu District Court.*[58] Here a widow stayed back in the matrimonial home after the death of her husband and had issue by another man to whom she was not married. It was held that the children belonged to the deceased husband's family and not to the lover.

This last decision is in true accord with customary law. Both are cases decided at first instance by customary (Native) courts which decided against the view taken by the High Court in *Edet v. Esien* on an appeal. *Nwaribe's case* went to the High Court, Owerri, on a writ of *certiorari.* The rule in it reflects the cherished values of the people of Nigeria and there is the likelihood that if both happen to be reviewed by a higher court *Nwaribe v. President, Orlu District Court* will be upheld. At the level of co-ordinate authority, however, it has won support.[59]

Decisions on Custody of Children Subject to Customary Law

By statute a High Court cannot exercise original jurisdiction in matters relating to the custody of children of a customary marriage.[60] In *Omodion v. Fasoro*[61] the High Court had occasion to consider the various statutory provisions and declined jurisdiction. But when under customary law it becomes necessary to grant custody of a child the proper party entitled is the family of the father into which

[57] (1932) 11 N.L.R. 47.
[58] (1964) 8 E.N.L.R. 24.
[59] *Amachree v. Goodhead* (1923) 4 N.L.R. 101.
[60] See Eastern Nigeria High Court Law, S. 14 and the High Court Laws of the respective States.
[61] (1960) W.N.L.R. 27.

the mother has married. Thus, in *Amachree v. Goodhead*[62] Berkeley, Ag. J., said:

> The Native Court was dealing with the question of the custody of a minor. They had to give the custody to one party or the other, and the fact that they gave it to the respondent is another indication of what the native law and custom is in this matter.

Earlier a native court had assigned the child in question to the family of the man who married his mother. This, as the learned judge said, indicated what the custom is. But in *Edet v. Esien*, *supra*, the custom of the people as laid down in the native court judgment was flouted. In each of the three cases above a native court had ruled in favour of the family into which the mother of each child was married, thereby showing that customary law enjoins that the right to ownership and custody emanates from marriage. *Edet v. Esien* ignored not only native customary law as expounded by the native court, but also the earlier case of *Amachree v. Goodhead.* Now that it has itself been distinguished (ignored in fact) in *Nwaribe's case* the legitimate conclusion to draw is that it is not a good authority.

Decisions on Chieftaincy Matters

Precedents also abound on questions relating to chieftaincy. The first thing to which we must direct attention under this heading is the self-imposed restraint on our courts against the determination of the question as to who is a chief as this involves a claim to a mere "title or dignity."

In *Adanji v. Hunvoo*[63] Packard, J., in the Full Court of Nigeria which dismissed an appeal against the ruling of the Divisional Court, had this to say:

> . . . no case has been cited in which such a claim has been held to lie either in the High Court of Justice of England or the Supreme Court of this colony.
>
> On the other hand cases have been cited in which it has been decided that similar claims will not lie (see *Cowley v. Cowley*, 1901 A.C.1.).

[62] (1923) 4 N.L.R. 101, 102.
[63] (1908) 1 N.L.R. 74, 80.

In *Ademola II v. Thomas*[64] the West African Court of Appeal followed the rule laid down in *Adanji v. Hunvoo* but extended it to cover a new situation where pecuniary rights were claimed along with the title of honour or dignity. Referring to the decision by the trial judge on the subject the court said:

> The learned judge felt himself bound by this decision but held that, if the plaintiff were seeking a title to a position of mere honour or dignity and also pecuniary rights cognisable by the Supreme Court, then the court must hear and determine the suit.

Approving the above statement of the law the West African Court of Appeal continued:

> . . . and we are of the opinion that this court should give further consideration to *Adanji v. Hunvoo* in the light of more recent cases and more especially the judgment of the Judical Committee of the Privy Council in *Laoye v. Ojetunde.*

The above decision represents a positive contribution to jurisprudence in at least two respects. One is the boldness of the trial judge in declaring, in effect, that although *Adanji's case* was binding on him he did not consider that its principle would apply to make the case before him non-justiciable as a legal claim involving pecuniary rights was attached to the "title of honour or dignity." The other was the condescension of the West African Court of Appeal in adopting the reasoning of the trial judge and investing it with a higher authority.

A third contribution is represented by the action of the legislature in intervening and adopting the rule laid down in the decided cases and enacting that "a court shall not have jurisdiction to entertain any civil cause or matter instituted for:

> (a) the determination of any question relating to the selection, appointment, installation, deposition or abdication of a chief.[65]

[64] (1946) 12 W.A.C.A. 81, 84.

[65] Chieftaincy Disputes (Preclusion of Courts) Ordinance, 1948, Section 3(a), No. 30 of 1948. Similar enactments are found in the Chieftaincy laws of the respective States.

This is a notable example of the courts guiding the hands of the legislature.

Under the Ordinance the holder of a Haza title—head of juju priests—was held to be a chief since section 2 of the Appointment and Deposition of Chiefs Ordinance defined a chief as "any native whose authority and control is recognised by a native community." Consequently, a suit which put his appointment in issue was held to be beyond the jurisdiction of the court.[66] But in *Odunsi v. Ojora*[67] the Federal Supreme Court held that the questions as to the effect of capping and of recognition by the Governor-General were issues that could "be settled without entering into any question relating to the selection, appointment, installation, deposition or abdication of a chief. . . ."

Odunsi v. Ojora followed the earlier case of *Onitolo v. Bello*[68] where property attached to a chieftaincy was treated differently from questions regarding the selection, etc. of a chief. Holding that the court had jurisdiction the Federal Supreme Court said:

> It cannot have been the intention of the Legislature to deny to a duly recognised chief the right to recover possession of property belonging to the Chieftaincy family and to seek the assistance of the court to that end. And yet unless the words of the section above quoted are given a restricted meaning no chief would be able to come to the Courts in regard to any such property. For these reasons I am of the opinion that the limitation imposed by Section 3(b) on the jurisdiction of the Courts applies only to property relating to the selection, appointment, etc., of a chief. This is not the case in the present action.

The importance of precedent also comes into prominence when questions of validity of appointment are raised. Thus in *Aromire v. Oresanya*[69] it was held that a person appointed as a family head by the family kingmakers and approved by the Oba is the proper chief as against another who was capped by a few supporters without the Oba's authority. In coming to this decision Graham Paul, J., said:

[66] *Osamor v. Izediuno* (1955–56) W.R.N.L.R. 118.
[67] (1961) All N.L.R. 283, 286.
[68] (1958) 3 F.S.C. 53, 57.
[69] (1938) 14 N.L.R. 116, 118.

> This is in my view established not only by the evidence in this case but by the decision in the case of *Akodu v. Omidiji and others (supra).*

Now the decision in *Akodu v. Omidiji*[70] was a decision on pure native custom. When the court in *Aromire's case* decided to follow it, it did not insist on frequent proof of that custom before it regarded the custom as law. This indicates a more sane approach than that in *Larinde v. Afiko* and *Odunsi v. Ojora* and assists in a rapid development of the law.

Taiwo v. Sarumi[71] is interesting from the point of view of original precedent. The case decided that recognition by the Governor was not necessary for the validity of the appointment of a chief. Osborne, C.J., delivering the judgment of the Full Court, said:

> We agree with the opinion of the court below that such a recognition was not a matter of native law, and we think that in the absence of specific legislation to the contrary, the want of recognition, however necessary it may be in practice, will not invalidate an election duly made according to native custom.

Decisions on Islamic Law

This is the last of the reserved fields which the common law has not occupied. Islamic law is customary law in a sense. In *Zaidan v. Mohssen*[72] where the question was which law applied to succession to the real estate of a Lebanese Moslem resident in Nigeria the Supreme Court said:

> . . . the applicable law is not the Administration of Estates Law (Cap. 1), but the (Moslem) customary law of Lebanon which is the one binding between the parties. . . .

The Supreme Court then proceeded to define customary law as:

> any system of law not being the common law and not being a law enacted by any competent legislature in Nigeria but which is enforceable and binding within Nigeria as between the parties subject to its sway.[73]

[70] (1922) 8 N.L.R. 55.
[71] (1913) 2 N.L.R. 106, 107.
[72] (1973) 11 S.C. 1, 21.
[73] See also Elias, *Groundwork of Nigerian Law*, 1954, p. 13.

We deal first with the procedure for the selection of a Chief Imam. In *Odebode v. Ashaka*[74] Brooke, J., held that the election to the post of a Chief Imam depended upon the vote of a Moslem community taken unanimously or by a majority. This principle was applied in *Asani v. Adeosun*[75] in which there were two contestants for the post, each contestant being supported by his well-wisher. The Supreme Court found that it was the first time there had been such a conflict. It was not proved that either of the contestants had a majority in his favour. Reversing the trial court the Supreme Court held that the candidate of the opposing group was not entitled to act as Chief Imam in the absence of a unanimous or majority vote in his favour.

Next we come to succession. In *Absi v. Absi*[76] Savage, J., held that the Statute of Distribution would govern the distribution of the intestate estate of a Syrian where the estate is situate in Lagos and not the Moslem law of the Syrian husband. But in *Zaidan v. Mohssen*[77] a contrary decision was given by the Supreme Court. The court said:

> The present appeal appears to be a case of first impression, except for the recent case of *Absi v. Absi* to which Dr. Odje drew our attention and to which we referred earlier. To the extent to which the case decides that the Statute of Distribution, which applies within Lagos State in common with the rest of the country outside the Western and the Mid-Western States, governs succession to an intestate estate of immovable(?), we can find little assistance from it because no reason was given by the learned trial judge in the Lagos High Court as to why the estate should be distributed in accordance with the Statute of Distribution, rather than the customary law of the Syrian husband and wife. It does not appear that section 12 of the High Court Law of Lagos by reference to section 20 of the Customary Courts Law was ever cited to the learned trial judge who must therefore be deemed to have given his judgment *per incuriam*.

Judging by the above remarks it is clear that *Absi v. Absi* has been overruled. The fact that the Supreme Court found that the judgment

[74] (1944) 17 N.L.R. 84.
[75] (1966) N.M.L.R. 268.
[76] (1973) L.L.R. 39.
[77] (1973) 11 S.C. 1, 17–18.

was given *per incuriam* removes all doubt to the contrary But the Supreme Court upheld the principle of law laid down in *Tapa Kuka*[78] and observed:

> We agree with the learned counsel that this is the rationale of *Tapa v. Kuka* 18 N.L.R. 5. Just as the court in Lagos is entitled to apply as between the parties before it a system of Tapa customary law in respect of immovable property in Bida, so can a Mid-Western Nigeria High Court apply Lebanese law to succession to immovable property in Warri in the case of Lebanese parties.

Decisions on criminal procedure in Moslem courts now have to be examined. In *Kaligari v. Bornu,*[79] counsel attacked the proceedings in the court of the Shehu of Bornu on the ground that the accused was asked for his defence before evidence against him was received. The then Supreme Court (now High Court) held that the procedure. though differing from English procedure, gave the appellant an opportunity of being heard and of putting forward his defence and that the requirements of natural justice were observed.

This case was followed and approved in *Kano N.A. v. Obiora*[80] in which the Federal Supreme Court said;

> A procedure is not contrary to natural justice merely because it is foreign to English law, so long as it is clear that substantial justice is done.

At page 229 of the Report the Federal Supreme Court intimated that the procedure adopted in Moslem courts should be corrected by the legislature if found to be wrong and not by the courts.

However, when the procedure adopted in Moslem courts has been found to be palpably wrong the higher courts have not failed to register their protest and set it right. In *Kano N.A. v. Obiora, supra.* the court said that the:

> stringent rule of procedure in the Moslem court has been modified by decisions in this court in two cases. The two cases which have been heard on appeal in this court have been decided on the grounds that certain procedure adopted by the Moslem court was repugnant to natural justice.[81]

[79] (1953) 20 N.L.R. 159.
[80] (1959) 4 F.S.C. 226.
[81] P. 228.

In *Guri v. Hadejia N.A.*[82] a rule of Maliki law applied in the Northern Nigerian Moslem Court of Appeal precluded persons accused of "Hiraba" (highway robbery) from having an opportunity to exonerate themselves. The rule was relaxed, however, in respect of the first appellant who sought to establish an *alibi*. The court had put questions to the man with whom the first appellant said he spent the night. But the defence of the second appellant was shut out. On appeal to the Federal Supreme Court, Ademola, C.J.F., delivering the judgment of the court, said:

> We have given this matter our most anxious consideration and we have considered the case *Danjuma Dan Buhari Rimin Auzinawa v. Kano Native Authority* (1) in the light of the present case. We approve of Danjuma's case which is an authority for saying that in a trial in a Native Court, an accused person must be given an opportunity to call witnesses to establish his defence of an alibi. We are of the opinion that the principle of Danjuma's case should not be limited to a defence of alibi alone, but that it is applicable in every case including a hiraba case. We are of the view that a procedure which does not permit an accused person to put forward his defence is repugnant to natural justice, equity and good conscience.

This cursory glance at decisions on Islamic law demonstrates beyond doubt that the doctrine is as operative in Islamic law as in common law and customary law in the superior courts. Not only have the superior courts used their powers on appeal to get the Moslem court to toe the path of rectitude,[83] but also they, as bodies of judges trained in the common law habit of legal thought, have used the doctrine to rationalise and systematise decisions on Islamic law, making it a body of consistent legal doctrine.

2. Reasons for the Application of the Doctrine of Precedent in Customary Law

We have seen in Chapter Four that the doctrine of judicial precedent is not part of the customary judicial process.[84] The present

[82](1959) 4 F.S.C. 44, 46.
[83] See *Kano N. A. v. Obiora* (supra), p. 227.
[84] Elias, *The Nature of African Law*, 1956, p. 258.

importance of the doctrine in decisions on customary law owes its existence, not to traditional customary law, but to the influence of the common law as received and applied in Nigeria and to five other ancillary factors.

Influence of the Common Law

We have already referred to the fact that the doctrine of judicial precedent has been deemed a peculiarity of the common law. This is due in a measure to the history of its development in England, for in the history of the evolution of the common law it became necessary for the judges to have regard to previous decisions to make sure that their conclusions on cases before them could be justified.[85] Again, if the common law was to achieve respectability and evolve into a science it was necessary that like cases should be decided alike.[86] It is also thought that the absence of a code might have influenced its development. In fact, Dias[87] has said:

> The lack of a code as important factor in bringing stare decisis about, but what part this still plays is doubtful.

Now if all the above considerations applied in England it was natural that they should also influence the development of customary law which was and still is in the same position as English common law in its early stages. Our customary law is not codified and decisions on them have to follow consistent lines if reliable rules have to evolve from them.

Professional Ethos of Judges and Lawyers

We saw in Chapter Four how our early judges were men with British background of birth and of social and cultural life. Their outlook on common law was influenced by two factors; they were born in it; they were trained in it. Similarly trained were the lawyers, both indigenous and expatriate, who practised before the higher courts (Magistrate's and High Courts). In the face of this it was natural that they should carry over their stamp of character and

[85] See Dias and Hughes, *Jurisprudence*, 1957, p. 54; T. Ellis Lewis, "The History of Judicial Precedent" (1932) 40 L.Q.R. 230, 237–238.

[86] Goodhart, "Precedent in English and Continental Law" (1934) 5 L.Q.R. 40, 52–53, 57.

[87] *Jurisprudence*, 3rd edition, p. 55.

training from the common law to decisions on pure customary law. In effect, therefore, both judges and lawyers bring their common law methods of legal thought to bear on decisions on customary law to the extent that the doctrine is as much applicable to customary law as to the common law.[88]

Need for Justice

Considerations of justice make it incumbent on judges to follow precedent. This applies particularly to judges of co-ordinate jurisdiction, for since one High Court judge is not bound to follow another[89] he can only do so if he considers the previous decision to be just, and for this purpose he may prefer the decision of one judge to that of another.[90] The same consideration explains why a superior court which has the power to overrule a court subordinate to it refrains from doing so and rather approves the subordinate court's decision.[91]

But one court may follow another not necessarily because the precedent promotes the interests of justice, but because it applies the law correctly, for a decision according to justice and one according to law are not necessarily the same thing.[92] The warning is necessary to prevent the illusion that in every case in which a decision of a court of subordinate authority is followed it is because it promotes justice.

Need for Consistency and Certainty

A decision on customary law may be followed in the interests of consistency and certainty. As is the case with the common law, inconsistency in decisions on customary law would rob that law of its character as a science It is this consideration of consistency and certainty that makes a higher court hesitate to overrule a wrong decision that has been followed for a long time and on which many

[88] For the influence of precedent in decisions on customary law see *Taiwo v. Lawani* (1961) All N.L.R. 703, 708 and *Salako v. Salako* (1965) L.L.R. 136.

[89] See for example *Olawoyin v. A. G. North* (1960) N.R.N.L.R. 53, 58.

[90] See *Sule v. Ajisegiri* (1937) 13 N.L.R. 146, 147.

[91] See for example the decision of Brooke, J., in *Katsina N.A. v. Kogo* (1930) 14 N.L.R. 49 followed in *Guri v. Hadejia N.A.* (1959) 4 F.S.C. 44.

[92] *Halliday v. Alapatira* 1 N.L.R. 7; *Benson v. Ashiru* (1967) N.M.L.R. 263, 267.

transactions must have been based.[93] It also explains why the judge continues to follow his previous decision even when a contrary decision of coordinate authority is brought to his attention, or when he is urged to hold the contrary and he finds no good reason to depart. Thus in *Ukaegbu v. C.O.P.*[94] a judge followed his previous decision and added:

> . . . nothing has occurred since the decision in that case to shift this court from that view

Sense of Obligation

As the doctrine of judicial precedent obliges a lower court to follow its superiors in the common law system we should also expect it to be applied to decisions on customary law. In Nigeria the same non-customary courts administer common law and customary law and we therefore find the same method of legal thought adopted in both cases.

The obligation to follow the decision of a higher court or, in some cases, courts of co-ordinate jurisdiction is, in the doctrine of precedent, known as *stare decisis*. This doctrine obliges a lower court to follow a higher court even if the latter is wrong. We have already referred to *Salako v. Salako*[95] where Adefarasin, J., criticised the decision of the Federal Supreme Court in *Danmole v. Dawodu*[96] and declared, however, that he was bound by it. In *Nwugwu v. Ogbonna*[97] the court, being confronted with a decision of the Supreme Court, said:

> I think I must be ruled by the attitude of the Supreme Court in the *Senuga case*. . . .

Udoma, J., in *Taiwo v. Lawani*, already referred to, found it impossible to decide against the application of Idi-Igi method of distribution of intestate estate because of the Federal Supreme Court decision in *Danmole v. Dawodu, supra.*

[93] See *In re Adadevoh* (1951) 13 W.A.C.A. 304, 310; *Johnson v. Lawanson* (1971) 1 N.M.L.R. 380, 388.
[94] (1972) 2 E.C.S.O.R. 207, 209.
[95] (1965) L.L.R. 136.
[96] (1958) 3 F.S.C. 46.
[97] (1972) 2 E.C.S.L.R. 213, 217, per Ikwechegh, J.

Thus we find that the sense of obligation to follow binding precedent also plays a part in introducing the doctrine of precedent into customary law decisions. The same objection to a subordinate court refusing to follow a higher authority which exists in the common law system also applies to decisions on customary law.[98]

Fear of Public Opinion

The influence of public opinion on the evolution of rules of law and of practice is unfathomable. If law or practice must command respect it must take account of popular sentiment. The masses of Nigeria would not feel that a real system of justice has prevailed if the superior courts' decisions on customary law had not been consistent and if like cases had not been treated alike.[99] Fear of public opinion may, therefore, be said to be one of the factors that have influenced the evolution of the doctrine in England and, later, in Nigeria.

It is difficult to find a judge who would not weigh his attitude to previous decisions on the scale of public opinion. He is being watched by Bench and Bar and the enlightened section of the public, and any departure from orthodox doctrine can be made the subject of adverse comment.

[98] See D. A. Ijalaye in (1971) N.B.J. 63.

[99] Goodhart, "Precedent in English and Continental Law" (1934) 50 L.Q.R. 40, 57.

7

JUDICIAL PRECEDENT AS A SOURCE OF LAW

1. A Legal Source

The most important contribution of a judicial precedent to legal theory is that it is a source of law. The expression "source of law" means the source from which legal rules derive their existence. Salmond recognises "legal" and "historical" sources. He writes:

> The former are those sources which are recognised as such by the law itself. The latter are those sources which are such in fact, but are nevertheless destitute of legal recognition.[1]

To explain further what historical sources mean, Salmond goes on to say that the origin of a rule of law is of long descent. He says that the immediate source of a legal rule "may be the decision of an English court of justice."

> But that court may have drawn the matter of its decision from the writings of some lawyer, let us say the celebrated Frenchman, Pothier, and Pothier in his turn may have taken it from the compilations of the Emperor Justinian, who may have obtained it from the praetorian edict. In such a case all these things—the decision, the works of Pothier, the corpus juris civilis, and the edictum perpetum are the successive material sources of the rule of English law. But there is a difference between them, for the precedent is the legal source of the rule and the others are merely its historical sources.[2]

On the above analysis Salmond concludes that the English law "knows nothing of Pothier, or of Tribonian, or of the Urban Praetor," but knows well the effect and nature of precedent. Dr. C. K. Allen takes Salmond to task on this submission. He agrees

[1] Salmond, *Jurisprudence*, 11th edition, p. 133.
[2] *Ibid.*

that the distinction is "very clear and exact," but submits that the courts do not maintain it in practice and cites cases in which Pothier has been quoted and relied upon in refutation of Salmond's thesis that "our Law knows nothing of Pothier."

On the question of whether Roman law was a source of English law in the legal sense Allen says:

> It is true that the voice of Justinian is heard once in our courts where the voice of our own legal authorities is heard a thousand times; and any counsel who based his argument solely on the Digest would occasion depression, if not a certain irritation, on the Bench. But it is going much too far to say that our law "knows nothing of Tribonian and the Urban Praetor," or indeed of any weighty exposition of a principle relevant to the case in hand. Some departments of our law have been settled almost entirely on the authority of the Digest.[3]

He then proceeds to illustrate his contention by reference to cases based exclusively on Roman law, and condemns Salmond for regarding Roman law as unauthoritative in the English courts.

It is true that the views of Pothier and portions of the Digest have been adopted by English courts and moulded into rules of English law as Allen rightly submits. In so far as this point is concerned he is in complete communion and agreement with Salmond. But their area of disagreement is where Salmond claims that such materials are unauthoritative and Allen says they are authoritative. Salmond says only the legal sources have a legal claim to recognition in our courts, that the historical sources have no claim and that although "they influence more or less extensively the sources of legal development" they speak with no authority [4] It is Salmond's thesis that when rules from foreign sources are incorporated into English law this is so at the option of the courts. Allen admits that "our courts are not obliged to accept them," but that "in fact they have so often done so when they are relevant that the rigid distinction between the 'binding' and the 'persuasive' becomes very shadowy and insub stantial."[5]

[3] Allen, *Law in the Making*, 7th edition, p. 272.
[4] Salmond, *Jurisprudence*, 11th edition, p. 134.
[5] Allen, pp. 269–270.

Dr. Allen has made a point. His point is most valid where the field is not covered by authority and the English courts have no English legal rule to fall upon. In these circumstances, the temptation to invoke relevant foreign rules and views may be difficult to resist and to this extent such rules and views may appear compelling and, therefore, binding. But as Dr. Allen himself admits, no obligation is cast upon our courts to admit them. They might easily be spurned and disregarded and a higher tribunal on appeal would not hold the case to have been decided *per incuriam* since these rules and views have never been binding rules of English law. The foreign rules and views of foreign writers at best afford guidance to the English courts, and to regard them as anything more would be to impress them with the character of English law which they do not possess.

Again, let us pursue the matter further from another angle. In strict legal practice only law books of English and Nigerian origin can be quoted in our courts.[6] Neither a book of Pothier nor the Digest can be permitted to be so quoted,[7] though the judge may, in his discretion allow such quotation or refer to the books himself. This being so we find that there is a discretion and a rule which depends upon discretion is not a legal rule. Foreign rules and the views of foreign textwriters only become English law upon incorporation either by legislation or by precedent.[8] Until then they have no enforceable claim to recognition in English or Nigerian courts, however persuasive they might be.

At this juncture a quotation from Dias and Hughes is pertinent:[9]

> A judge of the High Court, for example, will be bound to apply a decision of the House of Lords, even against his own opinion as to its merits, unless he can distinguish it; but he has no need to distinguish an utterance of Pothier. If he dislikes Pothier's observation he simply ignores it. On the other hand, the mere fact that he has accepted the statement of a writer because of its appeal does not in the least imply that he would have been bound to apply it against his inclination.

[6] *Adedibu v. Adewoyin* (1951) 13 W.A.C.A. 191.
[7] Dias and Hughes, *Jurisprudence*, 1957, p. 30.
[8] *Ibid.*
[9] *Jurisprudence*, 1957, p. 31.

To this we may add that a court that ignores Pother or the Digest will not incur the risk of reversal or of being overruled by a higher court which it will incur if it ignores a rule of English Law. If the decision is held to be wrong, it is so, not in law, but in reason, and the higher court will not say the reasoning is wrong because the lower court has not followed Pothier or the Digest. Its approval or disapproval of the decision will be predicated on some other ground.

Dr. Allen has raised two further controversial points. While still on the contribution of Pothier to English jurisprudence he says:

> The gist of the matter is whether it will be so applied, and not whether we dub it "binding" on the one hand, or "persuasive", "legal", or "literary" on the other. Thus of recent years American and Dominion decisions have been examined and followed with such respect that it is little more than a fiction to say that they are not regarded as authorities.[10]

The word "will" in the first sentence suggests inevitability. But is that correct? Which lawyer, however percipient, can say with confidence that the views of a foreign jurist "will be . . . applied" in a particular case going on before an English judge. Secondly, is it "little more than a fiction to say" that foreign decisions "are not regarded as authorities?" The influence of foreign decisions on English decisions is not doubted. They come into prominence when there are no English authorities on the point. But the question is whether they can compete successfully against the decision of an English court.[11]

Dr. Allen's preoccupation with equating historical sources of law with sources that are legal made him oblivious of the need to give separate consideration to the latter. Legal and material sources are clearly distinguishable. Where there is an English Court decision in point, all that the judge does is to compare the material facts and the issue of the precedent decision with those in the case he is handling and if he finds them to be similar he then decides the case in hand in accordance with the rule laid down in the precedent case. He thereby saves himself much trouble and dialectic. But where there is

[10] Pages 271–272.

[11] Professor Williams says that foreign decisions of common law countries will be listened to by English judges where "English authority is lacking or unsatisfactory": *Learning the Law*, 5th edition, p. 81.

no precedent he will have to grope for analogies, both local and foreign, and consult textwriters and "other forms of ethical or judicial doctrine"[12] which appeal to him. The process involves dilation and drudgery. And even after all this he will still be wondering whether he is on the right lines. It is only after his decision is upheld on appeal or followed by other judges that he considers his efforts worthwhile.

From the point of view of counsel, handling a case of first impression is really a tedious exercise and gives rise to anxious moments; and this is so even if he has at his disposal sources other than legal which may exercise persuasive influence upon the court. But with a clear authority—legal source—in point, the position is different. He can, from the outset, know what he has to meet at the trial and what the outcome will be and can then advise his client with optimism. This is one of the important differences between a source of law that is merely historical and one that is legal, namely, that in the one case there is uncertainty of outcome while in the other the outcome can reasonably be seen from the beginning.

Furthermore, where there is a clear authority in point the battle between opposing counsel shifts from what the law is to whether it applies to the case or not. On a point on which there is a dearth of authorities there will be much expenditure of energy on the part of counsel to prove and disprove a legal proposition submitted by one counsel to the court for acceptance and denied by the other. But where there is a clear authority instances are not unknown in which counsel on one side submits to a citation by the other side on the ground that he has no answer.[13]

2. Other Legal Sources

We have seen that precedent is a source of law. We have now to see what other sources of law there are. According to Dias and Hughes there are two principal sources: precedent and legislation;

[12] Salmond, *Jurisprudence*, 11th edition, p. 225.

[13] See *Atu v. C.O.P.* (1970–71) 1 E.C.S.L.R. 7, 8, where counsel for the State agreed with the procedure adopted by the counsel for the applicant for bail after conviction, thinking he was bound by *Okeke v. C.O.P.* (1959) N.R.N.L.R. 1.

the third—custom—is doubtful.[14] Salmond agrees that the law of England proceeds "from two legal sources, namely, legislation and precedent."[15] He has some reservations about custom, and to him:

> The only custom which can operate as a legal custom creating law *proprio vigore* in derogation of the common law, is ancient immemorial custom.[16]

According to Allen, custom is law when it satisfies certain conditions.[17] But all the authorities are agreed on precedent and legislation as sources of law.

> Legislation is the making of law by the formal and express declaration of new rules by some authority in the body politic which is recognised by the courts of law as adequate for that purpose.[18]

The three sources of law can be arranged in an ascending order of importance: custom, precedent and legislation. Custom is the lowest on the ladder. It may provide material for a legal rule but it is not a legal rule by itself without legislative or judicial recognition.[19] Either precedent[20] or legislation[21] can abrogate it, but it cannot abrogate either, though it may influence public opinion against their existence. Legislation can abrogate precedent.[22] It can create new legislative rules and alter or abrogate existing ones at its caprice.

Precedent can create a new rule;[23] it can also vary[24] or abrogate

[14] *Jurisprudence*, 1957, p. 32, where the learned authors say: "The binding sources of English Law, that stage in the evolution of a rule at which it is first quotable as English Law, are legislation and precedent. As to custom there is a doubt."

[15] *Jurisprudence*, p. 135.

[16] *Ibid.*, p. 251.

[17] *Law in the Making*, 7th edition, pp. 129–146.

[18] Salmond, pp. 135–136.

[19] *Odunsi v. Ojora* (1961) All N.L.R. 283.

[20] *Danmole v. Dawodu* (1958) 3 F.S.C. 46, *Edet v. Esien* (1932) 11 N.L.R. 47.

[21] See Abolition of the Osu System Law, 1956, which abolished social and legal disabilities among a class of people called Osu in Ibo area of former Eastern Nigeria.

[22] See *Adegbenro v. Akintola* (1963) 1 All N.L.R. 299.

[23] See for example, *Edet v. Esien* (1932) 11 N.L.R. 47, *Cole v. Cole* (1898) 1 N.L.R. 15, *Alake v. Pratt*, 15 W.A.C.A. 20.

[24] *Guri v. Hadejia N.A.* (1959) 4 F.S.C. 44, 46, in which the right to call evidence to establish alibi was extended to cover a hiraba case.

an existing judge-made rule.[25] But its ability to do this depends upon the accident of litigation[26] It cannot make a rule out of caprice, however expedient it may be to do so. Its law-making power comes into play when a dispute is brought before the court for a settlement. Even here it cannot make a new rule where there is a good precedent rule to follow. Precedent can only create law after its kind. A precedent on land tenure cannot create a precedent in respect of matrimonial causes. Thus, the power of precedent as a source of law is limited.

But what law prescribes that a precedent shall constitute law? No statute has declared this. But statute authorises the setting up of courts of law and permits these courts to adjudicate and pronounce judgments on disputes between subjects and between the subjects and the State. It does not go further and provide that such adjudications shall constitute law for the nation. From where) then does precedent obtain its authority as a legal rule? The generally accepted opinion is that it does so through the acquiescence of the legislature.[27]

Classification

Precedent as a source of law may be classified into original precedent, derivative precedent and declaratory precedent. A precedent is original when it establishes a new rule of law. It is derivative when it analogically extends an existing rule and makes it cover a new situation. It is declaratory when it merely follows an existing rule and makes no contribution of its own to legal development.[28]

Original Precedent

When the law of a case is not covered by a previous decision or the provision of a statute the court must make law for the occasion by looking for a legal principle that will govern the matter. A legal

[25] E.g. *Chief Oloto v. L.E.D.B.* (1950) 13 W.A.C.A. 57; *Motayo v. C.O.P* (1950) 13 W.A.C.A. 114 and other cases.

[26] Allen, pp. 302–311.

[27] Kiralfy, *The English Legal System*, 1954. p. 104.

[28] See Dias and Hughes, *Jurisprudence*, 1957, pp. 81–82.

principle evolved in this way comes into existence for the first time and is known as original precedent. To quote Dickinson:[29]

> There are cases . . . where the legislature has not spoken and for which no precedent is to be found. Obviously every precedent must have originated in precisely such a "case of first impression."

In Nigeria our legal system comprises the common law, the doctrines of equity and the statutes of general application which were in force in England on the first day of January, 1900, as well as native law and custom.[30] These four classes of law form the basic law of this country. Added to them are certain current English statutes and the statutes passed by the Nigerian legislatures. But where no express rule applies to any particular case the courts are mandated to apply "the principles of natural justice, equity and good conscience"[31] This is in effect an authority to the courts to devise legal rules where none already exists to meet the justice of the case before them.

This statutory mandate in Nigeria seems to be culled from the English common law. In England both textwriters[32] and the courts[33] are agreed that new rules can be created *ex improviso* to meet the situation that has arisen. If a judge does this, not only is he doing justice between the parties, but is also contributing positively to jurisprudence.

The kind of natural justice, equity and good conscience which the courts are expected to employ is the kind known to English law as received in Nigeria. It is not the type known to "the man on the Clapham Omnibus"; it is the kind with which a lawyer trained in the common law is deemed to be familiar.[34] To this we must add that

[29] "The Law Behind Law" (1929) 29 Columbia Law Review, 113, 117.

[30] Supreme Court Ordinance Cap. 211 in Vol. 6 Laws of Nigeria, 1948, SS. 14 and 17. This has been repealed and re-enacted in the High Court Laws of the States (see Chapter 4, footnote).

[31] *Ibid.*, S. 17(4).

[32] Salmond, *Jurisprudence*, 11th edition, pp. 225–226; Allen, *Law in the Making*, 7th edition, pp. 302–312; Paton, *A textbook of Jurisprudence*, 3rd edition, pp. 195–198.

[33] *Newbiggin-by-the-Sea Gas Company v. Armstrong* (1879–80) 13 Ch. D. 311, 312—per Lord Justice Brett; *A.G. v. Butterworth* (1963) 1 Q.B. 696, 719—per Lord Denning, M.R.

[34] Allen, p. 307.

these rules of "natural justice, equity and good conscience" must be adapted to suit the Nigerian situation and social background. Anything less will run counter to our ethics and social values.

This leads us on to a consideration of why our customary laws are preserved. We could not be governed by the received law alone. That would unsettle our society and provoke discontent. Customary law must be applied where the justice of the case requires it. In fact in most aspects of our family life, land tenure and chieftaincy institutions this is the law that is applied and has resulted in the emergence of a plethora of original precedents. Such precedents also abound in respect of statutory interpretations and Islamic law. We will briefly discuss the matter under each of the three heads.

Original Precedents On Custom. Soon after the setting up of courts in this country by the British administration in the last quarter of the nineteenth century decisions started to pour in. Many of those decisions were on our customs and the decisions rendered by the superior courts constituted precedents.[35] Those decisions which determine points of our customs for the first time constitute original precedents. The custom which provides the material from which a decision is derived is a source of law in the sense in which Salmond used the term—material source. According to Dias and Hughes:[36]

> Whether we ought to go further and regard it as a binding source is not easy to say.

We submit that as far as the law in Nigeria is concerned, custom is not a binding source of law[37] since it is a matter for evidence. It becomes a source of law only when judicial notice can be taken of it.[38] When custom is resorted to it is not because it is binding, but because there is nothing else to guide the court,[39] and the court will not hesitate to reject a custom which in its view is repugnant to

[35] See Dias, *Jurisprudence*, 3rd edition, p. 63, where the learned author says only superior courts create precedents.

[36] *Jurisprudence*, 1957, p. 41.

[37] *Odunsi v. Ojora* (1961) All N.L.R. 283.

[38] Evidence Act, S. 14(2).

[39] Paton, *A Textbook of Jurisprudence*, 3rd edition, p. 197, where the learned author says: "No developing system of law can avoid the influence of the general views of the community as to the end that law should pursue." See also Dias and Hughes, *Jurisprudence*, 1957, p. 43.

"natural justice, equity and good conscience" or "contrary to public policy."[40]

Once a custom is recognised and established judicially the raw materials of the custom recede into the background and the decision on it becomes pre-eminent. In other words, future courts do not have to look beyond the decision to the custom behind it as the custom has been swallowed up.[41]

Original Precedents from Statutory Interpretation. Sometimes the precedent lays down the meaning of individual words of the statute;[42] sometimes it explains its policy;[43] at other times it determines its limitations and scope.[44] Whichever function it performs, it makes a contribution to jurisprudence.

Original Precedents on Islamic Law. The decisions of the superior courts which determine points of Islamic (Moslem) law for the first time are original. In *Zaidan v. Mohssen*[45] a point of great importance involving succession to the property of a Syrian Moslem came before the Supreme Court for determination and the Supreme Court declared:

> The present appeal appears to be a case of first impression . . .

In that way the case was an original precedent on the point it decided. The case is also important for extending the ambit of customary law to include Moslem religious law.[46]

Precedents on Moslem law have also performed several other functions. They have helped to portray it as a body of consistent and ordered legal rules;[47] they have helped to show its analogy with

40 Evidence Act, S. 14(3).

41 But see Chapter 6 where the courts insist upon frequent proof before the custom becomes law; see also Aliott, *Essays in African Law*, 1960, p. 89.

42 *R. v. Adekanmi* (1944) 17 N.L.R. 99.

43 *Howard de Walden v. I.R.C.* (1942) 1 All E.R. 287, 289; *Brown v. Brass and Ambrose* (1949) 1 All E.R. 922, 925.

44 *Manama v. Bornu N.A.* (1961) N.N.L.R. 53; *Essen v. Ediok* (1936) 13 N.L.R. 99; *Isalomi v. Omunu* (1944) 17 N.L.R. 48.

45 (1973) 11 S.C. 1, 17.

46 *Ibid.*

47 *Guri v. Hadejia N.A.* (1959) 4 F.S.C. 44, 46.

English law:[48] and differences between the two systems have also been demonstrated by them.[49]

Derivative Precedent

While an original precedent creates a new rule of law where none previously existed, a derivative precedent extends an existing rule. This is possible because the facts of the case in hand are not on all fours with the facts covered by the original precedent, but contain additional matter which warrants an extension of the rule.

We have already referred in Chapter Five to Viscount Simond's *dictum* in *Scruttons v. Midland Silicones:*

> The law is developed by the application of old principles to new circumstances.

If a judge waits for exact precedents before he decides the cases pending before him he will nearly always wait in vain, but he can be sure of finding cases as near as possible to the ones in hand, and by drawing an analogy from these cases he can lay down a reasonably sound principle of law to govern the present case.[51] Salmond correctly appraised the situation when he wrote:[52]

> There is . . . one source of judicial principles which is of special importance and calls for special notice. This is the analogy of pre-existing law. New rules are very often merely analogical extensions of the old.

From the foregoing analysis we find that a decision derived analogically from an existing one is a source of law in a true sense. It may not be as revolutionary as that which stems from a case of first impression, but it does make a distinct contribution to jurisprudence. Dias and Hughes recognise the importance of rules of law extended in this way[53] We now proceed to make a brief reference to actual examples in our law.

[48] *Auzinawa v. Kano N.A.* (1956) 1 F.S.C. 27; *Anya v. The State* (1965) N.M.L.R. 62.

[49] *Kalioari v. Bornu N.A.* (1953) 20 N.L.R. 159; *Kano N.A. v. Obiora* (1959) 4 F S.C. 226.

[50] (1962) 1 A.E.R. 1, 7.

[51] See Lord Wright, *Precedents* (1944) 8 C.L.J., 118, 139.

[52] *Jurisprudence*, 11th edition, pp. 225–226.

[53] *Jurisprudence*, 1957, pp. 81–82.

Extensions from Existing English Common Law. In some cases, the rules of the common law as received in this country have been extended to fit in with local circumstances. Decisions on trade marks afford typical examples of such extension. Thus, in *MacIver & Co. Ltd. v. C.F.A.O*[54] the court found that the similarities between the trade mark of the plaintiffs and that of the defendants were such that the English public would not be deceived into thinking that the trade mark of the defendants was that of the plaintiffs. But in Nigeria where the masses of the population are illiterate there is a real likelihood of deception. Webber, J., delivering the judgment of the Full Court referred to several relevant English cases and remarked:

> These decisions are of course binding on us but they must be construed having regard to the local conditions which are widely different from those that obtain in England.

In the *United Kingdom Tobacco Co. Ltd. v. Carreras Ltd.*,[55] Butler Lloyd, J., observed:

> It is a well established principle, not only in this country, that the likelihood of deception varies with the intelligence and education of the consumers.

In the more modern case of *Gottschalck v. Spruce*[56] there has been a recognition of these double standards, Foster Sutton, F.C.J., saying:

> If the dispute regarding these marks was taking place in England I should have no hesitation in agreeing with the judgment in this case, but it is not, and I am of the opinion that the standards by which such matters must be judged in Nigeria are entirely different.

The above *dicta* fully illustrate our thesis. The Nigerian decisions are derived from English precedents, but local conditions have induced the Nigerian courts to adapt the English precedents for the purpose of doing justice to two classes of people—the merchant with a reputation for his goods and the consumer public whose ignorance must not be exploited to its disadvantage.

54 (1917) 3 N.L.R. 18, 22.
55 (1931) 16 N.L.R. 1, 2.
56 (1956) 1 F.S.C. 42, 43.

Apart from the above there is no known instance in which the common law has been stretched to suit local Nigerian conditions. We called attention in Chapter Five to instances in which our law needs reassessment and we specifically mentioned paternity, slander, seduction and cases of intestate succession. We, however, saw that the last is no longer a problem in view of the judgment of the Privy Council in *Bamgbose v. Daniel.*[57] But a critical view of our social conditions in the light of the received law would reveal what changes to the *status quo* are necessary.

Extensions from Existing Nigerian Cases. Instances are available in which rules laid down in previous Nigerian cases have been extended by subsequent cases. In *The Chairman, L.E.D.B. v. Olopinkwu*[58] a claimant of compensation for land compulsorily acquired included conveyancing expenses as part of the amount claimed as compensation. There was no authority directly in point, but the West African Court of Appeal in *Maja v. Chief Secretary to the Government*[59] had held that a claimant could not recover his past outlay in equipping a salt factory which had become moribund and the buildings derelict. In delivering the judgment of the Federal Supreme Court, Abbott, F.J., disallowed the claim for conveyancing expenses and observed:

> It is unfortunate . . . that there is such a dearth of authority in matters such as the present proceedings, and, indeed, I have been able to find no authority on the point raised by this ground of appeal. I have, however, obtained some guidance from the judgment of the West African Court of Appeal in *Maja v. Chief Secretary to the Government.*

The facts of *Maja's case* and those of *The Chairman, L.E.D.B. v. Olopinkwu* are similar but not exact. The only difference is that in the one case a past outlay on a salt factory which turned out to be a wasteful venture was claimed, while in the other case what was claimed was conveyancing expenses. In order to make one an authority for the other the court had to ignore this difference and bring the two cases within a common principle.

[57] (1954) 14 W.A.C.A. 116.
[58] (1959) 4 F.S.C. 53, 54.
[59] (1948) 12 W.A.C.A. 392.

That common principle appears to be that the government only pays for that from which it benefits. It does not benefit from the past outlay on the moribund salt factory, nor from the derelict buildings; hence there is no obligation to pay compensation. In the same way, conveyancing expenses in respect of the acquired land do not add to the value of the land; hence there was no obligation to pay them, and so the court held.

In so holding the later court applied the principle of *Maja's case* to the case before it in spite of the difference of facts and so widened the rule. In the process of extending the rule in this way the court is making law. To quote Dias and Hughes[60] when differences of facts between a precedent and the case in hand are ignored:

> The result is to extend the scope of the rule by making it cover new facts. This is one sense in which a judge may be regarded as "making law."

Dabiri v. Gbajumo[61] was a suit for forfeiture on the grounds of misconduct. The misconduct consisted in a claim by the defendants for partition in a previous suit. Earlier cases on forfeiture were consulted. Forfeiture is normally ordered where the occupant of the property does an act which amounts to a denial of the overlord's title such as granting a lease for a long term, say thirty years[62] or of granting a mortgage of the property and putting the mortgagee into possession,[63] but not a denial of plaintiff's title by the defendant under cross-examination in a previous suit instituted by the plaintiff's privies, which claim was unfounded.[64]

The facts in *Dabiri v. Gbajumo* showed no parallel with the facts in any of the earlier cases. There, under native law and custom, an occupant could obtain a partition of the property from that of the rest for his own beneficial use. But instead of doing it out of court the defendants in the later case partitioned it with others in a previous suit. The plaintiff claimed that this amounted to misconduct which justified a forfeiture. Taylor, F.J., delivering the judgment of the

[60] *Jurisprudence*, 1957, p. 84.
[61] (1961) All N.L.R. 225, 231.
[62] *Onisiwo v. Gbamgboye* (1941) 7 W.A.C
[63] *Adagun v. Fagbola* (1932) 11 N.L.R. 111.
[64] *Ashogbon v. Oduntan* (1935) 12 N.L.R. 7.

Federal Supreme Court, reversed the trial court's order for forfeiture even though he was "unable to find a case on all fours with the present."

The cases on forfeiture considered by the Federal Supreme Court did not cover the facts of the later case. None of them decided that forfeiture could be ordered in the circumstances of the later case. Although there was no actual authority in point which the court could follow out in reaching the decision it did reach, the cases the court had consulted had somehow indicated a track which *Dabiri v. Gbajumo* had to blaze. This blazed trail is a positive contribution to case-law.

The decision in *Akpan Owo v. Cookey-Gam*[65] that the court will not, in the exercise of its equitable jurisdiction, give effect to rules of native law which permit the plaintiff to assert his title against the possession of the defendant in which the plaintiff has acquiesced for at least 21 years, was applied and extended in *Eyamba v. Holmes* [66] In that case Berkeley, Ag. J., stated:

> This is a principle which seems to me to be eminently just, and applicable to the case before me. I am merely extending this principle when I say that I cannot allow the plaintiffs, though their title to the land is not disputed, to evoke a rule of native law which would enable them to dispossess the defendant of a piece of land which has been in the possession of her family for some 40 years, and which possession has been acquiesced in by the plaintiffs during the greater part of that period.

The difference between *Akpan Owo v. Cookey-Gam* and *Eyamba v. Holmes* is that the defendant in the former case disputed the title of the plaintiff while in the latter there was no such dispute as to title When the learned judge said that he was "merely extending this principle" he was laying down a rule of far-reaching importance far beyond that in *Akpan Owo v. Cookey-Gam*. This rule is that a plaintiff who has acquiesced in the possession by the defendant of a piece of land to which he clearly has a claim cannot be heard to say he wants to eject the defendant after the latter has been there for 40 years without showing misconduct on her part.

[65] (1913) 2 N.L.R. 100.
[66] (1924) 5 N.L.R. 85, 87.

In *Bassey v. Cobham*[67] the question was whether native law and custom conferred upon a donee of family swamp the title to the portion reclaimed by him. The nearest authority on the point was *Adam Duke IX v. Oku*[68] which held that a communal swamp filled in by a member of the plaintiff's family was not the property of the family but of the community as a whole. Webber, J., declared:

> I must now consider the effect of native law in the case of a gift of swamp land to a member of the family and that reclaimed by the donee. There is no direct authority on the point, although the case of Prince Adam Duke IX v. Asuquo Ekpenyon Oku, decided by Winkfield, J., in 1911, might be said to deal indirectly with it.

He decided against the donee and added:

> I am quite satisfied that the reclamation of land by the donee does not give him any special property in the land.

The difference in the two cases is this. In *Adam Duke's case* the reclaimer was not given the swamp reclaimed, but in *Bassey v. Cobham* the ancestor of the defendants was granted the swamp for beneficial use. In *Bassey v. Cobham* the court ignored this difference in order to govern its decision by the rule in *Adam Duke IX v. Oku*. By so doing the rule was extended to cover a new set of facts. Such an extension contributed to the development of case-law on customary land tenure in no small measure.

Many more examples could be given, but we have given enough illustrations to show how, notwithstanding differences in the facts, a previous legal principle can be extended to cover a new situation. But the most important thing to note is the influence of an existing principle over the evolution of a new rule of law. According to textwriters[69] this is a form of inductive logic by which a deduction is made from a particular instance or instances. The particular instance must have established a principle and the judge in a later case must find the principle helpful to the conclusion he has provisionally formulated. It does not matter whether the conclusion in the later case toes the same line as the conclusion in the former case,

[67] (1924) 5 N.L.R. 92, 96.

[68] Unreported, but decided by Winkfield, J., in 1911. See note 1 above.

[69] Dias and Hughes, *Jurisprudence*, 1957, pp. 82–85; Allen, *Law in the Making*, 7th edition, pp. 285–286.

or whether a different line is taken as in *Dabiri v. Gbajumo (supra)*. What matters is whether the previous decision has indicated a line of approach. It is by following the line so indicated that a new contribution is made to jurisprudence.[70]

Declaratory Precedent

This is the last of the classes of precedents recognised according to their degree of influence on the growth of the legal system. This class of precedents, as the name implies, simply declares existing law. To quote Dias and Hughes:[71]

> If it is only an application of the existing law its importance is very slight. . . .

It is true that a judicial decision that is a mere echo of an existing rule and which does not carry the law further is not as important as a decision that develops the law and makes a positive contribution to legal thought. But to stop here and not look further for its functions in the scheme of jurisprudence is to do it less than justice.

The importance of a declaratory precedent may not be as slight as might be thought at first sight. First, it gives weight to the precedent decision and invests it with greater authority than it would possess if it stood alone. The importance of this view is readily seen in cases where there are two conflicting precedents and one is followed and the other is not. A rival rule that is followed can justifiably claim orthodoxy and perfection over its counterpart.

Several examples of such conflict and following have occurred in our reports. In *Sule v. Ajisegiri*,[72] for example, counsel urged on the court that under native law and custom a male child of the intestate has a greater share of the father's estate than the female. Rejecting this submission Butler Lloyd, J., set the case of *Lopez v. Lopez*[73] which supported counsel's contention against the other partition cases which held the contrary and declared:

[70] In *re Hallett's Estate* (1879) 13 Ch.D. 696 where Sir George Jessel said: "The only use of authorities or decided cases is the establishment of some principle which the judge can follow out in deciding the case before him."

[71] *Jurisprudence*, 1957, pp. 81–82.

[72] (1937) 13 N.L.R. 146, 147.

[73] (1924) 5 N.L.R. 50.

> . . . while the case of *Lopez v. Lopez* N.L.R. Vol. 5 page 47 lends some colour to his suggestion, I prefer the reasoning of Mr. Justice Webber in *Andrei v. Agbebi* and N.L.R. Vol. 10 page 79 and I am not prepared to depart from the principle which has been followed in scores of partition actions before myself and other judges of this Court in accordance with which in cases of this kind partition or distribution of the proceeds of sale has been ordered equally between those entitled irrespective of sex.

But the rule that a declaratory precedent strengthens the authority of an earlier decision does not apply where the earlier decision and the one following it are shown to be manifestly erroneous. Thus in *Nwankwo v. Okoyeocha*[74] the question was whether a judge was entitled to dismiss an appeal for the failure of the appellant to attach to the copy of proceedings served on the respondent a certified copy of the notice of appeal even though such a copy was filed in court. Two earlier cases, *Okekembo v. Nwosu*[75] and *Onuegbu v. Okechukwu*,[76] decided that a judge was entitled so to dismiss. But a third case, *Dabipi v. Anyabogwu*,[77] held that non-compliance with the rule governing attachment rendered the appeal merely defective and that the defect could be cured under a different section of the rule of court.

Kaine, J., refused to follow the first two decisions and followed the last, and in doing so he observed:

> I am inclined to agree with Mbanefo, C.J., in his ruling in the case of *Dabipi v. Anyabogwu* mentioned above that failure to attach the certified copy to the notice of appeal served on the respondent makes the notice of appeal defective and could be cured by Order 56 Rule 15.

The latter view is what the profession has approved and the former is rejected.

[74] (1962) 6 E.N.L.R. 159, 160.

[75] Appeal No. O/37A/1960 decided at Onitsha on 30/9/60 by Reynolds, J. (unreported). See *ibid.* in note 1.

[76] Appeal No. O/29A/1961 decided at Onitsha on 29/11/61 by Betuel, J. (unreported). See *ibid.* in note 1.

[77] Appeal No. E/55A/61 decided by Mbanefo, C. J., on 8/5/62. See *ibid.* in note 1.

Another instance in which a declaratory decision cannot be said to strengthen the authority of the precedent decision owing to a common error affecting both is afforded by the case of *Inyang v. Teachers Disciplinary Council*.[78] That case followed a previous decision in *Mpi v. Secretary to Teachers Disciplinary Council*[79] which decided that a teacher whose conduct was the subject of enquiry before the council had an unqualified right to legal representation. The section of the Education Law which is deemed to have created this right is section 51(2) which reads:

> The Council may permit any person upon whose allegations an enquiry . . . has been instituted to be assisted by a legal practitioner in establishing the truth of his allegations, and shall permit the teacher whose conduct is the subject matter of the enquiry to be similarly assisted in meeting the charges against him.

Adopting a commonsense view of this provision one would conclude that the right of the teacher to legal representation is contingent on his accuser availing himself of one, but that if his accuser is not legally represented then the teacher is not so entitled. But *Mpi's* case held the right to be an unqualified one, and when in *Inyang v. Teachers Disciplinary Council* the counsel for the respondent had his attention invited to *Mpi's case* she conceded that the right was unqualified and the court entered judgment accordingly.

It is, however, to the judge's credit that he had started out to approach the case on the right lines when counsel for the respondent argued that the appellant's right to legal representation depended upon his accuser exercising that right. But when *Mpi's case* was brought to the notice of respondent's counsel she abandoned the interesting stand she had taken and allowed the judgment to go on the lines of *Mpi's case*. The judge himself had his reservations about *Mpi's case*, but was led to adopt its principle because "the fact has been conceded by the respondent."

Any lawyer can see how wrong the precedent decision is and why the later decision ought not to have followed its steps. But by so doing the principle of *communis error facit jus has been established*

[78] (1962) 6 E.N.L.R. 64, 65.

[79] Appeal No. E/26A/1960 by Palmer, J. (unreported). But see ibid in note 5 *supra*.

whereby several wrong decisions touching the same point of law create a rule of law. From this example it is clear that not only does a declaratory decision strengthen a good rule of law, but it also enables a bad law to pass as a good one.

A line of such decisions constitutes a great danger to the unwary judge and makes it impossible even for a higher court to overrule it for two reasons. One is where it has endured for a long time and becomes consecrated by age; another is where people have governed their transactions by the cases in the line.[80]

Another contribution of a declaratory precedent to jurisprudence is that it provides guidance in cases where it is not easy to get at the original precedent. A search through our law reports will show that most of the cases declare legal principles that have been determined times out of number. The reports containing the principles as originally determined may be out of reach and recourse has to be had to the re-echoed principles.

In sum, therefore, we find declaratory precedents useful for the following purposes. They are easy to come by and so furnish a handy source of law for the judge in a hurry. They clothe precedents of co-ordinate authority with weight even before higher courts.[81] They invest wrong decisions with a semblance of orthodoxy[82] and may serve to get later judges to toe their line.

[80] See *Admiralty Commissioners v. Valverda (Owners)* (1938) A.C. 173, 194.

[81] See note 1 above.

[82] *U.A.C. Ltd. v. Umeugo* (1959) 3 E.N.L.R. 30. In this case a previous case wrongly regarded a motion as an original proceeding, and, despite argument of counsel to the contrary, Reynolds, J., followed it saying: "I think this argument has considerable force but although I am not bound by the decision of Hughes, J., I think it is based on good sense and equity and is indistinguishable from the present application in principle."

8

THE DOCTRINE OF *STARE DECISIS*

The doctrine of judicial precedent involves two ideas. One is that a judge will respectfully examine a previous decision of another judge which is relevant to the case he is handling and follow it if he likes it. Another is that a judge is bound to follow the previous decision of another judge in a given set of circumstances. The first is called the loose doctrine of precedent because the judge before whom the precedent is invoked has a discretion regarding it and is not bound to follow it if it is not in keeping with his taste. The other is called the strict doctrine of precedent because the judge must follow it whether he likes it or not.[1]

This brings us to a consideration of one more classification of precedent—the classification into authoritative and persuasive. An authoritative precedent is a precedent which is the pith and marrow of the strict doctrine, otherwise called *stare decisis*. A persuasive precedent is the foundation of the loose doctrine; it is a precedent which a judge may consider, but is not bound to follow. It has a powerful influence on the mind of the judge and compels attention, but that is all. Each of these classes will now be discussed.

1. Authoritative or Binding Precedent

According to Dias and Hughes:[2]

> The doctrine of precedent in English law is of great antiquity; stare decisis, the doctrine of binding precedent is of more recent origin.

This statement is made about the position of things in England, and it is easy to see why that is so. Until the Judicature Acts, 1873–1875,

[1] See Lord Wright, "Precedents" (1944) 8 C.L.J. 118, 119.
[2] *Jurisprudence*, 1957, p. 53.

the hierarchy of the courts in England was not settled, but these Acts fused the courts into

> one Supreme Court of Judicature which was divided into two parts, the High Court of Justice and the Court of Appeal.[3]

With this arrangement there was, therefore, established a clear hierarchy of authority between the other courts and the Court of Appeal and it thus became clear which decision bound which court. Certainly the decision of the Court of Appeal bound all the courts below it with effect from the time the Acts came into force and all the other courts involved in the arrangement treated one another's decision as persuasive.

Nigeria did not have to experience this sort of arrangement and time-lag between precedent and *stare decisis* because the court hierarchy and the doctrine were introduced into the country at the same time.

At the risk of repetition[4] we will start by saying that all High Courts in the country are subject to the jurisdiction of the Federal Court of Appeal[5] and the Supreme Court and are bound by their decisions even when plainly erroneous.[6] In *Ngwo v. Monye*[7] the Supreme Court held that a decision that is "demonstrably wrong is however still binding on subordinate courts under the principle of *stare-decisis* which is the foundation on which the consistency of our judicial decisions in this country is based."[8]

The doctrine of *stare decisis* being an inseparable part of Nigerian judicial creed we find all the High Courts succumb to the Federal Court of Appeal and Supreme Court decisions even when they find them inconvenient. Thus in *Eziukwu v. President, Ibinta Improvement*

[3] Radcliffe and Cross, *The English Legal System*, 3rd edition, p. 288; see also Chapter 3 of this work.

[4] The operation of the doctrine of precedent was discussed in Chapter 5.

[5] Including its predecessors—The old Full Court of the Supreme Court, the West African Court of Appeal and the Federal Supreme Court.

[6] *Chairman, L.E.D.B. v. Oyewo* (1969) 1 N.M.L.R. 332; *Federal Administrator-General v. Adeshola* (1960) W.N.L.R. 53.

[7] (1970) 1 All N.L.R. 91, 100.

[8] See also *Ojosipe v. Ikabala* (1972) 1 All N.L.R. 128, 131, where the Supreme Court said "the principles of stare decisis . . . are a part of our law . . . by which we are enjoined to follow our previous decisions."

Union[9] Nwokedi, J., found himself obliged to follow the Supreme Court decision in *Ifegwu v. Ota Ukaefi*[10] and observed that until that case "is over-ruled by the Supreme Court itself or a Federal Decree is promulgated to set it aside, it remains a good binding law on all inferior courts in this country."

It is important to note that two things determine the binding force of a judicial decision in this context. One is the position of a court in the judicial hierarchy. Another is the nature of functions which a court performs in the hierarchy—is it an intermediate or final court of appeal? With regard to the first, the rule, as we have seen, is that all higher courts bind lower courts and not the other way round Thus in *Itsekiri Communal Land Trustees v. Warri Divisional Planning Authority*[11] Udoma, J.S.C., delivering the judgment of the Supreme Court happened to refer to the decision of the Western Nigeria High Court in *Minister of Lands and Housing v. Obe*[12] and remarked:

> . . . this was a decision by the High Court of Western Nigeria and therefore not binding on this Court. . . .[13]

With regard to the second, the rule in England is that all intermediate and final courts of appeal are bound by their decisions as well as by those of courts of co-ordinate jurisdiction. Thus in *R. v. Taylor*[14] Lord Goddard, L.C.J., said:

> I should like to say one word about the reconsideration of a case by this Court. A court of appeal usually considers itself bound by its own decisions or the decisions of a Court of co-ordinate jurisdiction. For instance, the Court of Appeal in civil matters considers itself bound by its own decisions or by the decisions of the Exchequer Chamber, and as is well known, the House of Lords always considers itself bound by its own decisions.

[9] (1972) 2 E.C.S.L.R. 494, 498.
[10] S.C. No. 225/71.
[11] (1973) 11 S.C. 235, 280–281.
[12] (1964) 2 All N.L.R. 61.
[13] See also *Zaidan v. Mohssen* (1973) 11 S.C. 1, 18, where the Supreme Court in referring to a Lagos High Court decision in *Absi v. Absi* (1973) L.L.R. 39 stated, "We do not consider ourselves bound by the decision. . . ."
[14] (1950) 2 A.E.R. 170, 172.

This statement of principle has been made by other appellate courts.[15] Exceptions have, however, been recognised and these form a subject of discussion later in this chapter.

Here we have to show that appellate courts in Nigeria have adopted and governed themselves by this principle. First of all let us refer to the Gold Coast (now Ghana) case of *Osumanu v. Seidu*[16] where the West African Court of Appeal adopted the principle enunciated by the Court of Appeal in *Young v. Bristol Aeroplane Co*[17] and laid down the rule that:

> the position, so far as this court is concerned, is that it is bound to follow previous decisions of its own, as well as those of courts of co-ordinate jurisdiction.

Although a Ghana decision, the principle is applicable in Nigeria for two reasons: (1) the West African Court of Appeal was a common court of appeal for Nigeria and the then Gold Coast; (2) the practice of the superior courts in England is also the practice of the superior courts in Nigeria on a matter on which Nigerian statutes do not make any provision,[18] so that, the doctrine of precedent being a matter of practice, whatever rule is adopted in England is binding on the Nigerian courts. And to remove all doubt the Federal Supreme Court held in *Layanju v. Araoye*[19] that *Young v. Bristol Aeroplane Co.* was a decision "which has been followed by this court also."

Both *Osumanu v. Seidu* and *Layanju v. Araoye* were civil cases, but the practice in criminal cases is the same. In *Motavo v. C.O.P.*[20] the West African Court of Appeal adopted the principle in *R. v. Taylor*, supra, and observed as follows:

> This court will adopt in criminal matters the principle enunciated by the Court of Criminal Appeal. . . .[21]

[15] Divisional Court in *Police Authority for Huddersfield Police Authority v. Watson* (1947) K.B. 842; Court of Appeal in *Young v. Bristol Aeroplane Co.* (1944) K.B. 718; *House of Lords in London Street Tramways v. London County Council* (1898) A.C. 373.

[16] (1949) 12 W.A.C.A. 437.

[17] See note 1 above.

[18] See Chapter 4, section 2.

[19] (1961) All N.L.R. 83, 85.

[20] (1950) 13 W.A.C.A. 114, 116.

[21] The principle has been stated above.

That principle is that it will not reconsider its previous decision except in cases where the liberty of the subject is concerned.

We may suppose that the Federal Court of Appeal will toe the same line. This is because it is the successor in functions of the two courts that had adopted the principle,[22] and also because when the Supreme Court in 1969[23] erroneously regarded itself as the same court as the Supreme Court in 1961[24] it governed itself by the same principle. The Supreme Court of 1960[25] was decidedly different from the Supreme Court of 1963:[26] the 1960 Supreme Court was an intermediate court of appeal with the Privy Council above it; the 1963 Supreme Court was a final court of appeal without a superior. So when in 1969[27] and 1972[28] it used words indicating identity with the 1960 Supreme Court it was committing an error of judgment.

Nevertheless this posture has taught us a significant lesson. By equating itself with an intermediate court it has adumbrated the attitude of the Federal Court of Appeal which is the legitimate successor of that court. It has also indicated to us that the Supreme Court as a final court of appeal is not bound by its previous decisions except in certain circumstances. In this regard it has equated its practice with that of an intermediate court of appeal. For this purpose it stands in contradistinction to the House of Lords up to 1966.

We have seen the two planes on which the doctrine operates. It operates to obligate lower courts to follow the decision of higher courts, and it also operates to keep appellate courts to their decisions, except in certain circumstances. Now we may ask: Is the practice in England on all fours with the practice in Nigeria? The answer is yes, except in one respect, for whereas in England the Court of Appeal does not normally consider a wrong construction of statute as an error justifying interference with its previous decisions,

[22] See Chapter 9, section 5.

[23] The Supreme Court as the highest court of Appeal for Nigeria came into existence under section 120 of the 1963 Republican Constitution.

[24] See *Adegboyega v. Igbinosun* (1969) 1 All N.L.R. 1, 9.

[25] From which appeals went to the Privy Council under section 114 of the 1960 Constitution.

[26] This court was a final court of appeal under section 120 of the 1963 Republican Constitution.

[27] See *Adegboyega v. Igbinosun* (1969) 1 All N.L.R. 1, 9.

[28] See *Nwafor v. Nduka* (1972) 1 All N.L.R. 307, 313.

in Nigeria this is not so. In *Young v. Bristol Aeroplane Co.*[29] Lord Greene, M.R., delivering the judgment of the Court of Appeal said:

> Where the court has construed a statute or a rule having the force of a statute, its decision stands on the same footing as any other decision on a question of law. But where the court is satisfied that an earlier decision was given in ignorance of the terms of a statute or a rule having the force of a statute the position is very different. It cannot, in our opinion, be right to say that in such a case the court is entitled to disregard the statutory provision and is bound to follow a decision of its own given when that provision was not present to its mind. Cases of this description are examples of decisions given per incuriam.

From the above passage it is clear that the Court of Appeal will adhere to its previous interpretation of a statute however wrong and that it will only feel bound to reconsider that decision if it was based, not a wrongful interpretation, but on ignorance of the existence of the statute or statutory provision. On this attitude of the Court of Appeal Salmond comments as follows:

> A precedent on the construction of statute is as much binding as any other, and the fact that it was mistaken in its reasoning does not destroy its binding force.[30]

In Nigeria the Supreme Court has taken a contrary position. It does not hold itself bound to a wrong decision on the meaning of statute even if the decision is that of the Privy Council. It was for this reason that in *Johnson v. Lawanson*[31] it disapproved the construction which the Privy Council in 1957 had placed on section 129 of the Evidence Act in the case of *Maurice Goualin Ltd. v. Aminu*[32] and overruled it on the ground that their Lordships had

> failed not only to give the material words of the statute their ordinary and natural meaning and import but also to explain

[29] *Supra*, p. 300.

[30] *Jurisprudence*, 11th edition, p. 204.

[31] (1971) 1 N.M.L.R. 380, 387–388; see also *Anya v. The State* (1965) N.M.L.R. 62, where a wrong construction of sections 287 and 288 of the Criminal Procedure Act was disapproved and *Oladimeji v. The King* 13 W.A.C.A. 275 overruled.

[32] Privy Council Appeal No. 17 of 1957, unreported.

> why those plain and unambiguous words of the statute should be discarded.

It is a thousand cheers to the Supreme Court that it has not adopted the attitude of the Court of Appeal or the House of Lords in clinging to its previous decisions in this regard despite their demerits. The saving graces open to the Court of Appeal and the House of Lords are not so easily open to the Supreme Court in this country. The Court of Appeal can well afford to follow its previous decisions known to be wrong because there is hope of their being corrected by the House of Lords.[33] The House of Lords could up to 1966 do so for its hope was in legislation to change them.[34]

But the Nigerian Supreme Court has no such advantages open to it. The right of appeal to the Privy Council had been abolished and no appeals lie from it to any other court.[35] Further, it has to interpret a written constitution which must be interpreted to suit the trend in national behaviour and in the political and economic circumstances of the country. In such circumstances, rigid adherence to precedent will impose undue hardship and spell disaster.[36]

Again, it is unlikely that the Nigerian legislatures would ever have their attention directed to a fault in statutory interpretation so as to have it corrected. The reason is that as a developing country she is too much occupied with pressing problems of development and administration to think of matters which have no immediate relevance to her objectives.

Before going on to consider the exceptions to the rule we have to ask and answer this question: What law prescribes that the doctrine of *stare decisis* shall apply? We shall look in vain for such a law, for there is none. It depends for its growth and authority upon the practice of the courts.

> That is what all decisions on precedent are: statements of judicial practice or tradition.[37]

[33] See *Young v. Bristol Aeroplane Co.* (1944) 2 A.E.R., p. 297.
[34] *Scruttons v. Midland Silicones* (1962) 1 A.E.R. 1, 7. Salmond, *Jurisprudence*, 11th edition, p. 180.
[35] Constitution, S. 120.
[36] See Lord Wright, "Precedents" (1944) 8 C.L.J. 118, 134.
[37] Salmond, *Jurisprudence*, 11th edition, p. 188. See also Dias, *Jurisprudence*, 3rd edition, p. 62.

We have to consider this point with regard to the practice of the courts from the High Court downwards and with regard to the practice of the Federal Court of Appeal and the Supreme Court separately. Courts below the Supreme Court are bound by the decision of the latter for the simple reason that there is a danger of overruling or reversal when they take a line antagonistic to the one drawn by a Supreme Court decision. There is also the fear of adverse comments and criticism by the higher courts, the profession and academic lawyers. The fear of denial of advancement on the Bench is also a possibility not to be discounted.[38]

But the position is not so clear when we consider why the Supreme Court itself should be bound by its own decisions and by those of the courts of co-ordinate authority. We are told, of course, that it does so in order to avoid "the alarming degree of instability which must follow in consequence of our failure or refusal to do this."[39] From the quotation we are aware that the rule is one of practical convenience only and not a statutory direction. There is therefore ample justification for the remark of a learned writer that:

> the obligation imposed upon the courts by the doctrine of stare decisis is a moral obligation only.[40]

We shall see later how far the Supreme Court is justified in imposing these fetters upon its own hands.

2. Exceptions to *Stare Decisis*

Under this heading we are going to consider the circumstances in which a judge is free to refuse to follow a previous decision which is technically binding on him.

Decision Per Incuriam

One of such cases is when the previous decision was given in ignorance of an applicable rule of law such as a statute or a rule having statutory force or a binding decision. When a previous court gave its

[38] See Ezejiofor, "Stare Decisis in the Nigerian Courts" (1972) 6 Nigerian Law Journal, 47.
[39] See *Ojosipe v. Ikabala* (1972) 1 All N.L.R. 128, 132.
[40] Freeman (1918) 18 Columbia Law Review, 230, 232.

decision in such circumstances we say the decision was given *per incuriam*. Such a decision is, of course, not binding because it does not carry the law with it.[41]

In Nigeria the Supreme Court does not follow a decision that was given *per incuriam*. Thus in *Ngwo v. Monye*[42] the Supreme Court said:

> Where a decision is given *per incuriam* it does not possess for this court any binding effect and this court is entitled to disregard it.

In *Onubaka v. The Queen*[43] the Federal Supreme Court refused to follow its previous decision in the unreported case of *The Queen v. Adelani*, saying:

> We are unable to agree with the decision and we are of the clear opinion that it was given per incuriam.

The West African Court of Appeal similarly discredited its previous decision in *In re Williams*[44] when in *Bamgbose v. Daniel*[45] Foster Sutton, P., delivering the judgment of the Court, remarked:

> We have also referred to the record in the case of In re Williams and I have no hesitation in saying that I agree with the view expressed by Verity, C.J., that the court acted per incuriam in that case.

The above examples show that the Supreme Court and those it called its predecessors would not take kindly to decisions which took no account of applicable legal rules. Such decisions though binding without this stigma, do not bind, when the stigma is present. But the impotence of a decision given *per incuriam* is limited in its effect to the Supreme Court and its predecessors; it does not extend to lower courts. Thus, in *Ngwo v. Monye*, *supra*, the Supreme Court declared:

> Such a decision is however still binding on subordinate courts under the principle of stare decisis which is the foundation on which the consistency of our judicial decision in this country is based.[46]

[41] See Salmond, *Jurisprudence*, 11th edition, p. 203.
[42] (1970) 1 All N.L.R. 91, 101.
[43] (1959) 4 F.S.C. 267, 268.
[44] (1941) 7 W.A.C.A. 156.
[45] (1952) 14 W.A.C.A. 111, 115.
[46] Page 100.

The obligation on the part of subordinate courts to follow a decision that is known to have been given *per incuriam* calls for comment. Clearly this is a decision that is wrong in law, and why should it be binding on a lower court that is called upon to apply it? As the practice is, this later court has no option but to follow it, and any attempt to question its validity will meet with stern rebuke from the higher court.[47] Perhaps the remedy of the unfortunate loser is to appeal so that a higher court may have an opportunity to reconsider the decision. This is what happened in ***Motayo*** *v. C.O.P.*[48] where the court below found itself bound by a decision *per incuriam* in *C.O.P. v. **Potts-Johnson***[49] and decided the case in tune with it. The West African Court of Appeal allowed the appeal and declared *Potts-Johnson's case per incuriam* and over-ruled it.

But how many people in this country can afford the cost of appeals?[50] It is not suggested that lower courts should not be bound by higher courts, nor that the lower courts should be allowed the liberty of declaring the decisions of higher courts *per incuriam*. That would reduce the doctrine to absurdity. That is why we do not agree with Dr. C. K. Allen when he says that the obligation of a lower judge to follow precedent disappears "where it is plainly and admittedly founded on error."[51] No case of error can be plainer and more admitted than the one founded on ignorance of an applicable legal rule.

But to preserve stability, consistency and certainty without having to rubber-stamp glaring errors a way out of the *impasse* must be found. There should be enshrined in the Constitution and the rules of procedure of the Federal Court of Appeal and the Supreme Court a procedure whereby the decisions of these courts considered by any subordinate court to have been given *per incuriam* should be referred to them for reconsideration. In practice the rules should provide for provision of particulars as to (a) express mention of the particular decision and the point of law decided; (b) what rule of law was

[47] See *Tsamiya v. Bauchi N.A.* (1957) N.R.N.L.R. 73, 83.

[48] (1950) 13 W.A.C.A. 114, 115.

[49] (1947) 12 W.A.C.A. 198.

[50] Except in murder cases where appeals lie to the FCA and the Supreme Court free of charge, appeals in other cases have to be paid for.

[51] *Law in the Making*, 7th edition, p. 295.

ignored in the process; (c) the summary of the facts in that case as proved in evidence; (d) the summary of the facts of the present case as proved in evidence; (e) the issues raised in the case, and (f) the intended decision thereon. Pending action on the reference, the subordinate court should adjourn the matter.

Armed with the above information the particular appellate court to which the reference is made should be in a position to reconsider the decision and either confirm, amend or vary that decision of itself or of a court of co-ordinate jurisdiction that has been questioned. The reconsideration should, where possible, be done by a full court. The decision on the reference should be reported in the Law Reports of the country in the ordinary way. The subordinate court judge that made the reference should then give effect to the decision in his judgment.

With a federal constitution such as we have and consequent multiplicity of legal systems the possibility of error *per incuriam* is a real one in our higher courts which can easily overlook statute and other laws. The suggested procedure is therefore an ideal way of retracing their steps from such error as they might have fallen into. The procedure, no doubt, involves a little protraction of cases, but it need not be much and it is a price worth paying for the maintenance of justice and respect for our judge-made law.

When the Liberty of a Subject is Involved

This exception applies chiefly in a criminal case. We have already referred to the relevant cases in this and other chapters.[52] But for the sake of completeness and analysis we have to quote from Lord Goddard, L.C.J., in *R. v. Taylor*:[53]

> This court, however, has to deal with questions involving the liberty of the subject, and if it finds, on reconsideration, that, in the opinion of a full court assembled for that purpose, the law has been either misapplied or misunderstood in a decision which it has previously given, and that, on the strength of that decision, an accused person has been sentenced and imprisoned, it is the bounden duty of the court to reconsider the earlier

[52] See Chapters 3, 4 and 5.
[53] (1950) 2 A.E.R. 170; (1950) 2 K.B. 368.

> decision with a view to seeing whether that person had been properly convicted. The exceptions applied in civil cases ought not to be the only ones applied in such a case as the present.

From the *dictum* quoted above three facts emerge and these are (1) that a precedent will be reconsidered when the liberty of the subject is involved, (2) by a full court assembled for that purpose, and (3) that the exceptions applied in civil cases are also applicable in criminal cases, but ought not to be the only ones applied. The Nigerian courts have adopted this practice of the Court of Criminal Appeal in England[54] and it is now part of our law.

We will now consider each of the facts we have elicited from the *dictum*. There is no doubt that human liberty is sacrosanct and that interference with it can only be justified when there is a clear and undoubted breach of the law. But it is not the only thing a man prizes. His pocket, his property and his reputation may and often are as important as his liberty. Should a wrong decision in a civil case which does not come within any of the exceptions in *Young v. Bristol Aeroplane Co.*[55] not be reconsidered where "the law has been either misapplied or misunderstood" and in consequence a subject has lost his property, his pocket or his reputation? Must our appellate courts which also exercise civil and criminal jurisdictions wait for inconsistency between their previous decisions, or with a later decision of a higher court or for the decision to have been made *per incuriam* before they can reconsider an obnoxious precedent?

Again, it is difficult to understand why reconsideration should be limited to cases where the liberty of the subject is involved and he has been wrongly and unjustly imprisoned. The public is as much interested in the freedom of the innocent person as in the incarceration of the recidivist. It will afford great interest to see a precedent which wrongly set a man free being reconsidered and not being allowed to afford umbrage to a guilty man.[56]

Further, it is salutary that the criminal courts have undertaken to be governed by the exceptions applied by the civil court of appeal. That extends the scope of the rule governing reconsideration of

[54] *Motayo v. C.O.P., supra.*
[55] (1944) K.B. 718.
[56] It is to the Supreme Court's credit that it has in fact done this. See the case of *Anya v. The State* (1965) N.M.L.R. 62.

precedents. But further extension should be possible. It is not necessary to spell out the specific circumstances in which reconsideration will be carried out. Each case should be considered on the merits, the real aim being to balance the interest of the accused against that of the society.

Lastly, the fact that reconsideration should be carried out by a full court is really comforting and reassuring. It will avoid a second error; the actual multiplicity of heads should give that assurance even if a full court has no greater powers than a division of the court.[57]

Special Cases of Expediency

There are cases both in England and in this country when a court on giving a decision expressly declares that that decision should not be regarded as a precedent.[58] This normally happens where there is an irregularity which may and may not violate a fundamental legal principle, but has not worked prejudice on the other party. In such cases, the appeal court pardons the irregularity but warns against its repetition.

Thus, in *Gachi v. The State*[59] the Supreme Court disapproved of the practice of defence counsel calling as a witness for a co-accused a person charged with the latter without the accused person's application to be so called. However, the court found that the procedure did not prejudice the witness. Brett, J.S.C., delivering the judgment of the court warned that "The example is one that should not be followed." In the same case the practice of defence counsel who gave evidence in support of his client's alibi was disapproved, but as this did not result in prejudice to the appellants it was pardoned, but the court warned that "This is another example that should not be followed."

Now let us ask: What would happen if, after this warning, similar practices were repeated in precisely similar circumstances and appeals are brought before the court that issued the warning on the grounds of such irregularities? Would the court say: "We have

[57] See Salmond, *Jurisprudence*, 11th edition, pp. 193–194; see also Chapter 3.

[58] *Solanke v. Somefun* (1974) 1 S.C. 141, 152, *R. v. Stockesley (Yorkshire) Justices, Ex parte Bartram* (1956) 1 A.E.R. 563.

[59] (1965) N.M.L.R. 333, 335-336.

warned against these practices before and you still indulge in them. We are going to allow the appeal this time even though no substantial miscarriage of justice has occurred?" Or would they repeat their warning and pardon as usual?

The answers to these questions depend upon what the effect of the warning is and whether the court has the necessary sanction to back its warning. If, as it is presumed, the warning is intended for lower courts which must henceforth refuse to permit such practices the possibility is that the practices will be discontinued and no occasion will, therefore, arise for the matter to be heard of again in the higher court. The warnings will invest the lower courts with authority to act and prevent repetition.

But if the warnings are ignored by the lower courts and the practices continue, the higher court under the principle of *stare decisis*, will, it is submitted, follow the case in which the warnings are contained and rebuke the particular lower court for intransigence. But as a temple of justice it is unlikely that it will allow any appeal on these grounds without proof of prejudice or miscarriage of justice. If such an appeal were allowed, the higher court would be cutting its nose to spite its face.

From this we deduce the conclusion that *Gachi v. The State* creates two rules. One is that when a court of appeal pardons an irregularity committed in the lower court that does not mean that every irregularity of that class has acquired a prescriptive immunity and should be continued. The decision which pardons it also disapproves of it and is a precedent against, and not for, its continuance. The other (a presumptive rule) is that a continuance of the irregularity will not necessarily result in an appeal on the grounds of such irregularity being allowed, but may evoke from the appellate court a rebuke of the judge that permitted it and of the counsel who perpetrated it.

Before ending this section there is another case we must consider. It is the case of *Solanke v. Somefun*.[60] This is a case in which a party who sought to amend his pleading filed a new statement of claim in place of the one sought to be amended and in his application to amend used the words "substitution" instead of "amend-

[60] (1974) 1 S.C. 141, 152.

ment." The High Court rejected the application on the ground that the rules provided for "amendment" and not for "substitution."

On appeal to the Supreme Court the Court said:

> We do not wish to decide whether the learned trial judge was right in rejecting "substitution" for "amendment" but we feel that if he had compared the two documents, he would have discovered that the use of the word "substitution" is a misnomer. We have adopted this most favourable attitude to effectuate a sooner determination in this case. It is not to be regarded as a precedent.

What is not to be regarded as a precedent? The answer is: The indulgence with which the Supreme Court treated the question raised in the appeal. Does this mean that the same indulgence will not be extended by the Supreme Court to a similar error made in similar circumstances as above if the matter happens again to be brought up on appeal? Or does it mean that lower courts would not be bound to show similar indulgence using the case as a precedent?

We submit that it means both. The decision of the Supreme Court was meant to do justice to the parties in the particular circumstances of the case and was not intended as a general principle of law binding the discretion of the courts for the future. But it is inconceivable that notwithstanding the warning against the use of the decision as a precedent a lower court or the Supreme Court would shut its eyes to the obvious injustice that might be done if a case based on similar facts were not to be sympathetically considered. The warning is probably no more than an invitation to counsel to desist from lax and ill-considered approach to their cases in the hope that mistakes arising therefrom will be overlooked. The sanction for a breach of the warning would, as we have seen, probably be a rebuke of the party responsible as well as of the court that permits it. It will not operate to lose for the party placed in circumstances similar to those in *Solanke's case* the right to have his case sympathetically considered. Considerations of justice are of more importance than technical legal points.

Decisions on Native Law and Custom

We saw in Chapter Six how the Nigerian courts treat decisions on native law and custom, and we saw that in *Larinde v. Afiko*[61] the West African Court of Appeal insisted upon "frequent proof in the courts" before such decisions could be regarded as precedents and therefore binding. The criticism of this doctrine in that chapter need not be repeated here. The point we are making here is that Nigerian courts purport not to regard first and even second decisions on the same custom as binding.[62]

Inconsistency Between Decisions of Same Rank

When two decisions of the same rank conflict, neither is binding upon a lower court. It would be impossible for either to bind because one is depriving the other of its authority and effect, or for both to bind because of the mutual exclusiveness of their character. Some authorities are of the view that in such circumstances the last decision should bind as it is deemed to represent a change of front.[63] That would be so only if the first decision had been considered[64] in the second and either dissented from or distinguished. Otherwise a subordinate court must exercise its freedom to pick and choose between the conflicting precedents.[65] But in doing so it must avoid comments which dub the precedent it has rejected *per incuriam*.[66]

A lower court would naturally follow a decision that appears to it to represent the law. Thus in *Ede v. Inspector-General of Police*[67] De Lestang, C.J., ignored the West African Court of Appeal decision in *R. v. Ajani*[68] and instead followed the English Court of Criminal Appeal decision in *R. v. Abbott*[69] on the question of a wrongful rejection of a no-case submission and subsequent conviction of the accused. The decision in *Ajani's case* and that in *Abbott's case* ended in the same conclusion but there was a difference as to premises. It was *Abbott's* premises that De Lestang, C.J., adopted.

[61] (1940) 6 W.A.C.A. 108, 110.
[62] *Odunsi v. Ojora* (1961) All N.L.R. 283.
[63] Salmond, *Jurisprudence*, 11th edition, p. 181.
[64] *Minister of Pensions v. Higham* (1948) 1 A.E.R. 863.
[65] See Salmond, p. 207; *Chime v. Elikwu* (1965) N.M.L.R. 70.
[66] See *Tsamiya v. Bauchi N.A.* (1957) N.R.N.L.R. 73. 83.
[67] (1960) L.L.R. 137.
[68] (1936) 3 W.A.C.A. 3.
[69] 39 C.A.R. 141.

Another High Court judge that followed *Abbot's case* was Quashie-Idun, C.J., in *Adisa v. C.O.P.*[70] in which he held that the lower court was wrong to have convicted the appellant on the evidence given after he was called upon for his defence even though there was no case for him to answer. The court in *R. v. Ajani* thought that such a conviction would be proper if the evidence in support was credible evidence.

Thus, at least two subordinate courts have supported *R. v. Abbott* in preference to *R. v. Ajani*. However, in *The Queen v. Asaba*[71] the Federal Supreme Court, the successor of the West African Court of Appeal, failed to note the rebuffs and adhered to *R. v. Ajani* and refused to say what status *R. v. Abbott* occupies in our law or what material difference exists between it and *Ajani's case*. This later re-affirmation of the rule in *R. v. Ajani* leaves in doubt the legality of the two High Court decisions we have noted above. But it cannot itself be said to be a convenient and just rule of law.

Later Contrary Decision of a Higher Court

This is the second of the exceptions to the rule in *Young v. Bristol Aeroplane Co.* A decision by one court on a given point of law is a precedent on that point. But if a higher court subsequently hands down a decision which is flatly contradictory to the precedent decision the authority of the later is thereby destroyed.[72] If its existence was not known to the higher court it is deemed to have been overruled by implication;[73] if the position is otherwise, the overruling is express. There is no difficulty with the latter as there is with the former. The difficulty lies in the possible lack of a consensus between two judges as to whether there is a conflict or not. We quote Goodhart:[74]

> It is possible to know with certainty when a case has been expressly overruled, but who can say with any confidence whether or not a case has been overruled by implication? One

[70] (1961) W.N.L.R. 81.
[71] (1961) All N.L.R. 673.
[72] This is so whether the higher court considered the first decision and overruled it or not.
[73] See Salmond, p. 201.
[74] "Precedents in the Court of Appeal" (1945–47) 9 C.L.J. 349, 358.

> judge may hold that there is a clear conflict between two cases while another may find no difficulty in reconciling them. It will therefore be impossible to say that a precedent, case in the Court of Appeal is absolutely binding until all analogous cases in the House of Lords have been considered, and until it has been determined that no implied conflict exists.

The picture, however, is not as grim as Professor Goodhart is trying to make it. To determine whether a later decision of a higher court has deprived a decision of subordinate authority of its force and potency it is necessary to look at the issues involved and the point of law decided in both cases. In *Uka v. Insp. Gen. of Police,*[75] Kassim, Ag. P.J., held that the safest way to prove whether a statement purported to have been made by an accused person was in fact made by him was to read the statement to the accused person in his own language who should then be asked whether he made that statement or not. But in a decision of the Supreme Court in *The Queen v. Mboho*[76] two years later a contrary opinion was reached, the court holding that:

> an accused person should not while the case for the prosecution is in progress, be asked or required by the court to make statements which normally should be made in the witness box on oath under S. 287(1) (a) (11), or from the dock under S. 287(1) (a) (1) of the Criminal Procedure Act.

The above illustration makes it plain beyond doubt that the two authorities are irreconcilably in conflict and that the decision in *Uka v. Insp. Gen. of Police* must surrender its ground to that in *The Queen v. Mboho*. The effect of this is obvious. The doctrine of *stare decisis* no longer operates to compel lower courts, such as magistrates' and customary courts, to govern themselves by the decision in *Uka's case* because the higher authority in *The Queen v. Mboho* has usurped their loyalty and allegiance.

Obiter Dicta

In England as in Nigeria the doctrine of *stare decisis* does not apply to an *obiter dictum* and no court is bound to apply it. Let us listen to Dias:

[75] (1962) 2 E.N.L.R. 7.
[76] (1964) N.M.L.R. 49.

Statements which are not part of the ratio decidendi are distinguished as obiter dicta and are not authoritative. Salmond says:

"that the authoritative influence of precedents does not extend to . . . obiter dicta.[78]

What then is *obiter* Guidance can be found in our law. A passage that is "not strictly necessary for the decision of" a point is *obiter.*[79]

In *Dede v. United Arab Airlines*[80] Holden. J., refused to follow a part of the judgement of the Supreme Court in *Ojemuyiwa v. Sun Insurance Office Ltd.*[81] on the ground that:

. . . it was obiter and not intended as a statement of the law.

The West African Court of Appeal in *Motayo v. C.O.P.*[82] overruled the case of the *C.O.P. v. Potts-Johnson*[83] on which the decision in the present case before it was based because that decision itself was based on an *obiter dictum* in another case.[84] Referring to the said passage, Blackall, P., delivering the judgment of the court, said:

that observation was no more than an obiter dictum: but the judges who sat on the Potts-Johnson appeal seem to have regarded it as a binding decision.

What is there in the character of an *obiter dictum* that makes it otiose as a legal principle? The answer is that it was not the issue to be decided in the case and was, therefore, not argued or deliberated upon by the court.[85] A case is only an authority for what it decides[86]

[77] *Jurisprudence*, 3rd edition, p. 63.
[78] *Jurisprudence*, 11th edition, p. 166.
[79] *Insp. Gen. of Police v. Mark* (1957) 2 F.S.C. 5, 6.
[80] (1969) 1 N.M.L.R. 75, 76.
[81] (1965) N.M.L.R. 451.
[82] (1950) 13 W.A.C.A. 114, 116.
[83] (1947) 12 W.A.C.A. 198.
[84] *Rex v. Eka*, W.A.C.A. 1945, unreported.
[85] See Allen, *Law in the Making*, 7th edition, pp. 260–268.
[86] Lord Halsbury in *Quinn v. Leathem* (1901) A.C. 495, 506.

and it can only legally decide the issue before the court.[87] But where a remark, though *obiter*, states the law correctly, later courts will follow it.[88] An *obiter dictum* may be adopted and affirmed as a statement of the law,[89] and in *Sule v. The Queen*[90] the Federal Supreme Court agreed with a *dictum* of the West African Court of Appeal which was expressed *obiter* in *R. v. Adegboyega*[91] and added:

> . . . we entertain no doubt that the view expressed in that case is correct.

The fact that an *obiter dictum* is approved and adopted is no reason to suppose that the court which approves and adopts it is bound by it. An *obiter dictum*, as we have seen is not binding even if it proceeds from the highest court of the land.[92] A court that accepts it does so as a matter of volition and in its discretion when it finds that it establishes the point of law it wants.

Foreign Decisions

By foreign decisions we mean decisions of courts outside Nigeria other than those of English courts, for the latter enjoy a special status in Nigerian courts.[93] The rule in England is that foreign decisions are not binding on English courts, but are of persuasive authority, especially those of the American Courts.[94] The rule in Nigeria is the same,[95] and there are decisions in Commonwealth countries outside Britain which have enjoyed high respect in our

[87] *R. v. Landow* (1913) 8 C.A.R. 218, 222; Salmond, Jurisprudence, 11th edition, p. 224.

[88] *Zeidman v. Owen* (1950) 1 A.E.R. 290, 291; Paton and Sawer in "Ratio Decidendi and Obiter Dictum in Appellate Courts" (1947) 63 L.Q.R. 461, p. 476, have this to say: "Of course if a judge positively agrees with an obiter dictum, it is a mere academic refinement to argue whether the dictum is binding or not; if he considers that a proposition correctly states the law, he will adopt it whether it be the dictum of a Lord of Appeal, a statement in a textbook, a conclusion of a note in a periodical, or even a dictum drawn from a foreign system of law."

[89] *The Queen v. Fadina* (1958) 3 F.S.C. 11, 12.

[90] (1959) 4 F.S.C. 89, 90.

[91] (1937) 3 W.A.C.A. 199.

[92] Allen, pp. 261–262; Lord Wright, p. 127.

[93] See Chapters 4 and 13.

[94] See authorities cited in *Haynes v. Harwood* (1935) 1 K.B. 155.

[95] See *Fulani v. Bornu N.A.* (1966) 1 All N.L.R. 260, 263.

courts.[96] Thus in ***Rex v. Adekanmi,***[97] Francis, J., deciding on the effect of provocation on a primitive and illiterate peasant and the meaning of "a reasonable man" as used in English law, observed:

> I have been unable to find any reported case in which the West African Court of Appeal has ruled on this question but, to my knowledge, the principle, as set out above, has been established by the Court of Appeal for Eastern Africa, which although not binding on this Court may, I think, with justice be followed as a guide in this case.[98]

Foreign decisions will be of the greatest value, therefore, whenever our courts are confronted with cases of first impression or cases for which there are no direct authorities in point. They are not binding as such, that is, in the sense that Nigerian courts are bound to follow them on pain of reversal or overruling; but they do at times settle conundrums for which we have no precedents in point.[99]

3. Merits and Demerits of *Stare Decisis*

Two separate and distinct schools of thought exist over the merits and demerits of the doctrine of *stare decisis.* Those supporting the doctrine do so on the grounds of the advantages it confers; those opposing it oppose because of the harm it does to the cause of justice and legal growth. Supporters are found within the rank and file of some judges of the appellate courts while its opponents are mainly the Bar and academic lawyers. Let us examine the grounds of support and opposition together.

Certainty

The principal ground on which the doctrine is supported is

[96] See for example cases like ***Mckenzie v. Findlay*** (1966) Victorian Reports page 3 at page 4 relied upon in ***Oyebajo v. Ogunlenu*** (1971) 1 N.M.L.R. 391 in deciding that a judge is free to move away from his decision in an interlocutory ruling and decide the contrary in his final judgment after he has had a better appreciation of what was involved in the case before him.

[97] (1944) 17 N.L.R. 99, 101.

[98] The status of English decisions in our courts will be treated separately in Chapter 13.

[99] For a comprehensive discussion of the influence of foreign decisions on our law see section 4, *infra.*

certainty and consistency.[100] This is the basis of its support by the English courts.[101] The same is applicable to Nigeria where it is "the foundation on which the consistency of our judicial decision is based"[102] and will produce instability if not observed.[103]

By way of comment we will say that certainty and consistency in judge-made law is desirable; it is essential that the subjects should know the contents and requirements of the rules to which they are subjected and by which their transactions are governed. But it is questionable whether a doctrine which requires lower courts to follow the decisions of higher courts which are plainly erroneous and in breach of statute is to be supported.[104]

Again, it is doubted where certainty or consistency resides where there are two inconsistent decisions on the same legal point and one decision is plainly acknowledged to have been *per incuriam* the other and despite this the Supreme Court refused to overrule it. This is what happened in *Nwafor v. Nduka.*[105] That was a case in which the plaintiffs claimed damages under the Fatal Accidents Law. Counsel for the defendants asked the Supreme Court to deduct the benefit which accrued to the dependants (plaintiffs) as a result of the death from the total amount awarded by the trial judge and adjudge the balance to be the amount payable by the defendants under the Law. He also invited the court to overrule *Anamali v. Ijirigho*[106] which decided the contrary and prefer *Layiwola v. Bello*[107] which favours

[100] "The final, and, from the English standpoint, the most important reason for following precedent is that it gives us certainty in the law"—Goodhart, "Precedent in English and Continental Law" (1934) 50 L.Q.R. 40, 58; see also Ellis Lewis, "The History of Judicial Precedent" (1931) 47 L.Q.R. 411, 421.

[101] See *Huddersfield Police Authority v. Watson* (1947) 2 A.E.R. 193, a Divisional Court decision where Lord Goddard said he could ". . . imagine nothing more disastrous than, where the court has given a decision on the construction or application of this Act, that another court should give a contrary decision so that there will then be two conflicting cases and no finality in the matter at all."—p. 195; see also *Young v. Bristol Aeroplane Co., supra* for the Court of Appeal; *Rex v. Taylor* (1950) 2 A.E.R. 170 for the Court of Criminal Appeal and *London Street Tramways v. London County Council* (1898) A.C. 375. for the House of Lords.

[102] *Ngwo v. Monye* (1970) 1 All N.L.R. 91, 100.

[103] *Ojosipe v. Ikabala* (1972) 1 All N.L.R. 128, 131–132.

[104] See note 102 above and Allen, *Law in the Making*, 7th edition, p. 356.

[105] (1972) 1 All N.L.R. 307, 313.

[106] (1960) 5 F.S.C. 97.

[107] (1965) 1 All N.L.R. 318.

such reduction. The latter decision was influenced by the English case of *Peacock v. Amusement Equipment Co. Ltd.*[108] Rejecting counsel's request the Supreme Court

> The court hereby reaffirms its previous decision in the ***Anamali case*** for the reason that, even though it was reached *per incuriam* of the ***Peacock case*** it is in accordance with established principle and with the provisions of the Fatal Accidents Law, Cap. 52.

Here is a court whose practice is to be bound by its previous decisions except where they were given *per incuriam.*[109] And here is an open admission that one of its decisions on a given point of law was given *per incuriam* and yet the Supreme Court refused to overrule it. By such refusal the Supreme Court allows both decisions which are in conflict to stand side by side. Which law governs the question? Is it that laid down in *Anamali v. Ijirigho* or that in *Layiwola v. Bello*? The position is uncertain.

The declaration that the decision in *Anamali's case* "is in accordance with established principle and with the provisions of the Fatal Accidents Law, is, with respect, meaningless in the absence of a finding as to which of the conflicting decisions is the law. Both interpretations of the same statute cannot be correct. If the Supreme Court has now discovered that *Peacock's case* has wrongly influenced its decision in *Layiwola's case* and that *Anamali v. Igirigho* should never have been departed from it should say so. On the other hand, if it is of the opinion that there is such a material difference between the facts of the two cases that it is impossible for the first case to be a precedent for the other this should have been so stated. True, the Supreme Court is still to say the last word on the matter.

Certainty in case-law can be impaired by three further factors. One is improper distinguishing; another is an oversight of authorities, and the third is a wrong interpretation of an existing precedent.

There is no objection to distinguishing a case. In fact, ability to distinguish properly is a very useful asset to a later court and imparts to case-law the consistency and predictability it should have. Trouble comes when a judge does not like a particular decision and

[108] (1954) 2 Q.B. 347.
[109] See *Ngwo v. Monye* (1970) 1 All N.L.R. 91; *Bamgbose v. Daniel* (1952) 14 W.A.C.A. 111.

tries to avoid it by distinguishing it on grounds that are not capable of being deciphered when, in fact, the cases are indistinguishable.

We have made reference to *Edet v. Esien*[110] and *Nwaribe President, Orlu District Court.*[111] In the first case a woman left her husband and produced issue for another man to whom she was not lawfully married. On a claim by the husband for the children the High Court held that the husband was not entitled to the children and that such a claim based on native law and custom was contrary to natural justice, equity and good conscience. In the second case the woman was a widow and stayed on in the matrimonial home and had a child by another man. The High Court held that the child belonged to the family of the deceased husband and not to the widow's lover.

The court in the latter case distinguished the first case on the ground that the wife in the first case had left the husband while in the latter case the wife of the deceased had stayed on in the matrimonial home. It is difficult to see where the distinction lies. Whether a woman stays on in the matrimonial home or deserts it does not alter her status; she is still a married woman. She cannot by her unilateral act convert herself into a *feme sole*. The yoke of marriage is still on her, according to native law and custom, so long as the bride price paid on her has not been refunded to the husband or the family of the husband if the husband is deceased. Any child born at this time by whomever born belongs to the husband.[112]

On this view, therefore, the decisions in *Edet v. Esien* and *Nwaribe v. President, Orlu District Court* represent opposing views. To this extent the legal position is rendered uncertain for purposes of the doctrine of precedent. If the judge in *Nwaribe's case* who himself is a Nigerian had simply refused to follow *Edet v. Esien* on the ground that it did not reflect the position at customary law the legal position would be tolerably certain. And this would be all the more so when it is realised that *Amachree v. Goodhead*[113] supports *Nwaribe's case*. But the legal position of *Edet v. Esien* was left unscathed.

[110] (1932) 11 N.L.R. 47.
[111] (1964) 8 E.N.L.R. 24.
[112] See *African Indigenous Laws*, 1975, p. 263.
[113] (1923) 4 N.L.R. 101, 102.

A second factor that introduces uncertainty into our case-law is an oversight of relevant authorities. Where a decision proceeds in a direction different from that taken by an antecedent decision deciding the same point of law the result is uncertainty. There is no real problem where the contradictory decisions proceed from courts of different ranks, the lower decision must submit to the higher one.[114] But this is so only if the oversight affects the lower authority and not the higher one. Where it is only the decision of the lower court that is concealed all courts can safely follow the higher court, since it is the higher court that binds all lower courts.

But if one High Court judge reaches a decision in ignorance of a previous decision of another High Court judge which contradicts the latter decision, lower courts are really in bewilderment. The conflict of decisions produces uncertainty. In this situation they must think for themselves and decide which to follow.[115] To a later High Court judge, the problem is not really acute since one High Court judge is not bound by another. He can decide for himself.

Where the conflicting decisions are those of a court which regards itself as bound by its previous decisions there is a problem for lower courts as well as for the court from which the conflicting decisions proceeded. When the conflict is later noticed the superior court might apply one of the exceptions to the rule in *Young v. Bristol Aeroplane Co.* and solve the problem. But until such solution lower courts will be placed in a quandary, perplexed as to which of the decisions to follow. The decision as to which to follow may be difficult to make since the lower courts may not know which of the conflicting decisions the higher court would select as good law.[116]

The third factor that creates uncertainty is a wrong interpretation of precedent. Every judge has to interpret a precedent cited to him in order to decide whether it is binding on him or not.[117] Much depends upon the conclusion he arrives at. If the precedent is correctly interpreted and followed the result will be certainty in the law. If, on the other hand the precedent is inapposite to the facts

[114] *Noble v. Southern Railway Co.* (1940) A.C. 538, 598.

[115] Salmond, *Jurisprudence*, 11th edition, pp. 169–170.

[116] On the problem of overlooked authorities see Allen, *Law in the Making*, 7th edition, pp. 315–318.

[117] Allen, p. 290.

and circumstances of the case, but the later court thinks it is apposite and follows it, the result is uncertainty. The uncertainty arises, not because the precedent decision is wrong, but because it is wrongly applied to inapposite facts and circumstances, thereby making the rule in the precedent case serve a purpose for which it was not intended.

Perhaps we cannot better conclude this discussion on certainty than by quoting from Dr. C. K. Allen:[118]

> We cannot, then, look for more "certainty" in case-law than is afforded by as much consistency as judges, faced with problems and circumstances of kaleidoscopic variety, can reasonably achieve; and lest, expecting too much, we suffer disappointment, we should be warned that this degree of certainty is limited and inconsistent. It cannot be otherwise when, as we have seen, the whole system of precedent must inevitably operate through the fluctuating, subjective medium of interpretation. It is necessary to enter this caveat because the claims made for the "certainty" of precedent are misleading to students.

Flexibility

Admirers of *stare decisis* claim for it the virtue of flexibility. This claim can at once be seen to be fallacious. How can a rule that ties up the hands of later courts be flexible? There is here an apparent confusion between case-law and *stare decisis*; it is the former that is flexible, not the latter. And the former is flexible so long as judges retain the freedom to decide cases before them in accordance with the demands of justice and are not tied to the apron strings of obnoxious precedents. But where, as in English and Nigerian systems, the latter practice operates, case-law must inevitably lose its flexibility. Flexibility and *stare decisis* are mutually exclusive.[119]

Convenience

Adherents of the doctrine also claim that it is a convenient mode of reaching decisions.[120] As we saw in Chapter Seven, the applica-

[118] *Law in the Making*, 7th edition, p. 350.

[119] See Allen, *supra*, p. 351; Goodhart, "Precedent in English and Continental Law" (1934) 50 L.Q.R. 40, 50.

[120] Goodhart, *ibid.*, p. 51.

tion of the doctrine may save the judge much trouble and dialectic, and as Kiralfy says:

> There is an obvious practical advantage in following precedent. It is a waste of time and energy to decide every point that arises in daily life by tracing it back to first principles.[121]

While this is true, it can also not be disputed that obedience to the doctrine encourages a feeling of ease and discourages the spirit of experiment in the individual judge. The result is that an error which may be embedded in a particular decision remains so embedded and is not discovered and corrected, and so bad law perpetuates itself.

Only the party which the precedent decision supports finds it convenient and such a party is likely to jubilate if the decision supports his bad case. But the other party with justice on his side will be disillusioned when he discovers after all that an unjust precedent stands in his way.[122]

Freedom from Bias

According to Professor Goodhart:

> . . . it is said that by requiring the judges to follow precedent we live under a government of laws and not of men.[123]

That being so, judges are restrained from exhibiting bias against any particular party or cause of action and are bound to toe the line of previous decisions. This is true. The watchful eye of the public and the profession and the possibility of reversal on appeal or of being overruled in a later case impose a restraining influence upon a judge actuated by prejudice.

But it cannot be denied that a judge can take shelter under the doctrine and perpetrate bias and injustice. Thus where there is a close point of law to be decided a biased judge might reject as immaterial certain conclusive facts in a case before him in order to follow a precedent which is against the party against whom or a cause of action against which he is biased. But if the doctrine of

[121] *The English Legal System*, 1954, p. 104.

[122] See Goodhart, "Precedents, in Divisional Courts" (1948) 64 L.Q.R. 40, 43–44.

[123] "Precedent in English and Continental Law" (1934) 50 L.Q.R. 40, 56.

stare decisis did not operate the particular judge would not claim justification for his action and counsel for his victim would be able to press the distinction between the facts before him and those in the precedent case and get such verdict as it is just that his client should have.

Freedom from Errors of Individual Judgment

No one denies the truth of this. The courts in this country have had occasion to question the legitimacy of certain decisions which proceed on lines different from those indicated by the authorities.[124] This serves to show that it is not always true that the presence of binding authorities will prevent a judge from proceeding on a frolic of his own.

But to support the doctrine on this ground one must show that the previous decision has nothing in law or reason for which it can be condemned, for if it is a wrong or unjust decision the doctrine will merely perpetuate it. However, this justification for the doctrine is not a perfect one. The doctrine would only be justified on this ground if the rule that is set down as a precedent is the result of a practice established by a series of independent decisions, for then there is something approaching a guarantee that the rule is perfect. The single decision of a single judge cannot afford this guarantee. with such a decision later judges will sink or swim.

Stability of the Law

This topic is closely allied to certainty, but in view of two important decisions of our appellate courts we must give it a special treatment of its own. These cases deal with the need of allowing decisions of long standing to continue undisturbed unless manifest injustice would be done by their continuance.

The first of such cases is *In re Adadevoh.*[125] This case held that the word "children" in England meant legitimate children and that

[124] See *Shokeye v. Insp. Gen. of Police* (1962) 2 All N.L.R. 119 where a conviction by a Magistrate was quashed because an English decision was not followed; *Okafor v. Ezeigbo* (1966-67) 10 E.N.L.R. 203, 206, where Oputa, J., refused to follow the unreported case of *Echefu v. Obi* on the ground that *Carpenter v. Ebblewhite* (1938) 4 A.E.R. 41 was not considered.

[125] (1951) 13 W.A.C.A. 304, 310.

"legitimate children" meant children who were legitimate according to the law of the domicile. Proceeding on this view of the law the case decided that the children of a polygamous union who in Nigeria were regarded as legitimate were entitled to share in the estate of their intestate father on the same footing as children who were the issue of a monogamous marriage. This was the result of the interpretation placed on section 35 of the Marriage Ordinance[126] which applied the Statute of Distribution to such estate. In so deciding, the case overruled *In re Williams*[127] which decided that the children of a polygamous union were excluded.

Although this was really a just decision the West African Court of Appeal regretted having to overrule *In re Williams* and Verity, C.J., declared:

> I am fully alive to the fact that grave inconvenience may arise from a judgment of this Court in such a matter which reverses a view of the law which has been held for upwards of ten years, but when the Court is faced with the alternative of perpetuating what it is satisfied is an erroneous decision which was reached per incuriam and will, if it be allowed, inflict hardship and injustice upon generations in the future or of causing temporary disturbance of rights acquired under such a decision, I do not think we should hesitate to declare the law as we find it.

The other case is *Johnson v. Lawanson*[128] in which four previous decisions (the first of them a Privy Council decision) on the meaning of section 129 of the Evidence Act were overruled because they failed "to give the material words of the statute their ordinary and natural meaning." The Supreme Court in that case expressed the same concern as was expressed by the West African Court of Appeal over *In re Williams*. Coker, J., delivering the judgment of the court observed:

> We are now faced with this situation in which the decisions to which we have referred have created a conflict of such a serious nature as to confuse practitioners and introduce a serious element of uncertainty into our law.

[126] Laws of Nigeria 1948, Vol. IV, Cap. 128.
[127] (1941) 7 W.A.C.A. 156.
[128] (1971) 1 N.M.L.R. 380, 387–388.

From these examples of overruling long-standing decisions of great authority, one of which was followed by a line of cases, we find that the so-called stability which the doctrine is said to introduce into case-law is a mirage. There is no stability where a decision which is supposed to settle the law and is subsequently followed is founded on error that will sooner or later be discovered and the whole line of cases thrown overboard. But stability would be a reality if the imperfections of human wit would allow judicial decisions to be perfect and unalterable.

4. Persuasive Precedent

The difference between authoritative or binding precedent and a precedent that is merely persuasive is not one of kind but of degree. As we have seen at the opening of this chapter a persuasive precedent is a judicial decision that does not place the judges under an obligation to follow it. It leaves with them a large element of discretion, but is a decision

> which they will take into consideration, and to which they will attach such weight as it seems to them to deserve.[129]

According to Salmond "persuasive precedents are merely historical" sources of law.[130] This statement is only true if the class of persuasive precedents is limited to foreign judgments, decisions of superior courts in the Commonwealth, judgments of the Privy Council and judicial *dicta*.[131] But it is of doubtful truth when the class is extended to include decisions of superior courts other than the House of Lords in England and the Supreme Court in Nigeria, for, as we have seen, judicial law-making starts with High Court decisions.[132] Can it then be seriously contended that decisions of courts other than the highest courts of the two countries do not constitute law for the land?

[129] Salmond, *Jurisprudence*, 11th edition, p. 165.

[130] *Ibid.*

[131] These are the examples of persuasive precedents which Salmond has mentioned in the passage from which the above quotation is taken.

[132] Dias, *Jurisprudence*, 3rd edition, p. 61; "Only decisions of the High Court and above are quotable as law."

In order to answer this question satisfactorily we must keep two situations clearly distinguishable. One is that so long as there is no contrary decision of a higher court the decision of a High Court judge or of the Court of Appeal is law for the whole of England. The other situation relates to the binding effect of this decision on the Court of Appeal or the House of Lords as the case may be. A court is not bound by the decision of a court lower than itself.[133] To that extent, therefore, while that decision is law for the land and for the court from which it proceeds, it is not law for the higher court.[134] It will only become law for the higher court when it is approved and adopted by the latter. It is only in this way and in this way only that this class of persuasive precedents can be said to be a historical source.

In Nigeria with twenty legal systems, however, the position is not as clear as it is in England. True, the decision of each High Court in Nigeria constitutes law. But whether a High Court in one State can bind lower courts in other States or—what comes to the same thing—whether the decision of a High Court in one State constitutes law for the whole country is problematical. There is no doubt that decisions of the High Courts in the different states are cited in courts all over the Federation, but the question is whether these latter courts regard them as binding on them or merely persuasive. Whatever the actual position is, it is beyond doubt that each State High Court binds all lower courts within the State.[135] As in England, High Court decisions in Nigeria are not law for the Supreme Court.[136] They only become law binding on the latter after adoption, and until then they are only historical sources *vis-a-vis* the Supreme Court.

We will now proceed to a discussion of the main types of persuasive precedents and show why each type has that character. The nomenclature "persuasive precedents" in the context of this chapter is limited to judicial decisions only.[137]

[133] *Zaidan v. Mohssen* (1973) 11 S.C. 1, 18.

[134] *Odiase v. Agho* (1972) 1 All N.L.R. 170, 177.

[135] See *Board of Customs and Excise v. Bolarinwa* (1968) N.M.L.R. 350.

[136] See Salmond, p. 211, see also *Zaidan v. Mohssen* (1973) 11 S.C. 1, 18.

[137] As to other forms of persuasive precedents see Allen, pp. 268–280; Salmond, pp. 225–226.

Decisions of High Courts before the Supreme Court

Enough has already been said about this above. The Supreme Court does not regard High Court decisions as binding on itself.[138] But instances are many in which the Supreme Court has approved and adopted High Court decisions—both English and Nigerian—thereby making them its own.[139] The Supreme Court will not, however, reject a High Court decision without giving it respectful attention and adequate scrutiny.[140]

Decisions of Courts of Co-ordinate Jurisdiction

The Supreme Court and the Federal Court of Appeal regard themselves as bound by the decisions of courts of co-ordinate jurisdiction.[141] So when we say that decisions of courts of co-ordinate jurisdiction are not binding we exclude those of courts of co-ordinate authority with these two courts and mean only the decisions of High Courts.

We have in our law reports a plethora of dicta which illustrate the point we are making here and a few examples will be given. In *Emodi v. Commissioner for Lands,*[142] Oputa, J., referring to a ruling of Ikpeazu, J., in *Chairman, L.E.D.B. v. Adewale*[143] stated:

> This ruling is a ruling of a court of concurrent jurisdiction and is therefore not binding on this court. It may however have a strong persuasive effect.

Araka, J., in *Administrator-General, East Central State v. Odumukwe*[144] also described a fellow judge's decision as persuasive when he said:

> I am fully aware that I am not bound by the said judgment and that it has only a persuasive effect over me.

[138] *Itsekiri Communal Land Trustees v. Warri Divisional Planning Authority* (1973) 11 S.C. 235, 280–281.

[139] See, for example, *Ademola II v. Thomas* (1946) 12 W.A.C.A. 81, 84.

[140] See Allen, *Law in the Making*, 7th edition, p. 257; *Zaidan v. Mohssen*, *supra*.

[141] *Tsamiya v. Bauchi N.A.* (1957) N.R.N.L.R. 73, 83; *Adegboyega v. Igbinosun* (1969) 1 All N.L.R. 1, 9.

[142] (1972) 2 E.C.S.L.R. 47, 49.

[143] (1966) N.M.L.R. 27.

[144] (1972) 2 E.C.S.L.R. 183, 185.

That the above judicial practice is universal throughout Nigeria is shown by examples from the High Court of Northern Nigeria in 1960. In *Olawoyin v. Attorney-General, Northern Nigeria*[145] Brown, C.J., commenting on other decisions of co-ordinate authority before him, observed:

> "It would therefore appear to be clear that while a judge sitting at first instance will accord great weight to a previous decision of a judge of co-ordinate jurisdiction, and will only depart from it with reluctance and after the most careful consideration, he commits no breach of principle if he does—for he is not bound by it.

The reason why one High Court judge will not lightly depart from the decision of a fellow High Court judge is that each High Court decision constitutes law, and since one of the characteristics of law is certainly the practice is a most desirable one. Departure is justified when close examination reveals that the decision does not represent the law. And when one judge cannot follow another there is a practice whereby he must give his reasons.[146]

The practice whereby one judge treats the decision of a fellow judge as merely persuasive and not binding is founded on good sense. If the doctrine of *stare decisis* applied here legal growth and development would be very much retarded and judge-made law would fall into disrepute. Again, the doctrine itself would not function with dignity and effect because the large number of independent decisions by different judges reached almost about the same time in a much-used area of the law would produce conflicts and create problems of solution. Conflicting decisions by different judges could not be binding at the same time. The present state of the law is the ideal thing in the circumstances.

Obiter Dicta

Under exceptions to *stare decisis* this matter was discussed. The discussion here will only be adventitious to the discussion under that heading. Both academic writers and judges agree that *obiter dicta* are not binding. The reason is that although they contain propositions

[145] (1960) N.R.N.L.R. 53, 58.

[146] *Odigbo v. C.O.P.* (1972) 2 E.C.S.L.R. 120, 125; *Adm.-Gen. v. Odunukwe* (1972) 2 E.C.S.L.R. 183, 185.

of law they are not legal rules. As legal propositions their influence does not extend beyond the persuasive.

Obiter dicta cannot alter established rules of law even if they proceed from the most eminent judges or the highest tribunal. Thus in *Williams v. Attorney-General of Nigeria*[147] Webber, J., in the Full Court of Nigeria said:

> I think the learned Chief Justice was wrong in law in concluding that these obiter dicta altered the well established principle of law that a petition of right will not lie against the Crown for the tortious acts of its servants.

But their importance is not as slight as might appear at first sight, for, as we have seen, they can influence future decisions and afford a perspective from which to look at a particular legal situation that has as yet not been regulated judicially or legislatively.

Foreign Decisions

Foreign decisions have not the status of law either in England or in Nigeria. Where they are apposite to the facts and circumstances under consideration they may influence the mind of the court and the principle of law stated therein may be adopted and transmuted into our law. It is only in this way that a foreign decision acquires recognition in our courts. But until transmutation it remains foreign and unbinding and only a historical and not a legal source of our law.[148]

The foreign decisions which are generally consulted are those of countries applying the common law, for the methods of legal thought of these countries show important similarities. Perhaps that is why Professor Glanville Williams says:

> American and overseas Commonwealth cases will sometimes be found cited in English legal treatises. Though not binding upon English courts, they will be listened to by the judges, particularly when English authority is lacking or unsatisfactory.[149]

[147] (1932) 11 N.L.R. 49, 53.
[148] See Chapter 7.
[149] *Learning the Law*, 5th edition, 1954, p. 51.

In the Norther States of Nigeria where the Penal Code and Criminal Procedure Code are in force the tendency is towards Indian decisions because these Codes are based on the Indian Codes. This is plain logic, for the interpretations which the Indian courts have placed upon their codes will act as guides to the Northern States' courts in interpreting their own.

Thus in *Offiong v. Commissioner of Police*[150] the Criminal Procedure Code by section 342 gave the High Court power to grant bail to an accused person remanded in custody by a magistrate. The Indian Code of Criminal Procedure in section 498(1) also contains a similar provision. The question was whether application should first be made to the magistrate before it was made to the High Court, or whether it could be made to the High Court direct. Referring to section 498(1) of the Indian Code, Bate, J., stated:

> The commentary on this sub-section in Sohoni's Code of Criminal Procedure (15th edition) shows that in India it has been construed to give the High Court the widest discretion to grant bail. But the learned editors go on to point out that it is a recognised and convenient principle that where two courts have concurrent jurisdiction, application should be made to the lower court first unless there are special reasons such as extreme urgency or a momentous question of public policy for reversing the usual order. I think that this principle and the reasons underlying it are as valid in Northern Nigeria as in India and must be recognised in the present case.

In *Ekechukwu v. C.O.P.*[151] the Appellate Division of the High Court of Northern Nigeria agreed with an Indian decision on sections of their Criminal Procedure Code which were identical with the Northern Nigeria Code and declared:

> We follow these Indian Authorities . . .

But where the Indian Code contains no provisions similar to the Northern Code the Northern High Courts will decide on "the provisions of our Code by themselves."[152] In the same way where

[150] (1966) N.N.L.R. 94, 95.
[151] (1966) N.N.L.R. 96, 101.
[152] *Muhammed v. C.O.P.* (1967) N.N.L.R. 30, 34.

words which had received judicial interpretation under the old Criminal Procedure Ordinance were re-enacted in identical terms in the current Criminal Procedure Code the court in Northern Nigeria has refused to follow Indian cases based on the Indian Code with similar but not identical wordings and instead followed the Nigerian interpretation.[153]

A foreign decision though merely persuasive may be preferred to a decision of a municipal court where the former has greater merits than the latter as a legal rule. This is what happened in *Anaho v. Keffi Native Authority,*[154] in which case Williams, J. preferred two Indian decisions to the Nigerian case of *Aba v. C.O.P.*[155] which declared the whole trial before a magistrate a nullity on the ground that the magistrate tried and convicted a person in the same trial of offences over which he had jurisdiction in some and none in others. But the Indian authorities decided the contrary, namely, that the trial is a nullity with regard to the offence over which there is no jurisdiction, but valid as to the others.

It must, however, be noted that the court accepted the Indian rule not because it was binding on it but because it was convenient and appeared to it to represent the true legal position. Again, the Indian rule was accepted not because there was no Nigerian decision in point but because that decision was unsatisfactory.[156]

5. Conclusion

In concluding this chapter we have to mention two other problems which the doctrine of *stare decisis* poses. We will also indicate which form of the doctrine of precedent claims our sympathy.

The first problem is the supression of the better judgment of the exceptionally qualified judge. If he is the first to decide the point he will have laid down good law and succeeding generations of judges and the profession will learn from him and the ends of justice will be served. But the problem arises where he comes later on the scene and

[153] *The State v. Dushi* (1967) N.N.L.R. 82.

[154] (1966) N.N.L.R. 37.

[155] (1962) N.N.L.R. 37.

[156] Williams, *Learning the Law*, 5th edition, p. 81. On the subject of influence of foreign decisions see Allen, *Law in the Making*, 7th edition, pp. 280–285.

finds his hands fettered by a decision he cannot, because of the doctrine, refuse to follow. The doctrine of binding precedent ties him to the apron-strings of a decision which is not in true accord with what his expert knowledge in the particular field of law tells him is right. It is easy to imagine how restive he can be in the circumstances.[157]

Another problem which we face under the doctrine is lack of adaptability to changed circumstances. Statutes are not passed for all time. Changes are brought in by Parliament as circumstances alter. There may be a repeal or an amendment whereby some provisions are deleted and others are introduced. But a judicial decision, unless overruled, remains for all time under the doctrine serving a good or an evil purpose. It is particularly objectionable in an era in which its doctrine has ceased to serve the interests of society.[158]

Lastly, we re-emphasise our point of view regarding the doctrine. We do not doubt the advantages which the doctrine possesses and the ends which it serves, but we think that its sphere of operation should be limited. Recently in England the Court of Appeal has given indications that the rule in *Young v. Bristol Aeroplane Co Ltd*[159] may some day be revised. In *Boys v. Chaplin*[160] Lord Denning said

> I foresee the time may come when we have to reconsider the self-imposed limitation stated in Young's case, especially in view of the recent change in practice in the House of Lords.

Now we have seen that the Court of Appeal in *Young's case* declared that it was bound by its previous decisions except in three instances, and we shall see[161] that the exceptions are not comprehensive enough to take account of all cases where justice requires previous decisions to be departed from. The above *dictum* shows that the court itself is painfully aware of the harm the doctrine is doing just as the House of Lords has been.

[157] See Goodhart, "Precedent in English and Continental Law" (1934) 50 L.Q.R. 40, 61, where the learned author asks: "But why should it be necessary to forge fetters for judges who are peculiarly able and powerful? The greater the skill and the professional reputation of the judges, the less necessary would it seem to be able to bind them by artificial rules."

[158] Stone, "Stare Decisis in the Divisional Court" (1951) 14 M.L.R. 219; Dias, *Jurisprudence*, 3rd edition, pp. 77–78; see Chapter 16.

[159] (1944) 2 A.E.R. 293; (1944) K.B. 718.

[160] (1968) 1 A.E.R. 283, 289.

[161] Chapter 9.

The plan for revision of the strict doctrine is gathering momentum. Thus in *Gallie v. Lee*[162] Lord Denning, M.R., again, said:

> We are, of course, bound by the decisions of the House, but I do not think we are bound by prior decisions of our own, or at any rate, not absolutely bound. We are not fettered as it was once thought. It was a self-imposed limitation; and we who imposed it can also remove it. The House of Lords have done it. So why should not we do likewise? We should be just as free, no more and no less, to depart from a prior precedent of our own, as in like case is the House of Lords or a judge of first instance. It is very, very rare that we will go against a previous decision of our own, but if it is clearly shown to be erroneous, we should be able to put it right.

We cite these instances of impending change of front by the Court of Appeal in England to illustrate the lesson which they pose to Nigeria and to show how welcome the proposal is. The strict doctrine should only be limited to compelling lower courts to toe the line drawn by the higher courts. To quote Salmond:

> As a compromise between the two opposing views, it is submitted that the strict doctrine should be retained in so far as it binds a court to follow the decisions of superior courts, but that courts should cease to be bound by decisions of courts of co-ordinate jurisdiction. In other words, the Court of Appeal and House of Lords should be given the power possessed by High Court judges to refuse to follow their own previous decisions.[163]

We agree with Salmond's views as expressed above subject to this qualification that an institutional machinery should be established whereby lower courts can refer to higher courts for reconsideration those decisions of the latter which the lower courts consider to be wrong. It is wrong for higher courts to insist upon lower courts rubber-stamping glaring errors in the name of *stare decisis* as happened in *Ngwo v. Monye.*[164] The machinery for reconsideration has been suggested earlier in this chapter.

[162] (1969) 1 A.E.R. 1062, 1072.
[163] *Jurisprudence*, 11th edition, p. 230.
[164] (1970) 1 All N.L.R. 91, 100, referred to earlier.

As regards the attitude of courts higher than the High Court to their previous decisions or those of coordinate authority we agree entirely with Salmond. As Lord Denning, M.R., admits,[165] the obligation to follow previous decisions is a self-imposed limitation. We will like to see the Federal Court of Appeal and the Supreme Court in Nigeria assume complete freedom to reconsider previous decisions of their own or those of courts of coordinate jurisdiction when the need arises.[166] Certainty and consistency will not thereby suffer since we do not advocate a capricious change of judicial attitude but rather a practice designed to correct obnoxious doctrines.[167]

[165] See above.

[166] In fact the attitude of the Supreme Court in this direction is very remarkable.

[167] See generally Salmond, pp. 228–230; Goodhart, "Precedents in the Court of Appeal" (1945–47) 9 C.L.J. 349; Lord Wright, "Precedents" (1944) 8 C.E.J. 118, 144; Freeman, "The Protection Afforded Against the Retroactive Operation of an Overruling Decision" (1918) 18 Columbia Law Review, 230, 231.

II

FACTORS THAT DETERMINE THE WORTH OF A JUDICIAL PRECEDENT

SUMMARY

Chapter 9 The Hierarchy of Authority

Chapter 10 The Ratio Decidendi

Chapter 11 The Attitude of Later Courts to the Precedent Decision

Chapter 12 Attitude and Contribution of Counsel

Chapter 13 The Special Relationship of English and Nigerian Law

Chapter 14 The Federal Character of the Country

Chapter 15 The Law Report

9

THE HIERARCHY OF AUTHORITY

The hierarchy of authority is one of the seven principal factors that determine the worth of a judicial precedent. By hierarchy of authority we mean that courts are hierarchically graded in Nigeria as in England and that the higher a court stands on the ladder of law-making courts the greater is the authority and weight of its decision. It follows that if a court is so low on the ladder as not to reach the status of being law-making it is otiose and irrelevant from the point of view of the doctrine of precedent. Apart from the hierarchy of authority the other principal factors are the *ratio decidendi*, the attitude of later courts to the precedent, the attitude and contribution of counsel, the special relationship of English and Nigerian law, the federal character of the country and the Law Report.

The hierarchy of courts in Nigeria is somewhat well settled. At the bottom in each State is the customary court or area court which applies and enforces local customary law.[1] Next come the Magistrate's Court, the higher grades of customary or area courts, the Sharia Court of Appeal (where applicable), the Customary Court of Appeal (where applicable), and the High Court where legal practitioners may appear. Placed above them at the federal level are the Federal Court of Appeal and the Supreme Court which surmounts the hierarchical structure. We shall now discuss the doctrine in relation to each category of courts in this ascending order.

[1] There is jurisdiction also to administer certain statute laws. See the Western Region of Nigeria Customary Courts Law, section 19; Cross River State Customary Court Edict No. 9 of 1969, s. 15; Eastern Nigeria Customary Courts (No. 2) Edict; 1966, s. 15. For Northern Nigeria see Keay and Richardson *Native and Customary Courts of Nigeria*, pp. 217–222.

1. Precedent in Customary Courts

Customary and Area[2] courts are grass-root courts operating mostly at the customary level and manned by persons most of whom are illiterate. Where they are literate they are not lawyers and their literacy is hardly of a standard that enables them to recognise and appreciate the importance of the doctrine of judicial precedent. They decide the cases before them according to their own idea of the customary law of the area over which the court exercises jurisdiction. Where statute authorises the enforcement of other laws than the customary law they interpret these laws as men of common sense. No regard is paid to precedent.

Professor Ezejiofor is of the opinion that customary "courts are not bound as a matter of law to follow decisions of the superior courts"[3] because "the principle of *stare decisis* which is a common law rule of practice has no necessary application in the customary courts." This hardly explains the position. There is no inherent trait in the common law that makes the application of *stare decisis* mandatory. The doctrine grew gradually in the common law and only became established when its value was recognised. If Professor Ezejiofor's formulation is accepted we shall find it difficult to explain why precedents abound in questions involving customary law[4] determined in the superior courts. The reason is rather that the judges of the lower grades of customary courts are not professional lawyers and have not acquired the professional ethos which impels lawyers to consider precedent, and customary law does not recognise this ethos.

Professor Ezejiofor thinks that "unless the law is changed these courts are not bound as a matter of law to follow decisions of the superior courts." We wonder what law has to be changed. No customary court law says customary courts should not follow the decisions of higher courts; nor will the substitution of common law for customary law as the enforceable law in customary courts bring about a disposition to follow precedent. The only change in the law that can produce this metamorphosis is the substitution of trained

[2] Area Courts only exist in the Northern States. (See Area Courts Edict 1968.)
[3] (1962) 6 Nigerian Law Journal. 53–54.
[4] See Chapter 6.

lawyers for lay natives which is most unlikely. Only trained lawyers by virture of their professional ethos have the inclination to follow precedent.

Again, it is incorrect to say that customary courts are not bound to follow the decisions of the superior courts. These grass-root courts may not recognise this sense of obligation, but it is there. It comes into prominence when their decision is tested on appeal to a higher court and a precedent in point is cited which goes the other way. When this situation arises the decision will be upset by the appeal court as being contrary to precedent. This is clear proof that customary courts are bound to follow the previous decisions of superior courts. Obligation to follow precedent is not a question of recognition but of fact.

A further point taken by Professor Ezejiofor is that a legally trained president of a higher grade customary court is entitled to ignore precedent "provided that by so doing he believes that he dispenses substantial justice." But what would be the legal worth of a decision of an inferior court that disregards a superior court precedent? And what consideration of "substantial justice" would render nugatory such a precedent? An inferior judge's idea of substantial justice is no better than, and not (as the law stands) even as good as, that of his superiors who must have determined a similar question in a previous judgment of their own court. The customary court rule that questions of customary law arising on appeal must be decided according to substantial justice without undue regard to technicalities cannot be indulged to the neglect of a valid precedent which must itself have been decided according to substantial justice.

Another jurist's opinion is that of Dr. Elias. According to him,[5] the magistrates' courts or even the Supreme Court are bound by a decision of the lowest customary court on questions of strict customary law on two conditions—that it is the only available decision on the point and that "it is not barbarous or otherwise against natural justice or any valid local law." With respect, this proposition is not right. It is an established rule of the doctrine of precedent that inferior courts cannot bind superior courts.[6] The law estab-

[5] British Colonial Law, p. 30.

[6] R. W. M. Dias, *Jurisprudence,* 3rd edition, p. 61: A. W. B. Simpson in (1959) 22 M.L.R. 453, 456.

lished by a higher court is of a higher status than that formulated by a lower court, and while the law laid down by the lower court is in certain cases the law of that court it is not the law of the higher court. The position is worse where the lower court is not a law-making court and such is a customary court.

Further, under section 14 of the Evidence Act customary law is a question of evidence. What a decision of a customary court does is to provide *prima facie* evidence of what the local customary law is on a particular point. Any higher court can only treat it as such, and it only becomes law after a superior court of record has endorsed it. It is not possible to point to an instance in which a superior court has declared itself bound by a decision of a customary court on a point of customary law. If a superior court agrees with a customary court's decision on a question of local customary law it does so because it considers the decision is right and not that it is bound by that decision. It will certainly set it aside just as it will set aside the decision of any other inferior court if it has a good reason to disagree.

The next question to consider is whether a customary court presided over by a legally trained president follows or should follow its own decisions. Such a court is an inferior court. It is not a law-making court and so need not follow its previous decisions.[7] There is, however, nothing to prevent it from toeing the same line as it toed in the past where there is no precedent binding upon it. That will show consistency, but it must depart from a previous decision of its own where precedent or the interests of justice require it.

Are the lower grades of customary courts bound to follow the decisions of the higher grades?[8] There are two basic problems which stand in the way. The first is that both the customary court of the higher grade (except the Customary Court of Appeal) and that of the lower grade suffer from the same infirmity—both are non-law-making. So the determination of one is as good as that of the other, and there is no obligation for the lower to follow the higher. The second is that the decisions of inferior courts are not reported and so there is no awareness of their existence. It is logical to suppose

[7] But see section 3 of the chapter.

[8] In former Western Nigeria there were four grades of customary courts, A, B, C and D. See Customary Courts Law, s. 18 in Cap. 31 of 1959 Laws of the Western Region. In 1964 the number was reduced to three grades.

that in states where appeals lie from the lower to the higher grade the latter should bind the former. This is true, but the power is limited. It can only be asserted on appeal when the higher court can strike down a decision of the lower court as being in conflict with a previous decision of its own on a point not determined by a higher court. But a decision of the lower court which has not gone on appeal to it cannot be overruled by a contrary decision it must have arrived at.

2. Precedent in Magistrates' Courts

Magistrates' courts like customary courts are inferior courts. As such they are not law-making.[9] But a magistrate's court differs from a customary court in three main respects. A magistrate's court administers English law,[10] while a customary court administers mostly customary law. Except in the customary courts of the higher grade, no legal practitioners are allowed to appear in the customary court, but they are free to appear in the magistrate's court. Except recently (in a few cases) the magistrates' courts are presided over by legally qualified persons whereas legal qualifications are required only for presidents of the higher grades of customary court.

These differences are important. When courts are presided over by legally qualified personnel and lawyers are allowed to represent parties before them, legal authorities will be cited. Following the citation of authorities comes attention to precedent. The authorities cited are statutes, text-books and the decisions of higher courts. All magistrates are bound by such decisions and if they have to distinguish them they must give reasons. Thus in *Board of Customs and Excise v. Bolarinwa*,[11] Thompson, J., held that a magistrate was bound by a High Court decision and that if he disagreed he must show in what material respects the facts of that decision differed from those before him.

One magistrate cannot bind another for the reasons we saw when considering the position in customary courts. Magistrates' courts,

[9] See Dias and Hughes, *Jurisprudence*, 1957, p. 61.
[10] Here we mean, not the law of England, but laws of the English pattern—Common Law and Statute Law.
[11] (1968) N.M.L.R. 380.

like customary courts, are courts of summary jurisdiction. The bulk of the cases which are handled by our courts is found in them. The cases are disposed of speedily, and although legal arguments are permitted they are not usually as thorough as they are in superior courts. Hence, their decisions cannot be relied upon as establishing the law. This is the preserve of the superior courts where time can be taken not only to listen to legal argument and for research, but also to discuss the law. On the other hand, the bewildering multiplicity of decisions would prevent the doctrine of precedent from working effectively; and the problem would be worse confounded by the fact that they are not reported. Attempts have been made from time to time by junior counsel to draw one magistrate's attention to the unreported decision of another in an effort to support their own cases. Such references have no value and they have been rightly spurned.

Can a magistrate follow his own decision? As a trained lawyer he can do so and many magistrates have done so when they are convinced the decisions are right. But, as we said earlier, they ought not to do so after they have discovered a contrary decision of a higher court, or after they have discovered that their previous decision was wrong. In each of these circumstances they should toe the path of honour by following precedent or the dictates of justice.

The last question to consider is whether a customary court binds a magistrate's court or *vice-versa.* This question can be considered in two parts. A customary court of the lower grade, i.e., those not presided over by legally qualified personnel, is obviously inferior to a magistrate's court conducted by a lawyer. The question as to whether such a court can bind a magistrate's court cannot, therefore, arise; nor can it arise even in connection with a court presided over by a lawyer-magistrate since the jurisdiction here is normally greater than that given to the customary court of the grade we are contemplating; so the only question to consider here is whether the magistrate's court can bind this lower customary court.

The question would not normally arise since their jurisdictions are different, the one administering English law while the other administers customary law and such statute laws as they are specifically empowered to administer. But in some cases their jurisdictions overlap where they have to administer the same statute laws. Would the determination of the magistrate on questions regarding the interpretation of such statute laws as fall within the province of a customary court to decide bind the customary court? For the reasons we have seen the answer is No. The magistrate's court is an inferior non-law-making court and in spite of its higher jurisdiction it cannot bind the customary court. But it can insist that the customary court should toe its line if it takes appeals from that court and knows of no higher authority overruling it. In this sense the magistrate can be regarded as having power to bind the customary court.

We now come to the second part of the question. Can a customary court of the upper grade and a magistrate's court bind each other? In areas where such courts exist side by side with one another their jurisdictions are so arranged that the magistrates deal exclusively with English law while the customary courts deal with customary causes and matters. The question of whether one court would bind the other would not normally arise because the doctrine of precedent presupposes identical points of law. But suppose a point of law common to both jurisdictions, say, in evidence, is determined in one way by one court, will the other court be bound to follow that determination? The answer is negative. Both are inferior courts without law-making capacity, and both are subject to the High Court or the Customary Court of Appeal, as the case may be, where law-making starts. None exercises jurisdiction over the other and so neither can insist that the other obeys its dictates.

3. Precedent in the Customary Court of Appeal and the Sharia Court of Appeal

The Customary Court of Appeal and the Sharia Court of Appeal are superior courts of record under the Constitution,[12] and, subject to the law of the House of Assembly, may exercise all the powers of such a court. Each of them is a court of appellate jurisdiction; the Sharia Court of Appeal exercises appellate and supervisory jurisdiction in civil proceedings involving questions of Islamic personal law; the Customary Court of Appeal is supposed to exercise

[12] 1979 Constitution, s. 6(3) and (5).

appellate and supervisory jurisdiction in civil proceedings involving questions of customary law.[13]

As superior courts of record[14] they should possess the capacity to lay down rules of law binding on lower courts, and such rules should be of quotable authority. But there is no known case in which their decisions have yet been reported, though it must be admitted that the Customary Court of Appeal is a new creation. Cyclostyled copies of the Sharia Court of Appeal judgments are available and there is evidence that it follows its precedents.[15] The Customary Court of Appeal is expected to do the same. But neither court is bound to follow its previous decisions though they must not lightly depart from them.

Are They Bound by High Court Decision?

It is unreasonable to expect them to be bound by the High Court. The reason is simple; they are all of equal status, being all of them superior courts of record. The question of the binding force of High Court decisions would not have arisen because of differences in their jurisdictions. But these differences had not always existed; there was a time when their jurisdictions overlapped. Secondly, even now in differences in jurisdiction they have certain things in common. The law of evidence and some points of practice and procedure are common to all three courts while customary law is common to the Customary Court of Appeal and the High Court.

The question is whether a decision of the High Court on any of these matters of concurrent jurisdiction binds the other two courts. Each of these two courts can determine such matters for itself and if it consults a High Court precedent it does so for purposes of guidance. It will not consider itself as strictly bound to follow it and it is submitted that it will reject it if it considers it wrong or inconvenient. Neither of these two courts will have anything to lose by disregarding a High Court precedent. No appeal goes from them to the High Court and so the question of being overruled does not arise. Before the Federal Court of Appeal all three courts appear to stand on equal pedestal.[16]

[13] Sections 242 and 247, respectively, of the 1979 Constitution.
[14] See section 4 for the meaning of a superior court of record.
[15]
[16] 1979 Constitution, s. 219.

4. Precedent in the High Court

The High Court has historically been regarded as a superior court of record with unlimited geographical and legal jurisdiction.[17] This fact and the fact that the King presided over it in its early days in England gave it a special authority and imparted to its decisions a legal imprint.[18] This explains the doctrine that law-making starts in the High Court.[19] "A decision of the High Court creates a binding precedent for all lower courts."[20] These latter courts are inferior courts with no law-making capacity.

The High Court Judge and his Attitude to his Own Decisions

Because law-making starts with the High Court and the High Court can bind lower courts with its own decisions, the High Court judge must consider his decisions with special care. He should be careful to lay down such rules of law as he would be prepared to follow in future cases for consistency is the essence of the doctrine. In *Ukaegbu v. Commissioner of Police*[21] Aniagolu, J., decided to follow his previous decisions on the limits of a defence of claim of right to damaged property and added:

> Nothing has occurred since the decision in that case to shift this court from that view.

De Lestang, C.J., in the High Court case of *Coker v. Jinadu*[22] stuck to his earlier decision on the question of forfeiture of a customary tenancy and observed:

> The Federal Supreme Court did not disapprove this view on appeal.

[17] It originated from "The Aula Regia restablished by William the First, which had universal jurisdiction in all matters of right and wrong throughout the Kingdom, and over which, in its early days, the King presided in person"—*Stroud's Judicial Dictionary*, Vol. 4, 3rd edition, p. 2934.

[18] Other courts which took their rise from the King's court possessed a similar authority, *ibid.*, p. 2935.

[19] Dias and Hughes, *Jurisprudence*, 1957, p. 60, "County Courts and Magistrate's Courts do not create binding precedents."

[20] Dias and Hughes, *Jurisprudence*, 1957, p. 61.

[21] (1972) E.C.S.L.R. 207, 209.

[22] (1958) L.L.R. 77, 78.

There is much to be said in favour of a judge being consistent with himself. It is part of the overall efforts to ensure certainty in the administration of justice and to obtain predictability and respect for the common law. But at the same time he must learn to cultivate a wider vision and examine respectfully the arguments of counsel and co-ordinate decisions tending the other way and must be prepared to change his ground when justice demands it.

We have some instances in the Nigerian system where a judge has departed from his previous decision in order to embrace a more plausible decision of a fellow judge. Charles, J., in *Barclays Bank D.C.O. v. Hassan*[23] had to do this when he said:

> I am satisfied from further consideration of my remarks in Ntiaghawo's case that non-compliance with the requirements of the Illiterates Protection Ordinance by the preparer of a document renders the document void, were too widely stated and inaccurate on that account.

Judges have departed from the position they took in interlocutory proceedings and have taken up a new position on a final judgment when the justice of the case so required.[24] In England a judge in shifting his ground from one case to another had said that the matter did not appear to him on the last occasion as it appeared on the first.[25] It is the concern for justice that produces such results.

We have nothing but commendation for a judge who takes this stand. It shows that he is not a bigot and that to him what matters is the need for justice and not self-aggrandisement. Lesser and arrogant professional men might regard this attitude as an exercise in self-effacement, but the noble judges who have chosen to tread this path of honour understand better. It might be further argued that such a change of front might cost judge-made law the much desired certainty. The answer to this is that certainty is not meant to be purchased at the price of justice.[26]

[23] (1961) W.N.L.R. 293, 296.

[24] See *Oyebajo v. Ogunlenu* (1971) 1 N.M.L.R. 391 which followed the Australian case of *Mekenzie v. Finlay* (1966) V.R. 3, 4.

[25] Bramwell, B., in *Andrews v. Styrap* (1872) 26 L.T. 704, 706.

[26] See Goodhart, *Precedents in the Court of Appeal* (1945–47) 9 C.L.J. 349, 351.

Whether a judge adheres to his previous decisions or departs from them should not be left to caprice. He should consult his common sense and his stock of legal knowledge and consider the ultimate consequences of his action before he makes a decision. When faced with such a choice he will do himself everlasting credit by reserving his judgment in order to consider the question more leisurely.

The High Court and its Attitude to Courts of Co-ordinate Jurisdiction

One High Court in Nigeria is of co-ordinate rank with the others and so also with the former Supreme Court.[27] It follows, therefore, that they cannot bind each other, and whenever one agrees with a decision of the other it does so because in its opinion that decision represents the law and not because it is binding.[28] But it has "a strong persuasive effect."[29]

When a decision reached by one division of the High Court is not acceptable to the other the latter can dissent from it, but it is the practice to give reasons for the dissent.[30] The practice in Nigeria is the same as the practice in England in this regard.[31]

The practice of giving reasons is a very desirable one and is an answer to those who would like to see uniformity in the decision of all divisions of the High Court because it tells them why certain decisions cannot be followed. Although certainty is not thereby obtained consistency is, however, achieved in that since all decisions on the point are intended to promote a particular legal doctrine the giving of reasons shows how the recalcitrant ones have fallen foul of this objective.

[27] See *Emodi v. Commissioner for Lands* (1972) E.C.S.L.R. 47, 49, *Salako v. Ordia* (1958) L.L.R. 66, 67.

[28] *George v. Walken & Co. Ltd.* (1962) 7 N.L.R. 64, 68; *MacIver & Co. Ltd. v. C.F.A.O.* (1917) 3 N.L.R. 18, 19.

[29] *Emodi v. Commissioner of Lands* (1972) 2 E.C.S.L.R. 47, 49.

[30] *Odigbo v. C.O.P.* (1972) 2 E.C.S.L.R. 120, 125, where Oputa, J., said: "I have . . . a duty to give my reasons for not agreeing with, and following a decision of a brother judge"; *Administrator-General v. Odunukwe* (1972) 2 E.C.S.L.R. 183, 185, where Araka, J., said: ". . . when a judge disagrees with a judgment of his brother judge it is only fair and desirable that he gives good reasons for so doing."

[31] *Foster v. Baker* (1910) 2 K.B. 636, 638.

It has been said that in England occasions are rare on which one High Court judge will refuse to follow another.[32] But in Nigeria the position seems to be the reverse. Occasions of conflict are many, and within a decade many conflicts have been recorded in certain areas of the law.[33] The alarming rate at which these conflicts develop seems to cause one to lose faith in the doctrine of precedent in the High Court. How do these disparities arise? In *Okafor v. Ezeigbo*,[34] Oputa, J., refused to follow the decision of a brother judge in *Echefu v. Obi*[35] because it did "not seem as though the case of *Carpenter v. Ebblewhite* was brought to the notice of the judge,"[36] This is a clear rebuke on counsel engaged in the case for not being thorough in their research and citation. But there are other instances where later courts have refused to follow other cases with poor merits and used language which indicated default on the part of the earlier judge. Thus in *Nwankwo v. Okoyeochia*,[37] Kaine, J., said of Reynolds, J., who failed to consider a certain provision of the rules of court in a case before him:

> I have to say that he did not consider the effect of Order 56, rule 15.

[32] Ekow Daniels, *The Common Law in West Africa*, 1964, p. 176.

[33] On jurisdiction in divorce see *Arinze v. Arinze* (1966) N.N.L.R. 103; *Okonkwo v. Eze* (1960) N.N.L.R. 80; *Machi v. Machi* (1960) L.L.R. 103, all of which opted for Regional jurisdiction and *Odiase v. Odiase* (1965) N.M.L.R. 196, and others which decided that there was a Federal jurisdiction, i.e. that a petition for divorce could be brought anywhere in the Federation. On procedure for the grant of bail to a convicted person some judges go by summons: *Okeke v. C.O.P.* (1960) N.R.N.L.R. 1; others go by motion: *Musa v. Insp. General of Police* (1962) 6 E.N.L.R. 149, and others go by application as in Form 35 rule 29A Article 963 at page 357 of 36th edition of Archbold: *Atu v. C.O.P.* (1970–71) 1 E.C.S.L.R. 7; *The State v. Odunsi* J/33C/1966, unreported; *Sam Offiong v. C.O.P.* HT/5CA/73, unreported.

[34] (1966–67) 10 E.N.L.R. 203, 206.

[35] Suit No. A/13/66, unreported, but see (1966–67) 10 E.N.L.R. 206.

[36] *Carpenter v. Ebblewhite* (1938) 4 A.E.R. 41 is an English decision which held that an insurance company cannot be joined in an action for negligence against the insured as no dispute has arisen between the insured and the company. In *Zaidan v. Mohssen* (1973) 11 S.C. 1, 18, the Supreme Court said: "It does not appear that section 12 of the High Court Law of Lagos by reference to section 20 of the Customary Courts Law was ever cited to the learned trial judge who must therefore be deemed to have given his judgment per incuriam."

[37] (1962) 6 E.N.L.R. 158, 159.

In each of the instances cited above the dissenting decisions are regarded as representing the law by the profession and those dissented from as bad law. And for the reasons given it appears that both Bench and Bar contribute to this state of things. It has been said that for the doctrine of precedent to work with dignity and effect there must be a strong Bar and a Bench of judges, more able than the Bar.[38] But where weaknesses are revealed in both and the trend continues it would no longer be "fallacious" to say with regard to precedent in the High Courts that "there is no such thing as judicial consistency, and that cases are decided solely by the 'bunche,' prejudices, idiosyncrasies, or sophistries of individual judges."[39]

When the task of dissent is "cleanly done"[40] the profession and lower courts are not left in doubt as to what side a particular decision belongs. But difficulty arises when a judge says in one breath that he does not agree with a decision of a fellow judge and in another he distinguishes that case from the case before him. Thus in *Bosah v. British American Insurance Co. Ltd.*,[41] Araka, J., while refusing to agree with the "conclusions" of a fellow judge[42] went further and said:

> Maybe there was the evidence before him which was not before me in this case . . .

With respect, if the learned judge found it impossible to agree with the decision shown to him he should limit himself to that fact and proceed to give his reasons for dissent as is the practice. He should not try to suppose the existence of facts which were not stated in the judgment and which he thought must have influenced the decision of the former judge.[43]

Before bringing this section of the chapter to an end we must look at a situation which arises when there is an unnoticed conflict

[38] Goodhart, "Precedent in English and Continental Law" (1934) 50 L.W.R. 40, 61.

[39] Allen, *Law in the Making*, 7th edition, p. 350.

[40] Salmond, quoting Bentham in his *Jurisprudence*, 11th edition, p. 180.

[41] (1972) 2 E.C.S.L.R. 134, 139.

[42] Odulami, J., in *Oyesanwen v. British American Insurance Co. Ltd.*, unreported Ibadan High Court Suit No. I/216/68 decided on 24/3/71.

[43] Though in fairness to him he said: ". . . even if that evidence had been before me it would not have made any difference to my conclusions." But why then the supposition?

of decisions. In *Igiokwe v. Nana*[44] and *Isalomi v. Omumu,*[45] two assistant judges came to opposite conclusions on the same question of law. The question was whether a magistrate had jurisdiction to try a case transferred from a native court to the magistrate's court under section 25 of the then Native Court Ordinance[46] where the case involved a question of title to land.

Jackson, Assistant Judge, in *Igiokwe v. Nana* held that there was no such jurisdiction and relied on the English case of *Pierce v. Hopper*[47] in which Fortescue, J., held that an "inferior court is not to be construed into a jurisdiction." In *Isalomi v. Omumu*, Jibowu, Assistant Judge, ignored any reference to English Law and remarked:

> The whole matter is a question of legal interpretation or construction of the Native Courts Ordinance, No. 44 of 1933, and of the Protectorate Courts Ordinance, No. 45 of 1933.

His Lordship then proceeded to ascertain the intention of the legislature, and started by finding that "the High Court and the Magistrate's Court are the creation of the Protectorate Courts Ordinance."[48] He enumerated the original civil jurisdiction which a magistrate was appointed to exercise under section 32 of the Ordinance and the exceptions provided for under a proviso. One of these was that a magistrate was not to exercise original jurisdiction in a case which raised "any issue as to title to land." Holding that the magistrate had jurisdiction under the proviso the learned assistant judge said:

> . . . the very presence of the proviso shows the intention of the legislature. If it had been the intention of the legislature that the Magistrate's Court shall not exercise any original jurisdiction in any land case it would not have provided exceptions to the prohibition.[49]

From the above reasoning of Jibowu, Assistant J., it is evident that his view is to be preferred to that of Jackson, Assistant J., but

[44] (1940) 17 N.L.R. 5, 7.
[45] (1943) 17 N.L.R. 48.
[46] No. 44 of 1933.
[47] 1 Stra. 260.
[48] (1943) 17 N.L.R. 49.
[49] *Ibid.*, p. 51.

Igiokwe v. Nana is not thereby overruled as both are decisions of co-ordinate rank. The accepted view is that "overruling is an act of superior jurisdiction."[50] The conflict is one to be settled by a higher court, and in *Toriola v. Arewa*[51] the conflict was quelled and the view of Jibowu, Assistant J., was upheld.

There is one danger which an unnoticed conflict may create for lower courts and that is that the latter will follow any of the decisions that is accessible, and the right one may not be the available one. In the meantime, the wrong decision may acquire ample support by being followed and acted upon, and when it is subsequently overruled all the transactions based on it and property acquired in reliance upon it become devoid of legal base and expectations are disappointed.[52]

Where, however, the conflict is noticed and commented upon as in *Flione v. Oladipo*[53] later courts are in a position to assess the relative merits of the conflicting decisions and decide on which side of the fence they want to be. But the comment to be useful must not amount to spurious distinguishing which leaves the precedent unscathed.[54]

Subordination of the High Court to the Federal Court of Appeal and the Supreme Court

The mere fact that the Federal Court of Appeal is higher than the High Court and takes appeals from it is enough evidence of subordination. High Court decisions can be disallowed by the Federal Court of Appeal;[55] they can also be approved.[56] The Supreme Court as the highest court in this country binds all inferior courts, including the High Court. The High Courts of this country have on many occasions expressly acknowledged the binding force of Supreme Court decision. In *Eziukwu v. President, Ibinta Improve-*

[50] Salmond, *Jurisprudence*, 11th edition, p. 167.

[51] (1949) 12 W.A.C.A. 505.

[52] Salmond, *Jurisprudence*, 11th edition, pp. 217–218.

[53] (1934) 11 N.L.R. 168.

[54] See the case of *Etiet v. Essien* (1932) 11 N.L.R. 47 fallaciously distinguished in *Nwaribe v. President*, Orlu District Court (1964) 8 E.N.L.R. 24.

[55] See *Ajayi v. The State* (1978) 1 L.R.N. 260.

[56] *African Pioneer Co. Ltd. v. Att.Gen.*, Rivers State: FCA/E/78/78 dated 5/2/79.

ment Union,[57] Nwokedi, J., admitted that a decision of the Supreme Court "remains a good binding law on all inferior courts in this country." Similarly, Oputa J., as he then was, remarked in *Chief John Odua II v. Akubeze*[58] when he was called upon to ignore a previous decision of the Supreme Court on certain grounds, that "by the theory of judicial precedent a lower court is bound by a ruling or judgment or decision or order of a High Court."

5. Precedent in the Federal Court of Appeal

The Federal Court of Appeal is a newcomer to the Nigerian judicial scene. It was established by Decree No. 43 of 1976 which is called the Federal Court of Appeal Decree. It is sandwiched between the High Courts of the Federation and the Supreme Court and takes appeals from the High Courts.[59] Under section 3 of the Decree the Western State Court of Appeal was abolished. Apart from hearing appeals from the High Courts it was vested with original jurisdiction to adjudicate on disputes "between the Federation and a State or between the States if and insofar as that dispute involves any question (whether of law or fact) on which the existence or extent of a legal right depends."[60]

Under the 1979 Constitution of the Federal Republic of Nigeria the jurisdiction of the Federal Court of Appeal underwent important changes. Section 212 of the Constitution now takes away the original jurisdiction of the court and vests it in the Supreme Court in precisely similar words, providing that this original jurisdiction shall be exercised "to the exclusion of any other court." Section 219 has added to the list of courts from which the Federal Court of Appeal shall hear appeals. The courts now are "the Federal High Court, the High Court of a State, Sharia Court of Appeal of a State and Customary Court of Appeal of a State." Thus, what is left of the jurisdiction of the Federal Court of Appeal now is exclusively appellate.

[57] (1972) 2 E.C.S.L.R. 494, 494.

[58] Onitsha High Court Suit No. O/82/69.

[59] These include the Sharia Court of Appeal and the Customary Court of Appeal.

[60] Constitution (Amendment) No. 2 Decree 1976, S. 1.

The FCA and its Attitude to its Own Decisions

No responsible court will depart from its previous decisions without a reason. The FCA is a responsible law-making court. Its supervisory and remedial role over subordinate courts is constitutionally guaranteed. Therefore the rules it lays down in its decisions should be certain and its attitude to these rules predictable. It is known to have followed its previous decisions.[61] But there is no warrant for the view that it has adopted a rigid attitude to precedent. It will depart from a previous decision of its own which it considers wrong in law in compliance with the mood of the age.[62] In fact it may be surmised that it will adopt the posture of the Supreme Court towards its own decisions.[63]

The Federal Court of Appeal and Courts of Co-ordinate Authority

We have said earlier that the Federal Court of Appeal is an intermediate court of appeal placed between the High Courts (including courts of co-ordinate status) and the Supreme Court. Now for the purpose of studying its attitude to precedents of co-ordinate authority we have to find out which of the defunct superior courts of record in Nigeria were co-ordinate with the Federal Court of Appeal. Without going far in our search we find an admission by the Federal Court of Appeal itself in *Koloko Imports and Exports Co. Ltd. v. African Continental Bank Ltd.*,[64] that the former Supreme Court established by the Supreme Court Act 1960 must be taken as its immediate predecessor. The chain can be extended until we reach the Full Court of the Supreme Court which was the first intermediate court of appeal between the former Supreme Court[65] and the Privy Council.

A brief trace of the link is of interest. The Supreme Court of 1960 was originally designated as the Federal Supreme Court,[66] and

[61] *African Pioneer Company Ltd. v. Attorney-General, Rivers State*: FCA/E/78/78.

[62] The House of Lords has changed its stand; so also have other appellate courts in England.

[63] See section 6.

[64] See FCA/L/26/77, decided 13th April, 1977.

[65] The pre-1954 Supreme Court was restyled High Court after each Region was empowered to establish its own High Court with the introduction of Federalism. See section 142 of the 1954 Constitution.

[66] See section 138 of the 1954 Constitution.

the word "Federal" was later dropped probably because there was no other Supreme Court that was not Federal.[67] In 1957 the Federal Supreme Court regarded itself as the successor of the West African Court of Appeal[68] and the latter had earlier declared itself the successor of the Full Court. The point of interest lies in the attitude of each succeeding court to the decisions of its predecessor. The Federal Supreme Court in *Layanju v. Araoye*[69] declared that it was bound by decisions of co-ordinate courts. A similar declaration of principle was made earlier by its predecessor, the West African Court of Appeal,[70] which followed the practice of the English Court of Appeal in *Young v. Bristol Aeroplane Co.*[71] and stated exceptions.

It is clear that the Federal Court of Appeal will follow a similar step. In *Ogbuanyinya v. Okudo*,[72] opposing counsel agreed and the Federal Court of Appeal, Enugu Judicial Division, impliedly consented that on the principle *of Osumanu v. Seidu*[73] the Federal Court of Appeal was bound by its previous decision, and a previous decision of that court at Ibadan was cited. But the Court only refused to follow that decision because the facts in that case and those in the one it was then handling were different.

There is, however, no doubt that in appropriate cases the court will follow not only its previous decisions but also those of co-ordinate authority. It is the only logical thing to do if the time-honoured doctrine of precedent is to continue to serve its purpose. A suggestion that a new court coming into the judicial arena should strike out on its own and blaze a new trail[74] is difficult to accept because it is difficult to see what innovation it can produce.

Any court of repute must pursue either of two alternative courses of action. It may follow its previous decisions or those of co-ordinate authority absolutely. In that event, the law can never develop since account cannot be taken of new situations and circumstances and since no opportunity can be taken to correct unjust decisions or

[67] See Supreme Court Act, 1960.
[68] See *Tsamiya v. Bauchi N.A.* (1957) N.R.N.L.R. 73, 83.
[69] 1961 All N.L.R. 83, 85.
[70] *Osumanu v. Seidu* (1949) 12 W.A.C.A. 437.
[71] (1944) K.B. 7, 8.
[72] F.C.A. E/135/78, dated 9th March, 1979, unreported.
[73] See Note 2, *supra.*
[74] See Allott, *New Essays in African Law*, 1970, p. 71.

those that fail to represent the law. Alternatively, it may decide to follow previous decisions conditionally upon their satisfying the requirements of justice and of the law. In this event, it will retain control over the trend of judicial doctrine and prevent the law from running in unhappy channels. Any third option would be "free law-finding." Here law would cease to be a science and decisions would be tantamount to the whims and caprices of the court. In that way, that certainty and predictability which constitutes a safe basis for business planning would be lacking, and law-suit would become a game of chance.

The Federal Court of Appeal and the Western State Court of Appeal (WSCA)

It is tempting to suppose that the Federal Court of Appeal will treat the Western State Court of Appeal as a court of co-ordinate authority.[75] But D. A. Ijalaye in comparing the relative status of the former Federal Supreme Court with that of the Western State Court of Appeal came to the conclusion that "the true legal position is not free from doubt";[76] so it is necessary to examine the pros and cons of the argument.

The WSCA was a regional court of appeal. Appeals went to it from all the divisions of the Western State High Court and from it to the Supreme Court. What will be the attitude of the FCA to the decisions of the WSCA? We submit that the attitude of the FCA will depend on its view of the status of the WSCA. If it treats the WSCA as a court of co-ordinate rank then its attitude to the decisions of that court will be the same as its attitude to those of the Federal Supreme Court, the West African Court of Appeal and the Full Court. But if it treats it as inferior to itself on the ground that the WSCA had its jurisdiction limited to the Western State the decision of the latter will be treated as persuasive only.

It does not appear that there is any warrant for regarding the WSCA as inferior to the FCA. Although a regional court, the WSCA

[75] This court was established for the Western State in 1967 following a power conferred by section 127 of the 1963 Constitution permitting the setting up of regional courts of appeal. See the Western State Court of Appeal Law, 1967, which came into force on 1/4/67, repealed by section 3 of the FCA Decree No. 43 of 1976.

[76] (1971) 9 Nigerian Bar Journal, p. 65.

was an intermediate court of appeal like the FCA with full jurisdiction to hear appeals from the High Court of the Western State It is, therefore, reasonable to hold that insofar as the Western States[77] are concerned, the FCA is of co-ordinate rank with the WSCA, but that in the rest of the States in the Federation where there were no regional courts of appeal between 1967 and 1976 the FCA has no equal. The decisions of the WSCA should, therefore, receive from the FCA the same treatment as those of its national predecessors.

But in *Omoluyi v. Akure Co-operative Plantation Society Ltd.*[78] the FCA wrongly assumed powers to sit on appeal over a decision of the WSCA under section 3(1) and (2) of the Constitution (Amendment) (No. 2) Decree No. 42 of 1976 and allowed the appeal against that decision. Sub-section 1 of the section provided that appeal pending before the WSCA on the 31st March 1976, when the WSCA stood dissolved were to be deemed to be pending before the FCA; and subsection 2 provided "Any notice of appeal, application or notice of application for leave to appeal, given or made or any other thing whatsoever done before or after the prescribed date with respect to any other thing whatsoever done before or after the prescribed date with respect to any proposed appeal to the Court of Appeal of the former Western State, with or without leave, from any decision of the High Court given in exercise of its original or appellate jurisdiction, shall be deemed for all purposes to have been given, made or done, as the case may be, with respect to a proposed appeal, with or without leave from a decision of the High Court given as aforesaid to the Federal Court of Appeal and such further action as may be necessary to be taken on the same by any person or authority in accordance with the provisions of this section and applicable rules of court shall be so taken."

This provision makes it clear that only pending appeals before the WSCA and applications and matters relating thereto can be handled and disposed of by the FCA. There is no power conferred on the FCA by this section to rehear an appeal already heard and

[77] The Western State was carved into three States in 1976 by the States (Creation) Decree, 1976.

[78] FCA/B/87/79 decided on 20/6/80 by the Benin Judicial Division of the FCA.

disposed of by the WSCA. But this is precisely what the FCA did in *Omoluyi's case* where it held that "This Court is vested with power to entertain this case by section 3(1) and (2) of the Constitution (Amendment) (No. 2) Decree No. 42 of 1976 . . ." By so misinterpreting its powers it regards the WSCA as inferior to itself. This goes far beyond what the Decree contemplated. The Decree merely set up the FCA as a court of appeal for all the States in the Federation, including the Western States, and, insofar as the latter States are concerned, the FCA is meant to replace the WSCA as a court of co-ordinate jurisdiction.

The WSCA and Non-Western State High Courts

But what, if a decision of the WSCA conflicts with the decision of a High Court in the rest of the States? It is tempting to argue that the FCA should be bound by the WSCA and reject the decision of the High Court. But that position is deceptively simple. If it is remembered that the High Courts elsewhere in the Federation had direct access to the Supreme Court in respect of their appeals under section 117 of the 1963 Constitution and that in this regard they enjoyed equal status with the WSCA it will be seen why the position is not so simple.

Since there was no hierarchy between these two systems of courts it is difficult to see how the WSCA should bind the courts in the other States. Its decisions are, at the best, of the most persuasive authority before them. It is, therefore, submitted that the FCA will use its discretion to decide which of the conflicting decisions is worthy of acceptance as establishing the correct legal rule.

Subordination of the Federal Court of Appeal to the Supreme Court

The Federal Court of Appeal is the subordinate of the Supreme Court by virtue of the fact that appeals lie from it to the latter court.[79] By this fact alone, the decisions of the Supreme Court should be binding on the Federal Court of Appeal, because it is an established rule that higher courts bind lower courts.[80] And the

[79] S. 213 of the 1979 Constitution.
[80] See Dias, *Jurisprudence*, 3rd edition, p. 61.

Federal Court of Appeal itself has acknowledged this fact in a number of its decisions.[81]

It is a matter of common sense that this should be so. Appeals go from the lower to higher courts so that the decisions of the former may be reviewed by the latter and be set right if found to be wrong. If a lower court would claim a right not to be bound by the decision of a higher court in these circumstances appeals would be an exercise in futility. The corrections made by the higher court bind the lower court, not only in the particular case, but also in similar cases in the future. It is only in this way that all the courts in the hierarchy can preach a consistent doctrine.

The Problem of the Federal Court of Appeal Sitting in Divisions

The Federal Court of Appeal sits in four divisions. This presents a problem to the doctrine of precedent. Can they always sing the same note on the same question of law? The position is uncertain. It may be argued that since the High Court also sits in divisions the position of the Federal Court of Appeal is not a peculiar one and that it will solve that problem in the same way as the High Court.

We have seen that one High Court judge is not bound to follow another, but that does not mean that they are free to decide similar points of law as differently as they like. Respectful attention must be given before a decision to diverge is taken, and we have seen cases where they have so diverged. But the higher we go on the judicial ladder the more certain and predictable the law should be. A situation where different Divisions of our intermediate court of appeal can afford to decide the same point of law differently is not an enviable one. Here certainty is required more than in the High Court and the necessity for certainty here is as acute as it is in the Supreme Court. For one thing, a large number of cases end their careers here and do not go beyond it to the Supreme Court,[82] and for another, the Federal Court of Appeal is expected to be an examplar for legal consistency and to resolve the antinomy created by High Court decisions.

[81] See, e.g. *Onome Okpalafe II and Ors. v. Efetitoroje & Ors*, FCA/B/88/78 delivered on 14/12/78; *Ajaji v. The State* (1980) 1 L.R.N. 260 263.

[82] The expenses of appeal make it so.

How then can this ideal and desirable state of affairs be achieved? One way is to reserve an unprecedented point of law for consideration by all the judges of the court and not merely those of the particular judicial Division. Such a meeting of brains will find an answer to the problem and establish one indivisible doctrine. Unless this is done it will not be surprising to find one Division in Enugu deciding one thing and another Division in Benin deciding another thing on the same question of law. In that event, lower courts would be faced with a conflict of decisions and would not know which is safe to follow. If the case is of the kind that can be taken to the Supreme Court the latter court might resolve the conflict, but the problem is incapable of solution where the case belongs to a class that ends in the Federal Court of Appeal.

Another way is to refrain from overruling settled authorities without consultation. In *Ajayi v. The State*[83] the FCA, Lagos Division, refused to follow the well-established case of *R.v. Wise*[84] which has been followed in a number of Nigerian cases[85] and which decided that one of the special circumstances to be taken into account in deciding whether to grant leave to appeal to a convicted person was whether the appeal had a prospect of success. In refusing to follow this decision the FCA said: "We are not prepared to prejudge issues before the appeal is heard." Leave to appeal was, however, granted on other grounds.

It is not likely that all the Divisions of the FCA will agree with this decision. The danger is that, if they disagree, the High Courts from where they take appeals will also disagree. Another danger is that unless all relevant superior authorities are considered by the FCA departure from settled authorities might bring them into collision with the Supreme Court. It is suggested that here again a Division that decides to overrule well-established doctrines should consult other Divisions on the need for such a step and only act where at least a majority of the Justices agree. But care should be taken to ensure that all relevant higher authorities are before the court and that nothing is done against them.

[83] FCA/L/2-4/77 decided by the Lagos Division of the FCA on 10/3/77.
[84] 17 C.A.R. 17.
[85] E.g., *Sam Offiong v. C.O.P.* HT/5CA/73 decided at Ikot Ekpene C.R.S. on 25/3/74, and other Nigerian authorities cited therein.

6. Precedent in the Supreme Court

This is the highest court of the land[86] and its decisions are final and conclusive. Appeals go to it from the Federal Court of Appeal on all classes of matters.[87] It is also vested with original jurisdiction in a dispute between the Federation and a State and between States if and insofar as that dispute involves any question (whether of law or fact) on which the existence or extent of a legal right depends. It is undesirable for the last court of the land to be vested with original jurisdiction in such matters. The former arrangement whereby the Federal Court of Appeal was given jurisdiction in such a dispute was preferable since an appeal could go to the Supreme Court against the determination of the Federal Court of Appeal; and freed from the burden and drudgery of having to investigate and determine the dispute at first instance the Supreme Court might, in an atmosphere free from strain, look squarely and freely at the determination of the Federal Court of Appeal and set right whatever error might be found in that determination. The present arrangement does not give this detachment and freedom of approach, and mistakes made as a result of plunging in *medias res* cannot be corrected.

The Supreme Court and its Attitude to its Own Decisions

The Supreme Court, like all courts of appeal in England,[88] is bound by its own decisions. Thus in *Ojosipe v. Ikabala* [89] the Supreme Court agreed with counsel that "the principles of stare decisis . . . are part of our law . . . by which we are enjoined to follow our previous decisions . . . ." Going further the court declared:

> . . . we cannot shut our eyes or ears to the alarming degree of instability which must follow in consequence of our failure or refusal to do this.

Two years earlier the court had described the principle of *stare*

[86] Section 215 of the Constitution of 1979. See also section 120 of the 1963 Constitution.

[87] See section 213(2) except where leave is required under sub-section 3.

[88] House of Lords, Court of Appeal (Civil and Criminal Divisions) and Divisional Court.

[89] (1972) 1 All N.L.R. 128, 131–132.

decisis as "the foundation on which the consistency of our judicial decisions in this country is based."[90]

The above passages show that the sole purpose of the application of the doctrine in Nigeria insofar as the Supreme Court is concerned is to ensure consistency in judicial decisions and to prevent the instability that would result from non-compliance. But the Supreme Court has recognised exceptions to the rule—at times expressly and at other times by implication. Thus, it will refuse to follow the principle where "the liberty of the subject is involved,"[91] or where the previous decision was given *per incuriam*,[92] or where the provision of a statute has been misconstrued.[93] In the latter case it has gone further than the Court of Appeal in England which does not consider an erroneous interpretation of a statute as a ground for interference by a later court.[94]

But as we remarked earlier[95] the consistency which the Supreme Court sets out to achieve through the doctrine sometimes escapes it. Thus in *Nwafor v. Nduka*[96] the Supreme Court failed to declare whether both of its previous inconsistent decisions cited to it were binding on it, or whether the one it chose to reaffirm was alone binding. In fact, the court failed to declare the status of the decision that it chose to ignore.[97] The two decisions now continue side by side as two parallel streams whose waters do not mix. Which of these two decisions is binding on lower courts and where is the consistency?

The Supreme Court is the last court of appeal for Nigeria,[98] and it is a happy circumstance that, as the last hope of the common man, it has decided not to fetter its hands in such a way as to preclude itself from reconsidering a previous decision of its own which is

[90] *Ngwo v. Monye* (1970) 1 All N.L.R. 91, 100.

[91] *Motayo v. C.O.P.* (1950) 13 W.A.C.A. 114, 116; *Maizabo v. Sokoto N.A.* (1957) 2 F.S.C. 13, 16.

[92] *Ngwo v. Monye* (1970) 1 All N.L.R. 91, 101; *Ombaka v. The Queen* (1959) 4 F.S.C. 267, 268.

[93] *Johnson v. Lawanson* (1971) 1 N.M.L.R. 380.

[94] *Young v. Bristol Aeroplane Co. Ltd.* (1944) K.B. 718.

[95] Chapter 8.

[96] (1972) 1 All N.L.R. 307, 313, discussed in Chapter 8.

[97] The ignored one was *Layiwola v. Bello* (1965) 1 All N.L.R. 318 and the one it reaffirmed was *Anamali v. Ijirigho* (1960) 5 F.S.C. 97.

[98] Appeals to the Privy Council from it were abolished in 1963; see 1963 Constitution, S. 120.

considered to be wrong. Writing of the position in England where the appellate courts consider themselves bound by their own decisions, Lord Wright asked:

> Why should not these Courts, each in its own sphere, have the same power of reviewing their own decisions as the Supreme Court of the United States, that august tribunal, or our own Judicial Committee of the Privy Council?[99]

The Nigerian Supreme Court should claim credit for its proclivity to reconsider its past decisions in the same way as the United States Supreme Court does and in circumstances in which the House of Lords before 1966, or the Court of Appeal would not consider it right to do so. The case of *Johnson v. Lawanson*[100] is an illustration of this principle. That is a case in which two of its own decisions, one Privy Council decision and one West African Court of Appeal decision were overruled by the Supreme Court on the ground that they placed a wrong construction on section 129 of the Evidence Act. In England the Court of Appeal would not overrule a decision of its own that misconstrued a statute.[101] It appears also that this was the attitude of the House of Lords,[102] but their attitude may now be different.

It is our humble suggestion that this happy trend on the part of our Supreme Court should be extended to cover all cases in which the law is not only misapplied or misinterpreted but also all cases in which justice demands that a different rule should prevail as against the precedent rule. An attitude such as this cannot destroy certainty in the law so long as justification can be found for every departure from precedent. Spelling out the circumstances in which the court will depart from precedent as was done by the English Court of Appeal in 1944 would not be helpful for two reasons. One is that the circumstances may not be exhausive;[103] the other is that the Bench and the Bar may find it difficult to agree on whether a particular

[99] "Precedents" (1944) 8 C.L.J. 118, 144.
[100] (1971) 1 N.M.L.R. 380, 387.
[101] *Young v. Bristol Aeroplance Co.* (1944) K.B. 718. Salmond, *Jurisprudence,* 11 edition, p. 204.
[102] *The Royal Court Derby Porcelain Co. Ltd. v. Russell* (1949) 2 K.B. 417, 429.
[103] Salmond, *Jurisdiction*, 11th edition, p. 192.

circumstance has occurred. It is, therefore, advisable to leave the matter in vague terms in order to avoid the pitfalls of detail.

Two other reasons exist for claiming for the Supreme Court complete liberty of action in matters of precedent. One is the dynamic character of the Nigerian society where life is growing fast and increasingly complex with twenty governments trying to regulate it with legislation. Opportunities for collision between the citizen and the law are, therefore, uncountable and, with a general rise in the level of wealth, more appeals against orders and convictions are likely to reach our highest tribunal. This emphasises the need for less rigidity in the application of the doctrine and the court should reserve for itself much elbow room to consider each case on its merit.[104]

The other reason which justifies the loose doctrine is that we have a rigid constitution to interpret and enforce. Every other law in the country takes its rise from it. All the governments and people live under it, and a difficult procedure is set for its amendment[105] which may not be easily carried through and yet it is meant to last for all time. Its provisions may be perfectly desirable and harmless at the time of promulgation, but circumstances and conditions are bound to change and its application may then become hazardous. Either through inertia or lack of the proper majority the legislatures may not act. It is here that the role of the Supreme Court as an impartial arbiter and protector of the constitution becomes evident.

It has been said that every law is the spirit of its age and environment.[106] But a constitution can only be the spirit of its age and environment through interpretation by the court, and if a rigid method of precedent is employed it will reflect the spirit of a bygone age and be out of tune with present circumstances and, to that extent, work injustice and hardship. At this juncture we quote Lord Wright:

> It seems clear that, generally speaking, a rigid method of precedent is inappropriate to the construction of a constitution,

[104] See Stone, "Stare Decisis in the Divisional Court" (1951) 14 M.L.R. 219, 224.

[105] Sections 4 and 5 of the Republican Constitution of 1963 provided for the alteration of the Constitution by special methods. So does also s. 9 of the 1979 Constitution.

[106] Allen, *Law in the Making*, 7th edition, p. 300.

> which has to be applied to changing conditions of national life and public policy.[107]

Added to this is the view of Paton and Sawer:[108]

> There is no field of law in which flexibility is, generally speaking, more desirable than the field of constitutional law.

From the foregoing statements we deduce the following conclusions. The Supreme Court ought to interpret the constitution in accordance with the spirit of every succeeding age in which its interpretation becomes necessary. In other words, it must adapt it to suit the public policy and needs of the times. This is exactly the goal which the legislatures would pursue if they could do so, and it is necessary to keep the law abreast of the times. It has been practised in the United States of America where

> The Supreme Court is not bound by its own previous decisions, nor are the State Courts bound by their own previous ruling.[109]

Perhaps it is this kind of fluidity of approach to precedent that has, as it is said, brought the Supreme Court into disrepute.[110] But it is, in fact, justified and necessary if the doctrine is not to degenerate into a tyrant.

The Supreme Court and its Attitude to Courts of Co-ordinate Authority

The Supreme Court of 1963 vintage had no equal, except the Privy Council of London, which it was created to replace. Under section 120 of the 1963 republican Constitution, the Supreme Court was made the final court of appeal for Nigeria. Earlier courts such as the Supreme Court of the 1960 vintage, the Federal Supreme Court,[111] the West African Court of Appeal and the Full Court, which were intermediate courts of appeal successively set between the High Court and the Privy Council, at once became its sub-

[107] "Precedents" (1944) 8 C.L.J. 118, 134.

[108] "Ratio Decidendi and Obiter Dictum in Appellate Courts" (1947) 63 L.Q.R. 461, 482.

[109] Gooderson, "The Rule in Young v. Bristol Aeroplane Co. Ltd." (1948–50) C.L.J. 432, 442.

[110] Salmond, *Jurisprudence*, 11th edition, p. 181.

[111] Created by section 138 of the 1954 Constitution.

ordinates. Each of these courts in its turn acknowledged the superior authority of the Privy Council and was ruled by its decisions. The 1963 Supreme Court acknowledged no superior and was the highest court of appeal for Nigeria.

If any of these courts had existed under the 1963 Constitution appeals would have lain from it to the Supreme Court which had replaced the Privy Council. That this would have been so is shown by the fact that the 1963 Constitution had made provision for regional courts of appeal to be sandwiched between the High Courts and the Supreme Courts. The Western State had established such a court of appeal.

It is therefore difficult to understand why the Supreme Court in 1969[112] treated a decision reached by the Supreme Court in 1961[113] as its own decision. This is so because a Supreme Court decision of 1961 was a decision of a subordinate court;[114] while that from the first day of October 1963 onwards was the decision of the highest court. The 1963 Supreme Court became the superior of the 1960 Supreme Court by being catapulted to fill the position from which the Privy Council was sacked by the 1963 Constitution.

So, in handling the decisions of the 1960 Supreme Court, the 1954 Federal Supreme Court and the West African Court of Appeal, the Supreme Court should have treated them as decisions of subordinate authority. They could not, for the reasons we have seen, be decisions of courts co-ordinate with the Supreme Court. Therefore, when the Supreme Court reversed those decisions it reversed the erroneous decisions of subordinate courts.

However, since the Supreme Court had treated itself as of co-ordinate rank with these earlier courts the ensuing enquiry is going to be conducted on that basis. The Supreme Court will depart from a decision of a court of co-ordinate jurisdiction if the latter misconstrues the extent of the powers which an appeal court possesses *vis-a-vis* the court of trial.[115] And of two decisions of a

[112] In *Adegboyega v. Igbinosun* (1969) 1 All N.L.R. 1, 9.

[113] The case was *Giwa v. Erinmilokun* (1961) All N.L.R. 294 decided by the 1960 Supreme Court.

[114] Because appeals could lie from such decisions to the Privy Council up to 30/9/63, whereas after this date the Supreme Court became the final court of appeal and took the place of the Privy Council.

[115] *Okwuwa v. The Queen* (1965) N.M.L.R. 53.

court of co-ordinate jurisdiction it may prefer one to the other.[116] In the same way it may adopt its reasoning in a previous decision in preference to that of a co-ordinate court.[117]

The statement of principle which the WACA adopted from the English Court of Appeal in 1949 binds the Supreme Court. That principle is the rule in *Young v. Bristol Aeroplane Co. Ltd.*[118] which states that the Court of Appeal is bound by its own decisions except in three instances: (1) where there are two conflicting decisions of its own the court is entitled and bound to decide which it will follow; (2) the court is not bound to follow a decision of its own which, though not expressly overruled, cannot stand with a subsequent decision of the House of Lords; (3) the court is not bound to follow a decision of its own if it is satisfied that the decision was given *per incuriam.*

The West African Court of Appeal adopted the rule in precisely the same terms as it was enunciated except that to the second exception it added "the Judicial Committee of the Privy Council" to "the House of Lords." The adoption was made in *Osumanu v. Seidu.*[119] Although there is no reported case of this principle having been adopted by the Federal Supreme Court (the immediate successor of W. A.C.A.) it declared *obiter* in 1961 that it was a principle "which has been followed by this court also."[120] The West African Court of Appeal has itself applied the rule to several cases.[121]

The merits and demerits of the rule have been exhaustively discussed elsewhere.[122] Here our duty is to discuss how the Nigerian Supreme Court has applied this rule that it inherited from WACA. As we saw in *Ngwo v. Monye*[123] the Supreme Court had recognised the principle of *stare decisis* as "the foundation on which the con-

[116] See *Anya v. The State* (1965) N.M.L.R. 62, 65, where it overruled *Oladimeji v. The King* (1951) 13 W.A.C.A. 275 and then said: We think that the construction adopted by the West African Court of Appeal in *Atunde v. Police* is the correct one (*Atunde v. Police* 14 W.A.C.A. 171).

[117] *Okwuwa v. The Queen* (1965) N.M.L.R. 53, 57.

[118] (1944) K.B. 718.

[119] (1949) 12 W.A.C.A. 437.

[120] *Layanju v. Araoye* (1961) All N.L.R. 83, 85.

[121] *Bamgbose v. Daniel* (1952) 13 W.A.C.A. 111, 115; *in re Adadevoh* (1951) 13 W.A.C.A. 304, 309.

[122] See Chapter 8.

[123] (1970) 1 All N.L.R. 91, 100.

sistency of our judicial decisions in this country is based." And in *Ojosipe v. Ikabala*[124] the Supreme Court was aware of the risk of "instability which must follow in consequence of our failure" to apply the principle. These remarks reassure us that the Supreme Court is painfully aware of the binding force of its decisions upon itself.

How about the exceptions? In *Johnson v. Lawanson*[125] the Supreme Court chose between a lone decision and a line of decisions (led by a Privy Council decision) which had construed the same section of a statute differently, and preferring the lone decision to the line of three, sanctioned the lone one as law and overruled the rest.[126] This was a courageous step on the part of the Supreme Court, especially as the decision had been followed for about fourteen years and was of the highest authority. The overruling, no doubt, disappointed expectations, but the Supreme Court felt justified in taking that course because its aim was to prevent greater evil.[127]

An important point to note about this exception is that the Court of Appeal was talking about two conflicting decisions. But in the actual application of the exception more than what was contemplated by it was done in the case of *Fisher v. Ruislip-Northwood U.D.C.*[128] when the Court of Appeal found four earlier decisions on the same point—three in agreement and one against—and preferred the single decision to the three. This is exactly what happened in *Johnson v. Lawanson.* Perhaps Salmond's warning is very pertinent here, namely, that the rule in *Young v. Bristol Aeroplane Co.* should not be construed like a statute.[129]

Another point to note is that the West African Court of Appeal said that it was "bound to follow previous decisions of its own as well as those of courts of co-ordinate jurisdiction," except in the

[124] (1972) 1 All N.L.R. 128, 131–132.

[125] (1971) 1 N.M.L.R. 380.

[126] The lone decision was *Omosanya v. Anifowoshe* (1959) 4 F.S.C. 94; the overruled line consisted of *Maurice Goualin Ltd. v. Aminu* (Privy Council Appeal No. 17 of 1957), *Odeneye v. Savage* (1964) N.M.L.R. 115; *Williams v. Akinwumi* (1966) 1 All N.L.R. 115.

[127] *Ibid.*. p. 388.

[128] (1945) 2 A.E.R. 458.

[129] *Jurisprudence*, 11th edition, p. 215.

three instances. In exercise of its rights under the first exception the Supreme Court has preferred one West African Court of Appeal decision to another[130] and its own decision to that of the West African Court of Appeal.[131]

But how will the conflict arise? According to Salmond[132] this will happen in two principal ways: (1) when the second decision is reached in ignorance of the first, and (2) when the first decision is improperly distinguished in the second. The case of *Omosanya v. Anifowoshe,*[133] one of the cases applied in *Johnson v. Lawanson*, appears to have been decided *per incuriam* the case of *Maurice Goualin Ltd. v. Aminu* because the Federal Supreme Court made no reference to the latter case. This view is further supported by the fact that the Supreme Court in *Johnson v. Lawanson* lamented the imperfection of "our system of law reporting in this country" which inevitably caused "a serious conflict in a most frequently used area of our law."

The conflict arising through improper distinguishing now claims our interest. In *Layiwola v. Bello,*[134] the case of *Anamali v. Ijirigho*[135] was distinguished. But when the same point came up again in *Nwafor v. Nduka*[136] the Supreme Court reaffirmed *Anamali's case*, saying that "it was in accordance with established principle and with the provisions of the Fatal Accidents Law, Cap. 52" even though it was reached in ignorance of an earlier English case[137] which later influenced their decision in *Layiwola v. Bello*. Under the first exception to the rule in *Osumanu v. Seidu* (*Young v. Bristol Aeroplane Co.*) the Supreme Court should make a categorical statement about the status of *Layiwola v. Bello,* but the matter is left at large. Therefore the conflict which was not noticeable before now becomes apparent.

The second exception is one that would not normally arise because since 1963 the Supreme Court has been the final court of

[130] *Atunde v. Police* (1952) 14 W.A.C.A. 171 preferred to *Olademeji v. The King* (1951) 13 W.A.C.A. 275.

[131] See *Okwuwa v. The Queen* (1965) N.M.L.R. 53.

[132] *Jurisprudence*, 11th edition, p. 206.

[133] (1959) 4 F.S.A. 94.

[134] (1965) 1 All N.L.R. 318.

[135] (1960) 6 F.S.C. 97.

[136] (1972) 1 All N.L.R. 307.

[137] *Peacock v. Amusement Equipment Co. Ltd.* (1954) 2 Q.B. 347

appeal and there is no court higher than it. No doubt, occasions of such conflicts must have arisen before 1963 when the Supreme Court was an intermediate court of appeal with the Privy Council above it.

The third exception has been frequently employed. In *Ngwo v. Monye*,[138] the Supreme Court said:

> Where a decision is impugned on the ground that it has been arrived at by the court only because the court had acted in ignorance or concealment of an authority, statutory or otherwise, which is binding on the court the decision is said to have been given per incuriam and constitutes a special case when the court is not bound to apply the principle of stare decisis.

As we have seen, the *per incuriam* doctrine as an exception to *stare decisis* originated with the decision of the Court of Appeal in *Young v. Bristol Aeroplane Co.* In 1955 the doctrine was more explicitly stated in *Morelle Ltd. v. Wakeling*[139] when Lord Evershed. M.R., observed:

> As a general rule the only cases in which decisions should be held to have been given per incuriam are those decisions given in ignorance of forgetfulness of some inconsistent statutory, provision or of some authority binding on the court concerned.

The Supreme Court in *Ngwo's* case adopted the above principle of law and declared:

> Where a decision is given per incuriam it does not possess for this court any binding effect and this court is entitled to disregard it.

On this ground, therefore, it held that an earlier judgment of its own given in 1964 was not binding on it.

Most people dislike the strict doctrine of precedent. It is comforting that some ways of escaping its evils have been found, but we have some reservations about the remedy. One is that more and more cases will be decided *per incuriam* because the great number of our judicial systems and consequent spate of legislations coupled with a notable improvement in the finances of the average Nigerian

[138] (1970) 1 All N.L.R. 91, 101.
[139] (1955) 2 Q.B. 379, 406.

and consequent ability to file more appeals will cause a great number of authorities to be overlooked. As Allen says, a

> difficulty, and one likely to increase in future with the ceaseless growth of recorded cases, is that exact and comprehensive citation cannot be ensured. If the judge is to be bound by precedents, he should have all the relevant authorities at his command.[140]

Another reservation is that the exceptions are not comprehensive enough. Many other situations could be envisaged in which adherence to precedent would be improper. They include changes in public policy, social and economic circumstances and the fact that we have a rigid constitution to interpret and which must be interpreted to suit the needs of the time.

Another point to note is that when the Court of Appeal laid down the rule and the West African Court of Appeal adopted it, neither court thought of the wisdom or basis of the rule.[141] What is every legal rule designed to achieve, at least, in a democracy? Is it not justice? Assuming that under the first exception the court will select a rule that is more in accord with justice and that under the second the doctrine obliges it to change its stand and follow the higher authority, can we find a similar plausible reason under exception (3) when it was a previous decision of the court (or of a court co-ordinate with it) and not a statute that was ignored?

According to this exception the last decision does not bind, but only the first does so, and the reason why the last does not bind is that it was given *per incuriam* the first. But what if the last decision furthers the interest of justice more than the first? If exception (3) is followed to its letter it will produce unjust results. Perhaps a justice-oriented court will treat the situation as a case falling under the first exception and prefer the latter decision.

The Supreme Court as the Highest Court of the Land

We have seen that the Supreme Court is the last and final court of appeal for the country.[142] This has important legal and con-

[140] *Law in the Making*, 7th edition, p. 315.

[141] See Goodhart, "Precedents in the Court of Appeal" (1945–47) 9 C.L.J. 349, 350–351.

[142] See *supra*.

stitutional consequences. Not only can no appeal be taken beyond it to any other court, but it also settles the law of the country just as the House of Lords settles the law of England.[143] After it has settled the law, all courts, persons and authorities in this country are bound by the law as settled.[144] It is doubtful whether a statute short of a constitutional amendment can alter the law settled by the Supreme Court or any other court for that matter. The reason is that the Constitution divides powers between the three arms of government and judicial powers are allocated to the courts.[145]

[143] *Robins v. National Trust Co. Ltd.* (1927) A.C. 515, 519.
[144] 1979 Constitution, s. 6(6)(b) and s. 215.
[145] Section 6 of the 1976 Constitution.

10

The Ratio Decidendi

Apart from the hierarchy of authority, another factor that determines the worth of a judicial precedent is the *ratio decidendi.* Every subsequent court pays particular attention to this part of the case because it is the only part that binds or persuades other courts. Thus, in *Osborne v. Rowlette*[1] there is the following dictum:

> . . . the only thing in a judge's decision binding as an authority upon a subsequent judge is the principle upon which the case was decided.

Both academic writers and the courts are agreed that it is the *ratio decidendi* that binds in a judgment. Dr. C. K. Allen[2] says:

> Any judgment of any court is authoritative only as to that part of it called the *ratio decidendi* . . .

According to Salmond, the "authoritative element is often termed the *ratio decidendi*" and it is the "*ratio decidendi* which alone has the force of law as regards the world at large."[3] The Supreme Court in Nigeria has decided that "it is the *ratio decidendi* of a decision of this court that binds all lower courts."[4]

The above remarks and *dicta* show conclusively that the *ratio decidendi* in a judicial decision is of overriding importance. This being so, it is incumbent on us to investigate its meaning and nature as well as the conditions it must fulfil in order to be clothed with so high an authority.

[1] (1879-80) 13 Ch.D. 773, 785-786.
[2] *Law in the Making*, 7th edition, p. 259.
[3] *Jurisprudence*, 11th edition, p. 223.
[4] *Odiase v. Agho* (1972) 1 All N.L.R. 170, 176.

1. WHAT IS A RATIO DECIDENDI?

Jurists have profferred different definitions of what a *ratio decidendi* is. Professor Hood Phillips defines it as "the reason for the decision, or the principle of law on which the decision was based."[5] According to Professor Glanville Williams:[6]

> **The *ratio decidendi* of a case can be defined as the materials facts of the case plus the decision thereon.**

Professor Llewellyn regards the *ratio decidendi* as "prima facie the rule of the case, since it is the ground upon which the court chose to rest its decision."[7]

All the above definitions have a common element which re-echoes in the writing of most of the other jurists.[8] That common element is that there is something (call it reason, principle, ground or material facts) on which the decision is based. But Professor Williams' definition, which is an adaptation of Goodhart's,[9] goes further than the rest in mentioning expressly material facts as the basis of the *ratio*. This gives some indication of how the rule, reason or principle on which the decision is based is formulated. To talk of reason for, or principle or ground of, the decision without mentioning the warp and woof from which the reason, principle or ground emanates is misleading.

As Goodhart himself explains[10] the *ratio decidendi* is not the reason for the decision nor the principle of law stated in the judgment, and he has reasons for this submission. First, the reason for the decision may be bad and yet later courts may still follow the decision. This is so where the precedent is technically binding on them. In support of Goodhart we submit that a judge may decide a case in a certain way for unexpressed reasons.[11]

Secondly, according to him no principle of law may be stated in the judgment, or judges in appellate courts may lay down different

[5] *A First Book of English Law*, 6th edition, pp. 202–203.
[6] *Learning the Law*, 7th edition, 1963, p. 71.
[7] *The Bramble Bush*, p. 66.
[8] See, for example, Allen, p. 259; Salmond, p. 223.
[9] *Essays in Jurisprudence and the Common Law*, 1931, Chapter 1.
[10] *Ibid.*
[11] *Isimekhai v. Insp. Gen of Police* (1966) 2 All N.L.R. 229 is a case in point.

legal propositions for the same conclusion, or the rule laid down may be wider than the facts of the case would justify. To Goodhart the *ratio decidendi* of a case consists in the decision based on the material facts of the case.

The criticism by Goodhart is justified and his definition is acceptable but it needs to be qualified somehow. First, as Dias and Hughes have stated:

> Goodhart's theory implies that it is the deciding judge who decides what are the material facts and that these can be discovered by a perusal of the judgment.[12]

The decision as to what are material facts does not rest exclusively with the deciding judge. We know of cases in which later courts have called attention to the facts the first judge had ignored.[13] Again, not all judgments set out the facts which must have influenced the judge's decision.[14]

Furthermore, it is wrong to suppose that the material facts of a case alone plus the judge's decision on them constitute the *ratio decidendi.* Account must be taken of the social policy of the day and the values which society has come to entertain with reference to the matter litigated before the court.

> If we attempt to ignore the impact of social life on the law and find our premises purely in the formal categories of the law, then inconvenience to society will result.[15]

Fourthly, Goodhart thinks only in terms of a jurisprudence of perfection. He has not extended his definition to include cases in which a judge constructs his *ratio decidendi* on wrong or non-existing premises.[16] A *ratio decidendi* is not necessarily a perfect principle of law; otherwise we would not hear of cases in which one judge says

[12] *Jurisprudence*, 1957, p. 74; see also Lloyd, *Introduction to Jurisprudence*, 2nd edition, p. 375.

[13] *Epi v. Aigbedion* (1972) 10 S.C. 53; *The Queen v. Ogodo* (1961) 1 All N.L.R. 700, 702, are examples.

[14] See *Isimekhai v. Insp.-Gen. of Police* (1966) 2 All N.L.R. 229; *Rex v. Sala* (1938) 4 W.A.C.A. 10.

[15] Paton and Sawer, "Ratio Decidendi and Obiter Dictum in Appellate Courts" (1947) 63 L.Q.R. 461, 481.

[16] See, e.g. *Zaria v. Small* (1973) 6 S.C. 61, 67, 68; *Federal Adm.-Gen. v. Adeshola* (1960) W.N.L.R. 53, 56; *Adelenwa v. The State* (1972) 10 S.C. 13, 19;

he will not follow another because of the latter's wrong *ratio*.[17] Yet the latter's decision has as much a *ratio decidendi* as the one that is correctly drawn.

Despite these criticisms, Goodhart's definition has some positive merits. One is that if a later judge accepts as material the facts found by the deciding judge to be material the definition will enable him to construct a legal principle to govern the case if the precedent decision does not contain such a principle. Another is that the definition accords with the theory that every legal decision must be based upon the facts of the case and not otherwise.[18]

No one has succeeded in producing a satisfactory definition of a *ratio decidendi*.[19] But Goodhart's own definition has provided an indication of the elements which a person in search of the meaning of the phrase should look for. These elements are: (1) that there must be facts upon which the case turns and that these facts or some of them, must be material; (2) that on the basis of these facts the judge must form his opinion of the liability of innocence of a party, and (3) that the opinion so formed influences his decision in the case. The second element is implied in Goodhart's definition, for there can be no decision without an opinion previously formed as to what the decision should be.

Now in attempting our own definition we must look away for a moment from perfection and consider what normally passes for a *ratio decidendi*. No court concedes to its predecessor the exclusive right to lay down a *ratio decidendi*. What one judge has laid down as a *ratio* may be modified or altered by another in a subsequent case in which the decision is cited as a precedent,[20] and sometimes the *ratio* of one judge may be an *obiter dictum* in the opinion of another.[21]

[17] *Onyama v. C.O.P.* (1970–71) 1 E.C.S.L.R. 10, 12; *Odigbo v. C.O.P.* (1972) 2 E.C.S.L.R. 120, 124–125.

[18] "The prerogative of judges is not to make law by formulating and declaring it—this pertains to the legislature—but to make law by applying it. Judicial declaration, unaccompanied by judicial application, is not of binding authority." Salmond, *Jurisprudence*, 11th edition, p. 224.

[19] Allen, *Law in the Making*, 7th edition, p. 259–260, supports this view.

[20] Dias and Hughes, *Jurisprudence*, 1957, pp. 77–76; Salmond, p. 224.

[21] See *Runka v. Katsina N.A.* (1950) 13 W.A.C.A. 98, 100 and *Chime v. Elikwu* (1956) N.M.L.R. 71, 77, which held the contrary view.

Thus, the *ratio* may be continually changing with each application.[22]

The *ratio decidendi* may be right or wrong. It may be too wide or too narrow. What matters is not whether every judge or writer would regard a particular rule or principle as the true *ratio* of the case, but what individual judges think is the *ratio* at different times. Thus, our attempted definition will run as follows: A *ratio decidendi* is a legal principle upon which a case is decided or ought to be decided, such decision being based upon a judge's view of the facts of the case and sometimes upon the social circumstances of his age and environment.

This definition may have its imperfections, but it also has the following merits. First, every legal decision should rest on a legal rule or principle. The fact that in some cases judges do not state on what legal rule their decision is based cannot preclude the inclusion of a legal rule as an element in the definition of a *ratio decidendi.* To omit it would be to give recognition to, and clothe with legality, the shortcomings of judges.

Second, the words "ought to be decided" are included to cover cases in which a later judge may refuse to recognise a rule formulated by the first judge as the *ratio* of the case and prefer a different rule. Third, the words "material facts" are designedly omitted since different judges may hold different views as to what facts are material in a given case. The words "judge s view of the facts of the case" are included to cover such cases.

Fourth, the facts of a case are not treated in isolation from the context of the society in which the dispute arose. It has been said that every legal rule is the product of its age and environment.[23] And since very judicial decision is supposed to lay down a legal rule, that rule must be related to the social circumstances of its age and environment.[24] A rule or decision that disregards these is regarded as anathema and provokes agitation for abrogation.[25]

[22] Allen, *Law in the Making*, 7th edition, p. 260, where the learned author says: "The *ratio* is thus in a constant state of flux. . . ."

[23] Allen, *Law in the Making*, 7th edition, p. 300.

[24] This point is illustrated by the trade mark cases discussed in Chapters 5 and 6. Even in England the circumstances of the society at a particular time are taken into consideration by the judges in giving their judgments. See Dias and Hughes, *Jurisprudence*, 1957, pp. 173–178.

[25] See *Nnaemeka-Agu in African Indigenous Laws*, 1975, p. 263.

The *ratio decidendi* of a particular case is the law of that case—the law which the case has laid down not only for the parties in the particular case but also to govern future transactions similar to those pronounced upon in the case. As a legal rule it is meant to be applied by later courts. Whether it will be so applied depends upon its inherent virtues. The virtues are: (1) that it must rest on facts; (2) that the rule drawn from the facts is not wider than the facts would justify; (3) that the facts must be material in the sense of helping to construct the *ratio* and to resolve the issue in controversy; (4) that it must be in accord with existing law; (5) that it must be in accord with public policy and social values, and (6) that it must be based on correct reasoning.

This epitomises the conditions for the validity and acceptability of a *ratio*. In the following pages we are going to apply the above criteria in order to show how some of the decisions of our courts fail to meet the conditions required for acceptability.

Facts as the Basis of a Ratio Decidendi

A ratio decidendi must be based on facts. The facts are those adduced in evidence by the parties in controversy and they seek to prove or disprove the allegations made by one party and denied by the other. The lifeblood of a judicial decision is the facts of the case on which it is based, and where the facts are non-existent the decision has no basis on which to operate and so is ineffective as a legal rule.

Decided cases demonstrate the dislike of higher courts for the attitude of judges who do not base their decisions on the facts before them. *Adelenwa v. The State*[26] is one of such cases. In that case the Supreme Court in allowing an appeal against a conviction for murder remarked:

> We think it right to point out that it is the duty of the court to consider the evidence produced before it and never to proceed to indulge in speculating as to what might have happened; a judge should not substitute his own supposition for the testimony of witnesses given on oath before him.

Similarly, the same court in *Ochonma v. Unosi*[27] declared:

[26] (1972) 10 S.C. 13, 19.

> In our view the judge was wrong to base his judgment on an interpretation of the transaction between the parties which neither of them had pleaded or testified to in evidence.

In each of the above instances the appeal was allowed and the trial judge's decision was set aside. This underlines the need for caution in the formulation of a *ratio decidendi*. It must be based on the facts actually put in issue by the parties and not on the judge's "supposition." A decision by a superior court is law-making, but it is law-making with a difference; it must be limited to the material before it. Only the legislature can make law "by formulating and declaring it."[28]

If a judge leaves the clear facts of the case to make a decision on what is not before him, two results follow. The dispute between the parties remains unresolved and the profession is robbed of an authoritative decision on the point. Another is that the decision arrived at on the non-existing facts amounts to no more than an *obiter dictum* and is to that extent unauthoritative.[29]

Ratio to Accord with Facts

Sometimes the judge, while being appreciative of the facts before him and trying to decide on their basis, casts his net too widely. That is, he makes a decision that goes far outside the ambit of the issues raised by the evidence before him. If that happens, later courts have the right to reassess the issues and reframe the *ratio*, cutting it down to suit the facts, for as Salmond says "courts do not concede to their predecessors the powers of laying down very wide rules."[30]

[27] (1965) N.M.L.R. 321, 323.

[28] Salmond, *Jurisprudence*, 11th edition, p. 224: Allen, *Law in the Making*, 7th edition, p. 309: "The legislature can project into the future a rule of law which has never before existed in England. The court can do nothing of the kind."

[29] See *Sun Insurance Office Ltd. v. Ojemuyiwa* (1965) N.M.L.R. 451, 454, where Bairamian, J.S.C. said: "At present it is usual to name the owner of the vehicle and his driver as the defendants to a suit claiming damages, and to leave the insurers, who control the defence, formally out of the suit; we would ask the solicitors of the parties to consider whether in these third party insurance cases it would not be better to have the insurers also joined." Compare *Olusanya v. Akintola* (1970) 2 All N.L.R. 229, 233, where the above remark was described as "obiter dictum," and ended in a refusal to follow.

[30] Salmond, p. 224.

This is what happened in *Akanbi v. Yakubu*[31] where the Supreme Court said:

> We are of the view that, in granting the relief sought, the learned trial judge seems to have done so in wide terms. On the facts as established in the lower court, we think we ought to vary the judgment of the learned trial judge so as to make it accord with the facts as found.

In the English case of *Scruttons v. Midland Sillicones,*[32] Lord Reid remarked that one of the cases in which the House of Lords would depart from their *ratio decidendi* is "where it is much wider than was necessary for the decision. . . ."

The above *dicta* show clearly that a wide *ratio* is not tolerated. To the extent to which it is wide, to that extent does it cease to represent the law. A *ratio* is law so long as it is limited to the requirements of the case. Courts are looking for guidance and are happy if they find it, but they will not take kindly to a *ratio* that overstates the law. As Dias and Hughes say, they exercise "a large measure of free discretion in deciding what propositions in earlier cases to accept, and which to castigate as being unnecessarily wide for the decision of that case."[33] In other words, in their anxiety for guidance they do not lose their sense of values and are not prepared to take stone for bread.

Material Facts

We have seen that the substrate of a *ratio* is facts. It is the facts as proved in the case that determine the result of the proceedings and decide what the *ratio* should be. But to achieve this end the facts must be material. According to Dias and Hughes, a fact may be material in one or two ways. It may help to establish its abstract form. It may also be material in the sense that it necessarily forms part of the proposition constructed out of the facts as opposed to those facts which are omitted and therefore regarded as immaterial.[34] To these we add that material facts are facts, a decision on which would dispose of the matter in issue.

[31] (1973) 12 S.C. 11, 21.
[32] (1962) 1 A.E.R. 1, 12.
[33] *Jurisprudence*, 1957, p. 78.
[34] *Jurisprudence*, 1957, p. 77.

How do we get at material facts? We do so by a process of elimination. We look at all the facts elicited in a given case against the background of what is to be decided as the issues in the case. Then we pick out those facts that bear directly on the issue, that is, those facts that will enable us to decide the case one way or the other. These are "the legally material facts."[35] The rest are not included in the decision, though they are important in making the material facts probable or improbable.[36]

After the froth of facts has been eliminated, a further process of elimination in respect of what remains is still necessary. This time the process is called abstraction. The material facts are abstracted, that is, divested of their concrete or particular forms and invested with more general or abstract forms. This is indispensable if we are to get a legal proposition constructed out of the material facts. The particular facts however material cannot give us a legal rule. It is the material facts in their abstract or general form that produce a rule of law. Professor Williams has truthfully stated that the higher the level of abstraction the wider the legal rule created.[37]

Let us illustrate our thesis with an actual example from one of our cases. In *Ogunbambi v. Abowab*[38] the plaintiff was in possession of a piece of land into which the defendant had trespassed. Both parties traced their claim to title to the Oloto family. The plaintiff claimed that his predecessor in title bought the land from the family in 1929 and had since been in possession up to the time he went into possession as his predecessor's successor. He tendered the purchase receipt in evidence and produced evidence to show that he was in possession at the time of entry by the defendant.

The defendant claimed that he bought the land from the Oloto family in 1948 and took a conveyance, by virtue of which he went into possession. He denied knowledge of the plaintiff's interest in or presence on the land.

On these facts, the question being one of trespass, the court had to determine: (1) who first purchased the land; (2) who was first in possession, and (3) who was in possession at the time the dispute

[35] Glanville Williams, *Learning the Law*, 5th edition, p. 64.
[36] Evidence Act, s. 12(b).
[37] See Williams, *ibid.*, p. 68.
[38] (1951) 13 W.A.C.A. 222, 223.

arose. It found that the plaintiff was first in possession and that he was still in possession at the time of defendant's entry. In the circumstances, the court found against the defendant in trespass. The defendant appealed to the West African Court of Appeal and his appeal was dismissed.

In arriving at this conclusion the court had to consider the actual issues raised in the case and whether in the light of these issues there was a case of trespass. To do so the court had to eliminate the less material facts such as the occupations and addresses of the parties and their witnesses, the length of time each has been in possession, the nature of activities carried out on the land, the boundaries of the land and names of adjacent owners as well as details of the evidence of witnesses.

After such elimination, the court is left with such facts as the of the parties, the respective dates of acquisition of interest in the land, the receipt and the conveyance and the purchase prices thereon, the fact of possession and entry, their respective dates, the location of the land and the question as to who was in possession at the time of dispute. These are the material facts of the case.

To see how clumsy a *ratio* based on the facts as they are would be, let us join up the above facts in one sentence as follows: If A purchased Blackacre from the Oloto family in 1929 for —— and took a receipt dated —— and went into possession for —— years until he was succeeded by the plaintiff, Abowab, who continued in possession until the dispute arose between him and the defendant and the defendant, Ogunbambi, only acquired the legal estate in the land in 1948 by means of a conveyance for —— he, Ogunbambi, will be liable in trespass to the plaintiff, Abowab, his entry being with knowledge of Abowab's equitable interest in the land.

Such a legal proposition is open to objection on several counts. First, it is cumbrous and almost unintelligible. Second, it is unnecessarily restrictive and confines the legal rule only to the parties in the case and does not provide a rule for future cases. A practice that sanctions that form of *ratio* formulation would inhibit jurisprudential growth.

To produce an ascertainable *ratio* and make the rule wide enough to cover other cases we have to eliminate the less material facts further. By elimination, as already stated, we mean expurgation of the less material facts of the case in the process of formulating the *ratio.* Thus the fact of a prior possession by the plaintiff's predecessor in title can be omitted. So also should the names of the plaintiff and the defendant as well as mention of receipt and conveyance and their dates,

Now let us attempt another proposition: If a plaintiff has acquired Blackacre for value from the Oloto family and has been in possession for a long time and later the defendant, knowing of the plaintiff's equitable interest, acquires the legal estate for value and enters the land while the plaintiff is still in possession he commits a trespass.

Although this is a better version than the first it is not altogether satisfactory for the following reasons. It lays down a rule that can only protect a plaintiff whose possession is disturbed by the defendant. It does not say what will happen if the trespasser is the plaintiff. Liability can only attach if the land is acquired by the plaintiff from a particular family—the Oloto family. A still wider rule can be obtained by abstraction thus: If a person has acquired a piece of land for value and is in possession at the time of entry by another whose title is subsequent the latter is liable in trespass even if he has obtained the legal estate for value.

The third version of the rule now lays down a rule of universal application which justifies the existence of the doctrine of precedent. But the *ratio* which the West African Court of Appeal based its decision is narrower than this:

> When in an action in trespass the plaintiff has obtained a conveyance from a predecessor who has been in possession under a claim of right for many years and has himself been in possession from the date of purchase the burden cast upon the defendant of showing a better title is not lightly to be passed over . . .

According to Professor Williams the *ratio decidendi* which subsequent courts, which are called upon to apply the case, lay down "may not be the *ratio decidendi* that the judge who decided the case would himself have chosen; but it may be the *ratio decidendi* that will be approved by a court that has to consider the matter in the future."[39] The case of *Orasanmi v. Idowu*[40] proved the opinion of

[39] *Learning the Law*, 5th edition, p. 69.
[40] (1959) 4 F.S.C. 40, 41.

Professor Williams quite right, for in that case the Federal Supreme Court, in restating the *radio decidendi of Ogunbambi's* case, had this to say:

> Now, to rely on *Ogunbambi v. Abowab* (1) there must be in addition to payment, an undisturbed and continuous possession for many years by the claimant or by his predecessor in title under whom he claims. In other words, it was not enough that the appellant should go into possession after the sale to him, but it is important for him to establish that he remained in possession.

The principle of the decision in *Ogunbambi v. Abowab* is not thereby affected, but the rule of the case is made simpler and less involved. Judges and even counsel who have to consider a precedent are not bound to express its principle in the same phraseology as the original judge, provided its spirit is maintained; and its spirit will be maintained if they agree with the first judge in his view of the material facts.

There is another very important point to not about material facts. All the facts material in the proceedings must be considered. If any material fact is ignored the rule is defective. Thus, where in a criminal case there is evidence of provocation which the first court has ignored a later court will upset the decision and base its judgment on all the material facts. This is what happened in *The Queen v. Ogodo*[41] in which the Federal Supreme Court treated the decision of the trial judge as "not in accord with the facts."

Accord with Existing Law

To commend itself to later courts a *ratio decidendi* must accord with existing law. According to Salmond:[42]

> New rules are very often merely analogical extensions of the old. The courts seek as far as possible to make the new law the embodiment and expression of the spirit of the old-of the ratio juris, as the Romans called it. The whole thereby becomes a single and self-consistent body of legal doctrine, containing with-itself an element of unity and of harmonious development.

[41] (1961) All N.L.R. 700, 702.
[42] *Jurisprudence,* 11th edition, p. 226.

It follows, therefore, that the criterion of validity is its consistency with a precedent that came before it. We have examples of decisions in our law which ignored or spurned pre-existing precedents and were in turn ignored or spurned. In *Idewu v. Hausa*[43] it was held that property inherited from the mother's side by an intestate who died without issue must go to the maternal relations of the deceased in preference to the paternal relations according to native law and custom. In the later case of *Suberu v. Sunmonu*[44] the proof of native law and custom was that property inherited from the father's side went to paternal relations in similar circumstances. The trial judge either ignored or spurned the rule in *Idewu v. Hausa* and awarded the property to the widows of the deceased and the plaintiff appealed.

Allowing the appeal and setting aside the judgment, the Federal Supreme Court held that the trial judge had violated two rules of pre-existing law. One was that in Yoruba customary law a widow could not inherit the property of her husband.[45] Another was the rule of customary law that the property of an intestate went to the side from which it was inherited if the intestate died without issue.

The Court approved the rule in *Idewu v. Hausa* and questioned why the trial judge did not have it and the other authorities in contemplation. Obviously the trial judge was violating a fundamental principle. He was not trying to make the new law "the embodiment and expression of the spirit of the old," and so violated a deeply entrenched customary rule of inheritance. Therefore, his decision not being in accord with pre-existing law was swept aside.

A further illustration of the attitude of later courts to a *ratio* that does not take account of pre-existing law is given–this time from the criminal law. In *C.O.P. v. Igwe*[46] the Federal Supreme Court overruled the High Court on the ground that its decision did not accord with the known rule as to the ejectment of trespassers. In that case the accused person had assaulted a constable who went to search his premises without a warrant. He was convicted by the Magistrate but on appeal to the High Court the conviction was set aside on the ground that the constable had no warrant to search the

[43] (1936) 13 N.L.R. 96.
[44] (1957) 2 F.S.C. 33, 35.
[45] *Aileru v. Anibi* 1952) 20 N.L.R. 46.
[46] (1961) All N.L.R. 9.

premises and was, therefore, a trespasser. Allowing an appeal against the acquittal the Federal Supreme Court held that as the constable was not told to leave the premises before the assault he could not be a trespasser and so the assault was unjustified.

The learned judge had ignored the rule in *R. v. Quinn*[47] which is that a police officer who enters premises without a search warrant only becomes a trespasser after he has been told to leave and he refuses to do so. If the decision of the learned judge of appeal were placed side by side with the West African Court of Appeal decision in *R. v. Quinn*, the error in the framing of its *ratio* would become noticeable. In the circumstances, a consistent legal doctrine would not emerge and "unity and harmonious development" would be imperilled.

Lastly, we consider the case of *Onwudinjoh v. Onwudinjoh*[48] where Ainly, C.J., of former Eastern Nigeria, decided that the issue of a customary marriage contracted subsequently to a monogamous marriage under the Nigerian Marriage Ordinance were not entitled to share in the estate of their intestate father. In so holding the learned Chief Justice stated that he was not deciding the case on the precedent of *Cole v. Cole*[49] and other authorities based on it as he thought that that authority and its line of cases would one day be overruled by the Federal Supreme Court. He rather based his decision on the ground that there was no native law and custom that permitted natural children to share the estate of their father with "the offspring of a lawful marriage."[50] Apart from the fact that this decision was reached *per incuriam*, being contrary to higher authorities, its *ratio* is clearly inconsistent with established legal rule on the subject.[51]

The legal position seems to be this. Every court framing the *ratio* of a case before it must have regard to existing authorities and must make sure that the new *ratio* can be reconciled with the old, especially where the later has been followed in a number of cases or is

[47] (1944) 10 W.A.C.A. 243.
[48] (1957–58) 2 E.R.N.L.R. 1.
[49] (1898) 1 N.L.R. 15.
[50] *Ibid.*, p. 5.
[51] See *Alake v. Pratt* (1955) 15 W.A.C.A. 20; *Bamgbose v. Daniel* (1952) 14 W.A.C.A. 111; in *re Adadevoh* (1951) 13 W.A.C.A. 304.

a higher authority. A conflict retards legal growth and makes the law uncertain. In such circumstances it is the clear duty of every "court which is presented with such a conflict to restore case-law discipline rather than to give way to the recalcitrant decision."[52]

But where a relevant pre-existing rule is clearly wrong the later court has a duty to justice to depart from its spirit and lay down the correct legal principle. But it is submitted that in doing so it must point out the flaws in the existing decision to show why it refuses to apply it. The practice of criticising previous decisions which are found to be wrong, pointing out their shortcomings and showing how they should have been decided, is by itself a contribution to jurisprudence. But to ignore them in silence is a disservice not only to justice but also to law as a science.

Accord with Public Policy and Social Values

Law does not operate in a vacuum. It exists to meet the needs and fulfil the purposes of society. This is particularly true of our customary law which governs the status and transaction of an overwhelming majority of Nigerians. Decisions on it must keep accord with the public policy and social values of the people. If not, they would be thrown into the limbo of bad law. According to Paton:

> No developing system of law can avoid the influence of the general views of the community as to the end that law should pursue.[53]

Actual cases will illustrate this point. In *Edet v. Esien,*[54] a wife left her husband to whom she was lawfully married according to customary law to live with another man and had children for the latter. The claim of the husband for the children was upheld by the Native Court on the ground that they were the lawful children of the appellant since the bride price paid by the latter on the mother of the children was not refunded. The Native Court said this was the customary law of the people.

On appeal to the then Supreme Court (now High Court), Carey. J., held:

[52] Winder, "Divisional Court Precedents" (1946) 9 M.L.R. 257, 272.
[53] *A Textbook of Jurisprudence*, 3rd edition, p. 197.
[54] (1932) 11 N.L.R. 47.

> . . . even assuming that the native law and custom as alleged by the appellant had been definitely established I am inclined to think it should properly have been overruled in this case as being repugnant to natural justice, equity and good conscience having regard to the circumstances.[55]

This decision has been trenchantly criticised. Nnaemeka Agu[56] has written:

> This raises the big question: Whose conscience? Is it the conscience of the past colonial masters influenced by their sociological background and their monogamous outlook which was obviously behind the decision in *Edet v. Esien* that we still have to impose on our people or is it the conscience of our indigenous, polygamous society which sees nothing wrong with this particular custom?

This decision ignored the earlier decision in the opposite direction in *Amachree v. Goodhead*[57] where it was held that a child conceived and born after the death of the mother's husband belonged to the family of the mother's husband and not to that of the mother before marriage. It can, therefore, be said that *Edet v. Esien* when it was decided was out of accord with pre-existing law apart from being inimical to the public policy and social values of the people. In fact it is revolting to native conscience to permit a man to own the children of another man's wife simply because they are the offspring of an adulterous union between him and the woman.

Later cases have systematically isolated *Edet v. Esien*. *Nwaribe v. President, Orlu District Court*[58] is the first case in point. That case involved similar facts to those in *Amachree v. Goodhead* and the decision was the same. The case went to the High Court on certiorari proceedings and the learned judge tried to distinguish *Edet v. Esien* on grounds that are not clear. But three years after the decision in *Edet v. Esien* a British judge, Graham Paul, J., had decided in *Chawere v. Aihenu*[59] that the mere fact of a woman leaving her

[55] *Ibid.*, p. 48.
[56] *African Indigenous Laws*, 1975, p. 263.
[57] (1923) 4 N.L.R. 101.
[58] (1964) 8 E.N.L.R. 24.
[59] (1935) 12 N.L.R. 4.

husband and living in adultery with another man did not make the woman the wife of the adulterer.

The splendid isolation of *Edet v. Esien* is warranted by the need to make the law on the subject fall in line with the popular sentiments and social values of Nigerians. In fact, *Edet v. Esien* has struck at the very root of social order and it is good comfort that it has not been followed. The observation of the learned judge who decided that the custom was "repugnant to natural justice, equity and good conscience" was more relevant to the situation he had created than to the rule of customary law which he rejected.

How can a custom that ensures peace and social order be said to be repugnant? If this decision were followed and acted upon it would lead to two evils. One is that no one would think of marrying, but would go about putting women, married or unmarried, in the family way and then claiming the children without shouldering the responsibility either of husbandhood or fatherhood. Another is that husbands and parents would take the law into their own hands and avenge their own wrongs with resultant danger to peace.

A learned jurist has told us when a custom should be so bad as to be rejected:

> It is not malus merely because it is an erratic exception to the general law, but only if it is so violent an exception, to the advantage of a small class of persons that it clashes irreconcilably with a principle which it is the policy of the law to apply to all persons whatsoever.[60]

The rule of customary law proved in *Edet v. Esien* has not posed this threat, nor is it a rule which operates among "a small class of persons." It is rather a principle which it should be "the policy of the law to apply to all persons" who are Nigerian indigenes.

Reasoning

The last of the six factors which induce a later court to accept or reject a judicial decision is the reasoning that backs it. Reasoning is the process of reaching conclusions by using one's reason.[61] The

[60] Allen, *Law in the Making*, 7th edition, p. 156.
[61] *Oxford Advanced Learner's Dictionary of Current English.*

purpose of reasoning is to determine right and truth.[62] The aim of every judicial reasoning should be to promote the interests of justice, and a subsequent judge will reject the decision of his predecessor if "the reasons which he gave for his decision have been shown to be erroneous."[63]

The importance of judicial reasoning comes into prominence when there is no precedent to which the present decision can be tied. The decision is then essentially a product of reasoning and has to justify its existence as a rule of law solely by its merits. That justification comes when the judge determines the question before him in accordance with "the principles of natural justice, practical expediency and common sense."[64] Where no guidance can be obtained from these principles regard can be had to persuasive influences like foreign decisions[65] and religious,[66] ethical and philosophical doctrines and the opinions of text-writers.[67]

In addition to the search for right and truth, every legal rule is formulated with the interest of the community in the background, and a decision which is absonant to these interests attracts condemnation[68] and criticism.[69] As Professor Paton says:

> There are no precise methods of discovering what the community really thinks, so we must trust the judge to be a typical representative of his day and generation.[70]

judge is reserved the sole prerogative of determining what is best for the community and that later judges have equal right to reason out

[62] *Chambers's Twentieth Century Dictionary.*

[63] *Fatoyinbo v. Williams* (1956) 1 F.S.C. 87, 89.

[64] Salmond, *Jurisprudence*, 11th edition, p. 225.

[65] *Rex v. Adekanmi* (1944) 17 N.L.R. 99, 101; *Doherty v. Abubakar* (1961) All N.L.R. 604, 614.

[66] *The State v. Edet Esien Ete*, unreported, but see Charge No. HU/20C/75 decided on 12/8/76 at the Uyo High Court by Akpabio, J., where the learned judge said ". . . it is true that from the Biblical point of view a sinner runneth when no man pursueth," in which a man who was accused of murder "consulted his safety by flight."

[67] Salmond, *ibid.*

[68] See *Nnaemeka-Agu in African Indigenous Laws*, 1975, p. 263, where *Edet v. Esien* is condemned.

[69] See *Salako v. Salako* (1965) L.L.R. 136, where Adefarasin, J., as he then was, criticised *Danmole v. Dawodu* (1958) 3 F.S.C. 46 for ignoring a custom approved by the people.

[70] *A Textbook of Jurisprudence*, 3rd edition, p. 116.

his conclusions and arrive at their own decision of what is best. When there is disagreement it is the first judge's reasoning that is attacked.

As we have seen, a decision will be supported when its reasoning is sound. It is the only merit upon which a decision depends for survival in the absence of a pre-existing rule to which the decision is subordinated. But where there is an acceptable rule of law in existence every subsequent decision must be judged by reference to it.

We are here considering a case in which the pre-existing rule does not provide a full answer to the existing dispute but deals with the problem peripherally. Here the judge reasons by analogy. The case which is used as an analogy provokes thought and, while not itself providing a solution to the problem involved, acts as a pointer to the direction in which the rule in the case in hand should bend.

In England, the case of *Donoghue v. Stevenson*,[71] a Scottish appeal was not decided on any single authority as there was none directly in point, but on the analogy of a number of cases, some for and others against the liability of a manufacturer of goods to the ultimate consumer where there was negligence. This decision proceeded from the reasoning from the analogies and established a far-reaching principle of liability. Three years later this decision was followed by the Privy Council in *Grant v. Australian Knitting Mills, Ltd.*,[72] the Board saying:

> It is enough now to say that their Lordships hold the present case to come within the principle of Donoghue's case.

That is what happens when a precedent is well reasoned. Later courts have no difficulty in agreeing with its conclusions and resting subsequent cases involving similar facts upon its principles. It is a sure sign of orthodoxy.

Where, however, a later court by negligence or design fails to consider an analogous precedent in point and arrives at a decision which is out of tune with that analogy the consequence is overruling[73] or refusal to follow.[74] We have already referred to a statement by Salmond that new rules are very often merely analogical extensions

[71] (1932) A.E.R. 1.
[72] (1935) A.E.R. 209, 219.
[73] *Suberu v. Sunmonu* (1936) N.L.R. 96.
[74] *Nwaribe v. President, Orlu District Court* (1964) 8 E.N.L.R. 24.

of the old and that the policy of the courts is to make the new law an embodiment and expression of the spirit of the old.[75]

As already stated, analogies tend to indicate the lines along which the new development should take place. The judge has to decide for himself whether the analogy is a good pilot or not. He does this by considering its merits as a legal rule in its own operative sphere before it can be depended upon as an infallible guide into another sphere. Thus in *Suberu v. Summonu*[76] the Federal Supreme Court approved the decision of the then Supreme Court (High Court) to the effect that property acquired by an intestate dying without issue from his mother's side went to the maternal relatives.[77] And later, when an analogous point came to be decided and was decided differently, the Federal Supreme Court set its face against it and reversed the decision, holding, on the analogy of *Idewu's case*, that it followed that property acquired from the father's side by an intestate dying without issue must go to paternal relations.

The action of the Federal Supreme Court in checking the devious reasoning of the trial judge and upholding the principle of the precedent analogous decision is commendable. But for such intervention not only would the law on the matter be twisted out of shape and become irrational and devoid of consistency and certainty, but also the basic norms of the people would have been destroyed. Commenting on the usefulness of analogical reasoning, Dias says:

> This type of reasoning is very popular in the common law, for it accommodates change with certainty as painlessly as possible. The pressure exerted by the desire for certainty is a powerful incentive to develop the law analogically wherever possible.[78]

We now come to a case in which there is a precedent directly in point. Here little reasoning process is involved, but the obligation to reason is not lacking even here. First, the judge has to reason out what the decision in the case before him should be. His mastery of the facts of the case and his training and knowledge of the law will present to his mind a practical answer. Then he consults his authori-

[75] *Jurisprudence*, 11th edition, p. 226.
[76] (1957) 2 F.S.C. 33, 35.
[77] See *Idewu v. Hausa* (1936) 13 N.L.R. 96.
[78] *Jurisprudence*, 3rd edition, p. 85.

ties where principles similar to those he is contemplating were laid down and applies those decisions to the case before him. At last he hands down his decision with confidence. Dias calls this approach the logic of justification.[79]

As we said earlier, some amount of reasoning is indispensable even here. In the course of hearing a case, the evidence, as it unfolds, reminds the judge of some precedent authorities which are directly relevant to and resolve the points that are being raised. But there may be other facts in the evidence which give the present case a different twist from those he has in mind and he must be prepared to resolve the differences. He can do this by ignoring them and treating them as immaterial and so base his decision on the precedents he has in mind. Alternatively, he may treat them as material and so reach a decision which is not actually in line with the precedent but somewhat near to it. The first approach preserves the law as it was while the second extends its principle.[80]

From what we have seen it is clear that reasoning plays a most important part in creating and shaping judicial decisions. It is therefore important to ask what type of reasoning judges employ. Certainly logic has a limited place.[81] But logical principles are not entirely ruled out; they come into prominence when syllogistic deductions are possible, that is, where exact precedents exist and all the judge has to do is to fit the facts of the case in hand into the principle established by the precedents.

But where there are no precedents to pray in aid the judge has to be guided by his common sense and by what is socially desirable.[82] Where analogies can be prayed in aid the considerations which actuate the judge are the need for consistency and certainty in the law. This, of course, has to be sacrificed if the interests of justice demand a contrary approach. To quote Salmond:

> Where justice so requires, it is the duty of the courts, in making new law, to depart from the *ratio juris antiqui*, rather than servilely to follow it.[83]

[79] *Ibid.*

[80] See *Akpobasa v. The State* (1969) 1 All N.L.R. 104, 111.

[81] Lloyd, *Introduction to Jurisprudence*, 2nd edition, p. 382.

[82] In *re Adadevoh* (1951) 13 W.A.C.A. 304, 309; Paton, *A Textbook of Jurisprudence*, 3rd edition, p. 197.

[83] *Jurisprudence*, 11th edition, p. 226.

Good reasoning can make the law designed for one environment serve the purpose of another where different conditions prevail. Thus close similarities between two trade marks which cannot deceive an educated and enlightened community may deceive an illiterate and primitive community. Therefore, precedents established for the first community must be modified to suit the second.[84] The concept of a reasonable man as understood in a civilised community for purposes of criminal responsibility is modified to suit the cultural status of a man in a primitive community.[85] The civilised idea of equality between man and wife does not apply in an uncivilised community where "the wife is still regarded as being under the rod of her husband."[86]

In each of the above instances the importance of sound and calculating reasoning comes into the forefront. If the rigid standards of England were transplanted into the Nigerian soil without modification to suit local circumstances the common law would certainly have lost its respect. But by marrying it to local conditions it becomes a tolerable system at least in these areas of the law. Good judicial reasoning is, therefore, an essential condition of justice and of obtaining respect and toleration for the common law.

Now what are the sanctions for bad reasoning? A decision that is not well-reasoned cannot claim authority as a good rule of law.[87] Such a decision is in danger of reversal on appeal,[88] or of being overruled in another case[89] or of being isolated by a court of coordinate jurisdiction which refuses to follow it,[90] or of being subjected to spurious distinguishing.[91]

After all this, let us go back to our starting point. A good *ratio* is a reasoned *ratio*—reasoned in the evaluation of the facts[92] as well as

[84] *MacIver v. C.F.A.O.* (1917) 3 N.L.R. 18.

[85] *R. v. Adekanmi* (1944) 17 N.L.R. 99.

[86] *The State v. David Egbe*, unreported, C/40C/1972, decided on 23/11/72 by Eno, J., at Calabar High Court.

[87] *Edet v. Esien* (1932) 11 N.L.R. 47 is of this class.

[88] *Fatoyinbo v. Williams* (1956) 1 F.S.C. 87, 89—reversal for erroneous reasons.

[89] In *re Adadevoh* (1951) 13 W.A.C.A. 304—to ensure "common sense and decency."

[90] *Sule v. Ajisegiri* (1937) 13 N.L.R. 146, 147.

[91] *Edet v. Esien. supra.*

[92] *Arayi v. Ojubu* (1955–56) W.R.N.L.R. 145.

in the application of the law. A good judge is one who can make his decision acceptable in this regard. Every legal rule that has survived owes its survival to sound reasoning. It is the reasoning and the principle evolved from it that constitutes the law of the case which later courts come to regard as a precedent,

2. Ratio and Dictum

To make this chapter self-contained we are bringing together and differentiating between *ratio* and *dictum* in the light of their importance in the scheme of precedent. There is a necessary difference between them. The authoritative part if the judgment is the *ratio.*[93] The *dictum* is unauthoritative.[94] It is the *ratio* that binds later courts; the *dictum* does not; but if sufficiently strong and well-reasoned it may persuade.[95]

According to Lord Sterndale:[96]

> Dicta are of different kinds and of varying degrees of weight. Sometimes they may be called almost casual expressions of opinion upon a point which has not been raised in the case, and is not really present to the judge's mind. Such dicta, though entitled to the respect due to the speaker, may fairly be disregarded by judges before whom the point has been raised and argued in a way to bring it under much fuller consideration. Some dicta, however, are of different kind; they are, although not necessary for the decision of the case, deliberate expressions of opinions given after consideration upon a point clearly brought and argued before the Court. It is open, no doubt, to other judges to give decisions contrary to such dicta, but much greater weight attaches to them than to the former class.

These remarks invite a search for, and an identification of, these different kinds of *dicta.*

We frequently come across the words "*dicta*" and "*obiter dicta*" and they are often used interchangeably. Here we want to show that

[93] Allen, *Law in the Making*, 7th edition, p. 259.

[94] Salmond, *Jurisprudence*, 11th edition, p. 166.

[95] Paton and Sawer, "Ratio Decidendi and Obiter Dictum in Appellate Courts" (1947) 63 L.Q.R. 461, 476.

[96] *Slack v. Leeds Industrial Co-operative Society* (1923) 1 Ch. 431, 451.

this use of the words is inappropriate. Each should be confined to the sphere to which it rightly belongs. "*Dictum*" means a saying; the *Chamber's Twentieth Century Dictionary* defines it as an "authoritative saying." *Obiter* means "indirect," "roundabout," "off the main point." When used as an epithet to *dictum* it limits the meaning of the latter to a saying that is not authoritative. From this it ought to be clear that the two expressions are not meant to refer to the same idea.

A *dictum* is a necessary step in a judge's argument towards a conclusion. It is like a link in a chain. If a link in a chain is cut the chain ceases to retain its integrity and falls into two parts. Similarly, if a *dictum* is taken out of a process building up a rule of law the resulting rule will cease to represent the intention of the judge and may be otiose for that reason. We therefore conclude that a *dictum* without its qualifying word is part of the law of the case and is authoritative.

Obiter dictum stands on a different footing. It is not a necessary step in the reasoning. It stands apart from the building-up process and is not part of the law of the case.[97] It is used to draw an analogy between the case in hand and an hypothetical case, to illustrate and to advise. It does not decide the particular issue between the parties.

Thus, in the unreported case of *The State v. Ogon*,[98] the charge against the accused person was false pretences. The learned trial judge dismissed the charge on the ground that it did not contain essential particulars and then added:

> If the charge had gone on to add after Ogoja the sentence "and by falsely pretending that the person who signed for the cheque aforesaid was A. O. Ewa" that charge would have been complete.

The above remark is an *obiter dictum*. It was not necessary for the decision which the learned judge reached in the case, namely, that the charge contained insufficient particulars and was therefore bad in law. It advised the prosecuting counsel on how the charge should have been framed. That was not an issue in the case and did not fall to be decided. The issue was whether the charge was complete with the necessary particulars, not how it should have been framed.

[97] Paton, *A Textbook of Jurisprudence*, 3rd edition, p. 180.

[98] Calabar High Court Criminal charge No. C/25C/72 decided on 30 10/72 by Kooffreh, J., as he then was.

A further example may be given. If a judge advises counsel in the course of his judgment to consider whether it would not be a good thing to join insurance companies in claims against insured defendants when the issue before him is whether an insurance company which was not a party to the original proceeding is entitled to appeal against the judgment in that proceeding, the judge is making the remark *obiter*. This is what happened in *Sun Insurance Office Ltd. v. Ojemuyiwa.*[99] In that case, an insurance company applied for leave to appeal against a High Court judgment which went against the insured defendant for damages for negligence. The insurance company was not a party to the original proceedings, but it applied for leave to appeal as an "interested person" under section 117(6)(a) of the 1963 Constitution of the Federation. The question before the Supreme Court, therefore, was whether the company was entitled to such leave.

The Supreme Court found that it was so entitled and granted the leave. Bairamian, J.S.C., who delivered the judgment of the court was, no doubt, concerned about the necessity to short-circuit matters in cases of this nature and so advised:

> The remaining reflection is that as in Nigeria civil cases are tried by a judge alone, there is no need to conduct these fatal accident cases in a world of make-believe. At present it is usual to name the owner of the vehicle and his driver as the defendants to a suit claiming damages, and to leave the insurers, who control the defence, formally out of the suit; we would ask the solicitors of the parties to consider whether in these third party insurance cases it would not be better to have the insurers also joined.

This admonition was clearly *obiter*; that is, though intended as a statement of the law it was not necessary for the decision of the issue before the court, which was whether the insurance company was entitled to leave to appeal against the judgment given against its insured client. The very point dealt with in the above *obiter dicta* was made the subject of express decision in the opposite direction in the English case of *Carpenter v. Ebblewhite*[100] when the point

[99] (1965) N.M.L.R. 451, 454.
[100] (1938) 4 A.E.R. 41.

arose. Oputa, J., in *Okafor v. Ezeigbo*[101] preferred the English decision to the Nigerian *obiter dicta* and declared:

> I will, with respect, prefer to be guided by the reasoning in the case of Carpenter v. Ebblewhite referred to above.

The *dicta* in the *Sun Insurance Office Ltd. v. Ojemuyiwa* proceeded from the highest court of the land; yet a lower court spurned it and preferred the English decision which, as we shall see in Chapter Thirteen, is not binding on it. This provides positive evidence that an *obiter dictum* as a rule of law is not binding.

But why does it not bind? We leave the answer to Professor Williams who says:

> The reason for not regarding an obiter dictum as binding is that it was probably made without a full consideration of the cases on the point, and that, if very broad in its terms, it was probably made without a full consideration of all the consequences that may follow from it.[102]

We have said that a *dictum* as a step in the reasoning is part of the *ratio* and therefore binding in a way *obiter dictum* is not. Everyone acquainted with practice knows that a judge does not simply recite the facts and then lay down the rubric of a case. In every well-written judgment the general practice is to recite the facts, then to make findings and later to lay down the law.

The setting down of the law is a reasoned process. The issue that has arisen for decision must be viewed in its legal context and the law applicalbe to it reasoned out in the light of the facts found to have been established. This means that the judge must see his legal conclusion from the beginning and then approach it by a step-by-step reasoning. We will cite an actual example[103] from an unreported decision of a judge of first instance:[104]

> I have carefully considered all the evidence adduced in this case as well as all the legal authorities cited by learned counsel on

[101] (1966–67) 10 E.N.L.R. 203, 206.

[102] *Learning the Law* 5th edition, p. 74.

[103] Not necessarily a perfect example, but it does afford the illustration we want.

[104] *The State v. Effiong Okon Akpan:* Charge No. HU/1C/76 decided on 15/10/76 in the Uyo High Court by Akpabio, J.

both sides, and find that the facts of the case are not in dispute. The only point of contention is whether these facts disclose a case of causing death through dangerous driving. In other words, whether the accused was driving dangerously on the night in question. It has long been stated in a line of cases starting with *Hill v. Baxter* (1958) 1 Q.B. 277 down to *R. v. McBride.*(1962) 2 Q.B. 167, that the test for Dangerous Driving must be objective. It is not what the accused says that matters; but what a reasonable man, standing by the road watching the accused, and taking all the circumstances into consideration would say, that matters. Dangerous driving may occur without a collision, or indeed without any indication from the speed or movement of the vehicle.

In the present case I have taken into consideration the fact that Aka Road along which the accident occurred, was traditionally a very busy road. It would appear to be much more congested than Uyo-Oron in that it is much narrower. It behoves every driver along this road therefore to be extra careful when driving along it. Furthermore, the time of the accident was about 10 p.m. in the night when visibility was much lower than in the day time. Finally, according to the evidence of accused himself, it had rained earlier that evening, so that the roads were naturally more slippery than it would have been on a dry day. This means that braking distance would be much longer. This is therefore another factor that a driver should take into consideration when determining his speed of operation. Now, the question is, was the accused going at a reasonable speed under all these circumstances? It would appear from the events of the evening that he was not. Even though P.W. 1, the only eye witness in this case had said that accused was driving normally, I must point out that in his verified statement which was made to the Police on 16/4/75 i.e. on the date of the incident when everything was fresh in his mind he stated as follows:

> The taxi car which caused the accident came from Aka Road towards the circus with a terrific speed.

Another eye-witness, the army man, who had also made a verified statement to the Police but unfortunately could not be got on the date of the trial to testify, had also used the same words, namely, that the vehicle was coming "with a terrific speed.' However, even putting aside all these words as they were not given on oath before me in this trial, I find that even the surrounding circumstances of this case are consistent with the fact that the accused must have been coming at a terrific speed inspite of the road hazard, already mentioned above. Accused not only left the tarred road completely to collide with a motor-cycle parked on the sand verge, but he went further and knocked down the deceased who was standing much further away. And as if this was not bad enough, he continued for another 60 feet 10 inches, dragging the deceased along until it further collided with an electric pole before coming to a standstill. These to my mind, are indicative that the accused must have been driving at a speed of not less than 80–100 kilometre per hour. To my mind, to have driven at this speed at that time of the night and under that type of weather and road condition, was clearly very dangerous to other road users.

An analysis of the above *dicta* will show that all that the judge is trying to establish is that the accused person has committed the offence of causing death by dangerous driving. He approaches that conclusion, first of all, by laying down the legal principle that "the test of dangerous driving must be objective" and then he illustrates what he means by "objective" by saying that it is what a reasonable onlooker thinks of the accused person's manner and circumstances of driving.

Secondly, the learned judge constructs from observable facts another legal principle out of the busy nature of the road, its congestion, the fact that driving took place in the night when visibility was poor and the fact that there was rain that day which made the road wet and slippery. This legal principle is that the circumstances were such that an extra duty of care was cast upon the accused person.

A third point of interest is that, despite the other circumstances which ought to have induced caution, the accused was driving at "a terrific speed" and left the road and went on to the sand verge and there knocked down a parked motor-cycle and, passing on, knocked down the deceased who stood much farther away and dragged him on the ground for more than sixty feet before hitting an electric pole and coming to a stop. The rule on this state of facts is that the accused was clearly guilty of negligence and dangerous driving.

Now each of these three propositions of law is a link in the chain of the learned judge's reasoning. None of them stands apart. None deals with extraneous considerations. Each is designed to lead ultimately to a finding in law that the accused has committed the offence of negligence and dangerous driving resulting in death. The concluding sentence shows that this is so. It says:

> To my mind, to have driven at that speed at that time of the night and under that type of weather and road condition, was clearly dangerous to other road users.

Now the point we are trying to make must be clearly understood. Each of the above propositions of law is what is properly called a *dictum*—an authoritative saving. Although each is looked upon as part of a chain,it is authoritative for what it actually decides. To that extent it is a *ratio* in its own right. It is wrong, absolutely wrong, to hold, therefore, that a *dictum* is only persuasive and not binding. It is only an *obiter dictum*—an "incidental remark or statement" (according to *Oxford Advanced Learner's Dictionary of Current English)*– that possesses this disability.

In the light of the situation as explained above, can anyone seriously contend that a *dictum* is not binding? A *dictum* as a statement of law married to the facts and circumstances of the case and the point in issue and pronounced after due deliberation is a *ratio* and is binding in respect of the point it has taken; and this is so notwithstanding the fact that it is part of a larger *ratio* which ultimately settles the issue in controversy between the parties.

But with an *obiter dictum* the position is different. It is a mere "aside." It has no direct relationship with the facts in issue and is no part of the reasoning leading up to the larger *ratio*. In so far as the controversy is concerned it contributes nothing to its solution. The meticulous argument and care in formulation which normally attend a *dictum* are not extended to it. For this reason it is not binding.

As long as the distinction between the two concepts is clearly observed, so long will the interchangeable use of the terms be avoided. But so long as judges and lawyers continue to confuse one with the other, to that extent will the differences between these two essentially distinguishable concepts remain blurred. And the consequences are serious. The general slight on *obiter dicta* also extends to *dicta* which share none of the infirmities for which *obiter dicta* are noted.[105]

It remains to add that in the traditional textbooks on jurisprudence this distinction does not appear to be recognised. Thus Allen[106] regards both as meaning the same thing—"*obiter dicta,* or simply *dicta*"—and continues:

> . . . it is extremely difficult to establish any standard of their relative weight.

Professor Paton[107] and Professor Lloyd[108] are clear in their minds about the disabilities of *obiter dicta*, but they do not distinguish this expression from its counterpart *dicta*, and do not appear to mention the latter at all. To Dias and Hughes, *dicta* and *obiter dicta* are synonymous,[109] they are also the same to Salmond.[110]

As we have shown, it is this confusing use of the terms that makes it impossible for us to recognise that a distinction exists and that a *dictum* is a *ratio* in its own right while an *obiter dictum* is not. To illustrate the kind of confusion we are complaining about we will quote Dias and Hughes:[111]

> In any case, dicta are frequently taken up by a subsequent court and followed as the correct expression of the law. This is especially so where they were careful and deliberate pronouncements upon a point of law which was raised and fully argued, even if that point was not essential for the decision of the earlier case.

We have no quarrel with the first sentence. It epitomises the sort of reception that *dicta,* properly so called, should receive. But we join issue on the second. It is difficult to imagine which court will

[105] Earlier use of the terms obiter dicta and dicta in this chapter and elsewhere in this treatise followed the popular usage which does not discriminate between them. In this chapter it is thought wise to show the differences so that the doctrine of precedent can benefit and so that statements of law which are relevant and lead up to the central issue may no longer be squelched as "mere dicta" or "obiter dicta."

[106] *Law in the Making*, 7th edition, p. 260.

[107] *A Textbook of Jurisprudence*, 3rd edition, pp. 180–184.

[108] *Introduction to Jurisprudence*, 2nd edition, pp. 373–378.

[109] *Jurisprudence*, 1957, p. 81.

[110] *Jurisprudence*, 11th edition, p. 166.

[111] *Ibid.*

permit a point of law that is "not essential for the decision" of a case to be "raised and fully argued." Would that not be sheer waste of time and an attempt to becloud the issues before the court? Of what jurisprudential value would a precedent created in that exercise be?

To Dr. Allen our answer is that it is not really difficult to establish any standard of the relative weight of *obiter dicta* and *dicta* so long as we appreciate the differences between the two concepts. It is *obiter dictum* that should have its persuasive efficacy determined by factors such as the eminence of the judge, the authority of the court and its proximity to, or remoteness from, the central issue. A *dictum* should be binding.

11

THE ATTITUDE OF LATER COURTS TO THE PRECEDENT DECISION

The attitude which later courts adopt towards a precedent determines the acceptability or otherwise of that precedent. It has been remarked earlier that courts do not concede to one another the right to treat rules of law as they like; later courts have a say in their promulgation. The mode of treatment to which earlier decisions are subjected by subsequent courts indicates the extent to which they are accepted or not accepted as rules of law.

1. Affirmation or Reversal

The first attitude is represented by affirmation or reversal. This occurs when a case is taken from a lower court to a higher court on appeal. The latter either affirms or reverses the decision.[1] When the decision is affirmed this indicates approval of the lower court's *ratio*. The decision now acquires greater authority, being a decision of the appellate court by adoption. When it is reversed, the authority of the decision is destroyed, the findings of fact and conclusions of law are wiped away and are replaced by the appellate decision.[2] Reversal indicates that the law was either wrongly applied or wrongly propounded and that it ought not to be allowed to subsist.

So far as affirmation or reversal is predicated on the grounds on which the decision was based in the court below there is no problem about the status of the decision as affirmed or reversed. Difficulties arise when the decision is affirmed or reversed on a ground different from that on which the lower court rested it. In England it has been held that a decision which was affirmed by the House of Lords on a

[1] Cases in which no decision is taken because of a tie are now rare because of the practice of appellate courts sitting with odd numbers of judges.

[2] *Nwokeleke v. Onicha* (1955–56) W.R.N.L.R. 87.

different point from that on which the Court of Appeal based it was of no authority.[3] But a decision tending the other way concerned the binding effect of a reversed judgment, and in *Curtis Moffat, Ltd. v. Wheeler*[4] it was held that a Court of Appeal decision which was reversed on a different ground by the House of Lords and whose *ratio* was even doubted by a Law Lord remained fully binding.

A similar situation has arisen in Nigeria. In *Odiase v. Agho*[5] the Supreme Court recognised the principle that a High Court decision remained an authority for what it decided and could even be cited before the Supreme Court even though it was reversed on some other point. In that case the Supreme Court said:

> Normally if there is an appeal against a judgment on one point then the appeal stands or falls on that one point. When we give judgment on that point we have not pronounced on points not argued and, though they rest as part of the decision of the High Court they remain open to argument as points of law in any other future appeal before us unfettered by any pronouncement of this court as to their validity. It is moreover important to appreciate this as it is only the *ratio decidendi* of a decision of this Court that binds lower courts.

It is salutary that in Nigeria the highest court of the land has made a pronouncement which avoids the confusion that has arisen in England as we saw above. A situation would be intolerable in which a decision reversed only on one point were to lose its authority on the other points on which it was rested. Salmond is, however, of the view that "a decision either affirmed or reversed on another point is deprived of any absolute binding force it might otherwise have had; but it remains an authority which may be followed by a court that thinks the particular point to have been rightly decided."[6]

It is clear from this that Salmond is saying that the authority of that decision does not go beyond the persuasive. This may be true

[3] *Hack v. London Provident Society* (1883) 23 Ch. 102, 112.
[4] (1929) 2 Ch. 224, 234.
[5] (1972) 1 All N.L.R. 170, 176.
[6] *Jurisprudence*, 11th edition, p. 203.

with regard to courts of co-ordinate or higher jurisdiction, but it is doubtful if his thesis applies to courts of inferior jurisdiction. We submit that it does not and that such courts are fully bound by the decision on the points unreversed.[7]

The position is different if the decision is affirmed "for reasons differing from those of the learned trial judge" and the reasons were examined by the appellate court and rejected.[8] In that event the decision of the High Court is no longer an authority on those points, but is replaced by the appellate decision. But where attack has been levelled against some grounds of the lower court's decision and not against others those not attacked are deemed to be correct and "they stand for the purposes of the judgment of the High Court" [9]

Another interesting problem arises when an appeal is allowed in part. When the appeal is against the whole of the judgment and some grounds succeed and the others fail, what is the relative status of the decision allowing part of the appeal and the decision dismissing the rest? Are both decisions to be regarded as decisions of the appeal court so that the lower court is counted out, or is there a differential treatment between both so that it is only the decision allowing part of the appeal that acquires the authority of the appellate court while that dismissing the rest is no more than a recognition of the lower court's authority and does not imprint it with authority of its own?

There is no problem as far as the decision allowing part of the appeal is concerned. That decision has reversed the lower court and stepped into the shoes of the latter's decision.[10] But the position is not so clear when we come to the part dismissing the appeal. This point would not normally arise but for the fact that appellate courts when making an order of dismissal do not follow a consistent practice. Sometimes we hear of dismissal *simpliciter*. At other times we hear of dismissal of the appeal and affirmation of the judgment of the lower court.

[7] For this reason we submit that *Curtis Moffat Ltd. v. Wheeler* is preferable to *Hack v. London Provident Society* (*supra*).

[8] *Makanjuola v. Khalil* (1958) W.R.N.L.R. 82, 84.

[9] *Odiase v. Agho (supra)*, p. 177.

[10] See *Nwokeleke v. Onicha* (1955–56) W.R.N.L.R. 87 already referred to.

What are the respective effects of these orders? When an appeal is dismissed there is no doubt that the decision of the lower court is left to stand.[11] When it is dismissed and the decision of the lower court affirmed it would appear that the appellate court also adopts the stand of the lower court and makes the decision of the latter its own decision by adoption. But what real difference exists between this and a dismissal *simpliciter?* It would appear that there is none and that when an appeal is dismissed the appellate court thereby implies that it has sanctioned the law laid down by the lower court unless the dismissal is on grounds which do not relate to the merits of the case. In other words, both are decisions of the appellate court and invested with its authority. But where the lower court's judgment has been fully reported there is nothing to prevent a future court from relying on that part of its decision that is unreversed. But that is law at the level of the lower court. The higher court's decision is preferable for obvious reasons.

The next point to consider is the status of the lower court's *dicta* in a judgment that has been reversed. It is possible for a decision to be reversed on appeal and yet the *dicta* employed by the trial judge as a step in his reasoning remain good for purposes of application in a later case.[12] But the *dicta* as *dicta* are not binding;[13] they are only prayed in aid when found to provide sufficient guidance for a solution of the problem in issue.[14]

In conclusion, we submit that when a judgment is affirmed or reversed as a whole, the court of appeal thereby shows affirmatively that the decision is right or wrong in its opinion. When it is affirmed or reversed on some other ground the implication is that in the case of affirmation there is a simpler and clearer point on which the decision ought to have been predicated; and in the case of a reversal there is an infirmity which affects the decision, which the trial court did not perceive. In both cases—affirmation and reversal—the appellate court is deemed to be of the opinion that the grounds upon

[11] See *Matthew v. The State* (1972) 10 S.C. 95, 100; *Ubom v. The State* (1972) 10 S.C. 101. In each of these cases the Supreme Court dismissed the appeal after finding that the appellants were rightly convicted of murder.

[12] *A.-G. v. Palm Line Ltd.* (1958) 3 F.S.C. 64, 65–66.

[13] *Motayo v. C.O.P.* (1950) 13 W.A.C.A. 114, 116.

[14] *Dede v. United Arab Airlines* (1969) 1 N.M.L.R. 75, 76. See Chapter 8 for a full discussion of this doctrine.

which the decision was based are not objectionable in any way, unless a contrary intention appears.

2. Overruling

When a decision is overruled this indicates that in the opinion of the overruling court the decision has never been good law; and the purpose of overruling is to wipe out the errant decision and to replace it with the decision of the overruling court. Overruling takes place when a case is considered as an authority in another case and the later court declares that the law embodied in it is bad law and so refuses to follow it or expressly declares that it is overruled. A case that is overruled has no authority whatsoever.

A case is not overruled for fun. It is overruled only because it is wrong, provided that it has not, "by the lapse of time or otherwise, ... acquired such added authority as to give it a title to permanent recognition notwithstanding the vices of its origin."[15] But in *West Ham Union v. Edmonton Union*,[16] Lord Loreburn held that where decisions "are plainly wrong, and especially where the subsequent course of judicial decisions has disclosed weakness in the reasoning on which they were based, and practical injustice" would result, there is a duty to overrule tnem.

The expedient of overruling, therefore, is not resorted to merely because a decision is wrong, but because it is so wrong that it subjects the subjects of the realm to a system of injustice and hardship. The problem is compounded in a legal system like England and Nigeria in which the doctrine of *stare decisis* compels later courts to follow precedent decisions with the result that whatever injustice and hardship the decision imposes tend to perpetuate themselves.

Elementary prudence, therefore, demands that such decisions should be wiped off the slate to make room for others that are more convenient and justice-oriented. The citizens should not be compelled to act irrationally or suffer unnecessary inconvenience simply because a judicial decision has so ordained.

The Supreme Court in Nigeria has overruled previous decisions both of its own and of its predecessors on various grounds and for

[15] Salmond, *Jurisprudence*, 11th edition, p. 220.
[16] (1908) A.C. 1, 4.

different purposes. When a statute has been wrongly interpreted a decision based on the wrong interpretation has been rejected and overruled. Thus in *Anya v. The State*[17] the Supreme Court disagreed with the interpretation placed on section 288 of the Criminal Procedure Ordinance by the West African Court of Appeal and observed:

> We must dissent from the use made of section 288 in Oladimeji v. The King, that decision must be overruled. The proper course in our view is to consider the effect of failure to comply with section 287(1) (a) without importing into it any implication from section 288.

In the above case the question was whether failure to ask an accused person if he had any witness to call rendered the trial null and void as was decided in *Oladimeji v. The King*[18] or only voidable as was decided in *Atunde v. C.O.P.*[19] Following the latter case, the Supreme Court decided that:

> the effect of such failure must depend on the circumstances of the particular case, and the appellate court is at liberty to allow the appeal and order an acquittal or retrial or dismiss the appeal if it considers that no substantial miscarriage of justice has occurred.

In the result the court dismissed the appeal and affirmed the convictions and sentences. This decision meets one of the objections to the rule in *R. v. Taylor*[20] which the West African Court of Appeal adopted for Nigeria in *Motayo v. C.O.P.*[21] The objection is that the rule talks of reconsidering a decision in which a person has been wrongly convicted without also reconsidering one in which he has been wrongly acquitted.[22] Assuming a power to overrule in these circumstances is really salutary since an accused person who is clearly guilty ought not to be acquitted on such technical grounds and since the public has an interest in the punishment of offenders.

[17] (1965) N.M.L.R. 62, 65.
[18] (1951) 13 W.A.C.A. 275.
[19] (1952) 14 W.A.C.A. 171.
[20] (1950) 2 K.B. 368.
[21] (1950) 13 W.A.C.A. 114.
[22] See Ezejiofor, "Stare Decisis in the Nigerian Courts" (1972) 6 Nigerian Law Journals 47, 59.

Johnson v. Lawanson[23] was another case in which a wrong construction was placed on section 129 of the Evidence Act and was followed in a line of subsequent cases. The Supreme Court overruled all of them and added:

> They are obviously steering a course which may be at present uneventful but which ultimately, when pursued to the logical conclusion, would be disastrous and an owner of property would find himself one day confronted with a deed of sale prepared by a stranger some twenty years back on his property and would be obliged to defend his title in the face of such a deed stored away all the time and which may well prove to be bogus.

Here the overruling was done in order to prevent the unpleasant social consequences that would emerge and which have actually started to emerge from perpetuation of bad law.

Where a decision in a criminal case has wrongly affected the liberty of a subject a later court of co-ordinate jurisdiction can overrule it. This is what happened in *Motayo v. C.O.P*[24] when the West African Court of Appeal which normally considered itself bound by its own decisions[25] decided to follow the English Court of Criminal Appeal and reconsider its previous decisions where the liberty of a subject was concerned. This attitude is commendable. Human liberty is priceless and *stare decisis* must not be allowed to stand in its way.

More sacrosanct even than liberty is life itself. In *Maizabo v. Sokoto N.A.*[26] a Native Court had power to impose a death sentence for murder under Maliki law which did not recognise provocation as a defence to the charge as is the case under English law. The Federal Supreme Court seized the opportunity to correct its earlier decision in *Tsamiya v. Bauchi N.A.*[27] in which it held that as provocation was not recognised as a defence under Maliki law it was not open for it to reduce the charge from murder to manslaughter.

[23] (1971) 1 N.M.L.R. 380, 388.
[24] (1950) 13 W.A.C.A. 114.
[25] *Osumanu v. Seidu* (1949) 12 W.A.C.A. 437.
[26] (1957) 2 F.S.C. 13, 16.
[27] (1957) N.R.N.L.R. 73.

Overruling the latter decision in the former case the Court said that *Tsamiya's case* was too wide and required qualification. Then it concluded:

> The position, therefore, as we see it is this. While a Native Court may and indeed must ignore the provisions of the Criminal Code in trying a case under native law and custom, it must not impose a punishment in excess of the maximum punishment permitted for that act or omission under the Criminal Code or other enactment.

Overruling is further justified when the effect of the overruled decision is to disinherit claimants to an intestate estate where their personal law—the law of the domicile—does confer a positive benefit upon them and does not permit disinheritance. It is for this reason that *In re Adadevoh*[28] overruled *In re Williams*[29] which denied such right of inheritance. Verity, C. J., remarked that the court was "entitled to examine the question as though there were no local authority binding upon it . . . with a desire to give effect to common sense and decency . . ."

Sometimes a decision of higher authority may overrule the decision of a subordinate court without the attention of the higher court being drawn to this fact. When a higher court decides a case in a way inconsistent with a subordinate decision but without the latter being brought to the notice of the higher court, the higher authority is deemed to have overruled the lower court's decision by implication.

Some examples of implied overruling can be found in our law. In *Uka v. Insp. General of Police*,[30] the question of ascertaining the authenticity of a statement made by accused persons arose for consideration. Kassim, Ag. P.J., said:

> The safest thing to do, therefore, is to get the statement of each of the accused persons read to him in Ibo and ask him whether or not he made the statement. The fact that the statement was read to him and the admission or denial of it in whole or in part should be recorded as a matter of the usual caution with which a

[28] (1951) 13 W.A.C.A. 304, 309.
[29] (1941) 7 W.A.C.A. 156.
[30] (1962) 6 E.N.L.R. 7, 8.

> criminal trial should be conducted and in order that it may appear that justice has been done.

A later decision is *The Queen v. Mboho*[31] which condemned the idea of an accused person being asked to make any statement while in the dock except in given circumstances. In that case the Supreme Court commented:

> As to the question put by the learned trial Judge to the accused. and the conclusion reached by the Judge as a result of the answer given, we wish to point out that an accused person even if represented by counsel, should not, while the case for the prosecution is in progress, be asked or required by the Court to make statements which normally should be made in the witness box on oath under S. 287 (1) (a) (ii), or from the dock under 287 (1) (a) (i) of the Criminal Procedure Act. Confirmation of a confessional statement is evidence which should be led in defence and not extracted in the manner in which it has, in the case on appeal.

It clearly appears from the quoted remarks in both cases that the approaches of the two courts were contradictory. The latter disapproves of the very practice which the former has advised. *The Queen v.. Mboho*, being a higher authority, has, therefore, impliedly overruled *Uka v. Insp.-General of Police.*.

A different form of implied overruling is observable in *Okoronkwo v. Insp.-General of Police*[32] That is a case in which the Federal Supreme Court described the lower court's construction of the word "enlarge" which appeared in a statute as "too narrow" without going further to say whether that decision is overruled or not.

When a case is expressly overruled it becomes clear at once that the overruled case has lost its authority. But the same cannot be said of a decision that is impliedly overruled. In fact, the question of whether a particular case has been overruled by implication by a subsequent higher authority may be a matter of controversy since no two persons may agree with the same interpretation [33]

[31] (1964) N.M.L.R. 49, 52.
[32] (1957) 2 F.S.C. 9.
[33] Goodhart, "Precedent in the Court Appeal" (1945-47) 9 C.L.J. 349, 358.

We now come to look at the dangers inherent in overruling settled authorities. Every judicial decision, as we have seen, is law for all the nation. On the basis of it, the subjects may enter into transactions and acquire property in the expectation that the law will continue as at present:

> Justice may therefore imperatively require that the decision, though founded in error, shall stand inviolate none the less. Communis error facit jus.[34]

It is for the above reason that courts are loathe to overrule decisions that have stood for many years without protest and acquired authority more and more with every adherence to their *rationes*. But Dias and Hughes say:[35]

> It is impossible to lay down any rules as to what guides and influences courts in the overruling of earlier authorities. The competing claims which courts must bear in mind are, on the one hand, the undesirability of too frequently overruling settled authorities which might disturb the conventional facade of the certainty of the law, and, on the other hand, the necessity for expunging decisions which are forcing the law into unhappy or unjust trends.

In Nigeria, the West African Court of Appeal and the Supreme Court have had occasion to balance one interest against the other before deciding to overrule. In *re Adadevoh*[36] the question was whether it was in the interest of justice that a decision that denied to children legitimate by the law of the domicile the right to inherit the intestate estate of their father should be maintained or overruled. The West African Court of Appeal decided in favour of overruling it because that course was dictated by "common sense and decency." In delivering the judgment of the court, Verity, C.J., observed:

> I am fully alive to the fact that grave inconvenience may arise from a judgment of this Court in such a matter which reverses a view of the law which has been held for upwards of ten years, but when the Court is faced with the alternative of perpetuating

[34] Salmond, *Jurisprudence*, 11th edition, p. 217.
[35] *Jurisprudence*, 1957, p. 89.
[36] (1951) 13 W.A.C.A. 304, 310.

> what it is satisfied is an erroneous decision which was reached per incuriam and will, if it be followed, inflict hardship and injustice upon generations in the future or of causing temporary disturbance of rights acquired under such a decision, I do not think we should hesitate to declare the law as we find it.

The Supreme Court in 1971 had occasion to overrule a line of decisions that had stood for twelve years because with another decision which went the other way "they have created a conflict of such a serious nature as to confuse practitioners and introduce a serious element of uncertainty into our law.[37] It also adopted the words of Verity, C.J., in *re Adadevoh* regretting the resolve to overrule a decision of such authority and long standing but consoled itself with the fact that this course was necessary to check possible large-scale fraud.

From the foregoing it is clear that the power to overrule is very sparingly exercised and that when it is exercised it is after the inconveniences of overruling have been balanced against the need for change. But however justifiable the change is, it cannot be denied that objections to it are weighty.

> Particularly is this so where a decision by the court upon principles of law or the construction of a statute will form the basis of dealings with respect to property, of contractual obligations, or, if the decision deals with the penal law, of future acts and conduct.[38]

To obviate such unpleasant consequences a new technique of overruling has been suggested.[39] This is the technique of prospective overruling. Proponents of this device suggest that courts should assume the power to overrule cases only for the future so that only future conducts, acts and transactions would be affected and not their antecedent counterparts as is the case with the present system.

Prospective overruling unquestionably has advantages. It leaves undisturbed the doctrine as settled by the overruled decision, and acts done, contracts entered into and property acquired in reliance

[37] *Johnson v. Lawanson* (1971) 1 N.M.L.R. 380, 387–388.

[38] Freeman, "The Protection Afforded Against The Retroactive Operation Of An Overruling Decision" (1918) 18 Columbia Law Review, 230, 231.

[39] See Freeman, *ibid.*; Dias, *Jurisprudence*, 3rd edition, p. 81.

upon the law as constituted before the overruling decision, retain their sanctity and protection under that law. Where the overruled decision settled a question of criminal law and exonerated from criminal responsibility prospective overruling will leave the position intact.

But it certainly has some disadvantages. The most glaring among them is the fact that the party seeking overruling does not stand to benefit from the fruit of his labour, and, this being so, he will find no incentive and encouragement in incurring the expenses and making the attempt. But incentive and encouragement can be found in a technique which permits the overruling decision to be effective not only for the future but also for the instant case. But the danger here is that if the overruled decision was a penal one which exempted from penal responsibility, a party to the overruling case would be made to suffer penal consequences for an act done under a legal regime in which such acts did not attract criminal responsibility.

The device of prospective overruling would be too revolutionary a doctrine to be invoked without statutory sanction. Our suggestion, therefore, is that, if the practice is worth invocation, legislation should be promulgated to regulate it. Among other things, there should be a special provision against the overruling case imposing penal responsibility on a party to it which the overruled case did not impose.[40]

One question about overruling has been reserved till last. That is the question of the court that has the power to overrule. One High Court judge cannot overrule another.[41] Overruling is an act of superior jurisdiction.[42] Only a superior court can overrule an inferior court; the converse is not true.

It is the practice of appellate courts to talk of overruling their own decisions and those of courts of co-ordinate jurisdiction. When one of their precedents is attacked, the practice is to empanel a full court to consider the precedent and, if necessary, overrule it.

[40] The position in Nigeria is not, however, affected because our Criminal Law is codified.

[41] *Sarkis v. Sarkis* (1923) 3 N.L.R. 133.

[42] Salmond, *Jurisprudence*, 11th edition, pp. 167, 199.

A full court of the Divisional Court was called to consider a previous decision of a division of that court in *Younghusband v. Luftig.*[43] The decision in *R. v. Taylor*[44] which overruled a previous decision of the Court of Criminal Appeal in *R. v. Treanor*[45] was reached bv a full court of seven judges. In *Young v. Bristol Aeroplane Co. Ltd.*[46] a full Court of Appeal considered two of its previous decisions that were being attacked and refused to overrule them.[47]

But in *Younghusband v. Luftig*, supra, Lord Goddard stated that "a Divisional Court of five judges has no greater powers than one of three or even two. This court is bound by its own decisions as is the Court of Appeal, whatever the number of judges that may constitute it." And in *Young v. Bristol Aeroplane Co.*,[48] Lord Greene, M.R. remarked:

> But we can find no warrant for the argument that what is conveniently but inaccurately called the Full Court has any greater power in this respect than a division of the court consisting of three members only.

In view of the above *dicta* it is questionable why a full court is necessary when a precedent has to be reconsidered. In his comments upon *Lord Goddard's dictum* in *Younghusband v. Luftig*, Stone said:

> the learned Lord Chief Justice did not enlarge upon the reasons why re-argument should be desirable before a full court which has no greater powers than any of its divisions.[49]

In the light of the foregoing it is clear that the word "overrule" is not a proper word to use; a better nomenclature would be "dissent" which implies a withdrawal of consent from, or a withholdment of consent to, the previous decision.

Perhaps the intention is not to bring the greater power of the full court to bear upon the precedent to be reconsidered, but to

[43] (1949) 2 K.B. 354, 360; (1949) 2 A.E.R. 72, 75.
[44] (1950) 2 K.B. 368.
[45] (1939) 1 A.E.R. 330.
[46] (1944) 2 A.E.R. 293.
[47] The decisions were *Perkins v. Stevenson* (1939) 3 A.E.R. 697; (1940) 1 K.B. 56; *Selwood v. Towneley Coal and Fireclay Co. Ltd.* (1940) 1 K.B. 180; (1939) 4 A.E.R. 34.
[48] (1944) 2 A.E.R. 293, 295.
[49] "Stare Decisis in the Divisional Court" (1951) 14 W.L.R. 219, 222.

obtain a broad-based opinion of all the judges of the court and to hold them bound to their opinion. If they, on second thoughts, decide to depart from the previous decision they are not thereby overruling it as overruling is an act of superior jurisdiction. They are merely disapproving that decision and holding that it no longer represents the law. As a learned writer puts it, such a decision "has only the status of a conflicting precedent when it refused to follow an earlier decision."[50]

In Nigeria, the practice of the Supreme Court and its predecessors follow the English practice which is to reconsider previous decisions in a full court. The so-called full court usually consists of five judges. But by statute the "court shall be duly constituted if it consists of three judges."[51] In *Motayo v. C.O.P.*[52] the West African Court of Appeal stated that although in local conditions it would be impracticable to hold a court of more than five judges, the practice would be that no previous decision of the court would "be reviewed save by a full court constituted of that number." In *Anya v. The State*[53] the case of *Oladimeji v. The King*[54] was overruled by a full court of five. A full court also overruled in *Johnson v. Lawanson*[55] a line of cases starting from the Privy Council case of *Maurice Goualin Ltd. v. Aminu.*[56]

But beyond this it does not appear that a consistent principle has been followed. Thus in *re Adadevoh* the decision in *re Williams*[58] was overruled by the West African Court of Appeal sitting with three judges. In *Maizabo v. Sokoto N.A.*[59] the Federal Supreme Court reconsidered and overruled its previous decisions in *Tsamiya v. Bauchi N.A.*[60] in a court of three.

[50] Winder, "Divisional Court Precedents" (1946) 9 M.L.R. 254, 264.
[51] Federal Supreme Court Ordinance No. 12 of 1960 section 9: Supreme Court of Nigeria Act 1960 section 9.
[52] (1950) 13 W.A.C.A. 114, 116.
[53] (1965) N.M.L.R. 62.
[54] (1951) 13 W.A.C.A. 275.
[55] (1971) 1 N.M.L.R. 380.
[56] Privy Council Appeal No. 17 of 1957.
[57] (1951) 13 W.A.C.A. 304.
[58] (1941) 7 W.A.C.A. 156.
[59] (1957) 2 F.S.C. 13.
[60] (1957) N.R.N.L.R. 73.

Later courts have had no occasion to quarrel with this change of practice. It would, therefore, appear that the so-called full court is not necessary before a break is made with a previous decision. This seems to vindicate the view that, since a full court has no greater powers than an ordinary division of the court, calling a full court is unnecessary. This is especially so since a full court has no statutory footing. It is only a convenient mode of ascertaining the views of as many judges of the court as possible with reference to the precedent which is under attack.

3 Distinguishing

A later court may distinguish a precedent cited to it as an authority to be followed in the case before it. The distinction takes the form that either the facts in both cases are different or that the principle in the precedent case is too wide. To quote Dias and Hughes:

> The process of distinguishing is that in which a court rejects an earlier case as an authority, either on the ground that the facts of the earlier case may be differentiated from the facts of the case in hand; or that the ruling of law in it is too wide.[61]

When a later court considers that the rule of law in a precedent is too wide and therefore incapable of application to the case in hand this is restrictive distinguishing..[62] It is called "restrictive" because the court called upon to apply it does not apply it as it finds it, but cuts it down to its own facts "by treating as material to the earlier decision some fact, present in the earlier case, which the earlier court regarded as immaterial".[63]

The purpose of restrictive distinguishing is to reshape the *ratio* of the case by cutting it down to suit its own facts and then applying it to the case in hand. In this way the case becomes a proper and acceptable authority in the hands of the court applying the pruning knife and is ready to be followed by any subsequent court that

[61] *Jurisprudence*, 1957, pp. 86–87.

[62] See Williams, *Learning the Law*, 5th edition, pp. 70–73 for a learned discussion of this question.

[63] *Ibid.*, p. 71.

agrees with the case as pruned. The power of restrictive distinguishing is of great importance in that it enables the courts "to preserve the flexibility of the law"[64] and prevent it from being put into a straight jacket.[65]

The power of restrictive distinguishing is exercised by a court over a decision of co-ordinate or inferior rank. In Nigeria there is no known instance of a High Court judge restrictively distinguishing the decision of a higher court, but criticisms which finally end in following the higher precedent are abundant,[66] and there is at least one instance in which a High Court judge has declared the decision of a higher court *per incuriam.*[67]

It is doubtful whether the decision of a lower court which restrictively distinguishes a higher authority will command enough respect to be followed. This is so because judges stand on different levels of vision and boldness, and while some may perceive the point and others not, not many judges will have the courage to lay down a rule that cuts down a Supreme Court decision.[68]

Another aspect of distinguishing relates to the facts. Professor Williams[69] calls this "non-restrictive distinguishing" and it "occurs where a court accepts the expressed *ratio decidendi* of the earlier case, and does not seek to curtail it, but finds that the case before it does not fall within this *ratio decidendi* because of some material difference of facts."

We illustrate the latter class of distinguishing with the case of *Akerele v. Atunrase.*[70] in that case the Supreme Court said:

> If the facts of this case fall within the principle of Abogunde's case we do not doubt that the decision must be followed in this case. We are clearly of the view, however, that the facts of this case do not fall within that principle.

[64] Salmond, *Jurisprudence*, 11th edition, p. 224.

[65] For examples of restrictive distinguishing see Chapter 10 under the heading "Ratio to Accord with Facts."

[66] *Federal Administrator-General v. Adeshola* (1960) W.N.L.R. 53; *Salako v. Salako* (1965) L.L.R. 136 are examples.

[67] *Tsamiya v. Bauchi N.A.* (1957) N.R.N.L.R. 73.

[68] But see *Chime v. Elikwu* (1965) N.M.L.R. 71, where Idigbe, Ag. C.J., Mid-Western Nigeria, as he then was, said that a WACA's statement regarding the decision of a differently constituted WACA as obiter was not obiter.

[69] *Learning the Law*, 5th edition, p. 70.

[70] (1969) 1 All N.L.R. 201, 209.

In other words, cases are alike and indistinguishable when their facts will support the same principle of law, not otherwise.

It is the practice to give reasons to show that a case whose *ratio* is being cited as a precedent is distinguishable from the case in hand. Thus in *Akpobasa v. The State*[71] the Supreme Court found that when the Federal Supreme Court in *R. v. Aliechem*[72] distinguished *Rex v. Aniogo*[73] it did not give any reasons and so proceeded to do so when counsel for the appellant urged the court to find a conflict between *R. v. Aliechem*, on the principle of which the trial judge convicted the appellant and *Aniogo's case*, on the principle of which his client would have a conviction of manslaughter substituted for that of murder. Giving reasons to show that there was no conflict the Supreme Court said:

> In our view that decision was not in conflict, as was submitted to us, either with *Aniogo's* case (supra) or *Obot's* case (supra) for the reasons that we have given and we think that the learned trial judge here was right to follow the principle enunciated in *Aliechem's* case (supra).

The practice of giving reasons for distinguishing one case from another serves to protect the doctrine of precedent from being an arid and inarticulate doctrine. It enables the profession and future courts to see why one case is decided differently from another, and if the distinction in fact exists it helps to present case-law as a self-consistent body of legal doctrine and not as an artificial and unscientific device of judges.

The practice is particularly valuable when a lower court happens to disagree with the *ratio* of a higher court whose decision is binding on it. Thus, in *Board of Customs and Excise v. Bolarinwa*,[74] Thompson, J., rebuking a Chief Magistrate for refusing to follow a High Court decision on the grounds that the facts in the High Court case were different from those before him, commented:

> It is not sufficient to say that the facts are different. A Magistrate who does not intend to apply a decision of the High Court must

[71] (1969) 1 All N.L.R. 104, 111.
[72] (1956) 1 F.S.C. 64.
[73] (1943) 9 W.A.C.A. 62.
[74] (1968) N.M.L.R. 350, 352.

> state (1) the Ratio decidendi of that decision (2) the facts proved in that decision and (3) show by Judicial reasoning in the body of the Judgment, in what manner the High Court decision is different from the case before him.

Such a rebuke is justified if the doctrine of *stare decisis* is to work with dignity and effect.

Sometimes, however, judges indulge in what Salmond calls "spurious distinguishing."[75] This arises when a judge who tries to avoid an obnoxious precedent differentiates if from the case in hand on grounds which scarcely exist. Resort to illogical distinction is not the answer. When a judge finds himself confronted with a decision he considers wrong there are two courses open to him. If the precedent is of co-ordinate rank he can refuse to follow it and say so expressly and give reasons. If it is a higher authority he can criticise it on clear grounds and then follow it. But to seek to distinguish it when it is indistinguishable is to complicate the law.[76]

Lastly, we may mention that cases are not only distinguished because of material differences of facts. The facts may be similar and yet the application of the principle of the first case may become inapposite in the other. This is due to the influence of an existing law over the facts of the later case.

In *The Queen v. Governor, Eastern Nigeria, Ex parte Warri*[77] a Western Nigeria decision was invoked before the Eastern Nigeria High Court as an authority that the court has jurisdiction to quash the recognition of a chief by a Governor in certiorari proceedings. Savage, J., refusing the application, observed:

> The learned Counsel for the applicants referred me to 1959 Western Region Law Report, page 44, The Queen v. The Governor, Western Region ex parte Alasan Babatunde, Ajaguna 11 of Ikare, to show that even if the Law takes away the civil jurisdiction of the Court to hear chieftaincy matters, the Court can still hear application for an order of Certiorari. In the case referred to, the Law of 1957 does not expressly exclude Certiorari. That was why the Court decided that it has jurisdiction to hear

[75] *Jurisprudence*, 11th edition, p. 180.

[76] Compare *Edet v. Esien* (1932) 71 N.L.R. 47 with *Nwaribe v. President, Orlu District Court* (1964) 8 E.N.L.R. 24.

[77] (1960) 4 E.N.L.R. 98, 100.

> the application. In this application before me section 7 of the Recognition of Chiefs Law, 1960, has expressly excluded application for an order of Certiorari. The Western Region decision referred to by learned Counsel for the applicants does not apply to this case.

The influence of an existing law prevented the English case of *Mary Kingston*[78] from being followed in the case of *Gokpa v. I. -G. of Police*[79] even though the material facts were similar. In the latter case, Mbanefo, C.J., remarked:

> Appellant's Counsel has asked the court to allow the appeal and acquit and discharge the appellant. For this submission he relies on Kingston. **Mary Kingston is an English case and the** court of Criminal Appeal had not at that time (1948) the power to order a new trial. Humphreys J. giving the judgment of the court said:
>
>> If that court had the power which the court times out of number has stated that it ought to have, namely, that of ordering a new trial . . . there is no question that this case is one which would cry out for a new trial.
>
> The High Court under the High Court Law section 38(1) (d) has the power to order a new trial and I am of the view that this is a case where such a power should be used without prejudice to the appellant.

The moral to be drawn from the above examples is this. Care should be taken when a precedent emanating from one legal system is being invoked in another. Every judicial precedent is the product of its environment and the pre-existing law of that environment gives it the colour and texture that makes transplant impossible.

4. Refusal to Follow

A later court may refuse to follow a precedent for various reasons. The precedent case may be wrong in law,[80] or in reason.[81] Or the case might have been rightly decided at the time in the light of the

[78] 32 C.A.R. 183.
[79] (1961) 5 E.N.L.R. 12, 14.
[80] *Ngwo v. Monye* (1970) 1 All N.L.R. 91, 101.
[81] *Odigbo v. C.O.P.* (1972) 2 E.C.S.L.R. 120, 124–125.

circumstances and conditions which then existed, but when prayed in aid later it is found to be unsuitable owing to change of circumstances.[82] Again, as we have just seen, it might have been decided in a different system of law which affected its *ratio*. In each of these instances a refusal to follow may be justified, though a court cannot refuse to follow a higher authority on any of the grounds mentioned above except the last.

A court may refuse to follow a decision of an intermediate court of appeal which is in conflict with that of the ultimate court of appeal.[83] In the same way, when two decisions of co-ordinate authority are in conflict a lower court is free to think for itself and decide which of the decisions to follow.[84]

Just as in distinguishing, the practice is that when one judge refuses to follow another he must give his reasons. In *Odigbo v. C.O.P.*,[85] Oputa, J., refusing to follow Egbuna, J.'s decision in *Okonkwo v. C.O.P.*[86] said:

> I have . . . a duty to give my reasons for not agreeing with, and following a decision of a brother judge.[87]

The mere fact of giving reasons indicates an awareness by the courts that case-law must hang together as a complete and undivided whole and that a decision that fails to contribute to this scheme must be shown to be otiose and unorthodox.

Refusal to follow is an act of co-ordinate jurisdiction. An exercise of the right of refusal to follow another judge preserves for the judge exercising that right freedom of judgment when it comes to following precedents of co-ordinate rank. In that way, he reserves

[82] Dias, *Jurisprudence*, 3rd edition, pp. 77–78.

[83] See *Thomas v. Ademola* (1945) 18 N.L.R. 12, 23.

[84] *Chime v. Elikwu* (1965) N.M.L.R. 71.

[85] (1972) 2 E.C.S.L.R. 120, 125.

[86] Appeal No. 0/6CA/70, unreported.

[87] See also *Adm.-General, East Central State v. Odumukwe* (1972) 2 E.C.S.L.R. 183, 185, where Araka J., said: "But when a judge disagrees with a judgment of his brother judge it is only fair and desirable that he gives good reasons for so doing." Again, see *Awe v. Alabi* (1970) 2 All N.L.R. 16, 23, where Taylor, C.J., of Lagos State gave reasons for disagreeing with his predecessor, De Lestang, C.J.'s decision in *Abeki v. Amboro* (1961) All N.L.R. 368 on the question of the power of one magistrate to set aside the judgment of another.

for himself free discretion to decide whether the precedent that he is being called upon to apply is in accord with reason or with pre-existing law, and if he finds the opposite he can depart from it and decide the case before him according to what he considers just or legally acceptable. In doing so, the judge preserves the objectives of law as a science.

5. Following by Later Courts

Precedents are meant to be followed, and, except where the strict doctrine applies, they can only be followed when found to be sound in law and reason. The fact that a decision is followed by later courts shows clearly that it has satisfied all the conditions laid down for a good rule of case-law. According to Dias and Hughes:[88]

> If a case has been repeatedly followed, this is a factor which enhances its authority.

Winder is of the opinion that

> A series of decisions has always carried greater authority than a single decision; at one time a series of decisions was the only strictly binding authority.[89]

But as we saw earlier[90] the fact that a decision is regularly followed is not always evidence of its virtue. The decision may be technically binding upon the courts that follow it, or it may be a case of *communis error facit jus*. Again, a later court may find it convenient to follow a precedent without critical thought. In each of these cases following is not indicative of merits in the precedent that is followed. It is through channels such as this that *inelegantia juris* finds its entrance into our case-law. Nevertheless such occasional lapses have not been effective enough to mar a system that has worked so well.

6. Approval by Later Courts

The *ratio* of an earlier case may be approved by a later court. Approval is the act of a court of superior or co-ordinate rank, and

[88] *Jurisprudence*, 1957, p. 91.
[89] "Divisional Court Precedents" (1946) 9 M.L.R. 257, 272.
[90] Chapter 8.

it involves a discretion. An inferior court cannot approve a decision of superior authority because it has no such discretion since the later is technically binding on it.

Approval vests the precedent with added authority and enhances the status of the deciding judge. And where there is a consensus among courts of co-ordinate jurisdiction on a given point of law a higher court may express an "unqualified approval of their decision."[91] Approval of a decision by a higher court which works under the doctrine of *stare decisis* may work an estoppel and prevent the higher court from overruling it.[92]

7. Explaining by Later Courts

A court called upon to apply the *ratio decidendi* of a previous decision may find it necessary to explain it, and the necessity to explain arises in the following sets of circumstances.

First, one court may misinterpret the earlier *ratio* of another court, and a later court may take occasion to correct the mistake by offering an explanation of what was decided. Thus, in *Oshodi v. Imoru*[93] the West African Court of Appeal said:

> In giving that decision the learned trial judge has misunderstood and misquoted the decision of this court. This court did not decide that there has been no acquiescence but merely that the defendant had failed to prove acquiescence, a very different thing.

Secondly, when counsel misconstrues precedent that he wants the court to apply, the court may explain the principle of the decision in the light of the facts thereof and either distinguish or refuse to follow it.[94]

[91] *MacIver v. C.F.A.O.* (1917) 3 N.L.R. 18, 19.

[92] *Admiralty Commissioners v. Valverda* (1938) A.C. 173, 194, where Lord Wright said: "The House of Lords has, no doubt, power to overrule even a long-established course of decisions of the courts, provided it has not itself determined the question."

[93] (1938) 4 W.A.C.A. 74, 75.

[94] See *Orasanmi v. Idowu* (1959) 4 F.S.C. 40, where *Ogunbambi v. Abowab* 13 W.A.C.A. 222 was explained; *Ekpendu v. Erika* (1959) 4 F.S.C. 79, 80–81, where the rules in *Esan v. Faro* 12 W.A.C.A. 135 and *Agbloe v. Sappor* 12 W.A.C.A. 187 were also explained.

Thirdly, a court may, when it foresees complications in its *ratio* when viewed against the background of an antecedent decision, take steps to explain right away what it has actually decided. Thus, in *Oshodi v. Balogun*[95] Lord Maugham, delivering the advice of the Privy Council, said:

> To prevent misconception it seems desirable to state that the present decision is not based on any doubt as to the possibility of a title equivalent to a fee simple being obtained as the result of a sale of family lands with the general consent of the family. Lord Dunedin in delivering the judgment of the Board in the Dakolo case did not say anything inconsistent with this.

The device of explaining is useful on several grounds. It brings into focus the material facts of the precedent case that is sought to be applied or that has been misapplied and restates its *ratio* in a clearer and less involved manner.[96] It gives later courts an opportunity to assist in the formulation of the *ratio* of a previous precedent and so increase its marketable value. As Dias and Hughes say:

> Explaining is one of the clearest manifestations of the power of subsequent judges to reshape the *ratio decidendi* of earlier cases.[97]

8. Inconsistency with a Decision of the Same or Higher Rank

If a later court finds that the decision with which it is confronted is in conflict with another of the same or higher rank its attitude to it depends upon the following considerations. If the decision is of co-ordinate rank with the one with which it is in conflict it is not bound to follow either, but has a discretion to pick and choose

> Where authorities of equal standing are irreconcilably in conflict, a lower court has the same freedom to pick and choose between them as the schizophrenic court itself.[98]

The above statement was quoted with approval by Idigbe, Ag. C.J., of former Midwestern Nigeria (now Bendel State) in the case

[95] (1934) 4 W.A.C.A. 1, 6.
[96] *Ofunne v. Okoye* (1966) 1 All N.L.R. 94 affords an example of this.
[97] *Jurisprudence*, 1957, p. 91.
[98] Salmond, *Jurisprudence*, 11th edition, p. 207.

of *Chime v. Elikwu*[99] when he was faced with a choice between conflicting decisions of the West African Court of Appeal. Adopting the above opinion the learned Ag. Chief Justice declared:

> . . . it is my view that in applying the principle of stare decisis, where there exist two conflicting decisions of a higher tribunal, it will not be improper for a Judge of first instance to review the points of law involved in the issue and thus select or adopt which line of decision he should follow.

This approach to the question of conflict has been criticised by Ijalaye.[100] His criticism does not seem to be well founded in view of the fact that the authority which he cites in support of his view[101] was not concerned with conflicting decisions, but with a single decision which the trail judge considered to be *per incuriam*. If it is the practice in England for a lower court to choose between conflicting decisions of a higher rank it is submitted that courts in Nigeria are entitled to the same privilege since our High Court Laws provide for adoption of English practice and procedure on matters on which local statutes are silent.[102]

But what happens when the conflicting decisions are not those of courts of co-ordinate rank, but of courts of a higher and lower rank, to both of which the court before which they are invoked is subordinate? The problem has been solved in England; it has also been solved in Nigeria. In *Noble v. Southern Railway Co.*[103] Lord Wright observed:

> What a court should do when faced with a decision of the Court of Appeal manifestly inconsistent with the decisions of this House is a problem of some difficulty in the doctrine of precedent. I incline to think it should apply the law laid down by this House and refuse to follow the erroneous decisions.

In Nigeria, Pollard, Ag. J., had said:[104]

[99] (1965) N.M.L.R. 71, 78.
[100] "*Chime v. Elikwu:* Judical Precedent: Conflicting Decisions of a Higher Tribunal" (1971) 9 Nigerian Bar Journal, 63, 64.
[101] *Tsamiya v. Bauchi N.A.* (1957) N.R.N.L.R. 73, 83.
[102] See Chapter 4, section 2.
[103] (1940) A.C. 538, 598.
[104] *Thomas v. Ademola* (1945) 18 N.L.R. 12, 23.

> Colonial courts must give precedence to the decisions of the Privy Council before those of any other tribunal It is apparent that part of the judgment of the West African Court of Appeal in Aminu Jinadu and others v. Salami Akiyele which dealt with the construction of the said subsection (2) is at variance with the .Privy Council's decision in Laoye and others v. Ameo Ojetunde and cannot be followed.

As far as we are aware the above *dictum* has not been disapproved by any court or condemned by any writer. It is considered to represent the true legal position. The end-result is then that, where two co-ordinate authorities conflict, a lower court is not bound to follow either, but must pick and choose the one that, in its view, more nearly represents the law. Where the conflict is between a lower and a higher authority a court that is subordinate to both must follow the higher authority in the interests of *stare decisis*.

9. Absence of Argument

Argument is the life of the law. A court of co-ordinate jurisdiction or higher authority can disregard a precedent on the ground that it was not argued. This is, of course, possible where absence of argument has concealed a defect that would have become apparent if the case had been argued. Thus, in *Onubaka v. The Queen*[105] the case of *The Queen v. Adelani*[106] fell to be considered. It was rejected as an authority because it failed to consider a relevant statutory provision which would have come to light if argued. The Supreme Court said:

> No authority was given for this statement of the law, and the record shows that the point was not argued and that judgment was delivered immediately upon the close of the hearing and not reserved. We are unable to agree with the decision and we are of the clear opinion that it was given per incuriam.

In England it has been held that a case that "was not argued for the defendants, who did not appear . . . has not the authority of a

[105] (1959) 4 F.S.C. 267, 268.
[106] FSC. 50/1959, unreported.

case which has been fully argued".[107] This shows that not only a total absence of argument but also an argument advanced only on one side can operate to forfeit for a decision the authority it would otherwise enjoy.

But let us conclude with Stone:[108]

> The ruling that a decision in a case argued only on one side has nothing like the weight of authority of one that has been fully argued seems to indicate a wide gulf between the authority of such a case and one fully argued, but the practical effect is said to be that the court will not "necessarily" be able to differ from the finding in previous cases, at least not always and not merely because the previous case was argued only on one side. The precise limit of these various provisions is obscure, and the resulting measure of uncertainty quite considerable.

To the same effect is a point not raised nor argued by the parties but decided by the judge. In *Egri v. Uperi*[109] the Supreme Court allowed an appeal against the trial judge's decision on the ground that a point on which the judge had rested his decision "was neither raised nor canvassed before him" and that the point was still open to argument.

A decision tending the other way is *Bryars v. Canadian Pacific Steamships, Ltd.*[110] an English decision, in which it was contended that an earlier decision was not binding on the judge of first instance because the point now canvassed before the Court of Appeal was not raised in the earlier case. Singleton, L.J., said:

> The point was there, if it was to be taken. . . . The case ought to be regarded as binding on the court in this case. It is no part of the duty of the court to look for a reason for not following a decision if the decision, on the face of it, covers the particular case.

Our conclusion is that when a point properly arises and is expressly decided by the judge the decision is binding if there is nothing that makes the decision defective. But when a point is

[107] Per Lord Goddard, in *Edwards v. Jones* (1947) 1 A.E.R., p. 833.
[108] "Stare Decisis in the Divisional Court" (1951) 14 M.L.R. 219, 222.
[109] (1973) 1 All N.L.R. 198, 207.
[110] (1956) 3 A.E.R. 560, 569.

neither raised nor argued by the parties a decision thereon goes to no issue and is not binding, because a case is only an authority for what it actually decides[111] and it cannot be deemed to decide a matter not in issue.[112]

On the all important question of bail for a person charged with an offence before a court inferior to the High Court no consistent procedure has been followed in applying for bail perhaps because of lack of reasoned argument as to the proper way of setting about the matter. In *Simidele v. C.O.P.*[113] a flawless argument was put forward in favour of a procedure by summons and affidavit. In deciding that the latter mode is the authorised one, Beckley, J., stated:

> The points raised by the Senior State Counsel in this case are incontrovertible and the learned Counsel for the applicant, quite rightly in my view, stated that he has no answer to the points raised. There can be no doubt that, in the past, applications of this nature have been brought to the court by way of motion and affidavit but the points now raised have not been raised in the previous applications.

10. DECISION PER INCURIAM

If a court takes the attitude that a decision to which its attention is drawn as a precedent was reached *per incuriam*, that is, in ignorance of a rule of law binding upon the court, the decision has no authority and does not bind. However, this rule applies to courts of co-ordinate jurisdiction with the court from which the precedent emanates.[114] It does not apply if the decision is that of a court of superior jurisdiction.[115] The status of decisions *per incuriam* has been exhaustively dealt with in Chapters 8 and 9, to which reference should be made.

[111] Dias, *Jurisprudence*, 3rd edition, p. 63.
[112] *Adelenwa v. The State* (1972) 10 S.C. 13, 19.
[113] (1966) 2 All N.L.R. 14, 21.
[114] *Ngwo v. Monye* (1970) 1 All N.L.R. 91, 101.
[115] *Ibid.*, *Tsamiya v. Bauchi N.A.* (1957) N.R.N.L.R. 73, 83.

12

ATTITUDE AND CONTRIBUTION OF COUNSEL

The fourth contributory factor to the infallibility and worth of a judicial precedent is the candour, care, diligence and industry of counsel engaged in the case. A successful precedent is, no doubt, the result of the joint efforts of Bench and Bar. But by far the greater part of the work should be done by counsel if they want justice for their clients, for the knowledge of what is in issue in every case is first available to counsel and it is on this basis that they advise their clients and prepare their cases. There are four qualities counsel must exhibit in order to bring a good precedent into being. These are: brilliant argument, thorough research, candour and expert conduct of the case.

1. Argument

Every judicial decision is the product of argument, not spineless argument, but argument proceeding from a given premise and geared towards a definite and clearly conceived objective. A lawyer with a command of this art has started on his way to success in his profession. Sound argument is a necessary concomitant of sound reasoning and the art is especially valuable where the matter is not covered by authority.

But from where does he derive the material for his argument? The materials are obtained from his observation of men and affairs—from his study of men in society—from common sense, natural justice, public policy and the values of society. But these are not all. A lawyer is not likely to approach his work with a blank mind; he must have had at the back of his mind the opinions of reputable writers, foreign decisions, analogies and so on.[1] A judge is likely to

[1] See Allen, *Law in the Making*, 7th edition, pp. 285–286; Salmond, *Jurisprudence*, 11th edition, pp. 225–226; Paton, *A Textbook of Jurisprudence*, 3rd edition, pp. 195–198.

be taken in by an argument that persuasively displays some or all of these materials. Where there is no precedent in point, three things attract a judge to an argument: one is that it must be exhaustive; another is that it must be well-reasoned, and a third is that there should be no possibility of a later court coming to a contrary decision.[2]

There are innumerable instances in which a court has openly acknowledged its gratitude for competent argument which has enabled it to arrive at a decision. On the interpretation of section 28 of the Native Courts Ordinance[3] the West African Court of Appeal expressed gratitude to counsel for the respondent for his "illuminating argument in regard to the true meaning of the section."[4] The same court was able to come to a decision as to who are legitimate children in Nigeria and entitled to intestate estate because of counsel's "careful and well-reasoned argument."[5]

Maizabo v. Sokoto N.A.[6] might have been decided on the same lines as *Tsamiya v. Bauchi N.A.*[7] which decided that a verdict of manslaughter was not available in Maliki law, but argument of counsel made the Federal Supreme Court "come to the conclusion that the decision in *Jalo Tsamiya's case* is too wide and requires qualification." In *Obaji v. The State*[8] the decision of the Supreme Court to interpret "a statute which is in the main declaratory of the Common Law" was influenced by counsel who referred the court to an English authority[9] which stated that the correct course was

> . . . in the first instance to examine the language of the statute and to apply its natural meaning, uninfluenced by any considerations derived from the previous state of the law, and not to start with inquiring how the law previously stood, and then assuming that it was probably intended to leave it unaltered.

[2] Compare Cowen, "The Binding Effect of English Decisions upon Australian Courts" (1944) 60 L.Q.R. 378, 380.
[3] Cap. 142, Vol. 4, Laws of Nigeria 1948.
[4] *Toriola v. Arewa* (1949) 12 W.A.C.A. 505, 508.
[5] In *re Adadevoh* (1951) 13 W.A.C.A. 304, 305.
[6] (1957) 2 F.S.C. 13, 14.
[7] (1957) N.R.N.L.R. 73.
[8] (1963) N.M.L.R. 417, 421.
[9] *Bank of England v. Veglians Brothers* (1891) A.C. 107.

In each of the above instances the court had nothing but admiration and gratitude for the ability of counsel to argue out points of law which made it possible for it to make positive contribution to the growth of Nigerian case-law. The argument in *Toriola v. Arewa* enabled the court to choose between two conflicting decisions of two judges in the lower court.[10] In *re Adadevoh*, counsel's argument made it possible for the court to find legitimacy in the law of the domicile. Counsel's argument in *Maizabo v. Sokoto N.A.* reminded the court that it was dealing with the liberty of a subject and that it should invoke the English practice which its predecessor had adopted in *Motayo v. C.O.P.*[11] and reconsider its decision in *Tsamiya's case.*

And perhaps without the D.P.P's. argument *Obaji v. The State* would have been based on English precedents to the disregard of the real meaning of our criminal code which clearly contradicted the English decisions. In the latter case our criminal code would have been given an interpretation which the legislature did not intend-with all the consequences that would arise therefrom.

Against this background of expert and illuminating argument we find arguments that are not so productive or that are completely barren of legal effect. Some are, consciously or unconsciously, designed to confuse rather than clarify issues. But for an astute lawyer on the Bench, Jibowu, J., letters of administration in *Aileru v. Anibi*[12] would have been granted to the wrong person contrary to customary law as a result of a citation of authorities which the learned judge found to be irrelevant. Misconceived arguments were again put forward in *Edet v. Att.-Gen.*[13] in a claim for damages for tort by a petition of right when counsel for the suppliant wrongly claimed that the English Crown Proceedings Act, 1947, applied in Nigeria.

Praying irrelevant authorities in aid is a conscious attempt by counsel to get the court to create wrong precedents, from which later courts on second thoughts may depart. Not only would the original decision work injustice and twist the law, but the legal

[10] The decisions were: *Igiokwe v. Nanna* (1940) 17 N.L.R. 5; *Isalomi v. Omumu* (1943) 17 N.L.R. 48.

[11] (1950) 13 W.A.C.A. 114.

[12] (1952) 20 N.L.R. 46.

[13] (1957–58) 2 E.R.L.R. 37.

position would become confused and uncertain when these decisions come to be dissented from or overruled.

Counsel are expected to note and understand the relevance between one case and another. But when counsel cites a case in support of his contention and the court has to reply by saying that "the facts of that case do not support counsel's contention"[14] what is meant is that the case he has cited is not an authority in point. But what would happen if the court were not shrewd enough to discover the irrelevance? The court would accept it as a precedent in point and put the law in bad shape.

It has not been decided in this country whether a sale by public auction constitutes notice to the world. But in *Omosanya v. Anifowoshe*[15] counsel put forward this proposition and had no authority to back it. Mbanefo, F.J., as he then was, delivering the judgment of the court said:

> I doubt whether any such authority exists, especially where, as in the present case, there is no evidence of how much publicity was given to the sale in each case.

This argument was, no doubt, ingenious, and if the court had accepted it, it would have made a positive contribution to jurisprudence. But the court rejected it partly because there was no precedent in support and partly because there was "no evidence of how much publicity was given to the sale. . . ." However under the Land Registration Act registration constitutes notice to the world when no one except the officials of the Land Registry and searchers of the Land Register ever have notice of registration. The development of the law is not for the legislature alone, the courts are its partners in the business of law-making. Since sale by public auction acquires greater notoriety than land registration it is submitted that the Federal Supreme Court has lost a first-class opportunity of effecting a most important development in our case-law.

Further, growth in our case-law is retarded by supine resignation by counsel to submissions made and authorities cited by his opposite partner. In *Atu v. C.O.P.*[16] counsel for a convicted person

[14] *Cole v. Folami* (1956) 1 F.S.C. 66, 67.
[15] (1959) 4 F.S.C. 94, 99–100.
[16] (1970–71) 1 E.C.S.L.R. 7, 9.

applied to the High Court for bail. The application was by summons supported by affidavit under section 123 of the Criminal Procedure Law which did not apply. Counsel for the State wrongly supported the application. Agbakoba, J., dismissing the application said:

> . . . I am unable to lean in favour of the procedure adopted by the applicant and supported by learned state counsel but have to look elsewhere for the procedure to be followed.

The learned judge found the right procedure in an unreported case of *The State v. Odunsi.*[17] The decision was subsequently followed in the Ikot Ekpene High Court case of Offiong *v. C.O.P.*[18] where the learned judge, Ette, J., described the above two cases as sound law.[19]

A similar uncritical attitude to precedent was manifested by counsel for the Crown in *Inyang v. Teachers Disciplinary Council.*[20] That was an appeal against an order of the Disciplinary Council removing a teacher's name from the Register of Teachers and the ground of complaint was that the appellant was denied the right to legal representation. Section 51(2) of the Education Law of the then Eastern Nigeria had permitted legal representation on the following conditions:

> The Council may permit any person upon whose allegations an enquiry . . . has been instituted to be assisted by a legal practitioner in establishing the truth of his allegations, and shall permit the teacher whose conduct is the subject matter of the enquiry to be similarly assisted in meeting the charges against him.

An earlier case of *Mpi v. Teachers Disciplinary Council*[21] had decided that a teacher's right to legal representation was unqualified under the section. But before this authority was shown to the counsel for the Crown she had rightly submitted that the appellant's

[17] J/33C/1966 decided in Ijebu-Ode on 25/11/69 by Abina, J. *ibid.*

[18] Unreported, but see HT/5CA/73 decided on 25/3/74.

[19] The procedure is found in Form 38, rule 29A, Art. 963 at p. 357 of the 36th edition of Archibold. That was the procedure in vogue in England on 30/9/60 which is the procedure section 16 of the former Eastern Nigeria Law (still in force in the four Eastern States) requires to be applied.

[20] (1962) 6 E.N.L.R. 64, 65.

[21] Appeal No. F/26A/1960 by Palmer J., *ibid.*

right to legal representation depended upon whether his accuser had availed himself of that right and that the words "similarly assisted" should be interpreted in that light.

But on being confronted with *Mpi's case* learned counsel shifted her ground and indiscriminatingly submitted to its authority. It is clear from the wording of the section of the Education Law that the interpretation which the learned counsel proposed was the correct one, but instead of adhering to it and exposing the fallacy in the reasoning in *Mpi's case* she allowed it to be used as a precedent with all its results.

2. Research

It is the duty of counsel to look for relevant authorities to support the case he is going to make at trial. The search for authorities may, however, be a tedious exercise in view of the proliferation of judicial decisions and law reports in recent years. But since many of the decisions are declaratory of other authorities counsel cannot find it too difficult to lay hands on the case he needs. The consequences of overlooking relevant authorities are often serious, espedially if the authorities are decisions of a higher rank, as where the West African Court of Appeal overlooked a Privy Council decision.[22] A similar result is obtained where counsel fails to bring to the notice of the court a relevant statute.[23]

When counsel is not industrious enough to look for relevant decisions to bolster his case the result may be a scathing remark from the court.[24] As the doctrine of precedent is a deeply entrenched practice in Anglo-Nigerian judicial system counsel should pursue the search for authorities with vigour. Nothing less than decided cases or relevant statutes would satisfy the court's quest for justice.

What we have said about counsel's responsibility for authorities does not mean that the judge is thereby relieved of the duty of looking independently of counsel for authorities to support his decision.

[22] *Chief Oloto v. Chairman, L.E.D.B.* (1956) 13 W.A.C.A. 57, 59.

[23] *Zaidan v. Mohssen* (1973) 11 S.C. 1, 18.

[24] The *Queen v. Itule* (1961) All N.L.R. 462, 464, where the Federal Supreme Court said: "The point of which . . . industry has enabled him to discover are of the most trivial kind."

The ultimate responsibility for the final decision is that of the judge and he does not have to rely solely upon what counsel are able to produce. From time to time we hear of subsequent courts saying of the first that it reached its decisions without any authority cited.[25]

An undue reliance upon counsel for authorities may spell disaster. Most judges in this country are aware that many lawyers go to court without the authorities they need for their cases. Even when they come up with authorities they are either irrelevant or not tied to any specific proposition of law which they submit to the court. This tendency is particularly noticeable in young lawyers.[26]

Not a few judges are disappointed at the attitude of some counsel who cite cases for what they do not decide. Sometimes they purport to cite from a report which they flaunt before the court. At other times they talk of "a case before your learned brother, Mr. Justice X, in which the decision was so and so" without mentioning the case by name or producing evidence that such a case exists.

The writer has held discussion with his colleagues about their attitude to this sort of "precedents," and he has found a consensus among them that such citations should be treated as balderdash. Ecoma, J., of the Calabar High Court, always regards such citations as a warning that the counsel has no authority in support of the view he is advancing and looks upon them as an attempt to mislead the court. Apart from having to consult the report which counsel has flaunted and often finding that it does not support counsel's argument he does not trouble himself about the decision by "your learned brother, Mr. Justice X," for often such decisions do not exist.

It is difficult not to support the learned judge's stand. If, in fact, there are authorities in favour of counsel's contention he would certainly produce them and will not cast upon the court the burden of looking for them. The fact that he has not done so and has not given the judge sufficient particulars to enable him to trace the particular decision shows that the decision exists only in the imagination of counsel. In the circumstances, therefore, the judge must decide the case in accordance with his own view of the law.

[25] *Onubaka v. The Queen* (1959) 4 F.S.C. 267, 268.

[26] This led to the banning of lawyers of less than seven years post-call experience from the Supreme Court a few years ago.

To do this, says Ecoma, J., he has to adjourn the case and read the authority which counsel has dangled before the court but which he has not cared enough to read. In the course of reading he will discover that the only things true about the case are the names of the parties, the volume of the report and the court that decided it, but that the facts bear very remote resemblance to the facts before him and that the decision is not as claimed.

In line with the above experience is the experience of Kooffreh, J., Chief Judge of the Cross River State, who told the writer that when such "authorities" are cited to him he often insists upon their production by the consel concerned and finds that they are not forthcoming. The experience of the writer during the five years he has so far been on the Bench agrees with what these two learned judges have met with. This trick is not, however, common; it is confined to a few bad eggs among the practitioners in each Judicial Division.

The practice is as dishonest as it is unprofessional. It is calculated to induce the undiscerning judge to predicate his decision on a non-existing principle of law. The counsel that practises the trick thinks only in terms of winning the case for his client and boosting his professional practice. He does not think of the interests of justice or of the development of the law as a science. It is better not to cite any authorities than to deceive the court with non-existing precedents. Failure to cite is the better of two evils.

Where authorities are not cited in support of a point the case is not being fully presented and counsel's research is not thorough. Writing of counsel's attitude to the issues involved in *Fairman v. Perpetual Investment Building Society*,[27] Dr. Ellis Lewis said:

> A brief statement, apparently without the citation of a single authority, is hardly the full presentation of an argument. If the point had been really in issue one would have expected counsel to advance some reasons in its support and to refer to the relevant cases.[28]

[27] (1923) A.C. 74.
[28] "The 'I think' Doctrine of Precedent" (1950) 66 L.Q.R. 374, 381.

3. Candour

Another quality on the part of counsel which contributes to an effective and respectable system of precedent is candour. Counsel must disclose to the court the authorities of which he is aware and which militate against his case[29] and a failure to do so may be regarded as misconduct.[30]

In *Ngwo v. Monye*[31] a judgment which purported to rest upon a previous case as *res judicata* was in issue. But unknown to the later court from which counsel concealed the fact that the first judgment was non-existing at the time of the proceedings the later court based its judgment on the first judgment. It was held by the Supreme Court that the later judgment did not constitute *res judicata* because the later court was "misled into thinking that judgment was still subsisting by the counsel who appeared before the court."

The evil arising from concealment of relevant authorities is too glaring to escape attention. Such concealment may cause later decisions to veer in a different direction and so bring confusion and uncertainty into the law. If this happened the doctrine of precedent would cease to be what its supporters claim for it.

But when counsel is candid enough to place at the disposal of the court a decision relevant to the point in issue even though that decision does not favour his case he is in fact trying to promote the interests of the doctrine as well as of justice and will earn commendation from the court. Thus in *Kajola v. C.O.P.*[32] counsel for the State announced that he did not support the conviction by the two courts below on the legal point both had advanced and drew the attention of the Supreme Court to an authority which contradicted the stand of the courts below. In commenting upon this attitude the Supreme Court said:

> We agree with him and commend his stand in this matter.

One further instance of counsel's candour remains to be noted. There was a claim for a declaration of title to land. The plaintiff's

[29] *Anani v. The King* (1951) 13 W.A.C.A. 196, 197.
[30] *Abraham v. Jutsun* (1963) C.L.R. 578.
[31] (1970) 1 All N.L.R. 91.
[32] (1973) 9 & 10 S.C. 25, 32.

land and that of the defendant were contiguous, but the plaintiff failed to prove the exact boundary between both pieces. The trial judge nevertheless gave judgment for the plaintiff. On appeal by the defendant to the Supreme Court on the ground that the trial judge was wrong to make the declaration in the circumstances, counsel for the plaintiff announced that he could not support the judgment.

The Supreme Court was understandably impressed by this attitude on the part of counsel and declared:

> With commendable candour, he admitted that he himself was not happy about the judgment and asked us to non-suit the plaintiff respondent.[33]

It is rare to find counsel who are prepared to admit that they have a bad case and submit to judgment on the case presented by their opponents. It is rarer still to find counsel who will not strenuously argue in favour of a case which, to all intents and purposes, has no merits. The worst comes when counsel cite authorities for what they do not decide. An admission by counsel that his case is bad has the effect of keeping the resultant decision in line with orthodox legal principles and so preserves the sanctity of the doctrine of precedent. But blind argument and an attempt to manipulate existing authorities to serve a purpose for which they are not intended aim at distorting the law.

4. General Conduct of the Case

The way and manner in which counsel conduct cases may enure for the benefit of law as a science. While the chief objective of counsel is to win cases for their clients they must also remember that the respect which case-law enjoys depends as much upon them as upon the judges who listen to them and the parties and then give their judgments.

In *Idahosa v. Oronsaye*[34] the Federal Supreme Court had occasion to commend the sense of responsibility with which counsel engaged in the appeal before it handled their respective briefs. The court, through Abbott, Ag. C.J.F., commented:

[33] *Epi v. Aigbedion* (1972) 10 S.C. 53, 58.
[34] (1959) 4 F.S.C. 166, 173–174.

> Finally, I should like both Mr. Okorodudu and Mr. Idigbe to know that we much appreciate the care and attention which they have both given to this case. Their arguments, well-reasoned and carefully prepared, have been of the greatest assistance. It is most refreshing to hear an appeal conducted in this way and particularly to find learned counsel with a sense of responsibility which leads them to give ground when it is obviously of no avail to prolong the struggle.

On the other hand, counsel with lax attitude to work have earned a rebuke. In the above case the same learned Ag. Chief Justice of the Federation rebuked counsel and their clients for the manner in which the proceedings were conducted in the court below in these terms:

> I have already pointed out some of the omissions and defects in the Defence filed and I regret to say that this lack of attention to essentials seems to have continued throughout the proceedings. Neither side is exempt from the criticism of the failure to call evidence on important matters, though again, this criticism must be levelled more weightily against the appellants and their then legal adviser than against their opponents. The lack of attention to essentials frequently puts the trial judge in difficulties which he would not experience were counsel to prepare and conduct the proceedings with proper care.

These comments are justified. Counsel when preparing pleadings are deemed to have certain authorities in mind. But if omissions of essential facts are made and material evidence is not called so that the present case does not contain similar material facts to those in the precedents, the latter will be inapposite when cited. Furthermore, this laxity of approach does not promote the interest of justice, and the judge, aware of the disservice which this lack of care and attention has done to a party's case, will not be able to pronounce his judgment with an easy conscience.

The debt of judges to counsel for their contribution to the development of case-law is invaluable. But a greater debt is possible if counsel appreciate their responsibilities from preparation of their cases to presentation. The nature of these responsibilities depends upon how well the cases they handle are covered by authorities. If fully covered, counsel should master these authorities and draw a comparison between them and the cases in hand. They should also make sure that the essential facts of existing authorities are either similar to or on all fours with those of the case in hand and take care to see that all essential facts in the latter are brought before the court.

If the case in hand is partly covered by authority, counsel should be prepared by sound and convincing inductive argument to show the analogies. He must show the court the extent to which the existing law has influenced the case in hand and remind it that the doctrine of precedent demands consistency of judicial approach to similar legal problems and that the law must develop as an integrated whole.[35]

On the other hand, there may be a complete lack of authorities on the point. Counsel should know this before hand and should be prepared to pray in aid of his proposition of law the opinions of eminent jurists, applicable foreign decisions, judicial *dicta*, ethical and philosophical writings, public policy, the rules of natural justice and the values which society holds dear.[36]

In urging these tenets upon the court, counsel must remember that what he wants the court to decide is a legal dispute and not ethical, philosophical, moral or policy dispute. He should, therefore, capitalise more and more upon the distinctive policy of Anglo-Nigerian law and urge the judge to employ "that kind of natural justice or common sense which he has absorbed from the study of the law and which he believes to be consistent with the general principles of English jurisprudence."[37]

[35] Salmond, *Jurisprudence*, 11th edition, p. 226; see also Chapter 10, section A(6) of this treatise.

[36] See Allen, *Law in the Making*, 7th edition, pp. 302–311; Salmond, *Jurisprudence*, 11th edition, pp. 225–226; Dias and Hughes, *Jurisprudence*, 1957. pp 169–198.

[37] Allen, p. 307; see also Chapter 7, section B(1).

13

THE SPECIAL RELATIONSHIP OF ENGLISH AND NIGERIAN LAW

A reference to Chapter Four of this treatise will show how English law was received in this country and Chapter Five traces its growth and development after reception. There thus exists a special relationship between English and Nigerian law. It is this special relationship and its influence on the doctrine of precedent that we set out to study in this chapter. It is true that the Nigerian courts do not form part of the same hierarchy with the English courts. For this reason, English decisions are not technically and directly binding on Nigerian courts. The exception was the Privy Council which, until 30th September, 1963,[1] was the final court of appeal for Nigeria and whose decisions were binding on Nigerian courts.[2]

Why, then, do the Nigerian courts have such indulgent regard for English precedents?

1. Influence of Colonialism and the Received Law

Why, then, do the Nigerian courts have such indulgent regard for English precedents? There would appear to be two principal reasons. The first is the special relationship which exists between the English and the Nigerian legal systems. The legal system of Nigeria is an offshoot of the English system, having been established by the British Colonial Administration[3] on lines similar to those in England and imbued with common law characteristics and ideals[4] and run by men trained in the common law methods of legal thought.

[1] But in actual fact this relationship started in 1874.
[2] *Thomas v. Ademola* (1945) 18 N.L.R. 12, 231.
[3] Elias, *Groundwork of Nigerian Law*, 1954, Chapter One.
[4] *Ibid.*, Chapter 2; see also Chapter 4 of this treatise.

The second reason is the influence of the received English law. We saw earlier that this received law provided the substratum of our system and exerted an influence which later dominated our indigenous system of justice.[5] Whenever any case came before the English-model courts, judges and lawyers thought of English precedents as guides to the solution of the problems posed by the cases. In many cases these precedents were regarded as conclusive.[6] Recourse to no other system was considered owing to lack of familiarity with such system.

It is generally thought that those English decisions reached before January 1, 1900, are alone binding and that decisions after this date are only of persuasive effect.[7] The reason was explained in Chapter 4. Only pre-1900 case-law was imported into this country by statute and it is this alone that ought to bind our courts. English precedents coming into existence thereafter do not form part of Nigerian case-law without the volition of Nigerian courts and these courts import such English precedents as guides.[8] But up to 1963 the decisions of the House of Lords and the Court of Appeal were binding.

Thus when in 1949 the West African Court of Appeal was asked not to follow its previous decision[9] because it was wrongly decided, the court observed that it was bound to follow its previous decisions and cited *Velasquez Ltd. v. Inland Revenue Commissioners*,[10] an English Court of Appeal decision, which it said governed its practice in this regard. In that case, Lord Cozens-Hardy, M.R., said:

> But there is one rule by which, of course, we are bound to abide—that when there has been a decision of this Court upon a question of principle it is not right for this Court, whatever its own views may be, to depart from that decision. There would otherwise be no finality in the law. If it is contended that the decision is wrong, then the proper course is to go to the ultimate tribunal, the House of Lords, who have power to settle the law

[5] See Chapter 5.

[6] E.g. *Shokeye v. Insp. Gen. of Police* (1962) 2 All N.L.R. 119, 121–122; *Okafor v. Ezeigbo* (1966–67) 10 E.N.L.R. 203, 206.

[7] Elias, "Colonial Courts and the Doctrine of Judicial Precedent" (1955) 18 M.L.R. 356, 368–369.

[8] But see section 2 with reference to the position before 1st October, 1963.

[9] *Osumanu v. Seidu* (1949) 12 W.A.C.A. 437.

[10] (1914) 3 K.B. 458

and hold that the decision which is binding upon us is not good law.

The principle of practice in that case was reaffirmed in *Young v. Bristol Aeroplane Co. Ltd.*,[11] but the latter case in the Court of Appeal stated exceptions to the rule. The West African Court of Appeal adopted and governed itself by the rule in *Young's* case when it declared:[12]

> . . . the position, so far as this court is concerned, is that it is bound to follow previous decisions of its own, as well as those of Courts of co-ordinate jurisdiction. The only exceptions to this rule (two of them apparent only) may thus be summarised:
>
> (1) The Court is entitled and bound to decide which of two conflicting decisions of its own it will follow.
> (ii) The Court is bound to refuse to follow a decision of its own which, though not expressly overruled, cannot, in its opinion, stand with a decision of the Judicial Committee of the Privy Council or the House of Lords.
> (iii) The Court is not bound to follow a decision of its own if it is satisfied that the decision was given per incuriam.

Osumanu v. Seidu[13] was a Gold Coast (now Ghana) case, but the Federal Supreme Court, the Nigerian successor of the West African Court of Appeal, said in *Layanju v. Araoye*[14] that the rule in *Young v. Bristol Aeroplane Co.* was a rule which it had followed.[15] Two points of interest deserve to be examined from the point of view of relations between English and Nigerian courts. One is the relish with which this Nigerian intermediate Court of Appeal governed itself by English Court of Appeal practice. The other is the declaration that a previous decision of its own would not bind it if a later decision of the Privy Council or of the House of Lords was inconsistent with it.

The undertaking to be bound by a decision of the Privy Council cannot trouble our thoughts, for up to 1963 the Privy Council was

[11] (1944) K.B. 718; (1944) 2 A.E.R. 293.
[12] See *Osumanu v. Seidu* (1949) 12 W.A.C.A. 437–438.
[13] Where the rule in *Young's case* was applied.
[14] (1961) All. N.L.R. 83, 85.
[15] Though there is no reported case on this point.

the ultimate court of appeal for Nigeria. But the position is not so clear when it said it was to be bound by the House of Lords. No appeal ever lay from any Nigerian court to the House of Lords. Why then this undertaking?

It cannot be denied that there is sound logic as well as common-sense in this declaration of policy. Where Nigeian law is the same as English law on a particular matter it would be wise for the Nigerian courts to follow the House of Lords; otherwise it would find itself reversed by the Privy Council whose composition was generally the same as that of the House of Lords.[16] The tenability of this submission is shown by the *dictum* of the Privy Council itself in the case of *Robins v. National Trust Co. Ltd.*[17] where it said that the supreme tribunal to settle English law was the House of Lords "and that being settled, the colonial court, which is bound by English law, is bound to follow it."

In fact, the Privy Council has consistently advised colonial courts[18] to follow the decisions of the courts in England where these have settled questions of law common to both countries. Thus, in *Trimble v. Hill*,[19] where a question of statutory interpretation was involved, the Privy Council advised colonial courts to follow the Court of Appeal precedent "where a like enactment has been passed by the (colonial) legislature." It was their Lordships' view that "in all parts of the empire where English law prevails, the interpretation of that law by the courts should be as nearly as possible the same."

Apart from rhetorics, the Privy Council has shown by example that on questions of English law it is inclined to the decision set down by the House of Lords. Thus the House of Lord's decision in *Donoghue v. Stevenson*[20] on the liability in tort of a manufacturer to the ultimate consumer of the product was followed by the Privy Council four years later in *Grant v. Australian Knitting Mills Ltd.*,[21] an appeal from Australia.

[16] See Daniels, *The Common Law in West Africa*, 1964, p. 177; Salmond, *Jurisprudence*, 11th edition, p. 167.

[17] (1927) A.C. 515, 519.

[18] By colonial courts we mean courts of former British colonies which still send appeals to the Privy Council.

[19] (1879–80) A.C. 342.

[20] (1932) A.C. 562.

[21] (1936) A.C. 85.

The moral of these admonitions and example is clear. They show what the attitude of the Privy Council is towards cases from Commonwealth courts going on appeal to it and involving questions of English law. Where Commonwealth courts have determined a point of English law differently from, say, the House of Lords, the decision is likely to be reversed on the principle of *Robins v. National Trust Co. Ltd.* It was, therefore, right and proper that the Supreme Court before 1963 should govern itself by the principle of *Young's case.*

In normal circumstances the Nigerian courts would not be bound to follow English decisions given after 1900—the date of reception of English law. But, as we have seen, the fact that the Privy Council was the ultimate court of appeal and that the latter governed itself by the decisions of the House of Lords on English law persuaded the Nigerian courts that it was sound prudence to follow English decisions up to 1963 when the Privy Council ceased to be a final court of appeal for Nigeria. It does not matter whether the Nigerian courts felt bound to do so; it is sufficient that the realities of the situation made it prudent that they should dance to the tune of English courts up to that date.

We have in our reports examples of cases of post-1900 but pre-1963 era which depend for their rules upon English decisions given during this period. They contain *dicta* which suggest that the English decisions are more than persuasive. They will be referred to later in this part of the chapter.

The foregoing discussion makes it abundantly clear why the relations between Nigerian courts and English courts were so close before 1963. But after this date the Nigerian courts felt no longer answerable to the Privy Council and through it to the House of Lords. In fact, after this date there are several *dicta* in our law reports which declare post-1900 English precedents either persuasive or not binding.

In *Chime v. Elikwu,*[22] Idigbe, Ag. C.J., of the then Midwestern State (now Bendel State) described post-1900 English decisions cited to him as "weighty and of considerable authority" but declared:

> I am not bound by them.

[22] (1965) N.M.L.R. 71, 80.

In *Ezeani v. Njidike*[23] the Supreme Court described the House of Lords' decision in *Rookes v. Bernards*[24] as "of strong persuasive authority." Beckley, J., in *Alli v. Okulaja*[25] said of a decision of Lord Denning in the Court of Appeal:[26]

> I do not think that this court can be held bound by that authority of the Court of Appeal of England, this country now being an independent sovereign state . . .

Beckley, J., is the only authority so far as we know that has stated why English decisions are not binding on Nigerian courts any longer. But, with respect, we submit that he has arrived at the right conclusion from the wrong premises. English precedents do not cease to be binding on Nigerian courts because of our political independence and sovereignty. The loss of binding force stems from our judicial independence declared on October 1, 1963, when the right of appeal to the Privy Council was abolished. With such abolition went the indirect obligation to follow English precedents. Now whenever English decisions are followed our courts do so, not because they are under a legal obligation to do it, but because they find them convenient and helpful to their efforts to do justice.

But regard to the character of our society rather than considerations of justice has caused the rejection of a laudable English precedent. Recently the newly established Federal Court of Appeal has had occasion to reject the *ratio* of the English Court of Criminal Appeal in *R. v. Wise*[27] in which the latter court decided that in deciding whether or not to grant bail pending an appeal it was necessary to consider whether there was any prospect of success in the appeal. The FCA disagreed with this test, observing: "We, ourselves, feel quite unable to embrace this particular test in respect of appeals pending before this court in view of the special and peculiar conditions and circumstances of our society. We are not prepared to prejudge issues before the appeal is heard".[28]

[23] (1965) N.M.L.R. 95, 98.
[24] (1964) 2 W.L.R. 269.
[25] (1970) 2 All N.L.R. 35, 44.
[26] *Edmeades v. Thames Board Mills Ltd.* (1969) 1 Lloyd's Report 221.
[27] 17 C.A.R. 17.
[28] *Ajayi v. The State*, FCA/L/2-4/77 of 10th March, 1977, unreported.

What is remarkable about this decision is that attention is once again being paid to the character of our society. This English courts did not do and could not be expected to do because their rules were fashioned solely for English society. They were extended to Nigeria merely through the accident of our legal and political history. Though the FCA did not say what the "special and peculiar conditions and circumstances of our society" were, we may venture to surmise that they were having in mind the Nigerian's propensity to impute unworthy motives. In Nigeria if a convicted person who was granted bail on the ground that his appeal had some prospect of success subsequently lost the appeal the situation would not be received in the same way as it would be received in England. Yet to throw overboard this laudable and easy reason for bail is a most unhappy development.

The contribution of English precedents to the development of Nigerian case-law is clearly discernible in two main fields—common law and statutory interpretation. It appears that Nigerian courts are always quick to import English precedents recently evolved in England whenever cases involving similar points of law come before our courts.

English Precedents On Common Law

At common law an example is *R. v. Sharp* and *Johnson*[29] which recognised for the first time in English law the defence of self-defence to a charge of affray.[30] The principle there laid down was followed in the Nigerian case of *Shokeye v. Inspector-General of Police*[31] where Onyeama, Ag. C.J., said:

> It is clear that the learned Magistrate did not consider that self-defence had any relevance to the charge and he convicted because it was shown that the appellant and others had been fighting in a public place. In view of the cases to which I have referred I think that this appeal should be allowed.[32]

In this way a recent English decision was used to decide a Nigerian case.

[29] (1957) 1 Q.B. 552.
[30] See Allen, *Law in the Making*, 7th edition, p. 307.
[31] (1962) 2 All N.L.R. 119.
[32] *Ibid.*, p. 122. The cases are *R. v. Sharp* and *R. v. Johnson*.

When an accused person pleads an *alibi* the law in England is that he has not assumed the burden of proving anything.[33] This rule has been adopted by the Nigerian courts.[34] Again, the English decision in *R. v. Golder*[35] that when a witness is shown to have made a previous statement inconsistent with his present testimony the jury should not only be told that the evidence of the witness is unreliable, but should be directed that the previous statement whether sworn or unsworn does not constitute evidence on which to act has been applied in Nigeria.[36] In *The State v. Ogon*[37] a witness made two previous statements which exonerated the accused persons and implicated himself. In court he gave evidence which implicated the accused persons and exonerated himself. Kooffrey, J., following *R. v. Golder*, remarked:

> On the authority of this case, Abang's evidence or statements sworn or unsworn are of no use to this court.

Quite apart from recent decisions, the Nigerian courts owe a big debt of gratitude to English precedents in developing their case-law. Random examples will illustrate the extent of the debt. In *The Queen v. Akpakpan*[38] Foster Sutton, F.C.J., delivering the judgment of the Federal Supreme Court said:

> In England it has repeatedly been held that a confession of adultery without more is never sufficient to reduce an offence which would otherwise be murder to manslaughter, and we are of the opinion that the same rule must be held to be applicable here.

In granting leave to appeal out of time the Supreme Court in *Aworeni v. Akinyele*[39] had to consider whether the reasons given by the appellant were "good and substantial" reasons. There were no local authorities in point, and Fatayi-Williams, J.A., (as he then was)

[33] *R. v. Johnson* (1962) 46 C.A.R. 45; *R. v. Denny* (1963) C.L.R. 191.
[34] See *Ikono v. The State* (1973) 5 S.C. 231.
[35] (1961) 45 C.A.R. 5.
[36] *Ikono v. The State* (1973) 5 S.C. 231, 253; *The State v. Okon Nelson* C/104C/1971 decided by Eno, J., at Calabar on 9/10/72 (unreported).
[37] Charge No. 18C/72 decided by Koofreh, J., as he then was, at Calabar on 30/10/72 (unreported).
[38] (1956) 1 F.S.C. 1, 2.
[39] (1967) N.M.L.R. 343, 348.

finding that three English cases[40] solved this problem declared: "Fortunately, we are not without guidance" and granted leave.

In *Evans v. Bakare*[41] the question of contributory negligence in a claim for damages for injury arising from a collision between two vehicles was decided solely on English authorities.[42] English precedents[43] solely decided the fate of the plaintiff in *Murmansk State Steamship Line v. Kano Oil Millers Ltd.*[44] which applied Russian law to the dispute arising under the Bill of Lading and also held that the English Statute of Limitations applied to an arbitration under the Bill of Lading.

To cite a few cases in illustration of the fact that post-1963 English precedents have contributed to the development of Nigerian case-law is to underrate the debt of gratitude which case-law in Nigeria owes to English precedents. In fact there is scarcely a Nigerian decision in the post-1900 era in which English decisions are not cited. The relationship, therefore, between the two systems is closer than might be expected by someone unacquanted with the trend of our decisions on common law.

English Precedents on Statutory Interpretation

Post-1900 English decisions have also been instrumental in construing our own statutes. In *Balogun v. Obisanya*[45] the English decision in *Chetwynd's Estate, Dunn Trust Ltd. v. Brown*[46] was invoked as a precedent for the interpretation of section 12(1) of the Nigerian Money-Lenders Ordinance[47] which the court found to be

[40] *Rumbold v. L.C.C.* (1909) 100 L.T. 259, *Codling v. Mowlem*, E. & E. Digest, Vol. 3, p. 387, *Gath v. Shoesmith* (1939) Ch. 841.

[41] (1974) 1 N.M.L.R. 78.

[42] *Lang v. London Transport Executive* (1959) 1 W.L.R. 1159; *Butterfield v. Forrester* (1809) 11 East 60; *Hicks v. British Transport Commission* (1958) 1 W.L.R. 493; *Stapley v. Gypsum Mines Ltd.* (1953) A.C. 663.

[43] *Norske Atlas Insurance Co. Ltd. v. London General Insurance Co. Ltd.* 43 T.L.R. 541; *Hamilton & Co. v. Mackie & Sons* (1889) 5 T.L.R. 677; *Perry v. Equitable Life Assurance Society* (1929) 45 T.L.R. 468; *Board of Trade v. Cayzer, Irvine & Co. Ltd.* (1927) A.C. 610; *Scott v. Avery* (1865) 5 H.L.C. 811; *Thompson v. Charnock* (1799) 8 Term Pep. 139; *Re Law* (1894) 1 Ch. 147; *Lloyd v. Guibert* (1865) L.R. 1 Q.B. 115.

[44] (1974) 1 N.M.L.R. 58.

[45] (1956) 1 F.S.C. 22.

[46] (1937) 3 A.E.R. 531.

[47] Cap. 136, Vol. IV of the Laws of Nigeria 1948.

"an adaptation of section 6 of the English Money-Lenders Act of 1927" and the court continued:

> . . . the effect of a failure to comply with the provisions of the sections in both our law and the English Law is to render a contract for repayment of a loan to a money-lender or security given for the loan unenforceable.[48]

In construing section 154(1) of our Criminal Procedure Ordinance (now Act)[49] the Federal Supreme Court relied upon the English case of *Hibbert v. Mckiernan*[50] in which Lord Goddard, L.C.J., held that "allegations concerning ownership of stolen property are, except in a few exceptional cases treated as immaterial."[51] On the nature of the onus of proof of insanity which rests upon an accused person under section 140(3) of the Evidence Act, the Federal Supreme Court drew assistance from the English Court of Criminal Appeal precedent in *R. v. Car-Briant*[52] and concluded:

> . . . we respectfully agree that that is a correct statement of the law on this subject.

In recent years more and more reliance has been placed on English precedents for the purpose of interpreting the provisions of our statute laws. The meaning of "revenue" in section 7(1) (a) of the Federal Revenue Court Decree 1973 was seen to be what Lord Tomblin said it was in *London, Midland and Scottish Railway Co. v. Anglo-Scottish Railways Assessment Authority*,[53] that is, incoming funds and not outgoing expenses.[54]

The *ejusdem generis* rule of interpretation was adopted by the Supreme Court to interpret the words "other measures" in section 7(1) (b) (iii) of the Federal Revenue Court Decree, 1973, when that section fell to be interpreted in *Jammal Street Structures Ltd. v.*

[48] P. 23.

[49] In each of the States, except the Northern States, identical local enactment is called Criminal Procedure Law, but the Act also applies.

[50] (1948) 1 A.E.R. 860.

[51] *See R. v. Elechi* (1958) 3 F.S.C. 17, 19.

[52] (1944) 29 C.A.R. 87.

[53] (1933) 150 L.T. 367.

[54] *Mokelu v. Federal Commissioner for Works and Housing* (1974) 1 N.M.L.R. 69.

African Continental Bank.[55] In doing so the Supreme Court relied upon several English authorities, the most important of which was *Coleshill and District Investment Co. Ltd. v. Minister of Local Government*[56] in which the Court of Appeal held that the words "other operations" in section 12(1) of the Town and Country Planning Act, 1947, meant operations similar to "building, engineering, mining" which appeared in the section. In adopting this method of interpretation the Supreme Court observed:

> We are accordingly of the opinion that in section 7(1) (b) (iii) of the Decree, the word, "other measures" must be construed *ejusdem generis* with the words "banking", "foreign exchange," and "currency".

From the above examples we have seen that English precedents on statutory interpretation are prayed in aid by Nigerian courts for two distinct purposes. In the first case, they are prayed to aid the interpretation of Nigerian statutes which are similarly worded and which cover the same subject matter as the British statutes. Secondly, even where the subject matters and the wordings are different they can still be of assistance where the lesson they teach is to indicate the right mental approach to the meanings of certain words and phrases as in the "revenue and *ejusdem generis* cases" referred to above.

In respect of the first case the Nigerian courts have entered warnings against overmuch indulgence of English decisions on English statutes. In *Obadara v. C.O.P.*[57] the Supreme Court said:

> Having regard to the origin of the Nigerian legal system and statute-book, decisions on English statutes will naturally carry great weight where the wording is identical . . .,

but the court warned that the correct way of interpreting our own statutes is not "to look to decisions on the meaning of English statutes with different wordings." In *Obaji v. The State*[58] the Supreme Court again ruled that:

> the duty of the courts in Nigeria is to interpret the Criminal Code

[55] (1973) 11 S.C. 77, 99.
[56] (1968) 1 W.L.R. 600, 605.
[57] (1965) N.M.L.R. 39, 42.
[58] (1965) N.M.L.R. 417, 420.

> free from interpolation and refrain from propounding the common law of England."

These warnings are very pertinent and timely. If they are not heeded two evils will follow. One is that the right precedents will be wrongly followed and in this way English precedents will be badly misrepresented in Nigeria, and this would be apparent to any percipient lawyer who would take the trouble to examine the English-oriented Nigerian decision in the light of the Nigerian statute. Another evil is that the policy and intent of our statutes would be defeated through interpretations not geared to their ordinary and natural meanings.

The above evils would be accentuated where citations are not made from the original reports but from textbooks. Textbooks are not always likely to present the full picture either of the cases or of the statutes the cases interpret. And a court which relies exclusively on the bowdlerised versions of the cases in the textbooks may miss the wood for the trees. At this juncture it is pertinent to quote Ayoola, J.,[59] as he then was:

> It is perhaps pertinent to emphasize here the need to treat quotations from Books with caution. One needs to read the reports of cases upon which such quotations are based: not infrequently one finds that the principles enunciated in such Books, particularly where they are Books setting out Laws which are Laws of England, and not necessarily of Nigeria, may have no application to Nigeria having been based on statutes of local application in England.

Two factors seem to be responsible for our overfree appeals to English precedents. One is our English common law training or system of legal education which is English-oriented; another is that English case-law is better developed and richer than ours and therefore commands greater confidence and respect. But we must heed the warning of Pollock:

> This just and necessary respect, if not informed by a due measure of intelligent criticism, tends to degenerate into mechanical slavery.[60]

[59] In *The State v. Customary Court, Oyo*, (1967) N.M.L.R. 267, 274.
[60] *The Genius of the Common Law*, p. 114.

There is wisdom in this warning. Every statute has a policy behind it, and this can only be discovered by a reading of the statute itself.[61] An unimaginative adherence to a precedent which the court thinks interprets the statutes, but which in fact does not, merely helps to defeat the intention of the legislature.[62]

2. Relations Between the Nigerian Courts and the Privy Council

From the inception of the right of appeal from Nigerian courts to the Privy Council[63] the decisions of the latter have been binding on Nigerian courts. Thus in *Osumanu v. Seidu*[64] the West African Court of Appeal recognised an exception to the binding force of its own decisions where these were contrary to later decisions of the Privy Council. And in *Thomas v. Ademola*[65] Pollard, Ag. J., said:

> Colonial Courts must give precedence to the decisions of the Privy Council before those of any other tribunal. It is apparent that part of the judgment of the West African Court of Appeal in Aminu Jinadu and Others v. Salami Akiyeki (II) which dealt with the construction of the said sub-section (2) is at variance with the Privy Council's decision in Laoye and Others v. Amao Ojectunde, and cannot be followed.

The *dictum* of Pollard, Ag. J., is in accord with the practice of the courts in the United Kingdom in cases where there is an unnoticed conflict between the decisions of a higher and a lower court. In *Rex v. Northumberland Compensation Appeal Tribunal*[66] Lord Goddard, L.C.J., said:

> I think that there we have a decision of the House of Lords which says one thing and a decision of the Court of Appeal, in

[61] See Craies on *Statute Law*, 7th edition, pp. 96–101. But this ascertainment of legislative intention only comes after attempt to get at the plain meaning of the words has failed – Lloyd, *Introduction to Jurisprudence*, 2nd edition, p. 385.

[62] Lord Wright, "Precedents" (1944) 8 C.L.J. 118, 137.

[63] The system of appeals was initiated in 1867; see Elias, *Groundwork of Nigerian Law*, 1954, p. 51.

[64] Referred to several times in this treatise. See, however, 12 W.A.C.A. 437.

[65] (1945) 18 N.L.R. 12, 23.

[66] (1951) 1 K.B. 711, 724.

which the decision of the House of Lords was not cited, which says another, our plain duty is to follow the decision by the House of Lords, and that we propose to do."[67]

This doctrine that when a lower court is faced with two conflicting decisions of courts of superior jurisdiction, one of which is higher than the other, the decision of the higher authority should be preferred is founded on commonsense. It gives meaning to the principle of the hierarchy of authority and ensures the much desired certainty of case-law and prevents the doctrine of precedent from being cast as rubbish to the void.[68] Furthermore, a lower court that applies the doctrine saves itself the embarrassment of having its decision reversed or overruled by the higher superior court.

The Privy Council up to 1963 was not a court of appeal for Nigeria only, but also for other Commonwealth countries and colonial territories.[69] Would its decision on, say, an appeal from Nigeria bind, say, an East African Court? It is true that Nigerian courts and East African Courts do not form part of the same judicial system. Consequently, a decision of the Privy Council on a case from Nigeria would not normally bind an East African court. But it is submitted that it will so bind where the law decided upon in the Nigerian appeal is the same as that which an East African Court is bound to apply.[70]

In *Bakhshuwen v. Bakhshuwen*[71] the Privy Council granted recognition to the principle that a decision by the Privy Council on a point of Muslim law on an appeal from India should be binding on an East African Court where the point of Muslim law was the same as in India. A contrary decision in *Negro v. Pietro Bread Co. Ltd.*[72] in which the Court of Appeal for Ontario refused to follow the Privy Council decision in *Victorian Railway Commissioners v.*

[67] See also *Noble v. Southern Rly. Co.* (1940) A.C. 538, 598.

[68] To use the expression in Salmond, *Jurisprudence*, 11th edition, p. 184 used in a different context.

[69] See Dias and Hughes, *Jurisprudence*, 1957, p. 72; Allen, *Law in the Making*, 7th edition, p. 249.

[70] See Elias, *Colonial Courts and the Doctrine of Judicial Precedent*, (1955) 18 M.L.R. 356, 362; see also Ekow Daniels, *The Common Law in West Africa*, 1964, p. 188.

[71] (1952) A.C. 1, 14.

[72] (1933) O.R. 112.

Coultas[73] is unsupportable. So also is the view of Ijalaye[74] that such decisions should be binding only on the courts of the country from where the appeal emanated "because the countries when sending appeals to the Judicial Committee constitute different legal systems."

Nationalist sentiment must be kept apart from the administration of justice. What matters is not whether the territories which send appeals to the Privy Council "constitute different legal systems," but whether the Privy Council is a common court of appeal for them and whether the point of law involved is the same in these countries. If the point of law is the same, elementary prudence demands that one country should be bound by a decision on appeal from the other to avoid the embarrassment of a reversal on appeal in the case in hand and of being overruled on appeal in a different case.

The position here is comparable to what obtains in a Federation like Nigeria where all appeals end up finally in the Supreme Court. Would a court, say, in Bendel State, be justified to hold itself not bound by the decision of the Supreme Court on appeal from, say, Niger State, on the ground that Niger State is a different State from Bendel State? If the point of law decided by the Supreme Court is the same in both States the answer is in the negative. The position can only differ if the question of law is different.

It is from this perspective that we should look at the decision of Adunwa-Bossman, J., in *Onogen v. Leventis & Co. Ltd.*[75] In that Ghana case, the learned judge followed a Privy Council decision on an appeal from India and declared that "as a decision of the Privy Council" it was "binding on the Supreme Court of Ghana." This decision is much criticised.[76] But in our opinion these criticisms are unmerited and unfounded for losing sight of two basic considerations. One was that the learned judge was deciding a point of English law which was the same in Ghana and India.[77] The other was that the Privy Council at the time was the final court of appeal for Ghana, so that any decision by a Ghana court that was out of harmony with

[73] (1888) 13 A.C. 222.

[74] See the Nigerian Bar Journal (1971) Vol. 9, p. 67, and the authorities he has relied upon.

[75] (1959) G.L.R. 105, 115.

[76] See Daniels, *The Common Law in West Africa*, 1964, p. 187; Ijalaye in (1971) 9 Nigerian Bar Journal, 63, 66–67.

[77] The Indian case was *Tewari v. Singh* (1908) 24 T.L.R. 884.

a principle it had laid down would be awry and in danger of reversal or of being overruled. The learned judge was, therefore, right to follow the Indian decision.

Some writers talk glibly of the Privy Council not considering itself bound by its previous decisions.[78] This creates the impression in the mind of the general reader that the Privy Council will capriciously reach its decisions without regard to precedent. But that is not the position and is not perhaps what the writers have intended. The Privy Council is aware of the differences in the legal systems over which it presides as a court of appeal and will not therefore rigidly follow its precedents; nor will it follow a previous decision of its own which it considers wrong in law. The Privy Council will not, for example, follow its previous decision on a mercantile contract if the principle of law there is "broadly laid down" and "their Lordships do not think that the case is one which it would be safe to follow."[79]

The flexible attitude of the Privy Council enables it to do justice in individual cases. Thus in *Nkambule v. R.*[80] it refused to follow its previous decisions in cases of murder. But it does not exhibit the same resilience when questions of constitutional interpretation are concerned. The *dictum* of Viscount Simon in *A.G. for Ontario v. Canada Temperance Federation*[81] is instructive:

> But on constitutional questions it must be seldom indeed that the Board will depart from a previous decision which it may be assumed will have been acted on both by governments and subjects. In the present case the decision now sought to be overruled has stood for over sixty years; the Act has been put into operation for varying periods in many places in the Dominion; under its provisions business must have been closed, fines and imprisonments for breaches of the Act have been imposed

[78] Daniels, *The Common Law in West Africa*, 1964, p. 177; Dias and Hughes, *Jurisprudence*, 1957, p. 72.

[79] *Mercantile Bank of India Ltd. v. Central Bank of India Ltd.* (1938) 1 A.E.R. 52, 58. The case which their Lordships thought it not safe to follow was a Gold Coast case—*Commonwealth Trust v. Akotey* (1926) A.C. 72, in which the Privy Council held that purchasers from a cocoa merchant who had no title and no authority of the owner to sell were not liable in conversion to the owner because by consigning the cocoa to the merchant the owner had invested him "with all the insignia of possession thereof and of apparent title."

[80] (1950) A.C. 379.

[81] (1946) A.C. 193.

> and suffered. Time and again the occasion had arisen when the Board could have overruled the decision had it thought it wrong. Accordingly, in the opinion of their Lordships, the decision must be regarded as firmly embedded in this constitutional Law of Canada, and it is impossible to depart from it.

By way of comment we submit that while certainty in constitutional decisions is desirable it must not be forgotten that the procedure for constitutional amendment is not as simple as the procedure used for amending other statutes. While the legislature drags its feet it should be possible for the courts to interpret the constitution in accordance with the spirit of the age and do justice in individual cases without too much regard to precedent. And account should be taken of change of circumstances from the time the constitution came into being up to the time it is being interpreted.[82]

It is a happy circumstance that the Privy Council has ceased to be a court of appeal for Nigeria. This attitude of the Privy Council to its previous decisions on constitutional issues would certainly not be ideal for Nigeria with a rigid constitution. We must not be taken as advocating a capricious attitude to precedents on constitutional questions. What we mean is that the constitution should bend from age to age and according to circumstances when the interests of justice so require, for a constitution that will not bend must crack.

As we said earlier the right of the Privy Council to take appeals from Nigeria came to an end in 1963. Nationalist sentiment brought this about. But the most immediate cause was the premiership tussle between Alhaji Adegbenro and Chief Akintola in Western Nigeria in 1962. What happened was this. Acting on an affidavit sworn to by sixty-six members of the House of Assembly expressing loss of confidence in Chief Akintola as premier and declaring that Alhaji Adegbenro enjoyed the confidence of this majority of members of the House the Governor of the Region, Sir Adesoji Aderemi, removed Chief Akintola from office and appointed Alhaji Adegbenro thereto.

Chief Akintola sued both the Governor and Alhaji Adegbenro and the Federal Supreme Court decided in favour of Chief Akintola.

[82] See Lord Wright, "Precedents" (1944) 8 C.L.J. 118, 132; G. Ezejiofor, "Stare Decisis in the Nigerian Courts" (1972) 6 Nigerian Law Journal, 47, 55.

Alhaji Adegbenro appealed to the Privy Council in London. The latter allowed the appeal and declared Alhaji Adegbenro validly appointed. On the day on which the Privy Council delivered its opinion the Western House of Assembly and House of Chiefs met and passed the Constitution of Western Nigeria (Amendment) Law, 1963. This law settled retrospectively the question of the premiership in Chief Akintola's favour.[83] In the following year, 1963, the republican constitution was introduced and appeals to the Privy Council were abolished.

We find here a parallel with what happened in South Africa before that country abolished appeals to Privy Council. According to Daniels:[84]

> In South Africa the immediate cause for the abolition of appeals to the Privy Council was as a result of Pearl Assurance Co. Ltd. v. Union Government, (1934) A.C. 570 where the Privy Council overruled the judgment of four members of the Appellate Division on what was a pure question of Roman-Dutch law.

Just as the maintenance of Roman-Dutch law in its traditional form was indispensable to the South Africans, so was complete freedom over constitutional processes a matter of life and death to Nigerian politicians in the first decade of independence. Chief Akintola's regime had the active support of the Federal Government which led the Federal Parliament to approve the amendment without hesitation and to launch the republican constitution the following year in which the amendment was introduced into all the regional constitutions.

In a very few words the Supreme Court of Nigeria was created by section 111 of the Constitution of the Federal Republic of Nigeria, and under section 120 of the same constitution the Supreme Court was made the final court of appeal for the country. This means that no appeal would lie to the Privy Council after the Constitution had come into force on 1st October, 1963. Pending appeals were, however, to continue in the Privy Council, but were to abate if not

[83] The Privy Council decision which was thus set aside by legislation was *Adegbenro v. Akintola* (1962) 1 All N.L.R. 465

[84] *The Common Law in West Africa*, 1964, p. 188 (footnote).

heard within a year, though appeals on chieftaincy and constitutional questions abated immediately.[85]

Status of Privy Council Decisions after 1963

At this juncture we ask two related questions. What is the status of decisions pronounced by the Privy Council before 1963, and what is the status of those pronounced after that date? We have already said that the Nigerian courts were bound by the Privy Council decisions.[86] But are they still bound by such decisions after the declaration of judicial independence from English precedents? The case of *Johnson v. Lawanson*[87] demonstrates positively that the binding force is not there again even where the Supreme Court has acted on such decisions. That is a case in which a decision of the Privy Council including three decisions of the Supreme Court which followed it were swept aside by the Supreme Court because they wrongly interpreted section 129 of the Nigerian Evidence Act.

There was a decision of the Federal Supreme Court which went the other way and was delivered after the inconvenient Privy Council judgment.[88] Clearly that decision which was given in 1959 after the Privy Council decision was *per incuriam* the latter, and if the Privy Council had remained a final court of appeal it would have been looked upon as a bad law by later courts and by the Privy Council itself. But change of circumstances saved it and today the Supreme Court has upheld it in preference to the decision of the Privy Council. From this attitude of the Supreme Court we deduce this conclusion that pre-1963 Privy Council decisions are not regarded as having absolute binding force even where they have been followed in a number of cases.

What about post-1963 decisions on appeals from other territories? We have seen earlier that the decisions of courts outside Nigeria are regarded as persuasive. In the same way, post-1963 Privy Council decisions have in our courts no more than presuasive efficacy. If the position were otherwise, the abolition of appeals to it

[85] 1963 Constitution S. 158 (3) (4).

[86] See the beginning of this section and the case of *Thomas v. Ademola* (1945) 18 N.L.R. 12, 23.

[87] (1971) 1 N.M.L.R. 380.

[88] *Omosanya v. Anifowoshe* (1959) 4 F.S.C. 94.

would be an exercise in futility. The right to take appeals from Nigeria carried with it the right to impose its decisions upon Nigerian courts, and an abolition of the first right necessarily meant the obsolescence of the second.

The 1963 Nigerian Constitution did not go as far as the 1960 Constitution of Ghana in providing for the binding force of the Supreme Court decisions upon the Supreme Court and upon the High Court, declaring that neither the Supreme Court nor the High Court shall

> be bound to follow the previous decisions of any court on questions of law.[89]

All that the Nigerian Republican Constitution did was to provide that no appeal shall lie from the Supreme Court to any other court.[90]

But in principle the omission does not matter. The fact that it is the ultimate court of appeal indicates clearly that no other court can bind it. And the fact that no other court can bind the courts in Ghana does not prevent these courts from consulting decisions external to Ghana for purposes of guidance, though they are not bound to follow them as a matter of obligation.

Again, what about the express enactment in the Ghana Constitution that the Supreme Court shall in principle be bound by its previous decisions and that the High Court shall be bound by the Supreme Court? Perhaps the intention is to avoid the experience of the United States Supreme Court which is not bound by its own decisions and whose vacillations on constitutional issues are deemed to have brought it into disrepute.[91] Equally possible is the view that the framers of the Constitution wanted the Supreme Court to copy the House of Lords which could not up to 1966 review its previous decisions.[92]

The provision is unnecessary. If the Nigerian courts, as we have seen, have refused to accord binding authority to decisions outside Nigeria without such a constitutional provision, why wouldn't the Ghana courts? Indeed, it would be preposterous for a court that is

[89] 1960 Ghana Republican Constitution, Art. 42.
[90] Section 120. See also S. 215 of the 1979 Constitution.
[91] Salmond, *Jurisprudence*, 11th edition, p. 181.
[92] *London Street Tramways Co. v. L.C.C.* (1898) A.C. 375. But review is now possible (see Practice Statement in (1966) 3 A.E.R. 77).

not answerable to another court to hold that it is bound by the decisions of that other court.

Nor is it necessary to provide that the High Court shall be bound by the Supreme Court. The binding force of the Supreme Court decisions upon the High Court stems from the latter's subordinate position on the hierarchical ladder. This is a practice inherited from the common law in which the courts of Nigeria and Ghana were brewed.

14

THE FEDERAL CHARACTER OF THE COUNTRY

The sixth factor that determines the worth of a judicial precedent in Nigeria is the federal character of the country. A unitary state has only one legal system and one hierarchy of courts, but in a federation there are several legal systems, each with its own peculiarities. Nigeria has twenty of them. Dr. Ekow Daniels[1] has written: "It has been established that the doctrine of precedent succeeds best in a country with a uniform and centralised judiciary. How the challenge is going to be faced in the Federation of Nigeria remains to be seen." In countries with only a single legal system there is a straight hierarchical structure of courts. In such a system it is easy to know which court binds which court, and the doctrine of precedent can work with dignity and effect. But the problem is not so easy in countries with a decentralised judiciary. Although we may have, as in Nigeria, a centralised Court of Appeal and Supreme Court at the apex, yet at the lower level each state in the Federation has its own system of courts, including the High Court.

Two problems arise from this structure. The enacted laws differ in their provisions from state to state though they cover the same subject matter and so give rise to varying interpretations. Secondly, lower courts in each state will feel bound only by what their higher courts have decided and will pay no respect to a contrary decision of higher courts in other states. In this way there will be a welter of conflicting authorities that will seriously affect inter-state commerce and transactions.

We will now consider each of these two problems one by one. The differences in the wording of similar statutes have caused a problem to the doctrine. A construction by the High Court of one state on the statute of that state is not necessarily a precedent for

The Common Law in West Africa, 1964, p. 194.

emulation by the courts of other states with similar statutes in force. Several cases will illustrate the problem involved. The High Court of the then Fastern Nigeria held[2] that the Western Nigeria case of *The Queen v. Governor, Western Nigeria*[3] was not an authority to follow in *certiorari* proceedings to quash the recognition of a chief in Eastern Nigeria. As the learned judge, Savage, J., explained, the Western Nigeria court made the order quashing the recognition because "The Law of 1957 does not expressly exclude certiorari," whereas in Eastern Nigeria "Section 1 of the Recognition of Chiefs Law, 1960, has expressly excluded application for an order of certiorari."

The second case is *Kalu v. C.O.P.*[4] where Umezinwa, J., refused to follow a Lagos High Court case of *Oyedele v. Awomodu*[5] which, under a differently worded statute, decided that "a magistrate has no jurisdiction in any cause or matter which raises any issue as to title to land and that such jurisdiction is ousted both in a criminal case and in a civil case." The learned judge found that the decision turned on the wording of "section 14(2) of the Magistrate's Court (Lagos) Ordinance Cap. 113 Laws of the Federation of Nigeria and Lagos" which was different from section 18(1) of the then East Central State Edict which excluded jurisdiction only in civil cases and had no application to criminal trials.

For purposes of clarification the provision of the Lagos Statute on which *Oyedele v. Awomodu* was based will be examined. It is section 14(2)(a) which enacts:

> Subject to the provisions of any other Ordinance, a Cheif Magistrate shall not exercise original jurisdiction in any cause or matter which:
>
> (a) raises any issue as to title to land, or to any interest in land.

What is of interest in this provision of the law is that the magistrate's jurisdiction is excluded "in any cause or matter." Section four of the Ordinance defines a cause as including "any criminal proceed-

[2] *The Queen v. Governor*, Eastern Nigeria (1960) 4 E.N.L.R. 98, 100.
[3] (1959) W.R.N.L.R. 44.
[4] (1972) 2 E.C.S.L.R. 738, 740.
[5] (1968) L.L.R. 118.

ing," and it can be seen from this that the decision that the magistrate's jurisdiction was excluded was clearly right.

Such a decision could not be used to support the construction of a differently worded provision that a magistrate "shall not exercise original jurisdiction in suits relating to trespass to any land whether or not any issue as to title to any land or as to any interest in land is raised therein." The crucial difference between the Lagos statute and the East Central State statute is that the Lagos statute uses the words "cause or matter" while the East Central State statute talks of "suits" simply, and suit is defined in section 2(1) of the Edict as "a civil proceeding commenced by writ of summons, or in such manner as may be prescribed by Rules of Court." Thus, an East Central State magistrate was precluded from exercising jurisdiction only in civil cases, and *Oyedele v. Awomodu*, imported from Lagos, was not an authority in point.

It is of interest to note that *Kalu v. C.O.P.* was not the only East Central State case in which this Lagos decision was invoked as a precedent. Earlier in the same year in which it was decided the Lagos decision was cited to and approved and followed in *Ukaegbu v. C.O.P.* by Aniagolu, J., in circumstances similar to those in which Umezinwa, J., rejected it. Both the Lagos decision and *Ukaegbu v. C.O.P.*[6] were cited as precedents to the latter judge who said:

> With respect. . . I find myself unable to follow Aniagolu, J., in Mohamadu Bello Ukaegbu's case (supra). I hold the view that the ouster of jurisdiction clause as provided for in our law only applies to a Magistrate in the exercise of his civil jurisdiction and does not apply to him in the exercise of his criminal jurisdiction.

The third case is a case in which a Federal Supreme Court decision was cited to a Northern State High Court judge. The decision was based on a common law rule which had been abrogated by legislation in the Northern States and so had ceased to exist. The judge quickly saw the ineptitude of the precedent cited to him and rejected it, basing his judgment on the applicable statute.

[6] (1972) 2 E.C.S.L.R. 207.

1. Solution to the Problem

It is the essence of federalism that each constituent unit makes such laws within its legislative competence as it pleases and words them the way it likes. As long as Nigeria remains a federal country these differences in the wording of similar statutes must occur, and this is in spite of efforts made at conferences of state functionaries to secure uniformity. How then can we guarantee that decisions tailored to suit one situation shall not be extended to a different and inappropriate situation?

One way of checking it is the continued vigilance of judges before whom precedents from a different jurisdiction are cited. We have seen above instances of this vigilance. It is commendable and should be stepped up. Of course, this is only possible with judges who are "on the whole, more able than the Bar."[7] Another is erudition and honesty on the part of counsel. They must be erudite enough to know when a precedent imported from one jurisdiction into another would be appropriate; and they must be honest enough not to mislead the court to follow the wrong precedent.

The third means of salvation lies with the Federal Court of Appeal (FCA). When cases involving the interpretation of statutes go before it, it should first of all ascertain the meaning and application of the statute and then consider any precedent from a different state with a similar statute cited in support of the decision to make sure of its aptness. If ineptitude is disclosed the precedent should be sundered from the case before it and both should be carefully interpreted in the light of their respective statutes. That will avoid confusing them again in future. In *Chiokwa v. The State*[8] the Federal Court of Appeal had done just this when it ruled that section 41 of the Evidence Law applicable in the Rivers State and section 250(1) of the Criminal Procedure Code applicable in the Northern States were not similar and that the cases of *Suwa v. The State*[9] and *Juwa v. The State*[10] which were decided on section 250(1) of the Criminal Procedure Code were not suitable precedents to be prayed in aid of

[7] Goodhart, "Precedent in English and Continental Law" (1934) 50 **L.R.Q.** 40, 61.

[8] *Chiokwa v. The State*, FCA/E/93/78 delivered on 25th January, 1979.

[9] *Suwa v. The State* (1965) N.M.L.R. 405.

[10] *Juwa v. The State* (1969) N.M.L.R. 168.

the construction of section 41 of the Evidence Law. In this way the Federal Court of Appeal has saved the sanctity of the two legal systems and enabled the doctrine of precedent to serve its purpose.

A fourth means of solving this problem of misapplied authorities lies in the technique of the editorial report of the case. Editorial comments on the reported case can point out what authorities from other jurisdictions have been misapplied and what the differences between the respective statutes are. In fact this has been done in some cases and the practice should continue on an increasing scale. Generations of lawyers and judges will benefit and the doctrine of precedent will maintain its purity and continue to serve its purpose.

2. The Problem of Multiplicity of Courts

The second problem to consider is that posed by the multiplicity of judicial systems. We have nineteen states and twenty judicial systems (when the Federal system is included). Each of the nineteen systems has a High Court as the first among its superior courts of record. There is also a Federal High Court. Both the High Courts and these other courts of record[11] are law-making courts operating at the same time and creating rules of law. Can they all agree? Can the doctrine of precedent work?

Professor Paton[12] has said: "An excess of precedents may easily lead to uncertainty unless they are uniform in result, and unless a satisfactory technique exists for discovering relevant cases." Certainly we cannot have uniformity of results, and in the present state of law reporting in the country[13] we do not have a satisfactory technique for discovering cases that are relevant to those that are presently under consideration.

The problem may not be serious in a country with a unitary constitution where there is only one legal and judicial system, but it is certainly acute in a Federation such as Nigeria or the United States with many systems of courts. In each state the lower courts are prone to follow the decisions of the higher courts of that state even if better precedents are available elsewhere. It is only reasonable that

[11] See section 3 of Chapter 9 and section 6 of the 1979 Constitution.
[12] *A textbook of Jurisprudence*, 3rd ed., p. 192.
[13] See post.

they should do so; otherwise their decisions could be upset on appeal to the higher courts of that system. The doctrine of precedent can only work on a national plane where the federal appellate courts have established rules of law common to all the states in the Federation, for in those circumstances all the courts in the country would be bound by these rules.

3. CONCLUSIONS

It is wrong and a disservice to the doctrine of precedent if a judge in one legal system follows a precedent imported from a different legal system uncritically. Every legal rule is the product of its environment and has all the trappings of that environment. So if a precedent is to serve its purpose of justice in a different environment the associated rules of that environment must be the same as those in the environment from which the precedent is imported. As we have seen, the rules in the component legal systems of a federation are not always identical.

One of the reasons which make a state willing to join in a federation is the freedom to keep its own laws. Its courts must interpret these laws in accordance with their letter and spirit. But this will not be the case if they fail to interpret the laws by themselves but begin to hunt for precedents from other jurisdictions. Ideas from extraneous systems may contaminate these laws and make them fail to represent the intention of the legislature of that state. If that happens the "federal principle" is violated. A safe approach is to construe the statute of a state according to its intention and policy as gathered from a reading of the statute[14] and form an opinion about its meaning. It is only when the meaning is not clear that similar statutes from other jurisdictions can be consulted with the decisions on them. Even then the decisions can be accepted as precedents only when the statutes which they construe are found to be similar in all material particulars to the one under consideration.[15]

An adherence to this practice will ensure that the laws of each state are properly interpreted. Junior courts in that system will

[14] See Dias, *Jurisprudence*, 3rd edition, pp. 131–132.
[15] But see Dias, *ibid.*, where the view is expressed that "the doctrine of *stare decisis* should not be applied to statute interpretation."

follow the right precedents and the doctrine of *stare decisis* will work effectively in the state. Both the legislature and the judiciary in each state will pursue a common aim, since the law of the legislature will also be the law of the courts.

Only precedents on such laws as are common to the whole country will operate at the federal level, binding all the courts in the Federation. Such precedents relate to such common law rules as are still common to the whole Federation, to such statutes as are exactly alike and to constitutional questions which are the same in every state.

From the above analysis we can see how the worth of a judicial precedent in Nigeria is determined by the federal character of the country. A precedent from one state in the Federation is worthy of application in another state if it has settled precisely the same question of law that is now in issue before the court. It is unworthy and should be rejected as a precedent where the question of law it has settled differs materially from the question presently calling for settlement, no matter what merits it has in its own right.

15

THE LAW REPORT

We have discussed the other factors which determine the acceptability and worth of a precedent and we have seen that they are: the hierarchy of authority, the *ratio decidendi*, the mode of reception by later courts, the contribution of counsel, the special relationship between English and Nigerian law and the federal character of the country. In this chapter we are going to discuss the seventh factor—the rolé of the Law Report in the scheme of precedent.

The original source of a decision is often difficult, if not impossible, to get at. Judges and the profession have therefore come to rely upon reports of the case by lawyers. What court decided the case, whether the *ratio* thereof is a good one and states the law correctly, what contribution the counsel engaged in the case made to the evolution of the rule that emerged and what the attitude of later courts is to the decision are facts obtained from no other source than from the Law Report. It is, therefore, easy to see the extent of the debt which the doctrine owes to law reporting.[1]

1. The Importance of Law Reporting

The primary purpose of the report is to make the decision on a particular legal issue available. Later courts faced with similar problems turn to the report for guidance. Judges have been known to be seriously handicapped by absence of reports of cases touching the points that claim their attention at the moment and have come to a decision without them.[2] In *Flione v. Oladipo*[3] Graham Paul, J.

[1] "A precedent is not a precedent unless it is accurately reported." Allen, *Law in the Making*, 7th edition, p. 312.

[2] See *P.Z. & Co. Ltd. v. Pepple* (1933) 11 N.L.R. 166, 167 where Carey, J., came to a decision that money in a savings bank account was not attachable by garnishee proceedings after "consulting such books of reference and reports as are accessible to me."

[3] (1934) 11 N.L.R. 168, 169.

refused to follow *P.Z. & Co. Ltd.v. Pepple*[4] because in that "judgement Carey, J., expressly suggests that no proper access to the authorities was possible. There is no law library at Aba," he concluded.

Availability of reports will place at the disposal of legal advisers a knowledge of what the law is on particular matters and may have the effect of avoiding litigation where the law is clearly against a particular claim. As Sir Carleton Allen says:[5]

> ...courts of law exist not to adorn learning by the elaboration of legal subtleties, but to do justice between citizens on concrete issues; and it is a blemish on the administration of justice that litigation should be protracted and parties put to expense because courts have not all the relevant material before them.

Furthermore, the doctrine of precedent would lose its meaning in the absence of reliable reports of cases bearing on particular points. According to Dias and Hughes:[6]

> That doctrine can only function with dignity and effect if there is something approaching a guarantee that all relevant cases will be brought to the notice of the courts.

If no record were kept of cases and no use were made of them, judges would waste valuable time and energy in deciding every legal point that arises "by tracing it back to first principles, like the propositions of geometry".[7]

Apart from what concerns the courts, litigants and their legal advisers, the Law Report is of inestimable value to a student of legal induction. Some authorities agree that the best way to study the law is to approach it from a study of cases.[8] The Law Report furnishes an admirable starting point, and without it such a study would be impossible.

The Law Report contains the acme of legal learning, and where relevant cases can be found they provide to the student and the lawyer that discipline in thinking which it is the aim of jurisprudence

[4] See note 2 above.
[5] *Law in the Making*, 7th edition, p. 315.
[6] *Jurisprudence*, 1957, p. 92, 8.
[7] Kiralfy, *The English Legal System*, 1954, p. 104.
[8] See Williams, *Learning the Law*, 5th edition, pp. 49–50.

to impart.[9] The orthodoxy of new decisions can be tested by reference to the cases already in the Report. In the same way, the perversion of the law can be discovered through a comparison of the new with the old.

Failure to report reportable cases can lead to unwelcome results. First, that guidance and certainty which it is the purpose of the doctrine of precedent to provide will be lacking. Secondly, lack of reporting presents us with the incidence of overlooked authorities which frequently leads to awry decisions that later courts have refused to follow.[10]

Sometimes lack of reported cases on a given point of law may induce the court to look for guidance from unrecognised legal sources such as "Historical Notes." In *Amodu Tijani v. Secretary, Southern Nigeria*[11] the Full Court of Nigeria in an appeal remarked:

> If this judgment had been known to the judges, surely they would not have accepted 'Historical Notes' as an authority

The evils of non-reporting are glaring enough, but sometimes it can be a positive blessing rather than a curse. Thus in *Johnson v. Lawanson*[12] the Supreme Court overruled a line of four cases headed by a Privy Council decision and sanctioned a decision of the Federal Supreme Court which correctly stated the law on the matter, but which was reached in ignorance of the Privy Council decision because the latter was not reported. Although the Supreme Court lamented:

> Our system of law reporting in this country are anything but perfect. . .,

our view is that the non-reporting had a salutary effect. If the case had been reported it would have come to the knowledge of the Federal Supreme Court which would have considered itself duty-

[9] Dias and Hughes, *Jurisprudence*, 1957, pp. 12–23.

[10] *Oloto v. L.E.D.B.* (1950) 13 W.A.C.A. 57, 59, where the West African Court of Appeal refused to follow its previous decision in *Kofi v. Twum*, 4 W.A.C.A. 187 because it was reached in ignorance of the then unreported Privy Council decision in *Moore v. Tayee* later reported in 2 W.A.C.A. 43, as well as the unreported W.A.C.A. case of *Kudiabor v. Kudanu* subsequently reported in 6 W.A.C.A. 14.

[11] (1915) 3 N.L.R. 24, 50.

[12] (1971) 1 N.M.L.R. 380, 388.

bound to follow it, and in these circumstances there would not have been "at least a single decision of the Federal Supreme Court running the other way" which undoubtedly illuminated the path of the Supreme Court.

In our system of judicial precedent a judge is bound whether the previous decision is reported or not rep ted.[13] The position is the same in England where an unreported decision of the Court of Appeal or of a Divisional Court is as binding as a reported one.[14]

2. Law Reporting in Nigeria

Of the earliest Law Reports in this country the best known is the Nigeria Law Report (N.L.R.) which started to be printed in 1915 and was published in 1916.[15] The reported cases date from 1880. Partly from the information given on the title page of Volume One of the Report and partly from *dicta* in the decided cases one gets the impression that more decisions were reached than found themselves in the Report. Although this Report is to be acclaimed as a first venture in serious law reporting it must not be assumed that it is in every way satisfactory.

First, the omitted cases might not have been thought worthy of being reported, but they still ruled the earlier courts from their limbo.[16] Secondly, the time lag between delivery of judgment and its report was so unreasonable as to make it impossible for the doctrine of precedent to work effectively, for, between pronouncement and report, other cases based on similar facts would necessarily have been decided in ignorance of the yet unreported decision, with the resultant tendency of the later cases going in a different direction.[17]

[13] *Oloto v. L.E.D.B.* (1950) 13 W.A.C.A. 57, 59.

[14] See Goodhart, "Precedents in the Court of Appeal" (1945–47) 9 C.L.J. 349, 354; Goodhart, "Precedents in Divisional Courts" (1948) 64 L.Q.E. 40, 43; see also *Palgrave, Brown and Son Ltd. v. S. S. Turid* (1922) 1 A.C. 397, 413, where Lord Summer said, "If it had not been reported at all, it would still have been a decision, which, when brought to light by any means, must have been regarded as authority."

[15] The first volume carries information to this effect.

[16] See *Oloto v. L.E.D.B.* (1950) 13 W.A.C.A. 57, 59.

[17] See *Oloto v. L.E.D.B.*, *supra*.

Dr. T. O. Elias[18] has referred to other Reports of the period between 1875 and 1933 which were partly private and partly official ventures in law reporting. But it does not appear from his account that these Reports established themselves in wide use or that they were anything to compare with the official Nigeria Law Report.[19] The Nigeria Law Report ran into twenty-one volumes and the last case it reported is dated 24th October, 1955.

Another Report of official character was the West African Court of Appeal Report (W.A.C.A.) which reported selected cases decided by the West African Court of Appeal sitting as a court of appeal for the four West African colonies of Nigeria, Gold Coast (now Ghana), Sierra Leone and Gambia. This series started in 1933 and ran into fifteen volumes by 1955 when further reporting stopped owing to improved constitutional status of Nigeria and consequent establishment of a separate court of appeal known as the Federal Supreme Court.[20]

Both the Nigeria Law Report and the West African Court of Appeal Report also contained reports of cases decided by the Privy Council to which appeals lay, first, from the Full Court, and later, from the West African Court of Appeal. In some cases the decisions of these courts were reported together with those of the Privy Council even where the Privy Council had overruled them.[21]

When publication of the West African Court of Appeal Reports ceased on December 30, 1955, its place was taken by a series known as the Federal Supreme Court Report (F.S.C.) which started publication in 1956 in annual volumes. The last of its volumes was published in 1960 as Volume Five. The series ontained selected judgments of the Federal Supreme Court delivered during the period from 1956 to 1960. Occasionally references have been made to unreported decisions of the West African Court of Appeal and the Federal Supreme Court which were as binding as those that had been repor-

[18] See *Groundwork of Nigerian Law*, 1954, pp. 28–30.

[19] This report was produced by the Judiciary and published by the Government Printer, Lagos.

[20] The Nigeria (Constitution) Order in Council, 1954. See also Elias, *Groundwork of Nigerian Law*, 1954, p. 169.

[21] See e.g. *Tijani v. Secretary, Southern Provinces* (1915) 3 N.L.R. 24–55 and pp. 56–66; *Bamgbose v. Daniel* (1952) 14 W.A.C.A. 111 and *Bamgbose v. Daniel* (1954) 14 W.A.C.A. 116.

ted. This shows that the problem of selection was such an intractable problem that the reporting authorities could not get into the Reports all cases that were influential enough to decide the fate of later cases.

When Nigeria became a federation in 1954[22] the need for more Law Reports arose. Each of the then constituent states in the Federation and the Federal territory of Lagos (as Lagos was known at the time) decided to publish the reports of their decisions. In this way the Eastern Region of Nigeria Law Report (E.R.N.L.R.), the Western Region of Nigeria Law Report (W.R.N.L.R.) and the Northern Region of Nigeria Law Report (N.R.N.L.R.) came into being. That of Lagos was known as the Lagos Law Report (L.L.R.).

On the country's independence the nomenclature of the respective reports changed accordingly. In each case the word "Region" was dropped and the Reports became known as Eastern Nigeria Law Report (E.N.L.R.), Western Nigeria Law Report (W.N.L.R.) and Northern Nigeria Law Report (N N.L.R.), respectively.

Nigeria became independent from Britain on October 1, 1960,[23] and in 1961 a new series replaced the Federal Supreme Court Report. This new series was known as the All Nigeria Law Report (All N.L.R.) and is still in vogue. Unlike the Federal Supreme Court Report the All Nigeria Law Report does not reserve its pages exclusively for the Supreme Court decisions, but reports High Court decisions throughout Nigeria as well.

A dominant private series came into existence in 1964 and is known as the Nigerian Monthly Law Report (N.M.L.R.). As the name implies,it was originally issued in monthly series, but now exists in annual volumes. There is another private series known as Federal Nigeria Law Report, not as popular as its counterpart, the Nigerian Monthly Law Report. A new series called The Law Reports of Nigeria came into being in 1980.

In the late sixties emerged Law Notes published under the aegis of the Nigerian Law School as part of its programme of continuing legal education. It did not contain a full report of the cases but only summaries of the facts and decisions and was issued in loose leaves. It attempted to cover the whole country and was very useful from

[22] See The Nigeria (Constitution) Order in Council, 1954.
[23] See Nigeria (Constitution) Order in Council, 1960, s. 2.

the point of view of students who, because of the bowdlerised accounts of the cases, were able to obtain a large measure of caselaw knowledge in a nutshell. It enjoyed varying measures of support from court to court, but the large measure of discrimination to which it was subjected caused the publishers to leave off publication in the first decade of its existence.

As from 1972 a new technique in law reporting was developed both by the Supreme Court and the Lagos High Court. These courts are issuing monthly unedited series of their judgements in cyclo-styled and bound copies. This makes it easy for as many cases as possible to get into the Report and reduces the chances of decisions being overlooked because of non-reporting.

At least two more states in Nigeria have published their own Law Reports after the Nigerian civil war. They are the Midwest State (now Bendel State) and the Rivers State. Bendel State published its first Report about 1972 and the Rivers State in 1976. The Cross River State has reached an advanced stage on the journey to publication, but is hampered by lack of personnel.

Three basic complaints can be made about law reporting in this country. One is that the percentage of cases which succeed in reaching the Law Report is infinitesimal in comparison with the total number of decided cases. Of the number unreported there are, without doubt, cases of the greatest value to the profession which only the industry of lawyers and judges exhume when similar points come up for litigation.[24] Sir Carleton Allen is quite right when he says:

> The chief complaints which are heard today are not so much about inaccurate reports as about their complete absence. In spite of the various concurrent series of reports which now exist, from time to time important cases seem to elude the vigilance of all reporters and editors.[25]

The next complaint is lack of promptitude. Between delivery of judgment in the case and its appearance in the Report a considerable

[24] See, e.g. the unreported Privy Council decision in *Maurice Goualin Ltd. v. Aminu*, 1957, overruled in *Johnson v. Lawanson* (1971) 1 N.M.L.R. 380.

[25] *Law in the Making*, 7th edition, pp. 312–313. See also Ezejiofor, "Stare Decisis in the Nigerian Courts" (1972) 6 N.L.J 47.

time must have elapsed. This problem was particularly acute in the days when the Nigeria Law Report and the West African Court of Appeal Report held the field. The danger posed by the problem is that by the time the case gets into the Report other decisions based on similar facts might have been reached, sometimes in the opposite direction.[26]

This criticism, however, must be sobered down when we remember two basic constraints. One is that our early Law Reports were the responsibility of officials of the judicial department who had other pressing duties to perform and not only those of law reporting. Another is that since these Reports were expected to cover decisions of courts all over Nigeria it was practically impossible in the circumstances of the time to travel with ease and speed from one provincial town to another to collect and select for publication the cases they needed.[27]

The third complaint is the undesirability of regionally based Reports. From the facts of experience those Reports are exclusively devoted to cases decided within the respective states and cases on appeal from those states. No attempt whatever is made to include cases from other jurisdiction and, but for the few nationally based Reports, the tendency of judges and lawyers in each state would have been to look exclusively to their own decisions for precedents. This would be a disservice to the doctrine of judicial precedent on a national level and would compound the problems which, as we have seen, federalism presents to *stare decisis* in Nigeria.[28] Looked at from another angle, however, regionally based reporting is not wrong in principle. It has the tendency and the potential of articulating the doctrine of precedent in the state insofar as decisions of the courts of that state are concerned. It may also help to prevent the importation of inapposite precedents from across the border.

[26] See *Oloto v. L.E.D.B.* (1950) 13 W.A.C.A. 57, 59, already referred to.

[27] Though I am told by Mr. U. U. Ekanem, one-time Principal Registrar of Uyo High Court, who worked with the Colonial Administration that the practice was for the European judges in the Divisions to train registrars in law reporting and that the reports in the Nigeria Law Report were the fruit of the efforts of the registrars so trained. But be it as it may, the system did not remove the constraints we have spotlighted above.

[28] See Chapter 14.

In the next section we examine what steps can be taken to reform law reporting in this country.

3. Reform of Law Reporting in Nigeria

From what we have seen above it is clear that law reporting in this country stands in need of drastic reform. The reform should, for present purposes, proceed along three main lines.

First, there should be promptitude in reporting. The time lag between judgment and its appearance in print should be reduced to a minimum. This should be possible if reporters are exclusively devoted to the duty of reporting and if there is at least one attachment to every judicial division. The duty of the reporter so attached would be the collection of judgments and processing them and transmitting for report all those that decide points of law.

This leads us to the second aspect of reform—that of reporting as many cases as possible. It is our view that all cases that decide points of law should be reported. There should be no question of discretion as there is no one with prophetic foresight who can tell whether a case that is thought unworthy of reporting today will not one day be decisive of the issue in controversy in a later case. We are aware, however, that the fact that all the cases are reported is not a guarantee that they will not be overlooked, for such an oversight has frequently occurred even when precedents are fully reported.[29] A comprehensive coverage is desirable, nevertheless, so that judges and counsel with the requisite industry and inquisitive mind can find the cases they need.

In recommending as we do we cannot lose sight of the question of expense. The inclusion of as many cases as decide points of law would necessarily lead to bulky volumes, costing paper, money and manpower,[30] but justice and its administration are so sacred that they should be attained at any price.

The third aspect of reform lies in the creation of one central body for law reporting. As we said earlier, the present tendency towards regional reporting is undesirable, for, even though we are operating

[29] See Allen, *Law in the Making*, 7th edition, Excursus, c. pp. 367–379; Dias and Hughes, *Jurisprudence*, 1957, pp. 91–92.

[30] See Allen, p. 376 where a similar concern is expressed.

a federal system of government with different legal systems, justice should not be compartmentalised or put into a straight jacket. It should be seen to be the same for everyone in every state of the Federation. Lawyers and judges should be encouraged to look for systems of justice beyond the frontiers of their own states to the Federation at large. Furthermore, it is doubtful if the policy of separate reporting of decisions on state basis will not create more problems for *stare decisis* with more than two hundred divisions of superior courts in the country.

For this reason we suggest that a National Council of Law Reporting be set up by the Federal Government with exclusive responsibility for law reporting in the country. The Council should have representative reporters in each Judicial Division or group of Judicial Divisions in the country for the purpose of a more efficient despatch of business. The chairman of the council, the reporters and the editorial staff should be experienced lawyers and should be employed full time. The council should be a statutory body and should adopt rules of procedure which, among other things, would place reporters under an obligation to send in reports of cases within a given time.

As the purpose of the Council would be to exercise exclusive jurisdiction and control over law reporting in the country all other law reporting agencies should cease to operate. Regional or state reporting of decisions should cease. Private reporters should be bought out. In this way, the diversity of Reports in the country will come to an end and judges and the profession will have only one source to look to—the Report of the Council.

The merits of this suggestion are, we suppose, at once apparent. First, all the law needed would be found in the same series. Secondly, judges and lawyers would be saved the distraction of looking for authorities in this, that or other Report. Thirdly, if the policy of reporting all cases deciding novel points or extending existing rules is adhered to the problem of overlooked authorities suddenly leaping into action from their limbo of oblivion and surprising judges and counsel with their dictates would be reduced to the minimum.

Given the establishment of a National Council of Law Reporting as suggested, we now turn our attention to the kind of cases the

Council should report.[31] Briefly these fall into five main classes. The first class consists of those cases which decide novel points of law, Such decisions make positive contribution to jurisprudence[32] and constitute original precedents.[33]

The second class consists of cases which extend existing legal rules. Such cases represent in no small way a notable contribution to our law, and while not as spectacular as those creating novel points, are invariably decisive when similar points come up for litigation.

The third class consists of decisions of higher courts which approve or disapprove lower authorities. Such decisions settle the law one way or the other and are a guide to the profession and lower court judges.

In the fourth class we have decisions of higher courts resolving conflicts in decisions from different jurisdictions. In the constitutional context of Nigeria such conflicts are inevitable and a decision on points of conflict really ensures the unity of the law and reduces the gap between one legal system and another.

Last but not least is the class of decisions in which a superior court in one state agrees or disagrees with a superior court in another state. Such decisions are important for two reasons. They show that justice cuts across state boundaries (where there is an agreement) and that the same system of justice prevails in the states concerned on the particular legal point. Where there is disagreement the judge disagreeing will naturally give his reasons, from which it can be ascertained how far the law in one state is different from that in the other state, or, where the law is the same, how far one or the other judge falls short of what is required.[34]

To ensure that the cases reported fall within the above classes and that no class is squelched the rules of procedure of the Council should spell out the classes of cases to be reported without prejudice to the Council's right to report other classes of cases which it considers to be of particular interest. Further, there should be a strong editorial committee of legal pundits to decide on whether particular

[31] Lewis, "The History of Judicial Precedent" (1932) 48 L.Q.R. 230, 235—cases of importance and utility to the profession should be reported.

[32] Allen, *Law in the Making*, 7th edition, p. 307.

[33] Allen, pp. 304–307; see also Chapter 7, section B(1).

[34] We saw in Chapters 9 and 11 instances of judges giving reasons for not following brother judges.

decisions fall within a given class. Where, for any reason, particular decisions cannot be reported, loose copies of such decisions should be made available to all courts in the country and kept in the court libraries. Sufficient copies should also be placed at the disposal of the Bar Association for the use of those of its members who would like to make use of them.

Apart from the Law Report there should also be published an annual alphabetical collection of rubrics of cases. The rubrics should be arranged according to subject matter and points decided. Under each rubric all cases deciding the point contained in the rubric during the year should be subsumed. One example will suffice. Under the rubric "A sale of family land by the head of the family without the consent of the principal members of the family is voidable, not void" should come all the cases (referred to by name, volume of Report and page number) deciding that point that year. This would ensure that decisions on particular points are spotted on a cursory glance through the pages and would solve the problem of overlooked authorities satisfactorily.

There is another point that deserves mention. It is the problem created by cases subsequently overruled. At present overruled cases continue undetected in our Reports and may be mistaken for legitimate rules of law. But if the suggested index of rubrics is compiled well it should mention in the appropriate group of cases those that have been overruled and by what cases and bold letters should be used to indicate this fact.

The above suggestions, if carried out, would create the problem of bulk. To report such a spate of cases issuing from over two hundred divisions of superior courts in the country, apart from the Federal Court of Appeal and the Supreme Court and to compile rubrics of cases of the nature contemplated in this treatise calls for no small space. But if the work of compilation is tackled with discrimination and insight the problem of space need not be enormous and it would be a worthwhile service to be rendered to justice.

4. FEATURES OF AN IDEAL LAW REPORT

Granting that the setting up of a National Council of Law Reporting is a desirable objective, what would be the features of the

Report it should produce? The Council should not just produce another Report; it should be a Report with a difference. The Report should contain features which are distinctively different from those of existing Reports, though the best in their features should be retained.

Dr. Ellis Lewis,[35] describing an ideal Law Report, has written:

> The report, to serve as an authority for subsequent cases, must give the material facts, a summary of the arguments which make the points at issue clear, and a full account of the judgment, disclosing the grounds and reasons upon which it proceeds. Further, it must enable cases to be cited with ease, by giving the names of the parties or a number, the year and the Court in which the decision was made, and reports of the same case must not differ in any material respects.

We cannot improve upon this statement of the qualities of a good Law Report. Many of our Reports are already resplendent with these virtues. But we have some additional features to suggest.

First, every Report of the series should carry clear and accurate headnotes with the facts of the case succinctly stated. The facts should be those upon with the *ratio* of the case is based—the legally material facts. So stated, the student or the busy practitioner will find the case easy to understand and will not miss the wood for the trees. As Professor Williams says:

> If the facts are adequately stated in the headnote it is to my mind quite permissible in ordinary cases to skip the facts as stated in detail by the judge, and to come forthwith to the part of his judgment that deals with the law.[36]

Secondly, the rubrics of the case should be clearly stated and displayed immediately below the condensed and pithy facts. If there are more than one *ratio* they should be serially numbered in the order in which they occur in the judgment. Ability to read a judgment and extract its *ratio* is an asset to every lawyer and only lawyers with such abilities should be employed by the Council. Another blemish on our Reports is that the rubrics below the headnotes do not

[35] "The History of Judicial Precedent" (1930) 46 L.Q.R. 207, 215.
[36] *Learning the Law*, 7th edition, 1963, p. 42.

state the rationes in full.[37] An ideal *ratio* is that which is constructed out of the material facts and presented in one sentence, if possible. It should be possible for the rule of the case to give a glimpse of the material facts.

The third suggested feature which we would expect the Council to exhibit in its Report is editorial comments. These comments should be so headed and should come below the rubrics. They should serve, among other things, the following purposes. They should call attention to authorities deciding a similar point where these authorities are not mentioned in the case that is being reported; and where the reported case conflicts with other authorities not referred to in the Report this should be stated and the authorities cited. The same thing should happen if a statute is ignored. Some volumes of our Reports have made efforts in this direction[38] and the practice should be promoted and encouraged.

Lastly, it would not be impudent for the Council to assume the freedom to offer alternative grounds upon which the decision should have been rested or to criticise the decision, showing what it should have been in the light of existing authorities or social circumstances. But care should be taken to warn the reading public not to mistake *editorial ratio* for that of the judge. Handled along these lines, the comments would make a distinct contribution to the growth of our case-law.

[37] Some do not even state them. See, e.g. the cases at pages 4, 5, 70, 89, 106, 108 of (1959) 4 F.S.C.

[38] See, e.g. *Odunjo v. Odunjo* (1964) L.L.R. 43; *Onwudinjoh v. Onwudinjoh* (1958–59) 2 E.R.N.L.R. 1.

III

THE FUTURE OF THE DOCTRINE IN NIGERIA

This closing chapter is devoted to a discussion of the future of the doctrine of precedent as received from England and applied in Nigeria. In Chapter Three we saw that the doctrine developed in three stages. The first stage was a period of "free law finding" when no court was bound to follow precedent. The second stage witnessed an epoch in which "we find the judges listening to citations of earlier cases, and no doubt being influenced by them in coming to their decision,"[1] but not yet bound to follow those cases.[2]

At the third and last stage we find judges declaring that they are bound by previous decisions in given circumstances.[3] It was at this stage that the doctrine received another name—*stare decisis*—because of its strict application and was received in Nigeria in that form, though as we saw in Chapter Eight the Supreme Court has tempered its strictness beyond that previously recognised in the Court of Appeal, Court of Criminal Appeal and House of Lords in England. The question now is whether the doctrine in its present form will continue in this country for the future, or whether we can foresee circumstances that will affect the operation of the doctrine for better or for worse.

We saw in Chapter Fourteen the influence which federalism has on *stare decisis* and we saw also what could be done to maintain the purity of the doctrine. The co-ordinating and reconciling role of the FCA and the Supreme Court was also emphasised. In Chapters Eight and Nine we suggested what attitude the Supreme Court is to adopt towards precedents on constitutional questions.

All this has a bearing on the future of the doctrine of precedent in this country.

We now deal with several other factors that are: the influence of individual and joint opinions in appellate courts, the influence of decisions from exotic sources and the dynamic character of the Nigerian society.

[1] Dias and Hughes, Jurisprudence, 1957, p. 54.

[2] Ellis Lewis, "The History of Judicial Precedent" (1930) 46 L.Q.R. 207, 212.

[3] This stage is generally thought to have been reached about the 18th century-Allen, Law in the Making, 7th edition, p. 210; Dias and Hughes, Jurisprudence, 1957, p. 57.

1. The Influence of Individual and Joint Opinions in Appellate Courts

Demands have from time to time been made for the delivery of individual opinions in the Supreme Court. The climax was reached when the Constitution Drafting Committee[4]) recommended that judges in our appellate courts should deliver individual opinions on the cases before them.[5] Arguments against individual opinions are that they make case-law unnecessarily bulky,[6] that it takes too much time to read several opinions, that lawyers in practice find the work of consulting several judgments on the same matter distracting, that it is sometimes difficult to find a common *ratio* in support of the decision since the judges may agree as to the conclusion but not agree as to the reasons on which the conclusions are based.[7]

It is further submitted by opponents of individual judgments that where there is a disagreement it is difficult at times to find a majority in support of the decision. The problem is embittered, they further submit, when the judges not only disagree as to the result, but also give conflicting reasons for their conclusions.[8]

Supporters of individual judgments claim for the practice certain advantages. Where the judges agree as to the conclusions and the reasons on which the conclusions are based it affords an interest to see the different ways in which the reasons, though similar, are formulated. Where they disagree it is equally interesting to see the point of view of the dissentients and their reasons for disagreeing. Such knowledge will help when filing an appeal against the decision.

For academic lawyers interested in research, individual judgments provide a veritable field for study. To quote Paton and Sawyer:[9]

> For persons such as Frankfurter, J., and the late Holmes and

[4] Appointed by the Federal Military Government in 1975 to produce a constitution for the return of the country to civilian rule.

[5] Section 192(2) of the 1976 Draft Constitution. Section 258(2) of the 1979 Constitution implements this recommendation.

[6] Paton and Sawer, "Ratio Decidendi and Obiter Dictum in Appellate Courts" (1947) 63 L.Q.R. 461, 483.

[7] Dias, *Jurisprudence*, 3rd edition, pp. 71–72.

[8] *Ibid.*

[9] "Ratio Decidendi and Obiter Dictum in Appellate Courts" (1947) 63 L.Q.R. 461, 485.

> Cardozo, J.J., to whom the study of judicial psychology and of the relation between law and society is an enthralling hobby, for those who take a keen intellectual delight in the play of ideas, and for university teachers who can devote their whole time to a minute analysis of opinions for purposes of research and for the stimulation of the better student—for such people, a multiplicity of opinions is valuable; the more there are and the more they conflict, the richer is the field for study.

It is also necessary to mention another reason for supporting individual judgments. While a joint opinion conceals the personalities of the participating judges, individual opinions bring such personalities to the fore and also such special abilities as each judge purports to possess. When opportunities for promotion occur they provide the criteria for selection.

In Nigeria, individual opinions are an exception rather than the rule today,[10] but the practice was very well known in the days of the Full Court of the Supreme Court where in most cases each of the judges delivered a separate opinion.[11] Nowadays when a justice of appeal delivers a separate judgment on the rare occasions on which this is done it is because he has a particular point to emphasise in a concurring judgment.[12] Dissenting judgments are even rarer.[13]

An overwhelming majority of the judgments delivered are joint judgments. No doubt joint judgments have their advantages. As Paton and Sawer have said[14] the chief purpose of the law

> is to provide a working guide for the citizen and in particular for his legal advisers. It is suggested that joint opinions would serve that purpose better than separate opinions. Joint opinions

[10] In 1961 only two opportunities occurred. In *Doherty v. Balewa* (1961) All N.L.R. 604, of the six justices participating, only Brett, F.J., delivered a separate opinion. In *Okechukwu v. Okafor* (1961) All N.L.R. 685 of the three justices sitting only one delivered an opinion and the two others simply concurred.

[11] See, for example, the cases in the first six volumes of the Nigeria Law Report (Volumes I–VI).

[12] See Paton and Sawer, *supra*, p. 483, see also *Doherty v. Balewa*, *supra*, p. 617 where Brett, F.J., said: "I agree that the questions referred to this Court should be answered in the way proposed in the judgment which has been read, and as the reasons which have led me to this conclusion differ only in emphasis from those already given I can be brief in stating them."

[13] See *Jammal Steel Structures Ltd. v. African Continental Bank Ltd.* (1973) 11 S.C. 77, 101 for the only dissenting judgment in the Supreme Court in 1973.

[14] See above, p. 485.

> would eliminate the difficulty of orders supported by conflicting reasons; it is believed that they would also reduce the difficulties caused by opinions resting on alternative grounds and by *obiter dicta* casting doubt on previous cases, because the judges in conference would be likely to submit the draft opinion to the kind of analysis which individual opinions frequently receive only after they are published.

In addition to the above advantages, joint opinions have the following merits.[15] They reduce the bulk of case-law and save expense, shelf room and the time of the practitioner and research worker. At a conference to discuss the draft there is usually a real attempt to find a common basis and a common language for the expression of the principle of the case and a joint principle has greater authority than that expressed individually. Lastly, a joint opinion enables the court's list to be disposed of more quickly as several cases may be disposed of at the same time.

Since the primary concern of a judgment is to dispose of the dispute and do justice between the parties to it and, secondarily, "to provide a working guide for the citizen," is it really desirable that some other method of achieving this purpose should be looked for when the present system is working well? We have already outlined generally the advantages and disadvantages of individual judgments. We have now to see what peculiar problems they will create for Nigeria in her present social and evolutionary context.

Supporters of individual opinions do not appear to have pointed out what is wrong with the present system. As far as we are aware, Nigerians, like other human beings in search of justice, have no interest in legal casuistry; what interests them is the final order, and the sooner that is made, the better it is for them.

Secondly, in view of shortage of lawyers in the country,[16] and consequent pressure of work on the few we have, it is doubtful if all of them can find the time to study effectively pages of Reports, each of which may run into tens or scores. Thirdly, the few that can do so may find it difficult to detect the grounds on which the case was

[15] Also given by the same learned writers at page 483.

[16] Not enough have been found to join the lower Bench as Magistrates or the Ministry of Justice of the various states, as State Counsel. The recent recruitment tour to other states by the Cross River State Attorney-General ended in failure.

decided if different reasons are given for the same conclusion.[17] In Nigeria, as elsewhere, judges are impatient with counsel who cite cases for what they did not decide.

Fourthly, opinions such as the above will present problems for the editor of a Report. Where there is an agreement as to the conclusion but not as to the reasons the editor will find it difficult to spell out a *ratio decidendi* when formulating his rubrics. If he puts down as the rule of the case what the majority of the justices have not put down as a rule, he will incur the displeasure, not only of the Bench, but also of the Bar, and may bring his Report into disrepute.

In the fifth place, the possibility that it may at times be difficult to find a majority in support of a decision is not too remote to be considered. We know that in Nigeria a tie in a judgment is a remote possibility, for the Supreme Court sits with an uneven number of judges and so also is the newly established Federal Court of Appeal.[18] But it is possible that the justices may in any particular case arrive at different conclusions in respect of the order to be made, even if they agree as to the reasons. The alternative, therefore, is a joint judgment which is always the result of a compromise not only as to the reasons but also as to the conclusions.

Sixthly, individual opinions might lead to prolixity in some justices, a tendency that might be curbed at a conference held to produce a joint opinion. A judgment commands respect and interest if it is concise, vivid and clear-cut—qualities that can only be attained through an economical use of words.

Seventhly, we said earlier that the system of individual opinions will enable justice to show his ability and expertise in particular branches of the law and so attract the attention of the authorities who might consider him for a higher appointment. But such a prospect is held out only to justices in the Federal Court of Appeal who have an eye on the Supreme Court; Supreme Court justices have no further advancement to look forward to, except the Chief Justiceship. But why should the personal interests and aspirations of the justices be allowed to interfere with a system that promotes the cause of justice best?

[17] See Dias already referred to.

[18] See Federal Court of Appeal Decree No. 43 of 1976, s. 9 and 1979 Constitution, s. 226.

Lastly, individual opinions will acerbate the problems of bulk and complexity of case-law that we tried to solve in Chapter Fifteen.

2. Influence from Exotic Sources

From time to time Nigerian courts pray in aid foreign decisions in support of their *rationes*.[19] More often such aid is sought when they are confronted with the interpretation of statutes whose words are not quite clear. Some of our statute laws have a foreign origin. Thus the Northern States Penal Code and Criminal Procedure Code are based on their Indian counterparts.[20] Our Criminal Procedure Act is based on the Queensland model.[21] Decisions on the different statutes from these jurisdictions have been instrumental in expounding our laws.

Thus in *Obaji v. The State*[22] the Supreme Court of Nigeria relied upon Australian decisions to rule on the criminal responsibility of an accused person who raised a plea of provocation to a criminal charge.[23] *Rex v. Adekanmi*[24] was a case in which Francis, J., had to rely on an East African case in the absence of a local decision as to whether the rule relating to provocation as a defence in a charge of murder should be the same for an enlightened and educated man as for "an illiterate and primitive peasant." In *Doherty v. Abubakar*[25] the Federal Supreme Court found "the decisions of the Australian courts helpful" in deciding whether the Nigerian Federal Parliament

[19] We defined foreign decisions as excluding decisions of English courts in Chapter 9.

[20] See Chapter 8 and *Offiong v. C.O.P.* (1966) N.N.L.R. 94, 95; *Ekechukwu v. C.O.P.* (1966) N.N.L.R. 96, 101.

[21] See footnote No. 23 below.

[22] (1965) N.M.L.R. 417, 421.

[23] In that case the Supreme Court said: "This view is supported by some decisions in the Australian Courts, and the Nigerian Criminal Code is based on the Criminal Code of Queensland (Australia) the wording of our sections 283 and 318 is identical with sections 268 and 304 respectively of the Queensland Code. We will make reference briefly to four Australian cases: (1) *R. v. Sabri* (5) (Digested in 1956 Supplement of the Australian Digest, Column 87–89). (2) *R. v. Herliky* (6) (Digested in 1956 Supplement of the Australian Digest, Columns 125 and 126). (3) *R. v. Young* (7) (Digested in 1957 Supplement of the Australian Digest, Columns 118 and 119). (4) *Mehemet Ali v. R.* (8) (1958 Australian Digest, Column 105)."

[24] (1944) 17 N.L.R. 99, 101.

[25] (1961) All N.L.R. 604, 613.

had a general power to pass an Act that permitted the holding of an enquiry on any matter anywhere in the Federation.

The above examples show the extent to which foreign decisions on statute laws help the Nigerian courts to interpret their own statutes. As Francis, J., said in *Rex v. Adekanmi* these decisions, though not binding on Nigerian courts "may . . . with justice be followed as a guide . . ." Dr. Allen says:

> Such decisions are not technically "binding" but in recent years there has been noticeable and increasing respect for them; and frequently there seems to be little real difference between praying them in aid to support a *ratio decidendi* and actually following them as authoritative statements of the law.[26]

As foreign decisions are not binding, our courts have occasionally maintained a sense of judgment and refused to follow them where the original reports are not available and it is doubtful whether the summaries in a textbook bear out the principle of law sought to be established. Thus, in *Fulani v. Bornu N.A.*[27] the Supreme Court refused to "attach high presuasive value to editorial summaries of isolated decisions on the Indian Penal Code when full reports of the decisions are not available."

So long as decisions culled from foreign jurisdictions are regarded as guides and not as masters, to that extent will our courts show a critical attitude and discrimination in their reception and treatment, and it must be remembered first and foremost that it is Nigerian statutes that are being interpreted and that where the foreign interpretations, though agreeing with the letter, do not agree with the spirit of our statutes they must be rejected and our decisions based on independent interpretation.

3. The Dynamic Character of Nigerian Society

A contrast must be drawn between a developed England and a developing Nigeria for purposes of the doctrine of precedent. The strict doctrine of precedent only emerged in England in the nineteenth century when the House of Lords declared that it was bound

[26] *Law in the Making*, 7th edition, p. 281.
[27] (1966) 1 All N.L.R. 260, 263.

by its own decisions.[28] Similar declarations were later made by the Court of Appeal, the Court of Criminal Appeal and the Divisional Court of the Queen's Bench.[29]

This strict stand has been pungently criticised by academic writers, on the ground, among other things, that it does not take account of change of circumstances.[30] According to Llewellyn:[31]

> Our society is changing, and law, if it is to fit society, must also change.

There is no doubt that the character of the Nigerian society has changed radically between the reception of English law on 1st January, 1900, and now. There have been changes in legislation, in public policy and social values, in **customs** and in education and intelligence level of Nigerians. These changes have affected in no small measure some decisions of the Nigerian courts. The English doctrine therefore appears to be too static for a dynamic situation.

Changes in Custom

Customary law recognises a claim for the return of a wife to her husband.[32] Bu- in *Egri v. Ukperi*[33] the Supreme Court held that such a claim was contrary to the wife's right to freedom of association under section 26(1) of the 1963 Constitution of the Federation. From this it is clear that all previous decisions to the contrary are overruled. It is legislation that has brought about this situation.

But our customs can change without legislative intervention, for other agencies of change are available, including contact with new ideas. Thus, in *Wokoko v. Molyko*[37] Pearson, Assistant J., said:

> It may be observed that in the past native custom has been by no means static; indeed a great many native customs in West Africa are manifestly of European origin, and it is eminently

[28] *London Street Tramways v. London County Council* (1898) A.C. 375.

[29] *Young v. Bristol Aeroplane Co.* (1944) K.B. 718; *R. v. Taylor* (1950) 2 K.B. 368; *Police Authority for Huddersfield v. Watson* (1947) K.B. 842.

[30] See Dias, *Jurisprudence*, 3rd edition, pp. 77–78.

[31] *The Bramble Bush*, p. 66.

[32] All customary courts in the country recognised this as restitution of conjugal rights.

[33] (1973) 11 S.C. 299.

[34] (1938) 14 N.L.R. 41, 44.

> desirable that native custom should be progressive, as in this case, where the older and, as I hold, superseded custom would restrain development.

Public policy, custom and social values change as society changes. Decisions based on these elements may some day fall out of focus with the needs of the time.[35] There is already a trend in this direction. In *Tijani v. Secretary, Southern Nigeria*[36] the Privy Council recognised the principle that the notion of individual ownership of land was "quite foreign to native ideas" and the land belonged to the community. But in *Lewis v. Bankole*,[37] Speed, Ag. C.J., observed:

> . . .family ownership is gradually ceasing to exist. In a progressive community it is of course inevitable that this should be so. The institution of communal ownership has been dead for years . . . .

This opinion was advanced some twelve years before the Privy Council decision in *Tijani's case*. Although Speed's decision was reversed by the Full Court it is indubitable that the trend from communal to individual ownership has been vindicated. The result of this is that the concept of communal ownership no longer monopolises Nigerian juristic thought and that individual ownership is steadily gaining recognition even in rural communities. In *Nwankwo v. Chukwueke*[38] Aniagolu, J., rejecting a plea of communal ownership, stated:

> Where there is predominating evidence establishing individual ownership in a community the court must declare in favour of individual ownership, the presumption of communal ownership having, in that case, been amply rebutted.

Communal ownership apart, other aspects of our customary law are undergoing modifications. This is due to changes in the mode of life and living conditions of the people. Custom holds sway mostly in the rural areas where most of the customary courts are situated. In recent years there has been a large exodus of people from the

[35] See Allott, *Essays in African Law*, 1960, p. 89.
[36] (1921) 2 A.C. 399, 404.
[37] (1908) 1 N.L.R. 81, 83.
[38] (1972) 2 E.C.S.L.R. 96, 99.

villages to the towns where new conditions of living prevail and new values are embraced. Even the stay-at-homes are not immune from the new influences.

The result is that they bring new usages and practices into being; and while these usages and practices cannot be said to be essentially the products of Western civilization they have the effect of so modifying the existing customs that new versions of customary rules are gradually replacing the existing social order. That is why we find attempts to use new customs to unseat the old, and in some cases the development is to be welcome.[39]

The new developments in the customary law of marriage in the four Eastern States of Nigeria have made the Eastern Nigeria law limiting dowry to £30 (now N60.00) practically a dead letter.[40] Fathers of brides now demand from their would-be sons-in-law all sorts of things ranging from a long, costly matchet *to open the road to the bride's house*, an Aladdin or Tilly Lamp *to illuminate the road*, a good foam chair *on which to sit and listen to the suitor* and so on. For the mother's part, there must be given a bag of salt, a bag of crayfish, four to six fathoms of loin cloth, etc. These gifts, very expensive in this era of inflation, only open the way for betrothal; they do not form part of the price which is finally paid after the necessary consent has been given by the parents and the girl.

The effect of this is that in the event of failure to meet these new customary obligations no marriage contract comes into existence even if the parents, owing to economic and financial pressure, take the bride price from the suitor. Without these preliminaries, the result is easily predictable. If a court of superior jurisdiction accepts the new custom[41] then all previous precedents which found for a marriage under the old custom of customary presents would be swept aside and become replaced by the new decision.

Again, some customary courts are now beginning to demand

[39] See *Dannole v. Dawodu* (1958) 3 F.S.C. 46 where the new development, though welcomed by lower court judges, was turned down by the Federal Supreme Court.

[40] Limitation of Dowry Law, 1956, is the Law in question.

[41] But see Allott, *Essays in African Law*, 1960, p. 90, where the learned author thinks that if such a change is allowed it will destroy the certainty which judicial recognition of a custom is designed to achieve.

writing as evidence of a transaction concerning land.[42] The superior courts have consistently ruled that writing is not essential to effect a sale of land subject to customary law.[43] But if all or most of the customary courts in all or any of the states in the Federation insisted upon writing as evidence of a land transaction then the superior courts would have no alternative but to accept this practice as evidence of the new custom.[44] This would lead them to have second thoughts on earlier decisions in which writing was held not to be required by customary law.

These illustrations show the influence of social and economic forces on rules of law. The change of practice in relation to customary presents before betrothal stems from the increased *per capita* income and inflation in the country. The change of practice with regard to writing as evidence of a transaction relating to land is due to the replacement of illiterate chiefs by literate elements as members of customary courts. Some day, however, it appears that the new trend may receive recognition if the practice is widespread.

This view, however, is mere speculation. In England the rule is that a new custom cannot unseat the common law. According to Salmond:[45]

> The public interest requires that modern customs shall conform to the law, and not that the law shall conform automatically to newly established customs.

Is it reasonable to expect that after a superior court in Nigeria has pronounced upon a custom and accorded it recognition a subsequent alteration of that custom can deprive the precedent of the superior court of its authority?

It is arguable that since Nigerian courts follow English courts in matters of practice and procedure where no provision is made in our laws the Nigerian courts will follow the English rule as stated above

[42] *Esien v. Okori*, Abak Magistrate Court Appeal No. AB/5A/73 is one out of many.

[43] *Ferguson v. Duncan* (1953) 14 W.A.C.A. 316, 317–318; *Ike v. Akujieze* (1970–71) 1 E.C.S.L.R. 145.

[44] In *Eleko v. Officer Administering the Government of Nigeria* (1931) A.C. 662, 673, the Privy Council observed that a modified custom must be shown to have received the assent of the community. "It is the assent of the native community that gives a custom its validity."

[45] *Jurisprudence*, 11th edition, p. 252.

It is also arguable that the Privy Council's *dictum* in *Eleko v. Officer Administering the Government of Nigeria*[46] does not apply to a case in which a custom has been recognised by a superior court, but only to cases in which no such recognition has taken place. In the circumstances, therefore, we may venture to conclude that no superior court in Nigeria will lay aside precedent in order to recognise and rubber-stamp the new custom. That will make the law uncertain and rob it of consistency.

There is a precedent in which the Federal Supreme Court refused to accept a new custom that had won popular approval, but chose to stick to the old. That case is *Danmole v. Dawodu.*[47] All the lower court judges before whom the same rival customs came up accepted the new custom in preference to the old one because it was more in accord with the principles of natural justice, equity and good conscience. But the Federal Supreme Court spurned their decisions and recognised the old rival.

In the above case the old custom was never at any time judicially recognised. At least there is no reported case to this effect. Yet the new custom failed to find favour with the highest court of the land. How much more vulnerable is the position of a new custom that is competing against an established custom that has won judicial recognition? There is the likelihood that the courts will learn their lesson from the attitude of the Federal Supreme Court to new customs.

Cultural and Educational Changes

A change in the standard of education and intelligence can make a precedent outdated, for a decision which takes account of poor education and intelligence may not be followed when the standard of education and general intelligence improves. It is for this reason that we think that in view of the universal free primary education scheme presently in force in Nigeria the time will soon come when the "divergence between English and local decisions" on trade marks will disappear because to that time "the local standard of education and intelligence" will improve.[48]

[46] (1931) A.C. 662, 673.
[47] (1958) 3 F.S.C. 46.
[48] *The U.K. Tobacco Co. Ltd. v. Carreras Ltd.* (1931) 16 N.L.R. 1, 2.

Dr. Allen has said that "changes and developments in human knowledge may greatly affect the application of precedent."[49] He cited the case of *M-T v. M-T*[50] which decided that a child born 340 days after the last possibility for intercourse between his parents could be legitimate. The decision proceeded on the ground that in recent years there have been considerable advances in the science of gynaecology and that earlier decisions based on more imperfect scientific knowledge were not to be followed. Dr. Allen concluded:

> It is a matter for speculation how far judges in the distant future will consider themselves free to disregard precedents in the light of what they believe to be larger and superior knowledge.[51]

Nigeria, of course, is a very good follower of Britain in matters of law and practice.[52] It is likely that whenever the point falls to be decided the Nigerian courts will follow the above decision. It is, however, unfortunate that when the point arose in 1972 there was no medical evidence to guide the court. In *Okpanum v. Okpanum*[53] a wife complained that the pregnancy she carried in 1972 was the result of her intercourse with the husband in 1970. Agbakoba, J., ruling against the wife observed:

> The age of the pregnancy was not stated but in any case I am bound to take judicial notice that human gestation enures for nine months and I cannot say that the pregnancy of the caveatrix in 1972 was as a result of association with the respondent in 1970 when he last had access to her.

The wife, in saying that the husband was responsible for her pregnancy in the above circumstances, might be telling the truth; she might equally be telling a lie. It is only medical evidence that might prove the actual position. But this was lacking. It would have afforded great interest to see how the English precedent would have been handled. In the present circumstances, it is impossible to say what contribution science has made to the development of judicial precedent in Nigeria.

[49] *Law in the Making*, 7th edition, p. 299.
[50] (1949), p. 331.
[51] *Ibid.*, p. 300.
[52] See Chapter 13.
[53] (1972) 2 E.C.S.L.R. 561, 565.

Our criminal law has treated with indulgence the "illiterate and primitive" peasants of this country by conceding to them a lower degree of tolerance than is required of "an educated and civilised person." On this basis it has been held that such a person is more easily provoked than one who is civilised and that words charging him with impotence and a sudden confession of adultery by his wife would reduce murder to manslaughter.[54] The rule was extended in *The State v. Egbe*[55] in which the learned judge said:

> . . .in . . .rural communities, the wife is still regarded as being sub verga viri (under the rod of the husband). Therefore, the act of a wife pointing her finger at a hungry husband who has a right to demand chop from her, and this followed with hard words, would in my view, be enough as I believe it did, to provoke the accused.

It would appear from the above decision that the concession is available to them only as long as the standard of education and civilisation and rural life remains what it has been. The concession will be lost when the standard improves. And improvement is setting in through measures adopted by the governments in the Federation to better the conditions of rural life. These measures are the universal free primary and adult education schemes and the taking of courts of justice—Magistrates' and Hight Courts—nearer to the people. Added to the list are the available modern facilities for easy communications which bring people of different nooks and corners and social strata together in mutual contact.

In the result, there is a visible tendency on the part of the rural peasants towards new ways of life and a higher degree of sophistication and enlightenment. Time is fast approaching in which no more claims of iracundity will be entertained and all tempers will be placed on the same level. At that time the concept of "ordinary man" as used in section 283 and 284 of our Criminal Code Act will acquire a connotation different from its interpretation in *Adekanmi* and *Egbe's cases*. In fact, law would be failing in its purpose of giving a

[54] *Rex v. Adekanmi* (1944) 17 N.L.R. 99, 101.

[55] Unreported, but see the Calabar High Court Judgment by Eno, J., in charge No. C/40C/1972 dated 23/11/72.

man his deserts if the meaning of the word were to remain constant despite change of circumstances.

In those days the theory that judges only declare law and do not make it[56] will be further shown to be fallacious, for a definite exercise of law-making power will be visible when outdated precedents will be rejected.[57] Again, the doctrine of *stare decisis* as known in England and imported into this country will operate far less rigidly then than it has done hitherto because decisions then will not necessarily follow the path of existing decisions which are reached under a different social order.

[56] See Goodhart, "Precedent in English and Continental Law" (1934) 50 L.Q.R. 44.

[57] "If, of course, the law-making function of courts is admitted, then it would be easy to reject out of date precedents openly on the grounds of changed conditions and not have to resort to the threadbare fiction that cases only reflect what always has been the law."—Dias, *Jurisprudence*, 3rd edition, p. 77.

www.ingramcontent.com/pod-product-compliance
Lightning Source LLC
Chambersburg PA
CBHW031319230926
51848CB00001B/18
* 9 7 8 9 7 8 1 5 6 0 1 7 0 *